PRENTICE HALL
WORLD STUDIES
THE ANCIENT WORLD

In association with
DK

PEARSON
Prentice Hall

Boston, Massachusetts
Upper Saddle River, New Jersey

Program Consultants

Heidi Hayes Jacobs

Heidi Hayes Jacobs has served as an education consultant to more than 1,000 schools across the nation and abroad. Dr. Jacobs serves as an adjunct professor in the Department of Curriculum on Teaching at Teachers College, Columbia University. She has written two best-selling books and numerous articles on curriculum reform. She received an M.A. from the University of Massachusetts, Amherst, and completed her doctoral work at Columbia University's Teachers College in 1981. The core of Dr. Jacobs's experience comes from her years teaching high school, middle school, and elementary school students. As an educational consultant, she works with K–12 schools and districts on curriculum reform and strategic planning.

Michal L. LeVasseur

Michal LeVasseur is the Executive Director of the National Council for Geography Education. She is an instructor in the College of Education at Jacksonville State University and works with the Alabama Geographic Alliance. Her undergraduate and graduate work were in the fields of anthropology (B.A.), geography (M.A.), and science education (Ph.D.). Dr. LeVasseur's specialization has moved increasingly into the area of geography education. Since 1996 she has served as the Director of the National Geographic Society's Summer Geography Workshops. As an educational consultant, she has worked with the National Geographic Society as well as with schools and organizations to develop programs and curricula for geography.

Senior Reading Consultants

Kate Kinsella

Kate Kinsella, Ed.D., is a faculty member in the Department of Secondary Education at San Francisco State University. A specialist in second-language acquisition and adolescent literacy, she teaches coursework addressing language and literacy development across the secondary curricula. Dr. Kinsella earned her M.A. in TESOL from San Francisco State University and her Ed.D. in Second Language Acquisition from the University of San Francisco.

Kevin Feldman

Kevin Feldman, Ed.D., is the Director of Reading and Early Intervention with the Sonoma County Office of Education (SCOE) and an independent educational consultant. At the SCOE, he develops, organizes, and monitors programs related to K–12 literacy. Dr. Feldman has an M.A. from the University of California, Riverside, in Special Education, Learning Disabilities and Instructional Design. He earned his Ed.D. in Curriculum and Instruction from the University of San Francisco.

Acknowledgments appear on page 297, which constitutes an extension of this copyright page.

ISBN 0-13-204144-8
13 14 15 V056 15 14 13

Cartography Consultant

Andrew Heritage

Andrew Heritage has been publishing atlases and maps for more than 25 years. In 1991, he joined the leading illustrated nonfiction publisher Dorling Kindersley (DK) with the task of building an international atlas list from scratch. The DK atlas list now includes some 10 titles, which are constantly updated and appear in new editions either annually or every other year.

Academic Reviewers

Africa

Barbara B. Brown, Ph.D.
African Studies Center
Boston University
Boston, Massachusetts

Ancient World

Evelyn DeLong Mangie, Ph.D.
Department of History
University of South Florida
Tampa, Florida

**Central Asia and
the Middle East**

Pamela G. Sayre
History Department,
    Social Sciences Division
Henry Ford Community College
Dearborn, Michigan

East Asia

Huping Ling, Ph.D.
History Department
Truman State University
Kirksville, Missouri

Eastern Europe

Robert M. Jenkins
Center for Slavic, Eurasian and
    East European Studies
University of North Carolina
Chapel Hill, North Carolina

Latin America

Dan La Botz
Professor, History Department
Miami University
Oxford, Ohio

Medieval Times

James M. Murray
History Department
University of Cincinnati
Cincinnati, Ohio

North Africa

Barbara E. Petzen
Center for Middle Eastern Studies
Harvard University
Cambridge, Massachusetts

Religion

Charles H. Lippy, Ph.D.
Department of Philosophy
    and Religion
University of Tennessee
    at Chattanooga
Chattanooga, Tennessee

Russia

Janet Vaillant
Davis Center for Russian
    and Eurasian Studies
Harvard University
Cambridge, Massachusetts

South Asia

Robert J. Young
Professor Emeritus
History Department
West Chester University
West Chester, Pennsylvania

United States and Canada

Victoria Randlett
Geography Department
University of Nevada, Reno
Reno, Nevada

Western Europe

Ruth Mitchell-Pitts
Center for European Studies
University of North Carolina
    at Chapel Hill
Chapel Hill, North Carolina

Reviewers

Sean Brennan
Brecksville-Broadview Heights
    City School District
Broadview Heights, Ohio

Stephen Bullick
Mt. Lebanon School District
Pittsburgh, Pennsylvania

William R. Cranshaw, Ed.D.
Waycross Middle School
Waycross, Georgia

Dr. Louis P. De Angelo
Archdiocese of Philadelphia
Philadelphia, Pennsylvania

Paul Francis Durietz
Social Studies
    Curriculum Coordinator
Woodland District #50
Gurnee, Illinois

Gail Dwyer
Dickerson Middle School,
    Cobb County
Marietta, Georgia

Michal Howden
Social Studies Consultant
Zionsville, Indiana

Rosemary Kalloch
Springfield Public Schools
Springfield, Massachusetts

Deborah J. Miller
Office of Social Studies,
    Detroit Public Schools
Detroit, Michigan

Steven P. Missal
Newark Public Schools
Newark, New Jersey

Catherine Fish Petersen (Retired)
East Islip School District
Islip Terrace, New York

Joe Wieczorek
Social Studies Consultant
Baltimore, Maryland

THE ANCIENT WORLD

Develop Skills

Use these pages to develop your reading, writing, and geography skills.

Focus on History

Learn about the geography, history, and cultures of the civilizations of the ancient world.

MAP·MASTER™	DK	Interactive Textbook
• Learn map skills with the MapMaster Skills Handbook. • Practice your skills with every map in this book. • Interact with every map online and on CD-ROM.	Maps and illustrations created by DK help build your understanding of the world. The DK World Desk Reference Online keeps you up to date.	The *World Studies* Interactive Textbook online and on CD-ROM uses interactive maps and other activities to help you learn.

Literature

Focus On

Skills for Life

Links

Citizen Heroes

Meet people who have made a difference in their civilization.

Eyewitness Technology

Detailed drawings show how technology shapes places and societies.

Target Reading Skills

Chapter-by-chapter reading skills help you read and understand social studies concepts.

MAP★MASTER™ Interactive

Go online to find an interactive version of every MapMaster map in this book. Use the Web Code provided to gain direct access to these maps.

How to Use Web Codes:

1. Go to www.PHSchool.com.
2. Enter the Web Code.
3. Click Go!

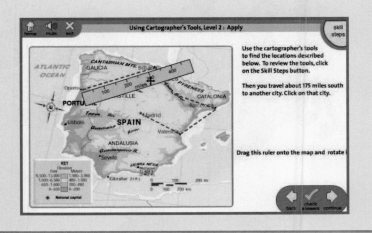

Charts, Graphs, and Tables

Building Geographic Literacy

Learning about a country often starts with finding it on a map. The MapMaster system in *World Studies* helps you develop map skills you will use throughout your life. These three steps can help you become a MapMaster!

The MAP★MASTER™ System

1 Learn

You need to learn geography tools and concepts before you explore the world. Get started by using the MapMaster™ Skills Handbook to learn the skills you need for success.

Location The Equator runs through parts of Latin America, but it is far from other parts of the region.
Locate Find the Equator on the map. Which climates are most common in Latin America, and how far is each climate region from the Equator?
Draw Conclusions How do climates change as you move away from the Equator?

Go Online
PHSchool.com Use Web Code **lfp-1142** for step-by-step **map skills practice.**

2 Practice

You need to practice and apply your geography skills frequently to be a MapMaster. The maps in *World Studies* give you the practice you need to develop geographic literacy.

3 Interact

Using maps is more than just finding places. Maps can teach you many things about a region, such as its climate, its vegetation, and the languages that the people who live there speak. Every MapMaster™ map is online at **PHSchool.com,** with interactive activities to help you learn the most from every map.

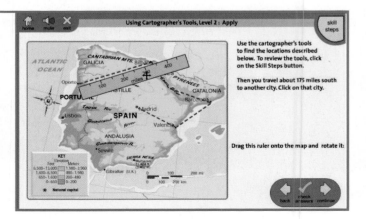

Learning With Technology

You will be making many exciting journeys across time and place in *World Studies*. Technology will help make what you learn come alive in your classroom.

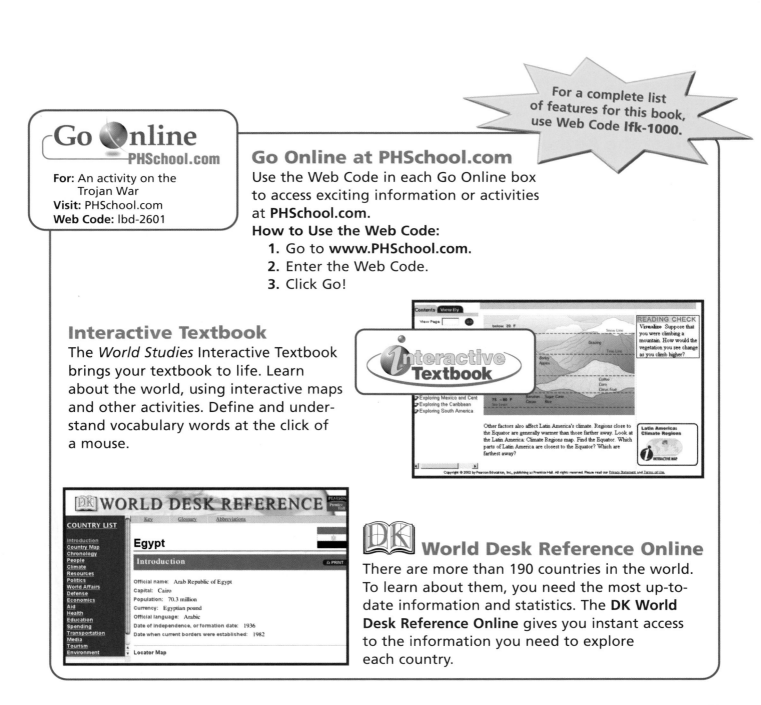

For a complete list of features for this book, use Web Code lfk-1000.

Go Online
PHSchool.com

For: An activity on the Trojan War
Visit: PHSchool.com
Web Code: lbd-2601

Go Online at PHSchool.com

Use the Web Code in each Go Online box to access exciting information or activities at **PHSchool.com**.

How to Use the Web Code:
1. Go to **www.PHSchool.com**.
2. Enter the Web Code.
3. Click Go!

Interactive Textbook

The *World Studies* Interactive Textbook brings your textbook to life. Learn about the world, using interactive maps and other activities. Define and understand vocabulary words at the click of a mouse.

World Desk Reference Online

There are more than 190 countries in the world. To learn about them, you need the most up-to-date information and statistics. The **DK World Desk Reference Online** gives you instant access to the information you need to explore each country.

Reading Informational Texts

Reading a magazine, an Internet page, or a textbook is not the same as reading a novel. The purpose of reading nonfiction texts is to acquire new information. On page M18 you'll read about some ⟳ Target Reading Skills that you'll have a chance to practice as you read this textbook. Here we'll focus on a few skills that will help you read nonfiction with a more critical eye.

Analyze the Author's Purpose

Different types of materials are written with different purposes in mind. For example, a textbook is written to teach students information about a subject. The purpose of a technical manual is to teach someone how to use something, such as a computer. A newspaper editorial might be written to persuade the reader to accept a particular point of view. A writer's purpose influences how the material is presented. Sometimes an author states his or her purpose directly. More often, the purpose is only suggested, and you must use clues to identify the author's purpose.

Distinguish Between Facts and Opinions

It's important when reading informational texts to read actively and to distinguish between fact and opinion. A fact can be proven or disproven. An opinion cannot—it is someone's personal viewpoint or evaluation.

For example, the editorial pages in a newspaper offer opinions on topics that are currently in the news. You need to read newspaper editorials with an eye for bias and faulty logic. For example, the newspaper editorial at the right shows factual statements in blue and opinion statements in red. The underlined words are examples of highly charged words. They reveal bias on the part of the writer.

> More than 5,000 people voted last week in favor of building a new shopping center, but the opposition won out. The margin of victory is irrelevant. Those radical voters who opposed the center are obviously self-serving elitists who do not care about anyone but themselves.
>
> This month's unemployment figure for our area is 10 percent, which represents an increase of about 5 percent over the figure for this time last year. These figures mean unemployment is getting worse. But the people who voted against the mall probably do not care about creating new jobs.

Identify Evidence

Before you accept an author's conclusion, you need to make sure that the author has based the conclusion on enough evidence and on the right kind of evidence. An author may present a series of facts to support a claim, but the facts may not tell the whole story. For example, what evidence does the author of the newspaper editorial on the previous page provide to support his claim that the new shopping center would create more jobs? Is it possible that the shopping center might have put many small local businesses out of business, thus increasing unemployment rather than decreasing it?

Evaluate Credibility

Whenever you read informational texts, you need to assess the credibility of the author. This is especially true of sites you may visit on the Internet. All Internet sources are not equally reliable. Here are some questions to ask yourself when evaluating the credibility of a Web site.

☐ Is the Web site created by a respected organization, a discussion group, or an individual?

☐ Does the Web site creator include his or her name as well as credentials and the sources he or she used to write the material?

☐ Is the information on the site balanced or biased?

☐ Can you verify the information using two other sources?

☐ Is there a date telling when the Web site was created or last updated?

Writing for Social Studies

Writing is one of the most powerful communication tools you will ever use. You will use it to share your thoughts and ideas with others. Research shows that writing about what you read actually helps you learn new information and ideas. A systematic approach to writing—including prewriting, drafting, revising, and proofing—can help you write better, whether you're writing an essay or a research report.

Narrative Essays

Writing that tells a story about a personal experience

1 Select and Narrow Your Topic

A narrative is a story. In social studies, it might be a narrative essay about how an event affected you or your family.

2 Gather Details

Brainstorm a list of details you'd like to include in your narrative.

3 Write a First Draft

Start by writing a simple opening sentence that conveys the main idea of your essay. Continue by writing a colorful story that has interesting details. Write a conclusion that sums up the significance of the event or situation described in your essay.

4 Revise and Proofread

Check to make sure you have not begun too many sentences with the word *I*. Replace general words with more colorful ones.

Main idea → In my last year of college, I volunteered for an organization called Amigos De Las Americas (Friends of the Americas). I was

Details → sent to a remote village in Brazil and worked with villagers to improve the community's water supply and sanitation systems. The

Significance of narrative → experience made me realize I wanted to work in the field of public health. When I went to Brazil, I never imagined what an incredible sense of purpose it would add to my life.

Persuasive Essays

Writing that supports an opinion or position

1 **Select and Narrow Your Topic**

Choose a topic that provokes an argument and has at least two sides. Choose a side. Decide which argument will appeal most to your audience and persuade them to understand your point of view.

2 **Gather Evidence**

Create a chart that states your position at the top and then lists the pros and cons for your position below, in two columns. Predict and address the strongest arguments against your stand.

3 **Write a First Draft**

Write a strong thesis statement that clearly states your position. Continue by presenting the strongest arguments in favor of your position and acknowledging and refuting opposing arguments.

4 **Revise and Proofread**

Check to make sure you have made a logical argument and that you have not oversimplified the argument.

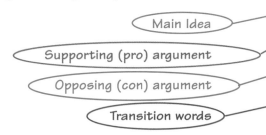

Main Idea

Supporting (pro) argument

Opposing (con) argument

Transition words

It is vital to vote in elections. When people vote, they tell public officials how to run the government. Not every proposal is carried out; however, politicians do their best to listen to what the majority of people want. Therefore, every vote is important.

Expository Essays

Writing that explains a process, compares and contrasts, explains causes and effects, or explores solutions to a problem

❶ Identify and Narrow Your Topic

Expository writing is writing that explains something in detail. It might explain the similarities and differences between two or more subjects (compare and contrast). It might explain how one event causes another (cause and effect). Or it might explain a problem and describe a solution.

❷ Gather Evidence

Create a graphic organizer that identifies details to include in your essay.

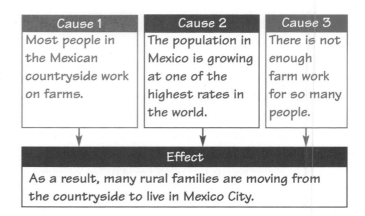

Cause 1	Cause 2	Cause 3
Most people in the Mexican countryside work on farms.	The population in Mexico is growing at one of the highest rates in the world.	There is not enough farm work for so many people.

Effect

As a result, many rural families are moving from the countryside to live in Mexico City.

❸ Write Your First Draft

Write a topic sentence and then organize the essay around your similarities and differences, causes and effects, or problem and solutions. Be sure to include convincing details, facts, and examples.

❹ Revise and Proofread

Research Papers

Writing that presents research about a topic

❶ Narrow Your Topic

Choose a topic you're interested in and make sure that it is not too broad. For example, instead of writing a report on Panama, write about the construction of the Panama Canal.

❷ Acquire Information

Locate several sources of information about the topic from the library or the Internet. For each resource, create a source index card like the one at the right. Then take notes using an index card for each detail or subtopic. On the card, note which source the information was taken from. Use quotation marks when you copy the exact words from a source.

Source #1
McCullough, David. *The Path Between the Seas: The Creation of the Panama Canal, 1870-1914.* N.Y., Simon and Schuster, 1977.

❸ Make an Outline

Use an outline to decide how to organize your report. Sort your index cards into the same order.

Outline
I. Introduction
II. Why the canal was built
III. How the canal was built
    A. Physical challenges
    B. Medical challenges
IV. Conclusion

Introduction

Building the Panama Canal

Ever since Christopher Columbus first explored the Isthmus of Panama, the Spanish had been looking for a water route through it. They wanted to be able to sail west from Spain to Asia without sailing around South America. However, it was not until 1914 that the dream became a reality.

Conclusion

It took eight years and more than 70,000 workers to build the Panama Canal. It remains one of the greatest engineering feats of modern times.

4 Write a First Draft

Write an introduction, a body, and a conclusion. Leave plenty of space between lines so you can go back and add details that you may have left out.

5 Revise and Proofread

Be sure to include transition words between sentences and paragraphs. Here are some examples:

To show a contrast—*however, although, despite.*

To point out a reason—*since, because, if.*

To signal a conclusion—*therefore, consequently, so, then.*

Evaluating Your Writing

Use this table to help you evaluate your writing.

	Excellent	Good	Acceptable	Unacceptable
Purpose	Achieves purpose—to inform, persuade, or provide historical interpretation—very well	Informs, persuades, or provides historical interpretation reasonably well	Reader cannot easily tell if the purpose is to inform, persuade, or provide historical interpretation	Purpose is not clear
Organization	Develops ideas in a very clear and logical way	Presents ideas in a reasonably well-organized way	Reader has difficulty following the organization	Lacks organization
Elaboration	Explains all ideas with facts and details	Explains most ideas with facts and details	Includes some supporting facts and details	Lacks supporting details
Use of Language	Uses excellent vocabulary and sentence structure with no errors in spelling, grammar, or punctuation	Uses good vocabulary and sentence structure with very few errors in spelling, grammar, or punctuation	Includes some errors in grammar, punctuation, and spelling	Includes many errors in grammar, punctuation, and spelling

CONTENTS

Go Online PHSchool.com Use Web Code **lap-0000** for all of the maps in this handbook.

Five Themes of Geography

Studying the geography of the entire world is a huge task. You can make that task easier by using the five themes of geography: location, regions, place, movement, and human-environment interaction. The themes are tools you can use to organize information and to answer the where, why, and how of geography.

▲ **Location**
This museum in England has a line running through it. The line marks its location at 0° longitude.

LOCATION

1 Location answers the question, "Where is it?" You can think of the location of a continent or a country as its address. You might give an absolute location such as 40° N and 80° W. You might also use a relative address, telling where one place is by referring to another place. *Between school and the mall* and *eight miles east of Pleasant City* are examples of relative locations.

REGIONS

2 Regions are areas that share at least one common feature. Geographers divide the world into many types of regions. For example, countries, states, and cities are political regions. The people in any one of these places live under the same government. Other features, such as climate and culture, can be used to define regions. Therefore the same place can be found in more than one region. For example, the state of Hawaii is in the political region of the United States. Because it has a tropical climate, Hawaii is also part of a tropical climate region.

MOVEMENT

4 Movement answers the question, "How do people, goods, and ideas move from place to place?" Remember that what happens in one place often affects what happens in another. Use the theme of movement to help you trace the spread of goods, people, and ideas from one location to another.

PLACE

3 Place identifies the natural and human features that make one place different from every other place. You can identify a specific place by its landforms, climate, plants, animals, people, language, or culture. You might even think of place as a geographic signature. Use the signature to help you understand the natural and human features that make one place different from every other place.

INTERACTION

5 Human-environment interaction focuses on the relationship between people and the environment. As people live in an area, they often begin to make changes to it, usually to make their lives easier. For example, they might build a dam to control flooding during rainy seasons. Also, the environment can affect how people live, work, dress, travel, and communicate.

◀ **Interaction**
These Congolese women interact with their environment by gathering wood for cooking.

PRACTICE YOUR GEOGRAPHY SKILLS

1 Describe your town or city, using each of the five themes of geography.

2 Name at least one thing that comes into your town or city and one that goes out. How is each moved? Where does it come from? Where does it go?

Understanding Movements of Earth

The planet Earth is part of our solar system. Earth revolves around the sun in a nearly circular path called an orbit. A revolution, or one complete orbit around the sun, takes 365 ¼ days, or one year. As Earth orbits the sun, it also spins on its axis, an invisible line through the center of Earth from the North Pole to the South Pole. This movement is called a rotation.

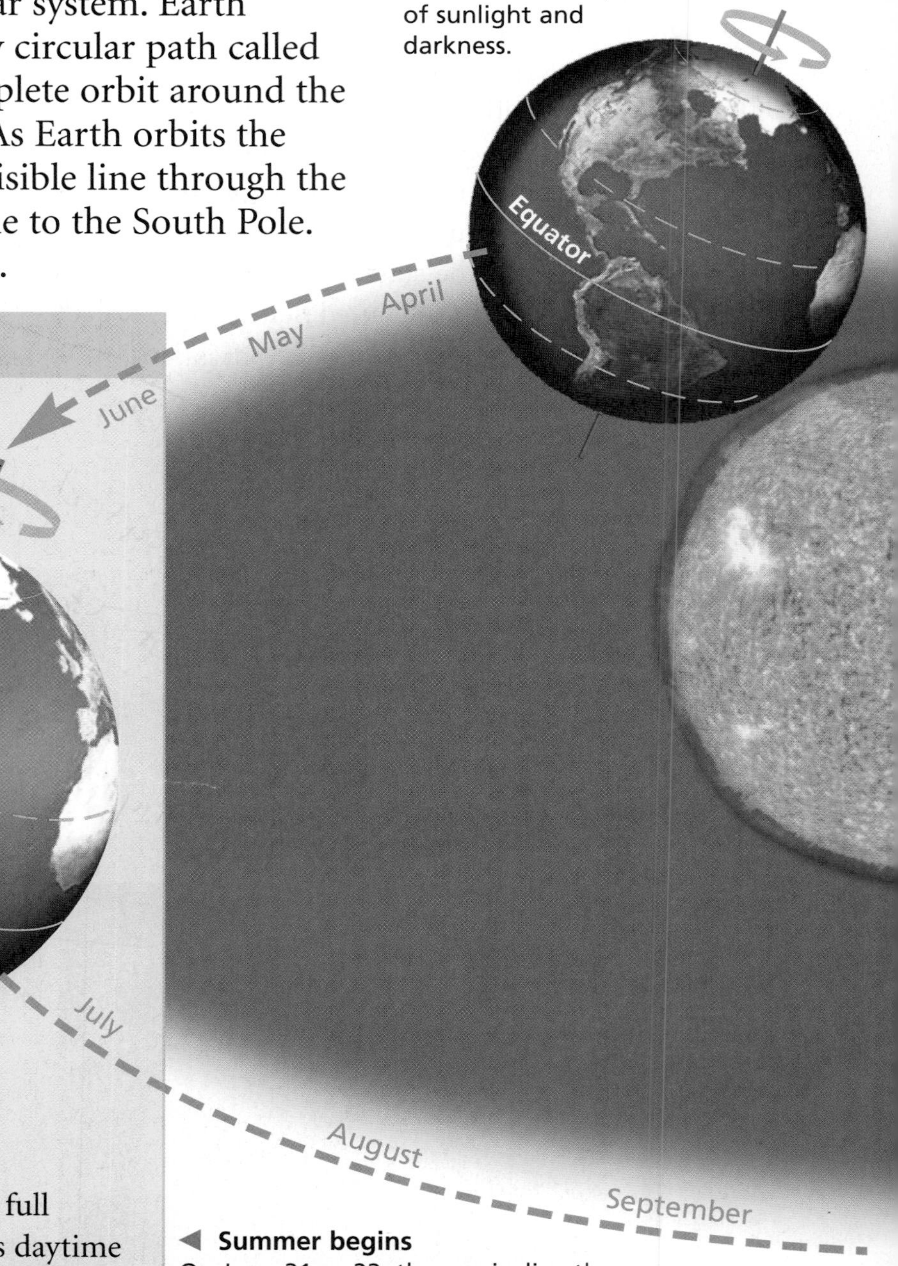

How Night Changes Into Day

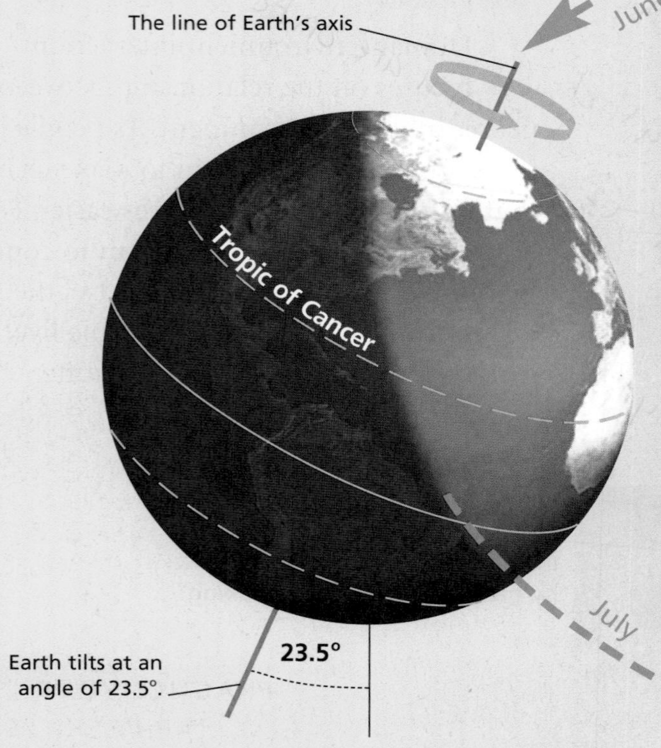

The line of Earth's axis

Tropic of Cancer

Earth tilts at an angle of 23.5°.

23.5°

Earth takes about 24 hours to make one full rotation on its axis. As Earth rotates, it is daytime on the side facing the sun. It is night on the side away from the sun.

▼ **Spring begins**
On March 20 or 21, the sun is directly overhead at the Equator. The Northern and Southern Hemispheres receive almost equal hours of sunlight and darkness.

Equator

June
May
April

July
August
September

◄ **Summer begins**
On June 21 or 22, the sun is directly overhead at the Tropic of Cancer. The Northern Hemisphere receives the greatest number of sunlight hours.

The Seasons

Earth's axis is tilted at an angle. Because of this tilt, sunlight strikes different parts of Earth at different times in the year, creating seasons. The illustration below shows how the seasons are created in the Northern Hemisphere. In the Southern Hemisphere, the seasons are reversed.

PRACTICE YOUR GEOGRAPHY SKILLS

1 What causes the seasons in the Northern Hemisphere to be the opposite of those in the Southern Hemisphere?

2 During which two days of the year do the Northern Hemisphere and Southern Hemisphere have equal hours of daylight and darkness?

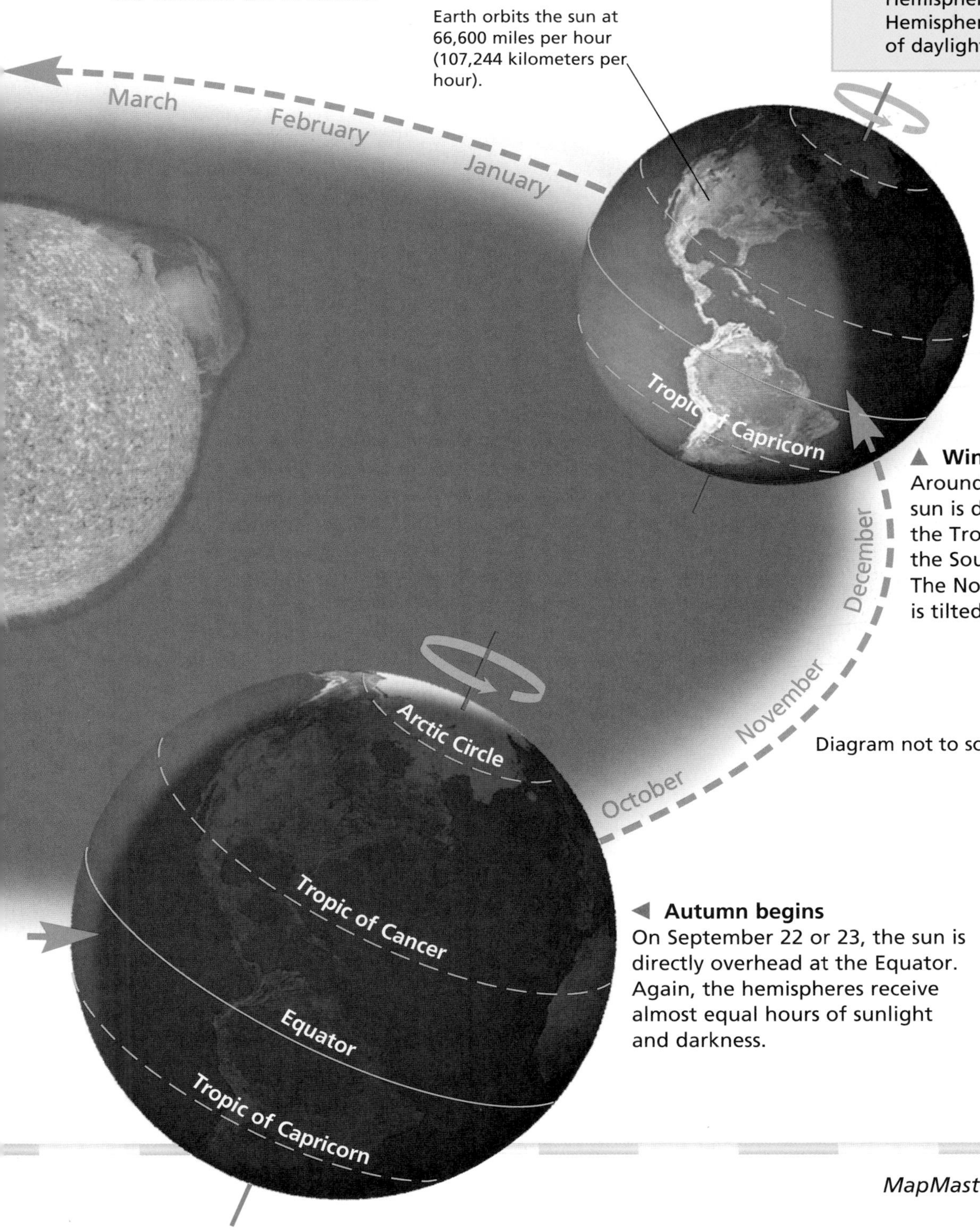

Earth orbits the sun at 66,600 miles per hour (107,244 kilometers per hour).

March
February
January

Tropic of Capricorn

December
November
October

▲ **Winter begins**
Around December 21, the sun is directly overhead at the Tropic of Capricorn in the Southern Hemisphere. The Northern Hemisphere is tilted away from the sun.

Diagram not to scale

Arctic Circle

Tropic of Cancer

Equator

Tropic of Capricorn

◀ **Autumn begins**
On September 22 or 23, the sun is directly overhead at the Equator. Again, the hemispheres receive almost equal hours of sunlight and darkness.

Understanding Globes

A globe is a scale model of Earth. It shows the actual shapes, sizes, and locations of all Earth's landmasses and bodies of water. Features on the surface of Earth are drawn to scale on a globe. This means that a small unit of measure on the globe stands for a large unit of measure on Earth.

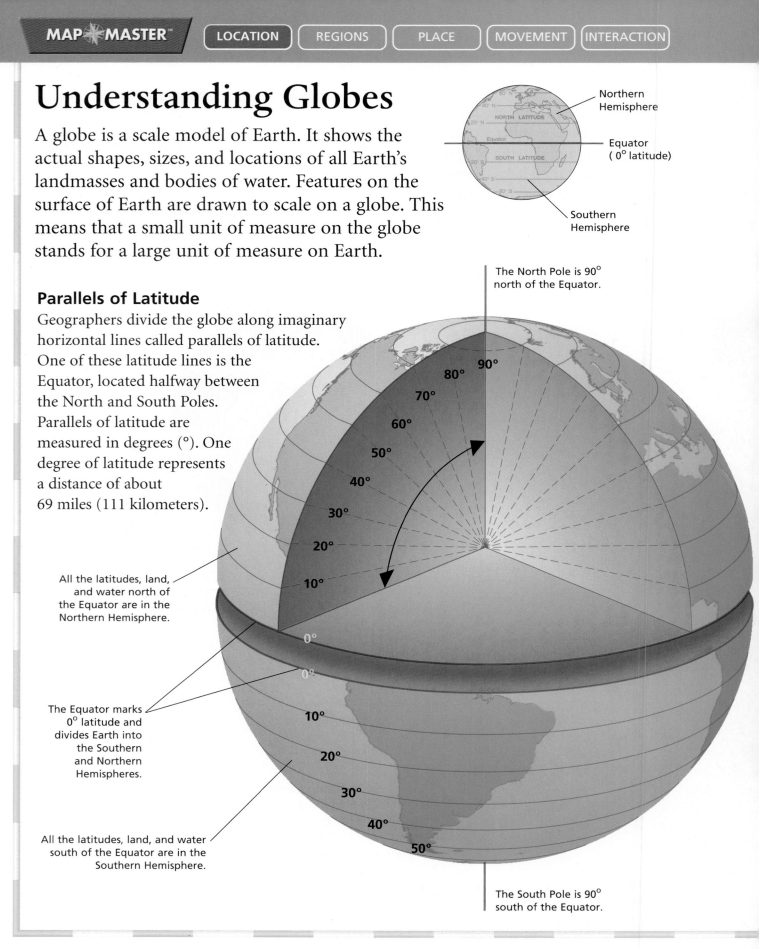

Northern Hemisphere

Equator (0° latitude)

Southern Hemisphere

Parallels of Latitude

Geographers divide the globe along imaginary horizontal lines called parallels of latitude. One of these latitude lines is the Equator, located halfway between the North and South Poles. Parallels of latitude are measured in degrees (°). One degree of latitude represents a distance of about 69 miles (111 kilometers).

The North Pole is 90° north of the Equator.

All the latitudes, land, and water north of the Equator are in the Northern Hemisphere.

The Equator marks 0° latitude and divides Earth into the Southern and Northern Hemispheres.

All the latitudes, land, and water south of the Equator are in the Southern Hemisphere.

The South Pole is 90° south of the Equator.

Meridians of Longitude

Geographers also divide the globe along imaginary vertical lines called meridians of longitude, which are measured in degrees (°). The longitude line called the Prime Meridian runs from pole to pole through Greenwich, England. All meridians of longitude come together at the North and South Poles.

PRACTICE YOUR GEOGRAPHY SKILLS

1 Which continents lie completely in the Northern Hemisphere? In the Western Hemisphere?

2 Is there land or water at 20° S latitude and the Prime Meridian? At the Equator and 60° W longitude?

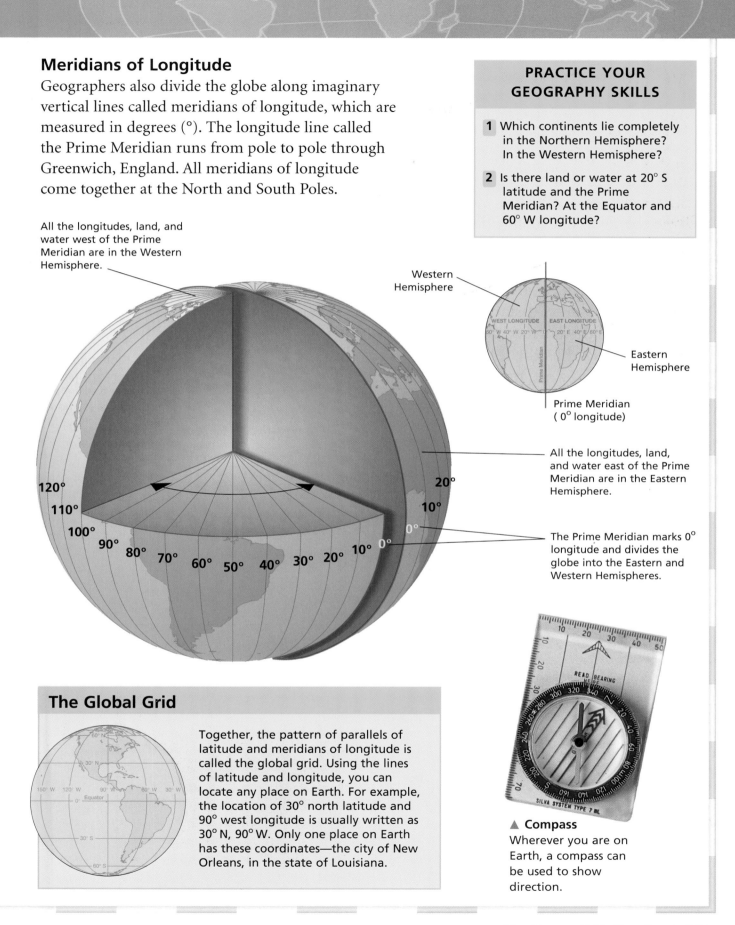

All the longitudes, land, and water west of the Prime Meridian are in the Western Hemisphere.

Western Hemisphere

Eastern Hemisphere

Prime Meridian (0° longitude)

All the longitudes, land, and water east of the Prime Meridian are in the Eastern Hemisphere.

The Prime Meridian marks 0° longitude and divides the globe into the Eastern and Western Hemispheres.

The Global Grid

Together, the pattern of parallels of latitude and meridians of longitude is called the global grid. Using the lines of latitude and longitude, you can locate any place on Earth. For example, the location of 30° north latitude and 90° west longitude is usually written as 30° N, 90° W. Only one place on Earth has these coordinates—the city of New Orleans, in the state of Louisiana.

▲ **Compass**
Wherever you are on Earth, a compass can be used to show direction.

Map Projections

Maps are drawings that show regions on flat surfaces. Maps are easier to use and carry than globes, but they cannot show the correct size and shape of every feature on Earth's curved surface. They must shrink some places and stretch others. To make up for this distortion, mapmakers use different map projections. No one projection can accurately show the correct area, shape, distance, and direction for all of Earth's surface. Mapmakers use the projection that has the least distortion for the information they are presenting.

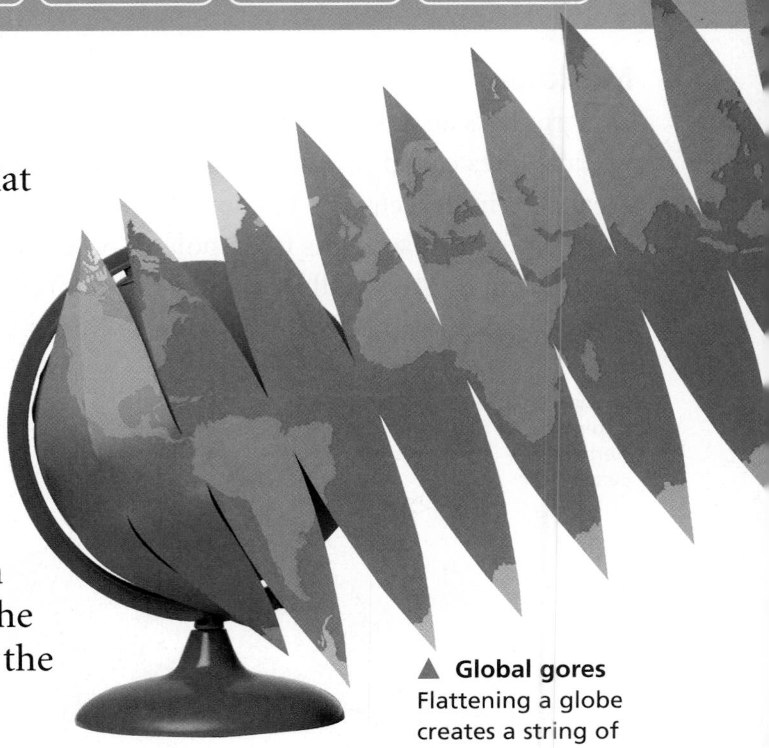

▲ **Global gores**
Flattening a globe creates a string of shapes called gores.

Same-Shape Maps

Map projections that accurately show the shapes of landmasses are called same-shape maps. However, these projections often greatly distort, or make less accurate, the size of landmasses as well as the distance between them. In the projection below, the northern and southern areas of the globe appear more stretched than the areas near the Equator.

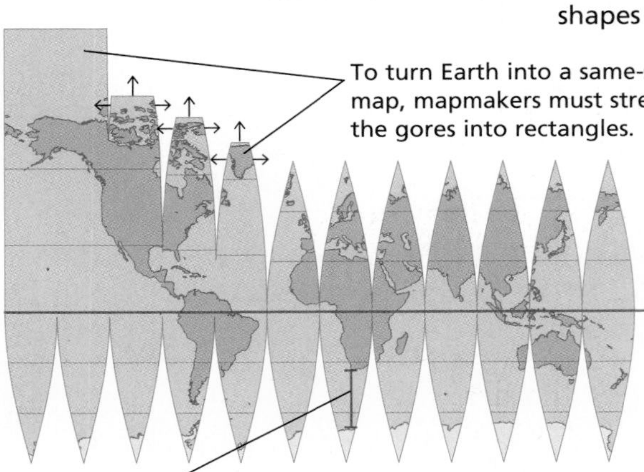

To turn Earth into a same-shape map, mapmakers must stretch the gores into rectangles.

Equator

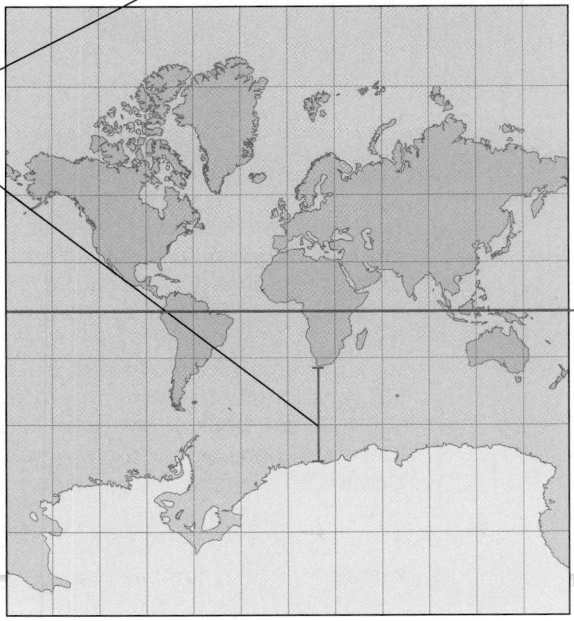

Stretching the gores makes parts of Earth larger. This enlargement becomes greater toward the North and South Poles.

Equator

Mercator projection ▶
One of the most common same-shape maps is the Mercator projection, named for the mapmaker who invented it. The Mercator projection accurately shows shape and direction, but it distorts distance and size. Because the projection shows true directions, ships' navigators use it to chart a straight-line course between two ports.

Equal-Area Maps

Map projections that show the correct size of landmasses are called equal-area maps. In order to show the correct size of landmasses, these maps usually distort shapes. The distortion is usually greater at the edges of the map and less at the center.

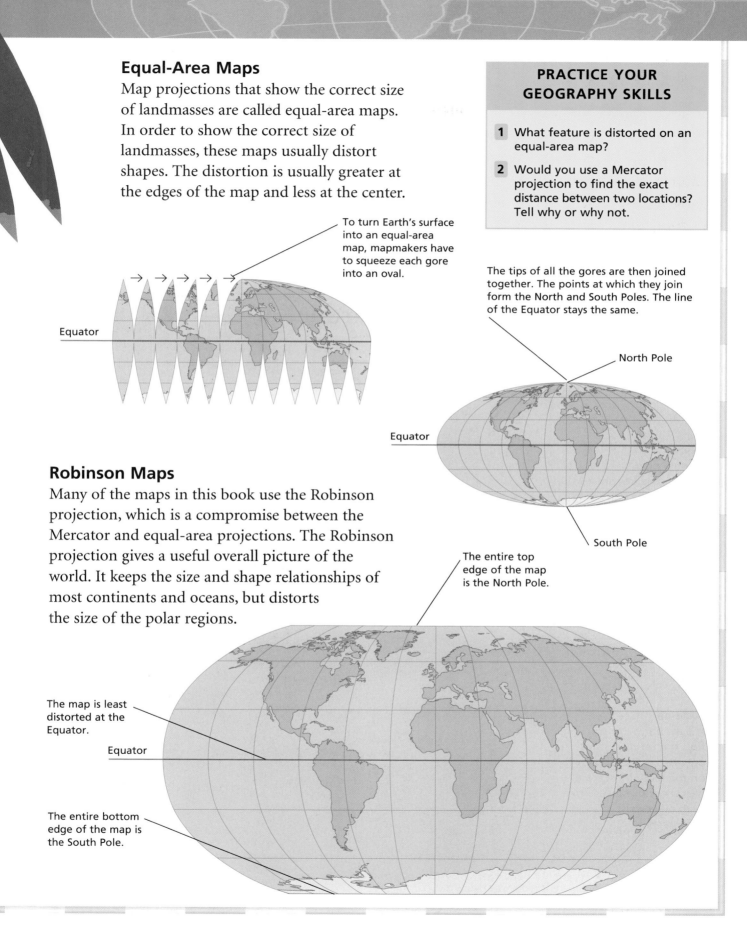

To turn Earth's surface into an equal-area map, mapmakers have to squeeze each gore into an oval.

Equator

The tips of all the gores are then joined together. The points at which they join form the North and South Poles. The line of the Equator stays the same.

North Pole

Equator

South Pole

Robinson Maps

Many of the maps in this book use the Robinson projection, which is a compromise between the Mercator and equal-area projections. The Robinson projection gives a useful overall picture of the world. It keeps the size and shape relationships of most continents and oceans, but distorts the size of the polar regions.

The entire top edge of the map is the North Pole.

The map is least distorted at the Equator.

Equator

The entire bottom edge of the map is the South Pole.

How to Use a Map

Mapmakers provide several clues to help you understand the information on a map. Maps provide different clues, depending on their purpose or scale. However, most maps have several clues in common.

Locator globe
Many maps are shown with locator globes. They show where on the globe the area of the map is located.

Title
All maps have a title. The title tells you the subject of the map.

Compass rose
Many maps show direction by displaying a compass rose with the directions north, east, south, and west. The letters N, E, S, and W are placed to indicate these directions.

Key
Often a map has a key, or legend. The key shows the symbols and colors used on the map, and what each one means.

Western Europe

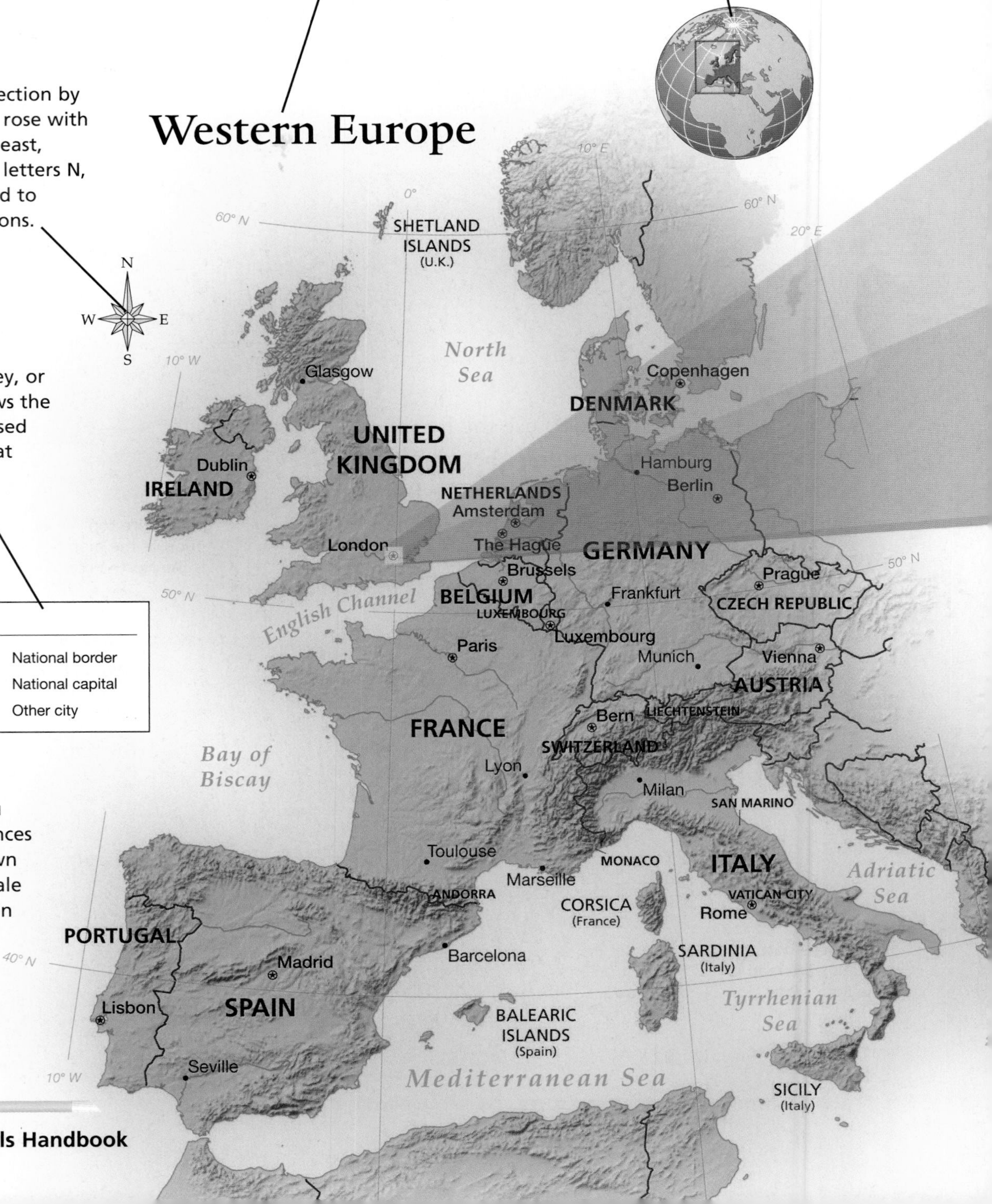

Key

——	National border
⊕	National capital
•	Other city

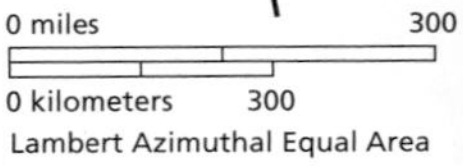

Scale bar
A scale bar helps you find the actual distances between points shown on the map. Most scale bars show distances in both miles and kilometers.

0 miles 300
0 kilometers 300
Lambert Azimuthal Equal Area

SHETLAND ISLANDS (U.K.)

North Sea

Glasgow

DENMARK Copenhagen

UNITED KINGDOM

Dublin Hamburg
IRELAND NETHERLANDS Berlin
Amsterdam
London The Hague GERMANY
Brussels
BELGIUM Frankfurt Prague
LUXEMBOURG CZECH REPUBLIC
Paris Luxembourg
Munich Vienna
FRANCE AUSTRIA
Bern LIECHTENSTEIN
SWITZERLAND
Lyon
Milan SAN MARINO

Bay of Biscay

Toulouse
Marseille MONACO ITALY Adriatic Sea
ANDORRA CORSICA VATICAN CITY
(France) Rome
PORTUGAL
Barcelona SARDINIA (Italy)
Madrid
SPAIN Tyrrhenian Sea
Lisbon BALEARIC ISLANDS (Spain)
Seville Mediterranean Sea SICILY (Italy)

English Channel

Maps of Different Scales

Maps are drawn to different scales, depending on their purpose. Here are three maps drawn to very different scales. Keep in mind that maps showing large areas have smaller scales. Maps showing small areas have larger scales.

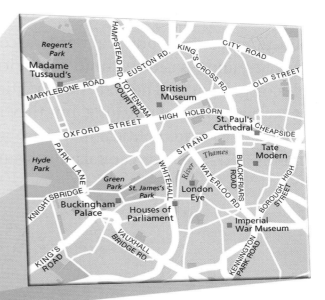

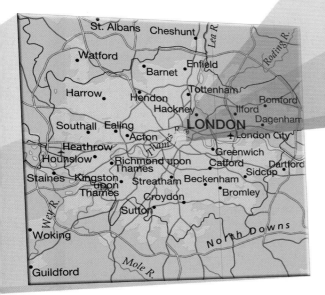

▲ **Greater London**
Find the gray square on the main map of Western Europe (left). This square represents the area shown on the map above. It shows London's boundaries, the general shape of the city, and the features around the city. This map can help you find your way from the airport to the center of town.

▲ **Central London**
Find the gray square on the map of Greater London. This square represents the area shown on the map above. This map moves you closer into the center of London. Like the zoom on a computer or a camera, this map shows a smaller area but in greater detail. It has the largest scale (1 inch represents about 0.9 mile). You can use this map to explore downtown London.

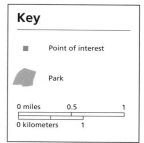

Key

■ Point of interest

▰ Park

0 miles   0.5   1
0 kilometers   1

Key

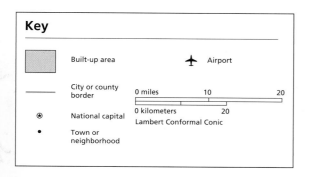

▨ Built-up area   ✈ Airport

— City or county border

⊛ National capital

• Town or neighborhood

0 miles   10   20
0 kilometers   20
Lambert Conformal Conic

PRACTICE YOUR GEOGRAPHY SKILLS

1 What part of a map explains the colors used on the map?

2 How does the scale bar change depending on the scale of the map?

3 Which map would be best for finding the location of the British Museum? Explain why.

Political Maps

Political maps show political borders: continents, countries, and divisions within countries, such as states or provinces. The colors on political maps do not have any special meaning, but they make the map easier to read. Political maps also include symbols and labels for capitals, cities, and towns.

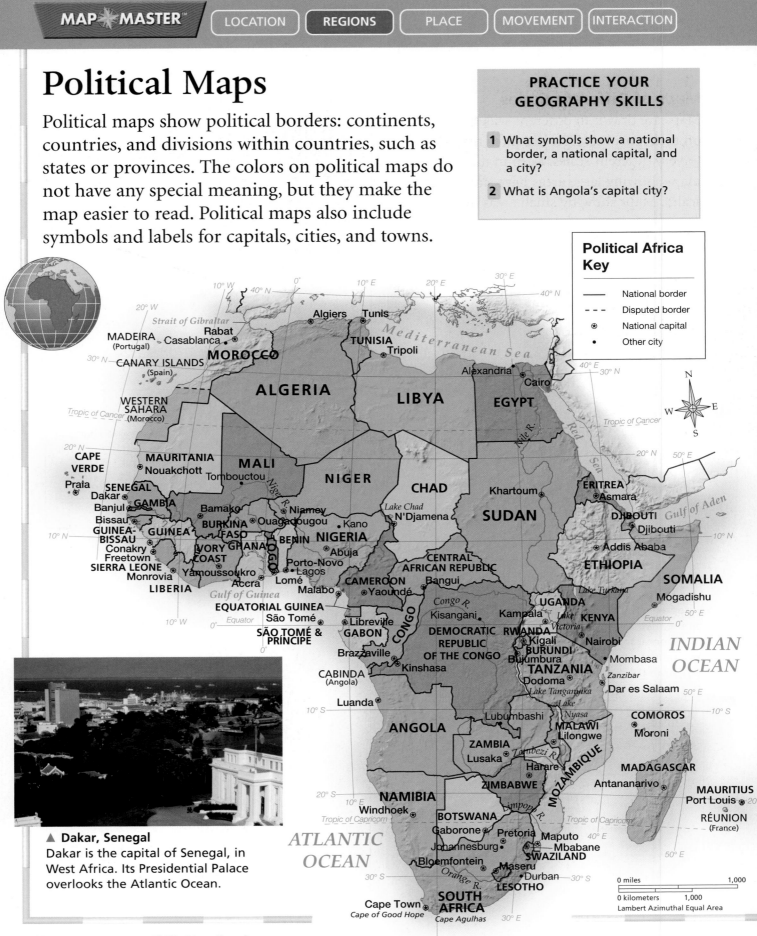

Political Africa Key

	National border
- - -	Disputed border
⊛	National capital
•	Other city

▲ **Dakar, Senegal**
Dakar is the capital of Senegal, in West Africa. Its Presidential Palace overlooks the Atlantic Ocean.

0 miles 1,000
0 kilometers 1,000
Lambert Azimuthal Equal Area

Physical Maps

Physical maps represent what a region looks like by showing its major physical features, such as hills and plains. Physical maps also often show elevation and relief. Elevation, indicated by colors, is the height of the land above sea level. Relief, indicated by shading, shows how sharply the land rises or falls.

PRACTICE YOUR GEOGRAPHY SKILLS

1 Which areas of Africa have the highest elevation?

2 How can you use relief to plan a hiking trip?

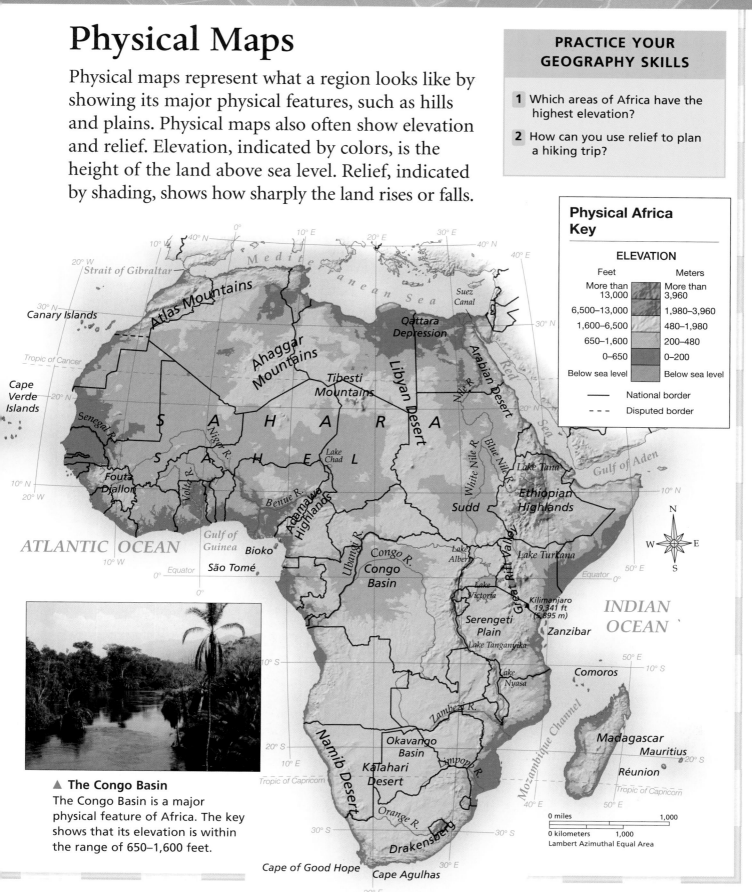

Physical Africa Key

ELEVATION

Feet		Meters
More than 13,000		More than 3,960
6,500–13,000		1,980–3,960
1,600–6,500		480–1,980
650–1,600		200–480
0–650		0–200
Below sea level		Below sea level

——— National border

- - - Disputed border

0 miles 1,000
0 kilometers 1,000
Lambert Azimuthal Equal Area

▲ **The Congo Basin**
The Congo Basin is a major physical feature of Africa. The key shows that its elevation is within the range of 650–1,600 feet.

Special-Purpose Maps: Climate

Unlike the boundary lines on a political map, the boundary lines on climate maps do not separate the land into exact divisions. For example, in this climate map of India, a tropical wet climate gradually changes to a tropical wet and dry climate.

PRACTICE YOUR GEOGRAPHY SKILLS

1 What part of a special-purpose map tells you what the colors on the map mean?

2 Where are arid regions located in India? Are there major cities in those regions?

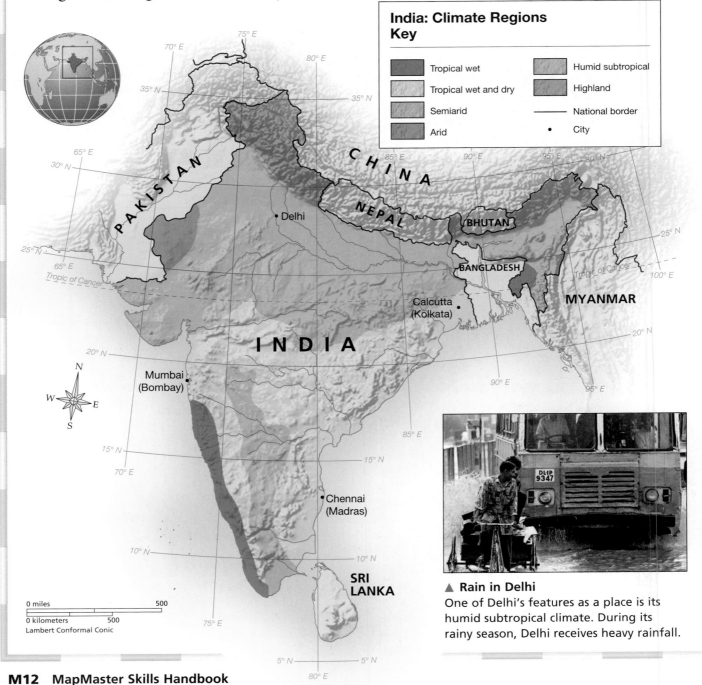

India: Climate Regions Key

Tropical wet

Tropical wet and dry

Semiarid

Arid

Humid subtropical

Highland

National border

City

PAKISTAN

CHINA

NEPAL

BHUTAN

BANGLADESH

MYANMAR

Delhi

Calcutta (Kolkata)

INDIA

Mumbai (Bombay)

Chennai (Madras)

SRI LANKA

Tropic of Cancer

0 miles 500
0 kilometers 500
Lambert Conformal Conic

▲ **Rain in Delhi**
One of Delhi's features as a place is its humid subtropical climate. During its rainy season, Delhi receives heavy rainfall.

Special-Purpose Maps: Language

This map shows the official languages of India. An official language is the language used by the government. Even though a region has an official language, the people there may speak other languages as well. As in other special-purpose maps, the key explains how the different languages appear on the map.

PRACTICE YOUR GEOGRAPHY SKILLS

1 What color represents the Malayalam language on this map?

2 Where in India is Tamil the official language?

The Hindi language ▶
Hindi is the most widely spoken language in India. It is also the most popular language in Delhi.

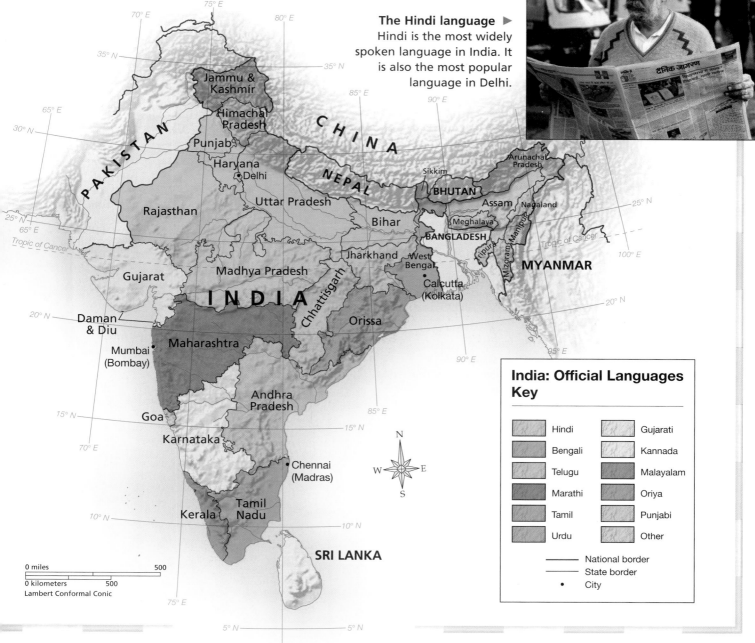

India: Official Languages Key

Hindi	Gujarati
Bengali	Kannada
Telugu	Malayalam
Marathi	Oriya
Tamil	Punjabi
Urdu	Other

— National border
— State border
• City

0 miles 500
0 kilometers 500
Lambert Conformal Conic

Human Migration

Migration is an important part of the study of geography. Since the beginning of history, people have been on the move. As people move, they both shape and are shaped by their environments. Wherever people go, the culture they bring with them mixes with the cultures of the place in which they have settled.

Explorers arrive ▼
In 1492, Christopher Columbus set sail from Spain for the Americas with three ships. The ships shown here are replicas of those ships.

▲ **Native American pyramid**
When Europeans arrived in the Americas, the lands they found were not empty. Diverse groups of people with distinct cultures already lived there. The temple-topped pyramid shown above was built by Mayan Indians in Mexico, long before Columbus sailed.

Migration to the Americas, 1500–1800

A huge wave of migration from the Eastern Hemisphere began in the 1500s. European explorers in the Americas paved the way for hundreds of years of European settlement there. Forced migration from Africa started soon afterward, as Europeans began to import African slaves to work in the Americas. The map at the right shows these migrations.

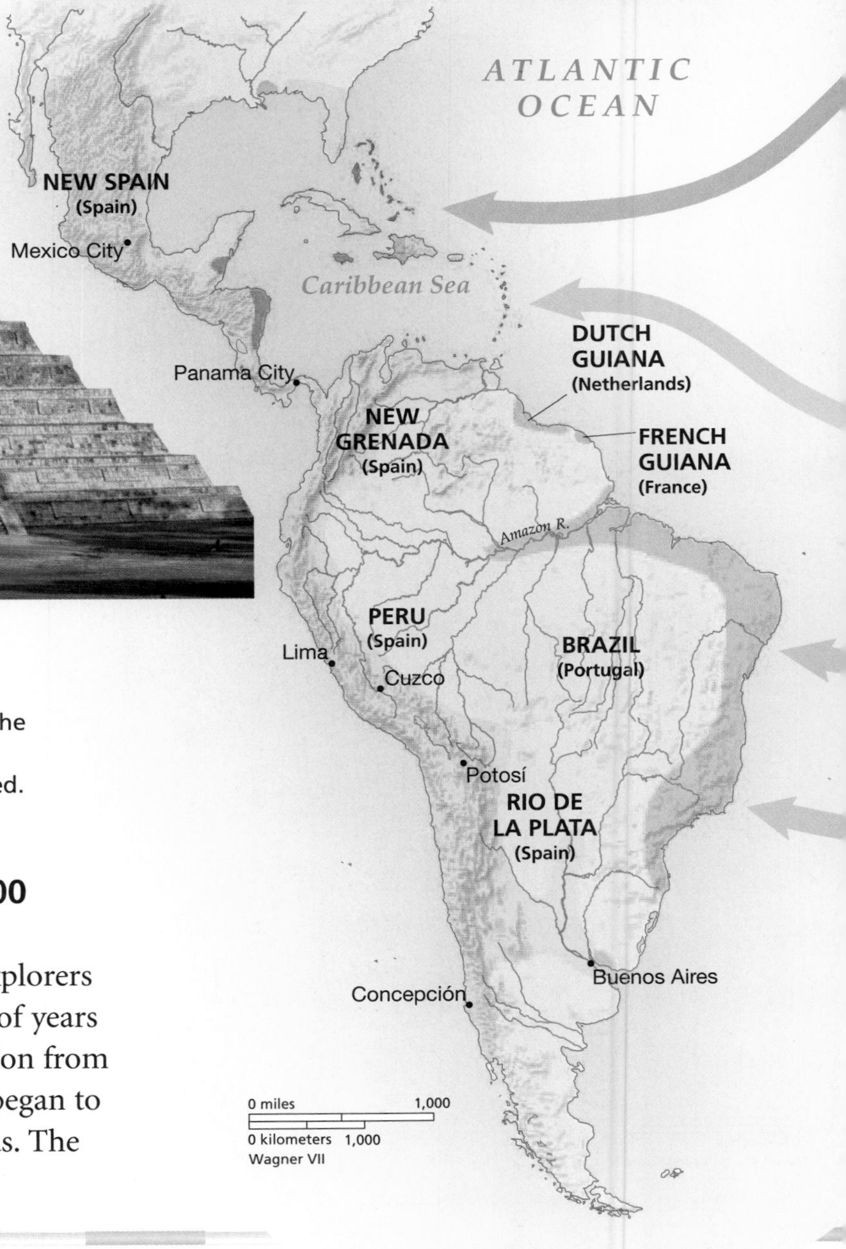

ATLANTIC OCEAN

NEW SPAIN (Spain)
Mexico City•

Caribbean Sea

Panama City•

DUTCH GUIANA (Netherlands)

NEW GRENADA (Spain)

FRENCH GUIANA (France)

Amazon R.

PERU (Spain)
Lima•
•Cuzco

BRAZIL (Portugal)

•Potosí

RIO DE LA PLATA (Spain)

Concepción•

Buenos Aires•

0 miles 1,000
0 kilometers 1,000
Wagner VII

SCOTLAND
IRELAND   ENGLAND
FRANCE   NETHERLANDS
EUROPE
PORTUGAL SPAIN

MOROCCO

N
W   E
S

WALO   **AFRICA**

Saint-Louis
Fort James
Cacheu   **AKAN STATES**   *Niger R.*

Elmina   Accra   **BENIN**
Axim

Congo R.
Congo Basin

KONGO
Luanda
Benguela

ATLANTIC OCEAN

Migration to Latin America, 1500–1800 Key

← European migration	Spain and possessions
← African migration	Portugal and possessions
— National or colonial border	Netherlands and possessions
···· Traditional African border	France and possessions
African State	England and possessions

PRACTICE YOUR GEOGRAPHY SKILLS

1 Where did the Portuguese settle in the Americas?

2 Would you describe African migration at this time as a result of both push factors and pull factors? Explain why or why not.

"Push" and "Pull" Factors

Geographers describe a people's choice to migrate in terms of "push" factors and "pull" factors. Push factors are things in people's lives that push them to leave, such as poverty and political unrest. Pull factors are things in another country that pull people to move there, including better living conditions and hopes of better jobs.

▲ **Elmina, Ghana**
Elmina, in Ghana, is one of the many ports from which slaves were transported from Africa. Because slaves and gold were traded here, stretches of the western African coast were known as the Slave Coast and the Gold Coast.

World Land Use

People around the world have many different economic structures, or ways of making a living. Land-use maps are one way to learn about these structures. The ways that people use the land in each region tell us about the main ways that people in that region make a living.

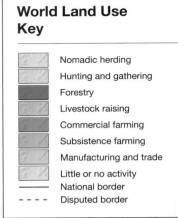

World Land Use Key

	Nomadic herding
	Hunting and gathering
	Forestry
	Livestock raising
	Commercial farming
	Subsistence farming
	Manufacturing and trade
	Little or no activity
——	National border
- - - -	Disputed border

▲ **Wheat farming in the United States**
Developed countries practice commercial farming rather than subsistence farming. Commercial farming is the production of food mainly for sale, either within the country or for export to other countries. Commercial farmers like these in Oregon often use heavy equipment to farm.

Levels of Development

Notice on the map key the term *subsistence farming*. This term means the production of food mainly for use by the farmer's own family. In less-developed countries, subsistence farming is often one of the main economic activities. In contrast, in developed countries there is little subsistence farming.

▲ **Growing barley in Ecuador**
Subsistence farmers like this one in Ecuador use hand tools to harvest barley. They use most of their crop to feed themselves or their farm animals.

NORTH AMERICA

SOUTH AMERICA

0 miles 2,00
0 kilometers 2,000
Robinson

▲ Growing rice in Vietnam
Women in Vietnam plant rice in wet rice paddies, using the same planting methods their ancestors did.

PRACTICE YOUR GEOGRAPHY SKILLS

1 In what parts of the world is subsistence farming the main land use?

2 Locate where manufacturing and trade are the main land use. Are they found more often near areas of subsistence farming or areas of commercial farming? Why might this be so?

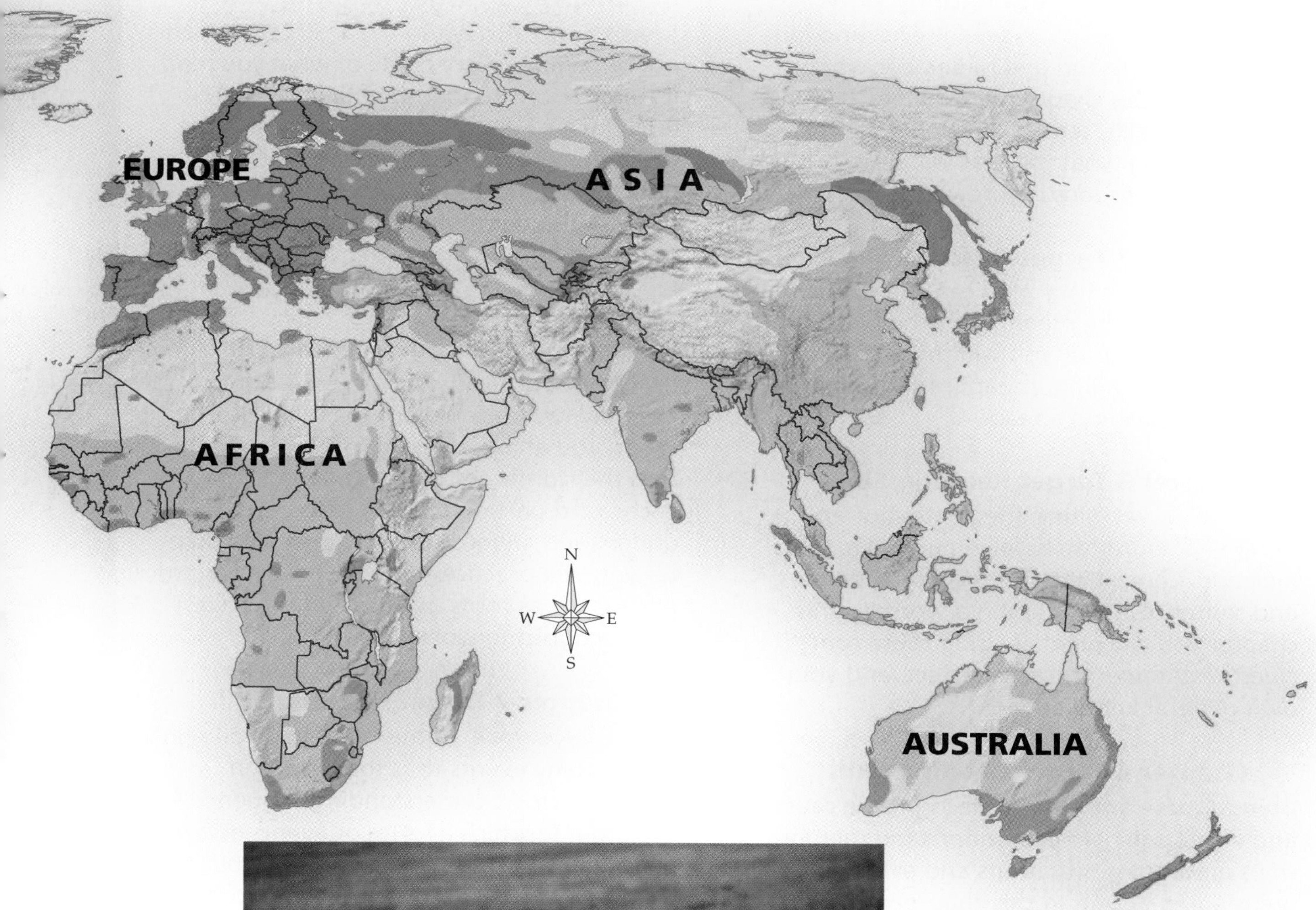

EUROPE

ASIA

AFRICA

N
W　　E
S

AUSTRALIA

◄ Herding cattle in Kenya
Besides subsistence farming, nomadic herding is another economic activity in Africa. This man drives his cattle across the Kenyan grasslands.

How to Read Social Studies

Target Reading Skills

The Target Reading Skills introduced on this page will help you understand the words and ideas in this book and in other social studies reading you do. Each chapter focuses on one of these reading skills. Good readers develop a bank of reading strategies, or skills. Then they draw on the particular strategies that will help them understand the text they are reading.

Chapter 1 Target Reading Skill

Using the Reading Process Previewing can help you understand and remember what you read. In this chapter you will practice using these skills: setting a purpose for reading, predicting what the text will be about, and asking questions before you read.

Chapter 2 Target Reading Skill

Clarifying Meaning You can use several skills to clarify the meaning of the word or idea. In this chapter you will practice these strategies: rereading, paraphrasing, summarizing, and reading ahead.

Chapter 3 Target Reading Skill

Using Context Using the context of an unfamiliar word can help you understand its meaning. Context includes the words, phrases, and sentences surrounding a word. In this chapter you will practice using these context clues: restatements, cause, effect, and your own general knowledge.

Chapter 4 Target Reading Skill

Using Cause and Effect Recognizing cause and effect will help you understand relationships among the situations and events you are reading about. In this chapter you will practice these skills: identifying causes and effects, recognizing cause-and-effect signal words, recognizing multiple causes, and understanding effects.

Chapter 5 Target Reading Skill

Identifying the Main Idea Since you cannot remember every detail of what you read, it is important to identify main ideas. The main idea of a section or paragraph is the most important point, the one you want to remember. In this chapter you will practice these skills: identifying both stated and implied main ideas and identifying supporting details.

Chapter 6 Target Reading Skill

Using Word Analysis You can analyze, or examine, words to determine their meaning. When you analyze words, you break them into their different parts. Knowing what each word part means will help you to understand a word's meaning. In this chapter you will practice these skills: using word parts (such as roots, prefixes, and suffixes) and recognizing word origins.

Chapter 7 Target Reading Skill

Using Sequence In this book you will read about many events that took place in ancient history. Understanding sequence—the order in which a series of events occurs—helps you to understand and remember the events. In this chapter you will practice these skills: identifying sequence and recognizing sequence signal words.

THE ANCIENT WORLD

The cities of ancient times bustled with activity. People shopped at markets, worked, and lived in families, as people do today. Builders, teachers, rulers, and thinkers invented objects, systems, and technology that we still know and use today. Who could have known how their beliefs and customs would affect the modern world?

Guiding Questions

The text, photographs, maps, and charts in this book will help you discover answers to these Guiding Questions.

1. **Geography** How did physical geography affect the growth of ancient civilizations?

2. **History** What historical accomplishments is each civilization known for?

3. **Culture** What were the beliefs and values of ancient peoples?

4. **Government** How did ancient peoples develop governments?

5. **Economics** How did ancient peoples develop economic systems?

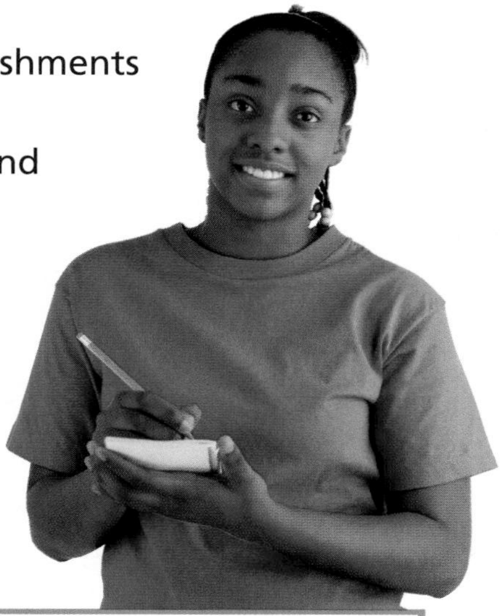

Project Preview

You can also discover answers to the Guiding Questions by working on projects. Several project possibilities are listed on page 244 of this book.

Investigate the Ancient World

The Ancient World is a phrase we use to describe the world during a long period of time. That period begins with prehistory—the time before writing was invented—and ends with the fall of the Roman Empire, an important ancient civilization. In the following pages, you'll locate the civilizations of the ancient world and investigate how they were shaped by geography and the movements of people.

Go Online Use Web Code **lbp-2000** for the
PHSchool.com **interactive maps** on these pages.

▲ **The Great Wall of China**
The ancient Chinese produced many great achievements in technology, the arts, and science. The Chinese also built the Great Wall, which extended thousands of miles across the country.

India, China, and Rome

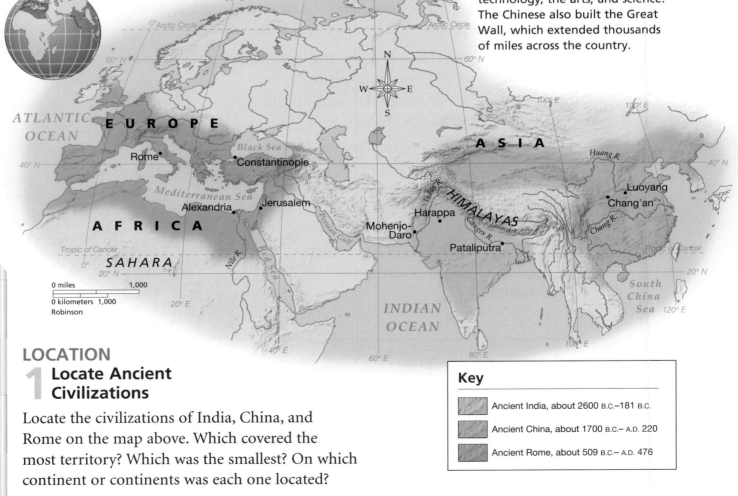

LOCATION

1 Locate Ancient Civilizations

Locate the civilizations of India, China, and Rome on the map above. Which covered the most territory? Which was the smallest? On which continent or continents was each one located?

Key

	Ancient India, about 2600 B.C.–181 B.C.
	Ancient China, about 1700 B.C.– A.D. 220
	Ancient Rome, about 509 B.C.– A.D. 476

Greece, Mesopotamia, Egypt, and Nubia

▲ **Ancient Nubia**
The ancient Nubians adopted many Egyptian practices, including burying their rulers in pyramids. The pyramids in the photo lie north of Khartoum in Sudan.

Black Sea

Athens

Aegean Sea

Mediterranean Sea

Tigris R.

Euphrates R.

Jerusalem

Babylon

Ur

Memphis

Thebes

Red Sea

Persian Gulf

Nile R.

Tropic of Cancer

0 miles 500
0 kilometers 500
Lambert Azimuthal Equal Area

Key

	Ancient Mesopotamia, about 3300 B.C.–539 B.C.
	Ancient Egypt, about 3100 B.C.–31 B.C.
	Ancient Nubia, about 3100 B.C.–A.D. 350
	Ancient Greece, about 2000 B.C.–146 B.C.

▲ **Egyptian fan**
This golden fan dates from 1336–1327 B.C.

PLACE
2 Understand Historical Dates

People have created different systems to help them study history. One is based on the year Jesus of Nazareth was born, and uses the symbols B.C. and A.D. The letters B.C. stand for "before Christ," and refer to the years before Jesus' birth. The letters A.D. stand for "anno Domini," and mean "in the year of our lord," or the years after Jesus' birth. Look at the maps above and on the previous page. Which civilization began first? Which one lasted the longest? Which ones existed at the same time?

Ancient India

INTERACTION

3 Investigate How Natural Barriers Affect Civilizations

Stretching south from the Himalaya Mountains, the kite-shaped land of India bulges out from Asia into the Indian Ocean. For thousands of years, India had limited contact with the rest of the ancient world. Look at the map below. How do you think mountains and seas helped to separate India from other civilizations? How might this separation have affected India's culture?

▲ **The Himalaya Mountains**
The Himalayas are the highest mountain system in the world. They form a natural barrier at the northernmost part of India.

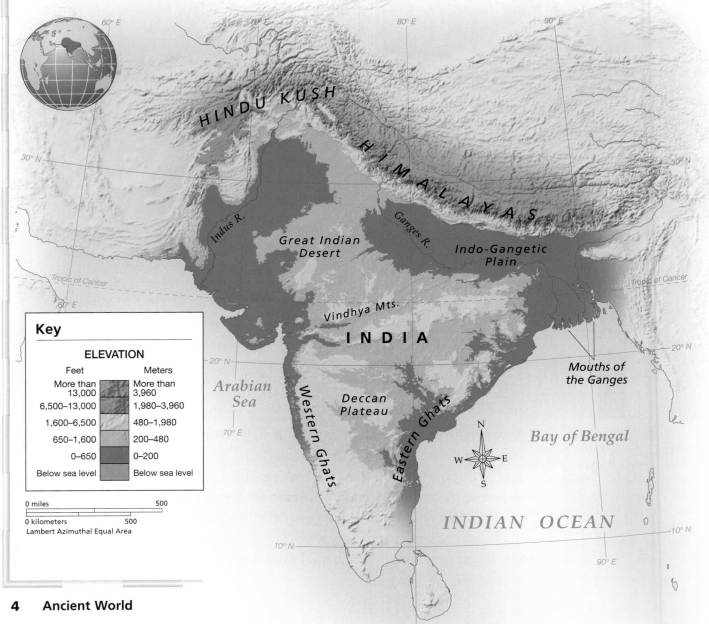

60° E   70° E   80° E   90° E

HINDU KUSH

HIMALAYAS

30° N   30° N

Indus R.
Great Indian Desert
Ganges R.
Indo-Gangetic Plain

Tropic of Cancer   Tropic of Cancer
60° E

Vindhya Mts.

I N D I A

20° N   20° N

Arabian Sea

Western Ghats

Deccan Plateau

Eastern Ghats

Mouths of the Ganges

70° E

Key

ELEVATION

Feet		Meters
More than 13,000		More than 3,960
6,500–13,000		1,980–3,960
1,600–6,500		480–1,980
650–1,600		200–480
0–650		0–200
Below sea level		Below sea level

N
W   E
S

Bay of Bengal

0 miles   500
0 kilometers   500
Lambert Azimuthal Equal Area

INDIAN OCEAN

10° N   10° N

90° E

80° E

The Fertile Crescent

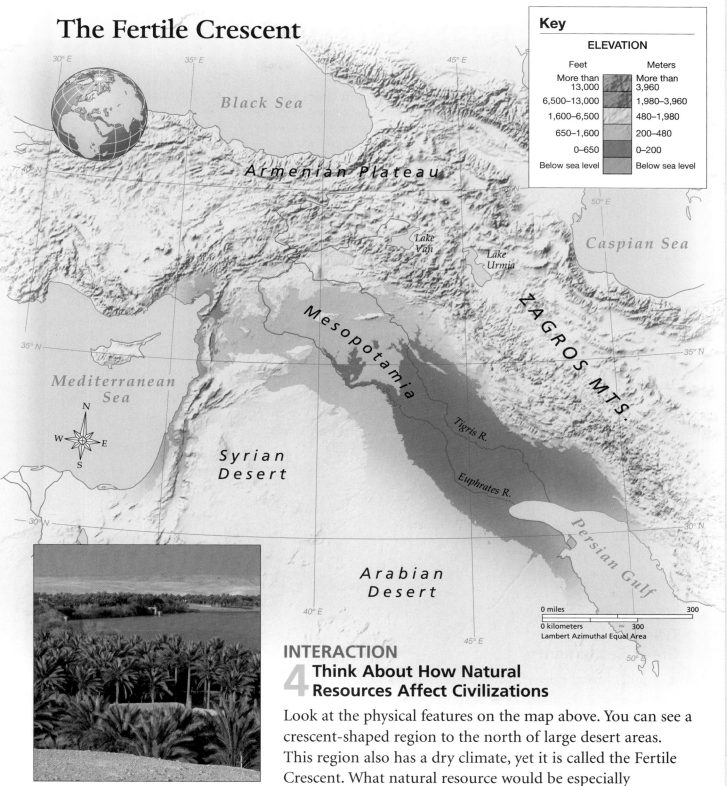

Key

ELEVATION

Feet		Meters
More than 13,000		More than 3,960
6,500–13,000		1,980–3,960
1,600–6,500		480–1,980
650–1,600		200–480
0–650		0–200
Below sea level		Below sea level

Black Sea

Armenian Plateau

Lake Van

Lake Urmia

Caspian Sea

Mesopotamia

ZAGROS MTS.

Mediterranean Sea

Syrian Desert

Tigris R.

Euphrates R.

Persian Gulf

Arabian Desert

0 miles 300
0 kilometers 300
Lambert Azimuthal Equal Area

▲ **The Euphrates River**
The Euphrates River was an important source of water for the people living in the Fertile Crescent.

INTERACTION

4 Think About How Natural Resources Affect Civilizations

Look at the physical features on the map above. You can see a crescent-shaped region to the north of large desert areas. This region also has a dry climate, yet it is called the Fertile Crescent. What natural resource would be especially important in a dry region? What two features on the map would make the region fertile? In what parts of the Fertile Crescent would most people have lived?

Greek Settlements

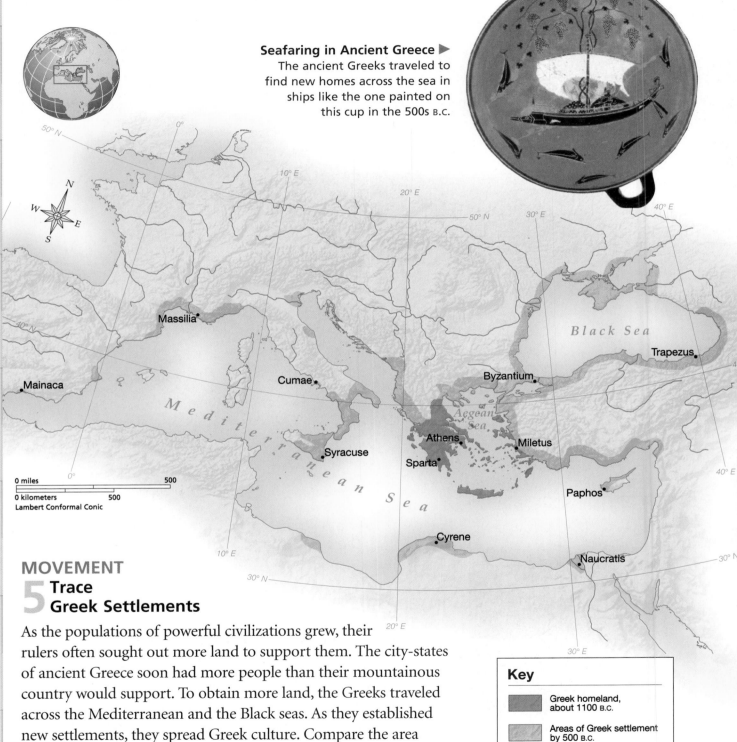

Seafaring in Ancient Greece ▶
The ancient Greeks traveled to find new homes across the sea in ships like the one painted on this cup in the 500s B.C.

MOVEMENT

5 Trace Greek Settlements

As the populations of powerful civilizations grew, their rulers often sought out more land to support them. The city-states of ancient Greece soon had more people than their mountainous country would support. To obtain more land, the Greeks traveled across the Mediterranean and the Black seas. As they established new settlements, they spread Greek culture. Compare the area of Greek settlements on the map with the area of the Greek homeland. Which is larger? Near what physical feature are all of the settlements located? Why do you think this is so?

Key

▨	Greek homeland, about 1100 B.C.
▨	Areas of Greek settlement by 500 B.C.
•	Greek city

Roman Roads

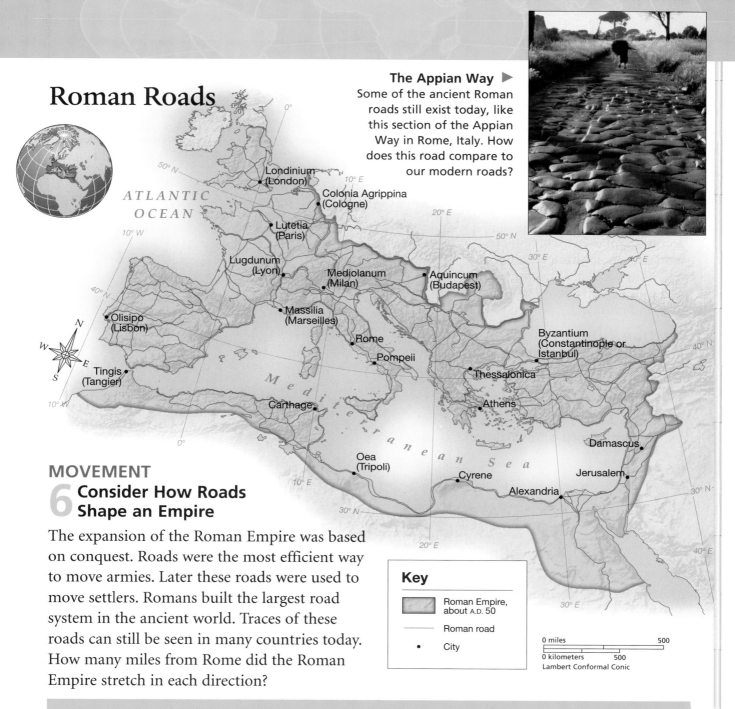

The Appian Way ▶
Some of the ancient Roman roads still exist today, like this section of the Appian Way in Rome, Italy. How does this road compare to our modern roads?

ATLANTIC OCEAN

Londinium (London)

Colonia Agrippina (Cologne)

Lutetia (Paris)

Lugdunum (Lyon)

Mediolanum (Milan)

Aquincum (Budapest)

Olisipo (Lisbon)

Massilia (Marseilles)

Rome

Pompeii

Byzantium (Constantinople or Istanbul)

Thessalonica

Tingis (Tangier)

Athens

Carthage

Mediterranean Sea

Damascus

Oea (Tripoli)

Jerusalem

Cyrene

Alexandria

MOVEMENT

6 Consider How Roads Shape an Empire

The expansion of the Roman Empire was based on conquest. Roads were the most efficient way to move armies. Later these roads were used to move settlers. Romans built the largest road system in the ancient world. Traces of these roads can still be seen in many countries today. How many miles from Rome did the Roman Empire stretch in each direction?

Key

Roman Empire, about A.D. 50

Roman road

• City

0 miles — 500
0 kilometers — 500
Lambert Conformal Conic

APPLY YOUR KNOWLEDGE

1 The world's highest mountains, the Himalayas, form a natural barrier to the north of this country. The people who lived there in ancient times were separated from the rest of the world for centuries by these mountains. What is the name of this Asian country?

2 This city, located between two rivers, was the home of a famous civilization of the Fertile Crescent. It has some of the oldest ruins in the world. What is the name of this city?

3 The world's longest river runs for 4,132 miles (6,648 kilometers) and empties into the Mediterranean Sea. Two ancient pyramid-building civilizations were located along this river's banks. What is the river called?

4 This city was settled by Greeks, but was not part of the Greek homeland. It was located on an island in the Mediterranean Sea, near the tip of a boot-shaped peninsula. What is the name of the city?

The Beginnings of Human Society

Chapter Preview

In this chapter you will find out how archaeologists learn about the past. You will also learn about the connections between geography and history.

Section 1
Geography and History

Section 2
Prehistory

Section 3
The Beginnings of Civilization

Target Reading Skill

Reading Process In this chapter you will focus on previewing to help you understand and remember what you read.

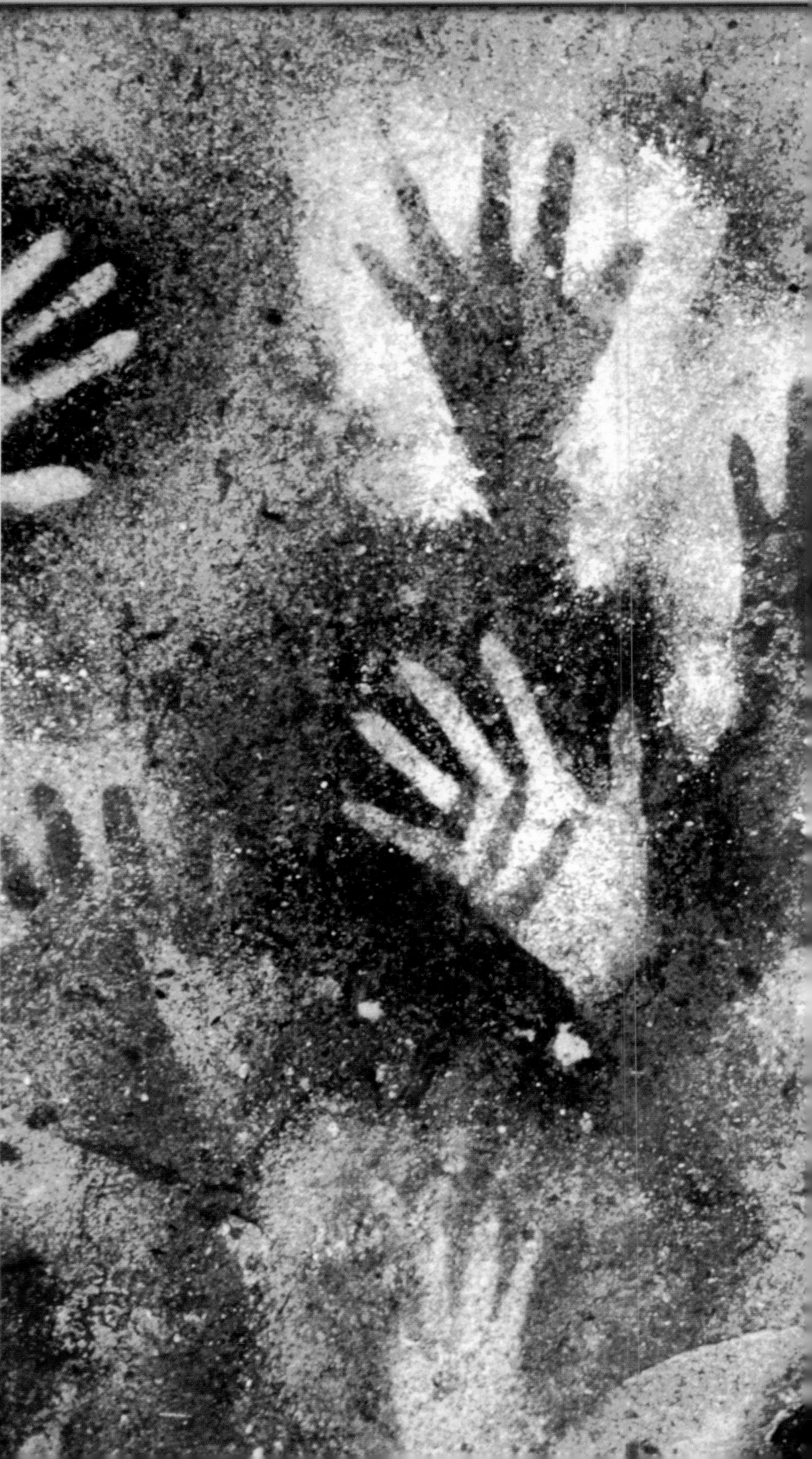

▶ Cave painting from about 5000 B.C., Argentina

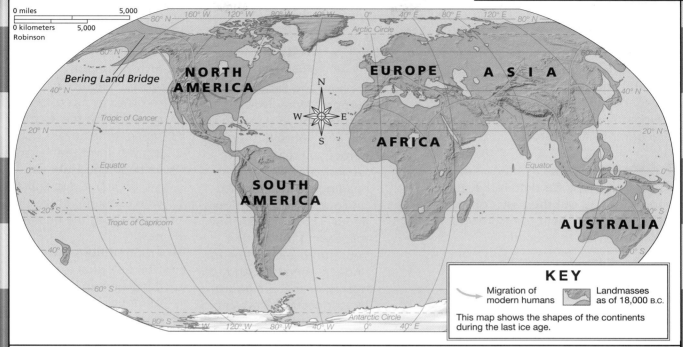

0 miles 5,000
0 kilometers 5,000
Robinson

Bering Land Bridge

NORTH AMERICA

EUROPE   **ASIA**

AFRICA

SOUTH AMERICA

AUSTRALIA

Arctic Circle
Tropic of Cancer
Equator
Tropic of Capricorn
Antarctic Circle

KEY

→ Migration of modern humans

Landmasses as of 18,000 B.C.

This map shows the shapes of the continents during the last ice age.

Movement Modern humans may have originated more than 100,000 years ago in Africa before spreading to other parts of the world. This migration most likely took place over many thousands of years. **Identify** What landmass did modern humans cross to travel from Asia into North America? **Infer** Why did the migration of humans from Africa to the rest of the world take place so slowly? Explain your answer.

Go Online
PHSchool.com Use Web Code **lbp-2111** for step-by-step **map skills practice.**

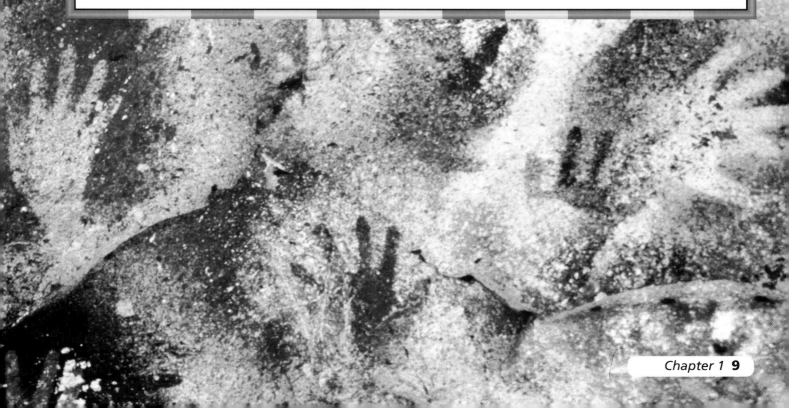

Prepare to Read

Objectives

In this section you will
1. Learn what tools are used to understand history.
2. Find out about the connections between geography and history.

Taking Notes

As you read, look for details that tell how people learn about the past. Copy the concept web below, and use it to record your findings. Add more ovals as needed.

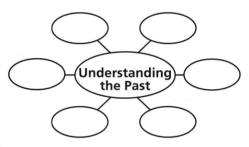

Understanding the Past

Target Reading Skill

Preview and Set a Purpose When you set a purpose for your reading, you give yourself a focus. Before you read this section, preview the headings and pictures to find out what the section is about. Then set a purpose for reading this section. Your purpose might be to find out about the study of history, or to learn about the connections between geography and history. Finally, read to meet your purpose.

Key Terms

- **history** (HIS tuh ree) *n.* written and other recorded events of people
- **prehistory** (pree HIS tuh ree) *n.* time before writing was invented
- **archaeologist** (ahr kee AHL uh jist) *n.* a scientist who examines objects to learn about the human past
- **oral traditions** (AWR ul truh DISH unz) *n.* stories passed down by word of mouth
- **geography** (jee AHG ruh fee) *n.* the study of Earth's surface and the processes that shape it

A scientist recovers the body of the ancient Iceman from a glacier in the Alps.

He is called the Iceman. His frozen body was found in a mountain pass in the Alps, on the Italian-Austrian border in Europe.

Two hikers discovered the Iceman by chance in 1991. His body and possessions were taken to a laboratory, where scientists learned more about him. His clothing, tools, and his body were well preserved. They provided clues about the Iceman's life and death. Scientists used these clues to build a story of his life. To learn how the Iceman died, see the Links to Science on the next page.

Scientists determined that the Iceman lived about 5,000 years ago, in about 3000 B.C. The Iceman's finely stitched animal skins showed that he probably came from a community that included people who were skilled in sewing.

The most important clue about the Iceman's life was his copper ax. Copper was the first metal used by Europeans, beginning about 4000 B.C. The ax left no doubt that the Iceman lived after people had learned to use copper. In many ways, the story of the Iceman helps us to understand the story of our past.

Understanding History

The scientists' curiosity about the Iceman's life was natural. As human beings, we are curious about our earliest origins. What was life like many thousands of years ago?

Before and After Writing About 5,000 years ago, peoples in Southwest Asia and in Africa developed systems of writing. They began to keep written records of their experiences. These developments marked the beginning of **history,** the written and other recorded events of people. By adding the prefix *pre-*, which means "before," you form the word *prehistory*. **Prehistory** is the time before history. Prehistory is the period of time before writing was invented.

Prehistory: Digging Up the Past To learn about life in prehistoric times, scientists must rely on clues other than written records. **Archaeologists** (ahr kee AHL uh jists) are scientists who examine objects to learn about past peoples and cultures. They sift through the dirt of prehistoric camps to find bones, tools, and other objects. These objects may tell them something about the people who lived there. For example, the size of stone spear points shows what kinds of game the people hunted. To kill big game, such as bears, hunters had to use large, heavy spear points. Such points, however, would not work very well with birds and small animals.

Links to
Science

Cause of Death At first, scientists believed that the Iceman had frozen to death. But ten years after the discovery of the Iceman, scientists found an arrowhead lodged in his shoulder. Later, they found a knife wound on his hand. Now scientists believe the Iceman may have died from injuries he received during an armed struggle.

The stone amulet, above, is similar to the one found with the Iceman. The knife and its grass case, left, were among his belongings.

A museum model of the Iceman, right, shows how he may have dressed.

Prehistoric rock painting in South Africa

History: A Record in Writing Historians do not rely only on the objects discovered by archaeologists to learn about the past. They also study the written records of human life and accomplishments to understand a society—its wars, its religion, and its rulers, among other things. Historians also look at what other groups living at the same time wrote about that society.

A Record of the Spoken Word The written records studied by historians often began as **oral traditions,** stories passed down by word of mouth. Oral traditions can include a family's history, such as stories of parents, grandparents, and great-grandparents. They can also tell stories about heroes or events in the past.

Oral traditions are still an important part of many societies today. Not all oral stories are historically accurate. Stories often change as they are told and retold. Like myths and legends, they often contain facts mixed with personal beliefs and exaggerations about heroes. Still, oral traditions tell how a society lived and what the people considered important.

Set a Purpose
If your purpose is to learn about the study of history, how does reading about oral traditions help you to achieve your purpose?

✓ Reading Check **Why are historians interested in oral traditions?**

Carrying on a Tradition
In West Africa, a professional storyteller called a griot (GREE oh) keeps oral traditions alive.
Draw Conclusions
How does a community benefit from knowing about its recent and ancient past?

Linking Geography and History

Knowing when something happened is important. Understanding why historic events took place is also important. To do this, historians often turn to **geography,** the study of Earth's surface and the processes that shape it. Geography also refers to the features of a place, including its climate, landscape, and location.

Knowing the connections between geography and history is often the key to understanding why events happened. Weather patterns, the water supply, and the landscape of a place all affect the lives of the people who live there. For example, to explain why the ancient Egyptians developed a successful civilization, you must look at the geography of Egypt.

Egyptian civilization was built on the banks of the Nile River in Africa. Each year the Nile flooded, depositing soil on its banks. Because the soil was rich, Egyptian farmers could grow enough crops to feed the large numbers of people in the cities. That meant everyone did not have to farm, so some people could perform other jobs that helped develop the civilization. Without the Nile and its regular flooding, Egyptian civilization would not have become so successful.

A farm in Egypt's Nile delta

✓ **Reading Check** **Give one example of geography's effect on history.**

Section 1 Assessment

Key Terms
Review the key terms at the beginning of this section. Use each term in a sentence that explains its meaning.

Target Reading Skill
How did having a reading purpose help you understand this section?

Comprehension and Critical Thinking
1. (a) Recall What do scientists study to learn about prehistory?
(b) Generalize What do we know about societies that leave behind written records?

(c) Draw Inferences Analyze the clothes you wear and the things you carry to school. What do they say about your life? How does your story compare to the Iceman's story?
2. (a) Identify Name some examples of familiar geographic features.
(b) Explain How can geography help us to understand history?
(c) Identify Cause and Effect What effect has geography had on the way people in your community live?

Writing Activity
Ask a classmate to share a story with you. The story should be about an important event in the person's life. Write the story from your classmate's point of view.

For: An activity on archaeology
Visit: PHSchool.com
Web Code: lbd-2101

A wall painting from the ancient city of Knossos, Greece, founded in 2500 B.C.

The post above was used to secure the reins on an animal's harness. It is from the ancient city of Ur, founded in 3500 B.C. in Mesopotamia.

When you study history, you must learn about many different events and the dates on which they occurred. However, a whole page filled with dates can be hard to follow. For that reason, writers often use a simple diagram called a timeline. A timeline shows the order in which events happened. At a glance, a timeline can give you a picture of a certain time period.

Learn the Skill

Refer to page 15 as you follow the steps below.

1 **Read the title of the timeline.** The title tells you what the timeline will show.

2 **Determine the time span.** Look at the beginning and the endpoint of the timeline to determine the time span. If the timeline shows ancient history, it is sometimes divided into two parts. The dates on the left side are marked with the letters *B.C.* The dates on the right side are marked with the letters *A.D.* The letters *B.C.* are an abbreviation of "before Christ" and refer to the years before Jesus' birth. The letters *A.D.* mean "anno Domini," which is Latin for "in the year of our Lord." The letters *A.D.* refer to the time after Jesus' birth.

Notice that with B.C., you count backward. The numbers get larger as you go backward in time. Also note the letter *c.* before some dates. An abbreviation for the Latin word *circa, c.* means "about." Historians often use *circa* or *c.* before dates.

3 **Determine the intervals of time.** A timeline is divided into intervals of time that are marked by vertical lines. Determine how many years occur between the vertical lines. Timelines that show a long span of time have longer intervals, such as 100 or 1,000 years. Timelines that show a short span of time have shorter intervals, such as 10 or 20 years.

4 **Study the events on the timeline.** Each event has a date and is connected to the timeline by a dot and a line. Notice when each event happened. Be sure to notice whether a date has more than one event.

Practice the Skill

Use the timeline below to practice the skill.

1 Find the title of the timeline. Based on the title, do you think this timeline will show a long or a short time span?

2 Determine the time span. Find the beginning of the timeline at the left. Notice that the first date is followed by B.C. Next, find the endpoint of the timeline. Notice that the last date is preceded by A.D. What is the span of time between these two dates?

3 Determine the intervals. Look at the dates marked by vertical lines on the timeline. How far is one date from another?

4 Study the events on the timeline. Notice the kinds of events that are shown and whether they are connected. How can you tell whether some events occurred closer together than others? Look at the abbreviations used with the dates on this timeline. Why is the event "Jesus is born" an important event to show on this particular timeline?

Apply the Skill

Turn to the table titled Early Cities on page 26. Create a timeline based on the information in the table. Follow the steps you used to practice this skill to help you create your timeline.

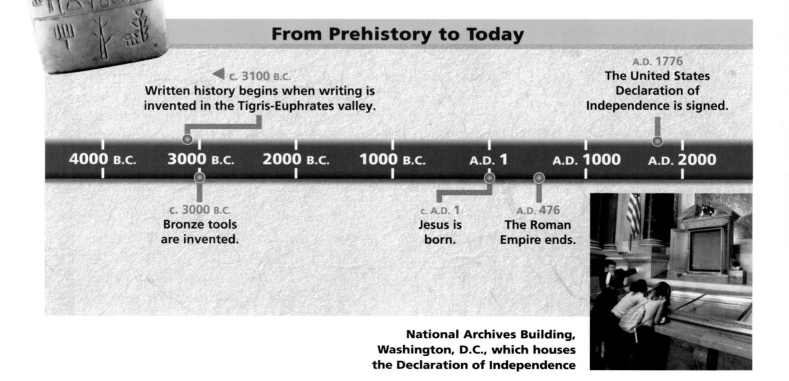

From Prehistory to Today

◀ c. 3100 B.C.
Written history begins when writing is invented in the Tigris-Euphrates valley.

A.D. 1776
The United States Declaration of Independence is signed.

| 4000 B.C. | 3000 B.C. | 2000 B.C. | 1000 B.C. | A.D. 1 | A.D. 1000 | A.D. 2000 |

c. 3000 B.C.
Bronze tools are invented.

c. A.D. 1
Jesus is born.

A.D. 476
The Roman Empire ends.

National Archives Building, Washington, D.C., which houses the Declaration of Independence

Prepare to Read

Objectives

In this section you will
1. Discover how hunter-gatherers lived during the Stone Age.
2. Learn about the beginning of farming.

Taking Notes

As you read, look for details about survival during the Stone Age. Copy the table below, and use it to record your findings.

Topic	Details
Tools	
Hunting	
Gathering	
Fire	
Settlement	
Farming	
Animals	

Target Reading Skill

Preview and Predict
Making predictions about your text helps you to remember what you read. Before you read this section, preview it by looking at the headings and pictures. Then predict what the text might discuss about prehistory. For example, you might predict that the text will explain important events that happened in prehistory. As you read, connect what you read to your prediction. If what you learn doesn't support your prediction, revise your prediction.

Key Terms

- **hominid** (HAHM uh nid) *n.* a modern human or a member of an earlier group that may have included ancestors or relatives of modern humans
- **Stone Age** (stohn ayj) *n.* a period of time during which hominids made lasting tools and weapons mainly from stone; the earliest known period of prehistoric culture
- **nomad** (NOH mad) *n.* a person who has no settled home
- **domesticate** (duh MES tih kayt) *v.* to adapt wild plants or tame wild animals and to breed them for human use

About three and a half million years ago, a huge explosion shook a part of East Africa. A volcano spit out clouds of fine ash that fell on the surrounding land. Then rain came. It turned the blanket of ash into thick mud. Before the mud dried, two individuals walked across the landscape. As they walked, they left their footprints in the mud.

In 1976, a group of scientists discovered the footprints, preserved in stone. They were amazed at their find. The footprints are almost identical to those made by modern humans walking in wet sand. Such evidence may help scientists understand early **hominids**, a term that refers both to modern humans and to earlier groups that may have included ancestors or relatives of modern humans.

Scientists think that hominids made these footprints about 3.5 million years ago.

Stone Age Hunting and Gathering

A million years after the footprints were made, early hominids began making stone tools. By studying these tools, we learn about the development of prehistoric culture.

Stone Age Culture The first use of stone to create tools began the earliest period of human culture: the Stone Age. The Stone Age was a period during which hominids, including modern humans, made lasting tools mainly from stone. They also made tools from wood and animal bones. Scientists think that the Stone Age continued for hundreds of thousands of years, until people learned to use metal for tools.

Archaeologists divide the Stone Age into three periods: the Old Stone Age, the Middle Stone Age, and the New Stone Age. During the Old Stone Age, modern humans and other hominids did not yet know how to farm. They were hunter-gatherers who survived by hunting animals and gathering wild plants. Almost all of human prehistory took place during the Old Stone Age.

Fire! Between about 1,400,000 and 500,000 years ago, early hominids learned how to use fire. No one knows for sure how they learned. Perhaps one day a small band of hunters saw a grass fire caused by lightning on the open plain. Although terrified by the fire, they learned how to keep it going. With fire, they could ward off dangerous animals, who were also afraid of the flames.

Finally, early hominids discovered how to create fire. They probably did this by rubbing two sticks together or by striking stones together to produce a spark. The ability to create fire was an important step for our ancestors. With this great advance, they could move to areas with colder climates.

Links to Science

How Old Is It? After archaeologists find bones, tools, or other objects, they ask themselves that question. Scientists use different tests for dating different objects. One very useful test is called radiocarbon dating. All plants and animals have tiny amounts of a substance called radiocarbon in their bodies. After they die, the radiocarbon changes into another substance. Scientists know how long this change takes. They have tests that measure how much radiocarbon remains. Scientists can then calculate the age of the material. Because the ancient comb, below, is made from the antler of a deer or an elk, radiocarbon dating could be used to determine its age.

A wildfire on the grasslands of Africa

Predict
Based on what you have read so far, is your prediction on target? If not, change your prediction now.

Settling New Areas As early hominids developed the use of tools, they left their original homes in Africa. Their move may have begun as early as one million years ago. Many early hominids were nomads. **Nomads** are people who have no settled home. They moved around to places where they thought they would find food and stayed there for several days. When they had gathered all the food around them, they moved on.

Early hominids eventually spread out over much of Earth. There is evidence that early hominids were living in Asia and Europe at least 500,000 years ago. Many scientists believe that modern humans originated more than 100,000 years ago in Africa and then spread to other parts of the world. Perhaps 30,000 years ago humans crossed from Asia into North America. By 10,000 B.C., humans had reached Chile in South America. Compared with today, humans then were few in number. But as we can today, they survived in all sorts of geographical conditions. They lived in the steamy rain forests of Asia, the cold lands near the Arctic Circle, and the mountains of South America.

✓ **Reading Check** **What was life like during the Stone Age?**

The Beginning of Farming

For tens of thousands of years, our ancestors continued to live as hunter-gatherers. However, some societies entered the Middle Stone Age, which was characterized by the use of more refined, or advanced, tools. Those who began the practice of farming would enter the New Stone Age.

Nomadic Herding
A young shepherd guides her flock to graze in the Taza Province of Morocco in North Africa. **Predict** What factors might influence this nomad's decision to move the sheep from one area to another?

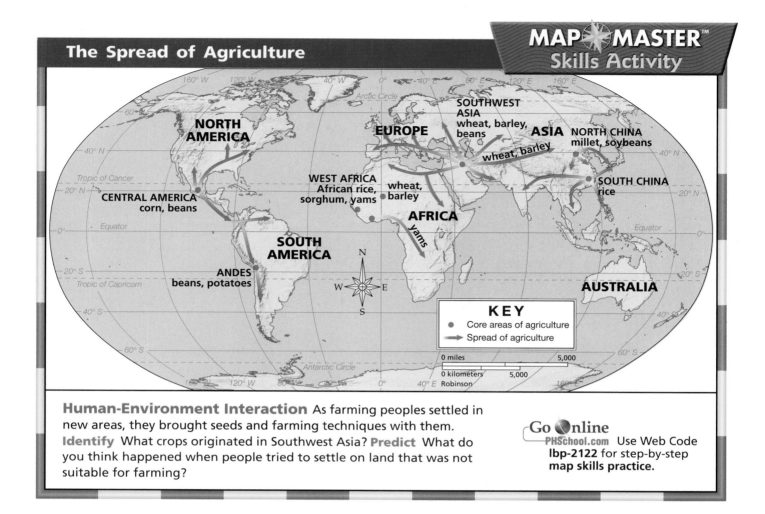

The Spread of Agriculture

Human-Environment Interaction As farming peoples settled in new areas, they brought seeds and farming techniques with them. **Identify** What crops originated in Southwest Asia? **Predict** What do you think happened when people tried to settle on land that was not suitable for farming?

Go Online PHSchool.com Use Web Code lbp-2122 for step-by-step map skills practice.

Early Farmers About 11,000 years ago, people in Southwest Asia made an amazing discovery. They learned that if they planted the seeds of wild grasses, new crops of grasses would come up. Thus began the New Stone Age in Southwest Asia. It was called the New Stone Age because people began to grow their own food. They did not have to be nomads, although they still depended on stone tools. However, in many other parts of the world, the Old and Middle Stone Ages continued for many thousands of years. In some areas, Old Stone Age societies even existed into the 1900s.

At the same time that people began to grow their own food, some people became pastoral nomads. That is, they raised livestock and traveled from place to place in search of grazing areas for their animals. Many people, such as the desert-roaming Bedouins of present-day Iraq, Syria, and other areas, are still pastoral nomads.

In most societies, women were responsible for gathering plants and seeds. Therefore they may have been the first to plant seeds. Men usually were the hunters. Women began planting and harvesting their crops in the same place year after year.

Farming Techniques

Over time, people have made important advances in farming. In Bali, Indonesia, top, farmers build terraces, or platforms, into the hillsides for growing rice. In 5000 B.C., people grew ears of corn, above left, about 1 inch (2.5 cm) long. By A.D. 1500, years of careful breeding produced much larger corn, above right, about 5 1/3 inches (13.6 cm) long. *Analyze Images What advantages do farmers gain from such techniques as terrace farming and plant breeding?*

Farming Around the World Some places were better for farming than others. Soil in some areas was very fertile, or rich in the substances that plants need to grow. Because plants also need light and warmth, areas that had long springs and summers were good places to farm. Gentle rains are important sources of water for plants. People gradually discovered that the soil, the water, and the length of the growing seasons in several places around the world were good for plants. These people took up the farming way of life.

About 9,000 years ago, Chinese farmers began planting rice and other crops. A little later in Central America, people began to grow corn, beans, and squash. The map on page 19 shows where certain crops were first planted and how their use spread.

Plant Selection While the kinds of plants grown by those first farmers are still important today, the plants looked very different then. When people first began to plant crops, they carefully chose seeds from the biggest, best-tasting plants. In doing so, they began to **domesticate** plants, or adapt wild plants for human use. Very gradually, this careful selection of seeds and roots from each crop led to the kinds of food that we eat today. The photograph of ears of corn on this page shows the domestication of corn over time.

Raising Animals Just as humans learned to domesticate plants, they also learned to domesticate animals. During the New Stone Age, humans learned to tame wild animals and breed them for human use. The first domesticated animals may have been dogs, because they were valuable in hunting. By taming larger animals such as sheep, goats, and pigs, people developed ready sources of meat, milk, wool, and skins. Through gradual and careful breeding, herders developed animals that were gentler than their wild ancestors and provided more milk or wool. By about 2500 B.C., cattle, camels, horses, and donkeys were trained to carry heavy loads.

The Challenge of Domestication Over the course of history, humans have tried and failed to domesticate many species. Since ancient times, many animals have been captured in the wild and tamed. The people of ancient India tamed wild elephants for use in battle. Ancient Assyrians and Egyptians trained wild cheetahs for hunting. But these animals and many other species are not easy to breed in captivity. In fact, only a few species of large animals have been suitable for use in agriculture or transportation.

A caravan of camels used by nomads in Iran

✓ **Reading Check** **What skills did people develop during the New Stone Age?**

Section 2 Assessment

Key Terms
Review the key terms at the beginning of this section. Use each term in a sentence that explains its meaning.

Target Reading Skill
What did you predict about this section? How did your prediction guide your reading?

Comprehension and Critical Thinking
1. (a) Recall Describe how hominids of the Old Stone Age survived.

(b) Infer What important skills did hominids of the Old Stone Age use to find food?
(c) Synthesize How did survival skills change as people began to settle?
2. (a) Identify What marked the beginning of the New Stone Age?
(b) Contrast How was life in the New Stone Age different from life in the Old Stone Age?
(c) Apply Information What are the effects of geography and climate on farming?

Writing Activity
Suppose you are a hunter-gatherer. You think of an idea for growing your own food. Write a journal entry describing what gave you the idea, and how your idea might affect your people.

Go Online
PHSchool.com

For: An activity on the Stone Age
Visit: PHSchool.com
Web Code: lbd-2102

Hunter-Gatherers

Spears ready, they hide behind rocks and trees. Their hand axes have been sharpened to a fine edge. They are hungry, and the wait seems endless. Then one of them spies the prey and gives a signal to the group. The hunt is on!

Hunter-gatherers lived in the wild. They built their own shelter and made their own clothes. They ate fruits, roots, leaves, and nuts. When they wanted meat, hunting in groups worked best.

Hunting in Groups Big game, such as the mammoth shown here, was valuable for its meat, hide, and bones. Mammoths—now extinct—thrived during the last ice age, which ended about 10,000 years ago.

Hunting big game was dangerous and required team-work. A hunter could easily be crushed by a mammoth, or speared by its sharp tusks.

Scientists have different ideas about how such game was hunted. The animals may have been wounded by spears and then lured into hidden pits and killed. Or, hunters may have attacked the animals near watering holes. Some evidence suggests that hunters would herd animals until they were forced over bluffs, falling to their deaths.

The illustration above shows the mammoth being butchered after a hunt. Once the hide was removed, it was stretched and scraped clean. Damaged weapons were then repaired and made ready for the next hunt.

Prehistoric flint tool (left) and flaked stone spear tip (right)

Ancient Art

During the Ice Age, a time when glaciers covered much of Earth, hunter-gatherers painted animal forms and symbols on cave walls. Charcoal and other materials were used for pigments. Paintings have been found in Africa, Europe, and Australia. The painting above is from a cave in Alsace, France.

Creating Shelter

Hunter-gatherers lived in caves or human-made shelters. Long ago, hunter-gatherers in parts of Europe made huts of mammoth bones and tusks, like the model shown above. The shelters were probably covered by large animal hides. Firepits, dug into the hut floor, provided heat.

Tools

Hunter-gatherers made their own tools and weapons using stone, wood, bone, and animal sinew.

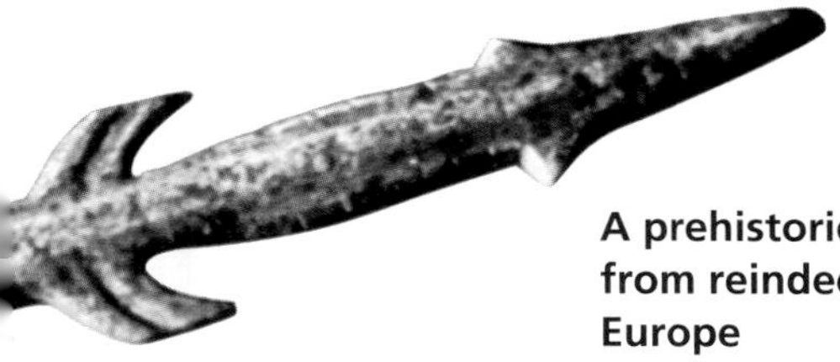

A prehistoric harpoon made from reindeer bone, found in Europe

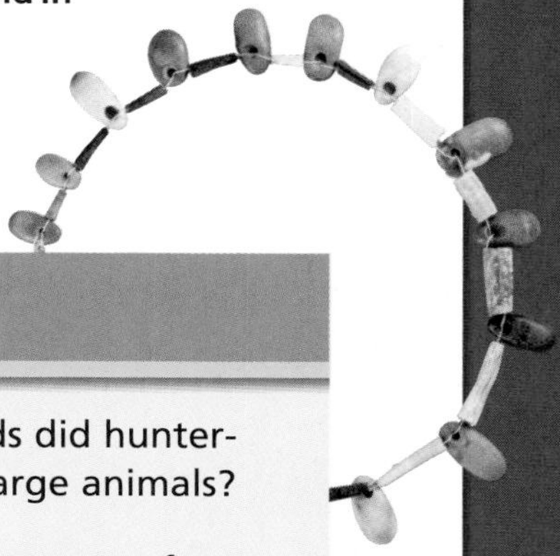

A shell and bone necklace found in Israel

Assessment

Describe What methods did hunter-gatherers use to hunt large animals?

Infer Describe the importance of animals to the survival of hunter-gatherers long ago.

The Beginnings of Civilization

Prepare to Read

Objectives

In this section you will

1. Find out about the advantages people gained from settling down in one place.
2. Learn about the growth of early cities.
3. Understand how the first civilizations formed and spread.

Taking Notes

As you read, summarize changes that lead to the growth of civilization. Copy the chart below, and use it to record your findings.

The Growth of Civilization

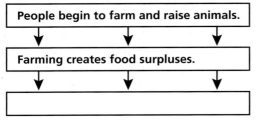

| People begin to farm and raise animals. |
| Farming creates food surpluses. |

Target Reading Skill

Preview and Ask Questions Before you read this section, preview the headings and pictures to find out what the section is about. As you read, write two questions that will help you remember something important about the beginnings of civilization. For example, you might ask yourself, What is a city? Or, How did early civilizations form? Find the answers to your questions as you read.

Key Terms

- **irrigation** (ihr uh GAY shun) *n.* supplying land with water through a network of canals
- **surplus** (SUR plus) *n.* more than is needed
- **artisan** (AHR tuh zun) *n.* a worker who is especially skilled at crafting items by hand
- **civilization** (sih vuh luh ZAY shun) *n.* a society with cities, a central government, job specialization, and social classes
- **social class** (SOH shul klas) *n.* a group of people with similar backgrounds, incomes, and ways of living

Caring for irrigation trenches in Libya, North Africa

Under a fierce desert sun, long lines of people are digging a trench that will soon become a deep canal. Other people lift heavy baskets of dirt dug from the canal onto their shoulders. They dump the dirt near the river where another crew is building a huge earthen dam.

These are some of the world's first construction workers. They are building a system of **irrigation,** supplying land with water from another place using a network of canals. One person directs the work at each site. Like the big construction projects of today, this job takes teamwork.

Soon, the dam will hold back the spring floodwaters of the river. A group of people are building wooden gates in the dam. Officials will open the gates in the dry season, allowing water to flow through the canals and irrigate the growing crops. Farming techniques like this irrigation system were important in creating early communities.

Advantages of a Settled Life

Farming was much harder work than hunting and gathering. However, it had far greater rewards. People who produced their own food could have a steady supply of food year-round. This meant they no longer had to travel from place to place. People often even had a food surplus—more than what is needed. Surplus food could be stored for use at another time.

The Population Grows Having surplus food also affected the size of families. The hunting-gathering life did not allow parents to have many children. How could they feed them all? Now, food surpluses would feed many more people.

Larger families brought rapid population growth. Scientists estimate that about 10,000 years ago, the population of the world was about 5 million people, which is about the number of people living in Minnesota today. By 7,000 years ago, many people had settled into the farming life. The world's population then was as much as 20 million.

Early Villages and Towns People lived in New Stone Age farming settlements for many centuries. Gradually, as the population increased, the settlements grew into towns.

With food surpluses, people did not have to spend all their days producing food. Some people were able to switch from farming to other kinds of work. For example, some people became artisans. An artisan is a worker who is especially skilled in crafting items by hand. Artisans make items such as baskets, leather goods, tools, pottery, or cloth.

✓ Reading Check **What effect did food surpluses have on people living in settlements?**

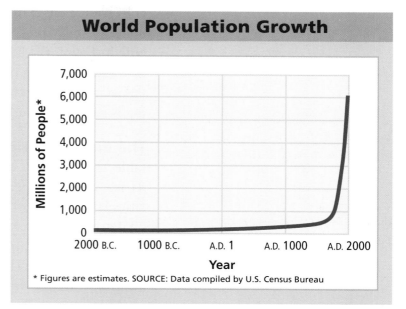

World Population Growth

Millions of People*

7,000
6,000
5,000
4,000
3,000
2,000
1,000
0

2000 B.C.   1000 B.C.   A.D. 1   A.D. 1000   A.D. 2000

Year

* Figures are estimates. SOURCE: Data compiled by U.S. Census Bureau

■ **Graph Skills**

By A.D. 1000, the world's population had reached about 275 million.
Identify By what date had the population reached more than 6 billion?
Generalize How would you describe the rate of population growth before the year A.D. 1?

The ruins of Çatal Hüyük in Turkey, a settlement from around 7000 B.C.

The Growth of Cities

Although some farming settlements grew into cities, many others did not. Cities were more likely to develop in areas where rich soil created large surpluses of food. People also needed a dependable source of drinking water and materials to build shelters. Some of the earliest cities grew up along large rivers, such as the Nile in Egypt, the Tigris (TY gris) and Euphrates (yoo FRAY teez) in Iraq, the Huang (hwahng) in China, and the Indus (IN dus) in Pakistan. Cities grew up in these areas because the soil for farming is rich near riverbeds.

The Earliest Cities Look at the table titled Early Cities. The table shows when some of the first cities developed in Asia, Africa, and Europe. You will learn more about some of these cities later.

Early cities were different from farming villages in some important ways. Cities were larger, of course. Cities also had large public buildings. There were buildings to store surplus grain, buildings for the worship of gods, and buildings where people could buy and sell goods. In villages, most people were farmers. In cities, workers had a wide variety of occupations. Most worked at a craft. As new skills developed, so did new occupations.

Chart Skills

Cities arose at different times in different places. Ruins from Knossos, right, are part of a palace built circa, or around, 1550 B.C. In the table, *c.* stands for *circa*.
Identify Where were the cities of Ur and Anyang located, and when were these cities founded?
Compare In the text, you learned about the geographic conditions in the areas where the earliest cities developed. What geographic factor do you think the cities of Ur and Anyang had in common?

Early Cities

City	Present-Day Location	Date Founded
Ur	Iraq	c. 3500 B.C.
Memphis	Egypt	c. 3100 B.C.
Mohenjo-Daro	Pakistan	c. 2700 B.C.
Knossos	Greece	c. 2500 B.C.
Anyang	China	c. 1700 B.C.

Governments Form As the population of cities grew, governments formed. Governments kept order in society and provided services. They also settled disputes and managed public building and irrigation projects.

✓ Reading Check **Along which rivers did early cities grow?**

The First Civilizations

Over time, some New Stone Age societies grew into civilizations. A **civilization** is a society that has cities, a central government run by official leaders, and workers who specialize in various jobs. Writing, art, and architecture also characterize a civilization.

The Bronze Age By 6600 B.C., artisans in Europe and Asia had learned a key skill. They discovered that melting a certain rock at high temperatures would separate the metal copper from the rock. By 3000 B.C., artisans had learned to mix copper with another metal, tin, to make a mixture called bronze. Ancient peoples may have discovered bronze-making by accident. In nature, small amounts of tin are sometimes found with copper deposits. This discovery marked the beginning of the Bronze Age.

The first people to refine copper with tin had discovered a valuable new metal. Because bronze is much harder than copper, it could be used to make items more durable, or long-lasting. For example, bronze was used to make weapons, tools, helmets, and shields more durable.

Bronze Tools
Shown are half of a stone mold for pins and a bronze pin, top, from Switzerland, around 1000 B.C., and a bronze razor from Denmark, bottom. **Infer** *How are these tools signs of early civilizations?*

Trade and the Spread of Ideas Traders took valuable items such as pottery, tools and weapons, baskets, cloth, and spices to faraway cities. They traded these items for food and goods that people at home wanted.

By around 3500 B.C., some civilizations had developed a simple but amazing invention: the wheel and axle. An axle is a rod on which a wheel turns. With the wheel and axle, trade goods could be loaded into carts and pushed through the city to market. More goods could be transported farther and more easily.

Social Status
Ancient jewelry can provide clues to the social status of its owner or to the type of artisans in a society. The decorative bracelet above comes from the area of present-day Iran. **Infer** *What does the bracelet tell us about the ancient society it came from?*

Trade over water also developed. Merchant ships now carried goods across seas and rivers. With all this travel, people of many different cultures came into contact with one another. New tools and ideas from one society soon spread to other societies as people traded information along with goods.

Social Classes Develop Growing trade links brought new prosperity to the cities. Prosperity led to another major change in society—the development of social classes. A **social class** is a group of people having similar backgrounds, incomes, and ways of living.

In the large cities, the king was the most powerful person. Next in importance were two classes of people. One class was made up of the priests of the city's religion. The other class was made up of nobles, who were government officials and military officers. Below them were the artisans, small traders, and merchants. Common workers and farmers were the lowest ranked free members of society.

Slaves, human beings owned as property by other people, formed a separate social class. Most slaves worked in cities, often as household servants and as laborers. Their status, or rank, was beneath that of free people.

✓ **Reading Check** **What skills and practices were important in the growth and spread of early civilizations?**

Section 3 Assessment

Key Terms
Review the key terms at the beginning of this section. Use each term in a sentence that explains its meaning.

Target Reading Skill
What questions did you ask to help you learn or remember something about this section?

Comprehension and Critical Thinking
1. (a) Describe How did people's lives change when they began to produce their own food?

(b) Identify Effects What effects did food surpluses have on people and populations?
2. (a) Recall What resources were necessary for villages to grow into cities?
(b) Compare and Contrast What were the similarities and differences between villages and cities?
3. (a) Name What developments occurred as societies grew into civilizations?
(b) Draw Conclusions How did prosperity lead to the development of social classes?

Writing Activity
Suppose you are an early trader bringing tools and weapons made of bronze to people who have never seen bronze before. Write a speech in which you try to persuade these people to trade for your bronze goods.

Writing Tip Write an opener for your speech that will grab the listener's attention. Write a list of reasons why bronze tools are better than tools made of copper. Refer to this list when writing your speech.

Review and Assessment

◆ Chapter Summary

Section 1: Geography and History

- The study of tools, bones, and other objects can help to explain prehistoric life.
- The development of writing marks a turning point in the story of our past.
- The geography of a place can explain why historic events happened there.

Section 2: Prehistory

- During the Old Stone Age, our ancestors survived by hunting animals and gathering plant foods.
- Gradually, our ancestors moved from Africa and spread out over much of Earth.
- During the New Stone Age, some people began to farm and to domesticate animals.

Section 3: The Beginnings of Civilization

Knossos

- The advantage of a steady food supply helped early farming settlements to prosper.
- Farming settlements grew into cities because of their geographical locations.
- The first civilizations developed in cities and spread with the help of trade.

Camel caravan

◆ Reviewing Key Terms

Fill in the blanks in Column I using the key terms from Column II.

Column I

1. Stories passed down by word of mouth are _____.

2. The _____ was the earliest known period of human culture.

3. Human ancestors learned how to _____, or tame, animals.

4. Making items such as baskets, jewelry, and pottery is the job of a(n) _____.

5. A society that has cities, a central government, and specialized workers is a(n) _____.

6. _____ is the period of time before writing was developed.

Column II

civilization
archaeologist
oral traditions
artisan
Stone Age
prehistory
domesticate
irrigation

◆ Comprehension and Critical Thinking

7. (a) Identify What is the difference between history and prehistory?
(b) Explain How can we learn about people who lived before written history?
(c) Draw Inferences Suppose that large, heavy spear points are found at a prehistoric site. What might they tell us about the people who once lived there?

8. (a) Describe How did early hominids find food during the Old Stone Age?
(b) Make Generalizations What characterized the Old Stone Age, the Middle Stone Age, and the New Stone Age?
(c) Sequence What is the connection between farming and the growth of early cities?

9. (a) Recall What survival skills did our human ancestors learn throughout the Stone Age?
(b) Identify Effects How did the discovery of the use of fire affect early hominids?
(c) Identify Causes What developments allowed early nomads to move from Africa to many parts of the world?

10. (a) Recall Describe aspects of the earliest cities.
(b) Explain How did cities benefit from a central government?
(c) Draw Conclusions What was the relationship between government and the social classes of early civilizations?

◆ Skills Practice

Using Timelines In the Skills for Life activity in this chapter, you learned how to use a timeline to gain a better understanding of a certain time period. You then created your own timeline. Review the steps you follow for this skill and study the timeline on page 15. Then reread Chapter 1 looking for events that fit within the timeline span. Redraw the timeline with the additional events.

◆ Writing Activity: Science

Form conclusions the way archaeologists do. Choose a place you know well, such as your classroom. Then, pick two or three objects found there and make detailed notes on them. What do your notes tell you about the people who use the objects?

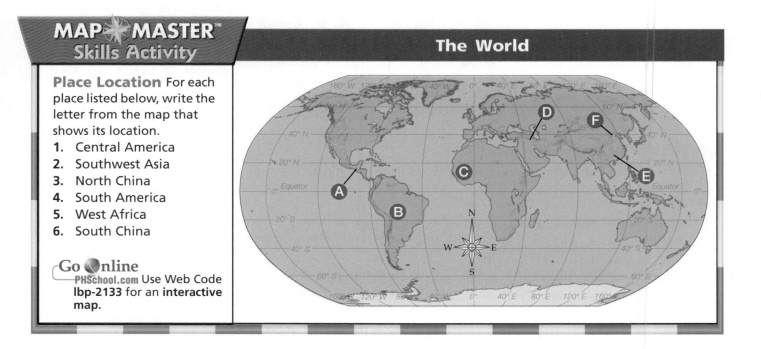

MAP✦MASTER™
Skills Activity

The World

Place Location For each place listed below, write the letter from the map that shows its location.
1. Central America
2. Southwest Asia
3. North China
4. South America
5. West Africa
6. South China

Go Online
PHSchool.com Use Web Code **lbp-2133** for an **interactive map**.

Standardized Test Prep

Test-Taking Tips

Some questions on standardized tests ask you to analyze a reading passage for causes and effects. Read the paragraph below. Then follow the tips to answer the sample question.

> The Sumer civilization arose in the region between the Tigris and Euphrates rivers. Similarly, early Egyptian civilization developed along the Nile River. Ancient China had its origins along the Huang River. A fresh water supply and rich soil made these river valleys "cradles of civilization."

TIP Identify the main idea, or most important point, as you read a paragraph or passage.

Pick the letter that best completes the statement.

TIP Restate this as a question: Which effect was the author writing about?

The author wrote this passage to give information about the effect of

- A geography on early civilizations.
- B agriculture on early civilizations.
- C geography on the economies of early civilizations.
- D migration on the environment.

Think It Through Start with the main idea: Early civilizations developed near rivers in many places. Keep the main idea in mind as you try to answer the question. Rivers are a part of geography, so you can eliminate B and D. Rivers do have an effect on economies, but the paragraph does not discuss that topic. The correct answer is A.

Practice Questions

Use the tips above and other tips in this book to help you answer the following questions.

1. Prehistory describes the time period before
   - A people existed.
   - B people used tools.
   - C clothes were made from animal skins.
   - D writing was invented.

2. During which time period did farming develop?
   - A the Bronze Age
   - B the Old Stone Age
   - C the Middle Stone Age
   - D the New Stone Age

3. As food surpluses developed,
   - A population growth increased.
   - B towns grew into farming settlements.
   - C people left the cities.
   - D more artisans became farmers.

Read the passage below, and then answer the question that follows.

Oral history, while important, does not give an accurate history of a society. Stories may exaggerate or only focus on certain things. Archaeology is also incomplete. Bones and objects tell us only part of the story of the past. Any accurate history must take into account the written records of human life.

4. Which statement best reflects the main idea of the passage?
   - A Historians must have written records to fully understand the past.
   - B Written records are not very important.
   - C Written records are almost as important as stories and archaeology.
   - D Historians value oral stories the most.

Go Online
PHSchool.com

Use Web Code lba-2103 for **Chapter 1 self-test.**

Chapter 2

The Fertile Crescent

Chapter Preview

This chapter will introduce you to the civilizations of an ancient region of the Middle East known as the Fertile Crescent.

Section 1
Land Between Two Rivers

Section 2
Fertile Crescent Empires

Section 3
The Legacy of Mesopotamia

Section 4
Mediterranean Civilizations

Section 5
Judaism

Target Reading Skill

Clarifying Meaning In this chapter you will focus on clarifying, or better understanding, the meaning of what you read.

▶ A shepherd grazes his sheep along the banks of the Euphrates River in Syria.

MAP MASTER™
Skills Activity

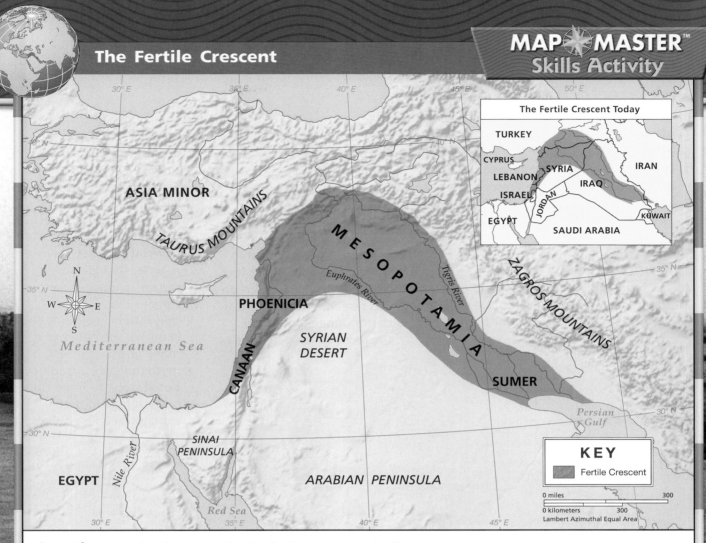

The Fertile Crescent Today

TURKEY
CYPRUS
LEBANON
ISRAEL
EGYPT
SYRIA
JORDAN
IRAQ
IRAN
KUWAIT
SAUDI ARABIA

ASIA MINOR

TAURUS MOUNTAINS

M E S O P O T A M I A

Euphrates River

Tigris River

ZAGROS MOUNTAINS

PHOENICIA

CANAAN

SYRIAN DESERT

Mediterranean Sea

SUMER

Persian Gulf

SINAI PENINSULA

Nile River

EGYPT

ARABIAN PENINSULA

Red Sea

KEY

Fertile Crescent

0 miles 300
0 kilometers 300
Lambert Azimuthal Equal Area

Location A region known as the Fertile Crescent stretched in an arc from the Mediterranean Sea to the Persian Gulf. It had many attractions to the people of the ancient world. **Identify** What kinds of geographic features do you notice in the Fertile Crescent? **Apply Information** Which areas of the Fertile Crescent might attract invaders? Explain why.

Go Online
PHSchool.com Use Web Code
lbp-2211 for step-by-step
map skills practice.

Land Between Two Rivers

Prepare to Read

Objectives

In this section you will

1. Find out how geography made the rise of civilization in the Fertile Crescent possible.
2. Learn about Sumer's first cities.
3. Examine the characteristics of Sumerian religion.

Taking Notes

As you read, look for details about Mesopotamia and Sumer. Copy the outline below, and use it to record your findings.

> **I. The geographic setting**
>   **A. Mesopotamia**
>   1.
>   2.
>   **B. The Tigris and Euphrates rivers**
> **II.**

Target Reading Skill

Reread Rereading is a strategy that can help you to understand words and ideas in the text. If you do not understand a certain passage, reread it to look for connections among the words and sentences. When you reread, you may gain a better understanding of the more complicated ideas.

Key Terms

- **scribe** (skryb) *n.* a professional writer
- **Fertile Crescent** (FUR tul KRES unt) *n.* a region in Southwest Asia; site of the first civilizations
- **city-state** (SIH tee stayt) *n.* a city that is also a separate, independent state
- **polytheism** (PAHL ih thee iz um) *n.* the belief in many gods
- **myth** (mith) *n.* a traditional story; in some cultures, a legend that explains people's beliefs

The Work of Scribes
The language on this tablet—Sumerian—is the oldest known written language. **Analyze Information** Why were scribes important in Sumer?

The following words from the past come from a student at one of the world's first schools. He tells what happened to him when his homework was sloppy or when he spoke without permission.

> **❝My headmaster read my tablet and said, 'There is something missing,' and hit me with a cane. . . . The fellow in charge of silence said, 'Why did you talk without permission?' and caned me. ❞**
>
> —*A Sumerian student*

The first known schools were set up in the land of Sumer (SOO mur) over 4,000 years ago. Sumerian schools taught boys—and possibly a few girls—the new invention of writing. Graduates of the schools became **scribes,** or professional writers. Scribes were important because they kept records for the kings and priests. Learning to be a scribe was hard work. Students normally began school at about the age of eight and finished about ten years later. The writings Sumerian scribes left behind help to tell the story of this early civilization.

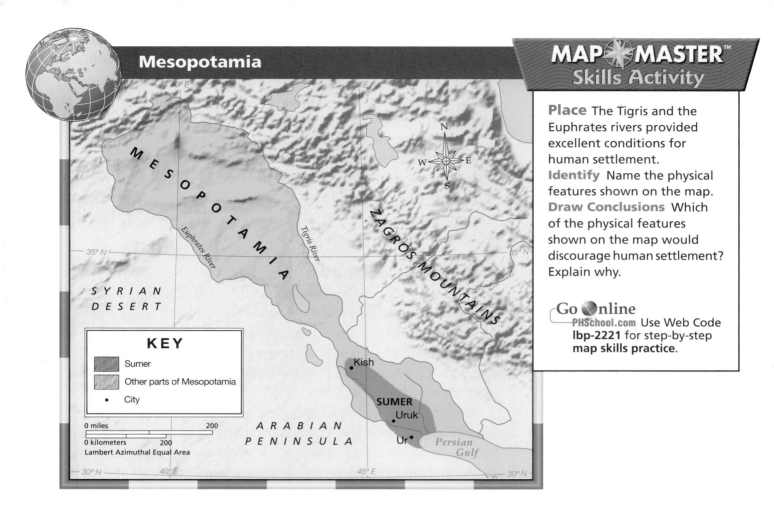

Mesopotamia

KEY

Sumer

Other parts of Mesopotamia

• City

0 miles 200
0 kilometers 200
Lambert Azimuthal Equal Area

The Geographic Setting

Sumer was located in a region called Mesopotamia (mes uh puh TAY mee uh). Look at the map titled Mesopotamia. Like the place where you live, ancient Mesopotamia had special attractions that drew people to settle there. Most important, it had rich soil and life-giving rivers. These attractions drew people who became farmers and city builders. Sumer's central location within the ancient world drew many traders from other regions. Sumer became one of the most prosperous areas of the ancient world.

The Location of Mesopotamia

Mesopotamia's name describes its location. The word *Mesopotamia* comes from Greek words that mean "between the rivers." The map above shows that Mesopotamia lies between two rivers, the Tigris and the Euphrates.

The ruins of Uruk, an ancient Sumerian city on the Euphrates River, northwest of Ur

Mesopotamia is part of the **Fertile Crescent,** a region in Southwest Asia that was the site of the world's first civilizations. Turn to the map titled The Fertile Crescent on page 33. To see how this region got its name, place your finger at the eastern edge of the Mediterranean Sea (med uh tuh RAY nee un) on the map. Move eastward from the Mediterranean coast to Mesopotamia. Then move southeast to the Persian Gulf. Notice that the region you've traced is shaped like a crescent moon. The rivers of this crescent-shaped region helped to make it one of the best places in Southwest Asia for growing crops.

Rivers of Life and Death   The Tigris and the Euphrates rivers were the source of life for the peoples of Mesopotamia. In the spring, melting snow picked up tons of topsoil as it rushed down from the mountains and flooded the land. The floods left this topsoil on the plain below. Farmers grew crops in this soil. The rivers also supplied fish, clay for building, and tall, strong reeds used to make boats.

The floodwaters sometimes brought sorrows as well as gifts. The floods did not always happen at the same time each year. Racing down without warning, they swept away people, animals, crops, and houses. Then, the survivors would rebuild and pray that the next flood would not be so destructive.

✓ Reading Check   **How did flooding rivers affect people who settled in Mesopotamia?**

Peacetime in Sumer
Around 2500 B.C., artists from the Sumerian city-state of Ur created this mosaic recording of peacetime activities. Shown are two out of the three rows of figures.
➊ The king sits facing members of the royal family at a banquet.
➋ Servants stand ready to wait upon the royal family.
➌ A musician playing a harp and a singer provide entertainment.
➍ Servants deliver animals, fish, and other items for the feast.
Infer *How do the activities shown provide clues about jobs and social classes in Ur?*

The First Cities

As farming succeeded in Mesopotamia, communities began to build up surpluses of food. In time, food surpluses encouraged the growth of cities. By 3500 B.C., some of the earliest known cities arose in the southern region of Sumer, along the Tigris and Euphrates rivers.

Independent Cities Form Although cities in Sumer shared a common culture and language, they did not unite under a single ruler. Instead, they remained politically independent city-states. A **city-state** is a city that is also a separate, independent state. Each Sumerian city acted as an independent state, with its own special god or goddess, its own government, its own army, and, eventually, its own king.

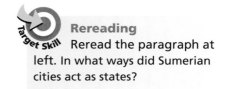

Rereading Reread the paragraph at left. In what ways did Sumerian cities act as states?

A Brief Tour of a Sumerian City Public squares bustled with activity. In the marketplaces, merchants displayed goods in outdoor stalls. Musicians, acrobats, beggars, and water sellers filled the streets. For a fee, scribes wrote letters for those who could not read or write. Sumerian houses faced away from the crowded streets, onto inner courtyards where families ate and children played. On hot nights, people slept outdoors on their homes' flat roofs. Oil lamps supplied light for Sumerian homes.

√ Reading Check **How were the cities of Sumer governed?**

Sumerian Religion

A stranger coming to a Sumerian city could easily notice a giant brick building at the heart of the city. It was the ziggurat (ZIG oo rat), the site of the temple to the main god or goddess of the city.

Sumerian Temples Religious, social, and economic activities all took place at the temple sites. Ziggurats were pyramids made of terraces, one on top of another, linked by ramps and stairs. Some were more than seven stories high. At the top of each ziggurat was a shrine. The Sumerians believed that gods descended to Earth using the ziggurat as a stairway.

Ancient Religious Beliefs The people of Sumer worshiped many gods and goddesses. This practice is known as **polytheism,** a belief in many gods. To understand this word, break it up into its parts. *Poly-*, a Greek prefix, means "many." *Theism* means "belief in a god or gods."

Sumerian **myths,** or stories about gods that explain people's beliefs, warned that the gods would punish people who angered them. The myths also promised rewards to people who served the gods well.

Sumerians placed prayer figures on altars. The eyes of the worshiping figures were made wide, as though they were fixed on the gods.

Stairway to the Heavens
This partially restored brick ziggurat was part of the ancient city of Ur. **Analyze Images** *Why do you think the Sumerians believed the gods could use the ziggurat to descend to Earth?*

Honoring the Gods The Sumerians honored their gods in religious ceremonies. Temple priests washed the statues of gods before and after each meal was offered. Music sounded and incense burned as huge plates of food were laid before them. In most ancient religions, the food was often eaten after it was presented to the gods. Perhaps the worshipers thought that by eating the offering, they would be taking in the qualities they admired in the gods. The religious beliefs of the Sumerians give us an idea of what was important to them. Poetry was also used to express what was important to them:

> "Behold the bond of Heaven and Earth, the city. . . .
> Behold . . . its well of good water.
> Behold . . . its pure canal."
>
> *—A Sumerian poem*

A reconstructed musical instrument called a lyre (lyr), about 2500 B.C., from Ur

The Fall of Sumer Unfortunately for Sumer, its wealth became its downfall. Sumerian city-states fought each other over land and the use of river water. Rulers from various city-states won and lost control of all of Sumer. Around 2300 B.C., Sumer was conquered by the armies of neighboring Akkad (AK ad). Its ruler, King Sargon, united the Sumerian city-states and improved Sumer's government and its military. Sumer remained united for about 100 years until it dissolved once more into independent city-states. Sumer was no longer a major power after 2000 B.C. It fell to a northern rival, Babylonia, in the 1700s B.C.

✔ Reading Check What weakened the cities of Sumer?

Section 1 Assessment

Key Terms
Review the key terms at the beginning of this section. Use each term in a sentence that explains its meaning.

Target Reading Skill
What word or idea were you able to clarify by rereading certain passages?

Comprehension and Critical Thinking
1. (a) Recall Describe the geography of Mesopotamia.

(b) Find the Main Ideas How did Mesopotamia's geography help civilizations to develop in the area?

2. (a) Compare In what ways were Sumerian cities alike?
(b) Contrast In what ways were the cities of Sumer different?

3. (a) Explain How did Sumerians practice religion?
(b) Infer What do the religious practices of the Sumerians tell us about their values?

Writing Activity
Write a journal entry from the viewpoint of a student scribe in Sumer. Describe what you see on your walk to school.

For: An activity on Sumer
Visit: PHSchool.com
Web Code: lbd-2201

Farming in Mesopotamia

Farming the land "between the rivers" required skill and determination. The life-giving rivers could be generous one year and stingy the next. Frosts, droughts, floods, weeds, or insects could bring starvation. For survival, families worked together in farming communities. As cities rose above the Mesopotamian plain, governments created huge farms. From the river-fed land, farmers cultivated the crops—wheat, barley, cucumbers, and figs—that nourished kingdoms for many years to come.

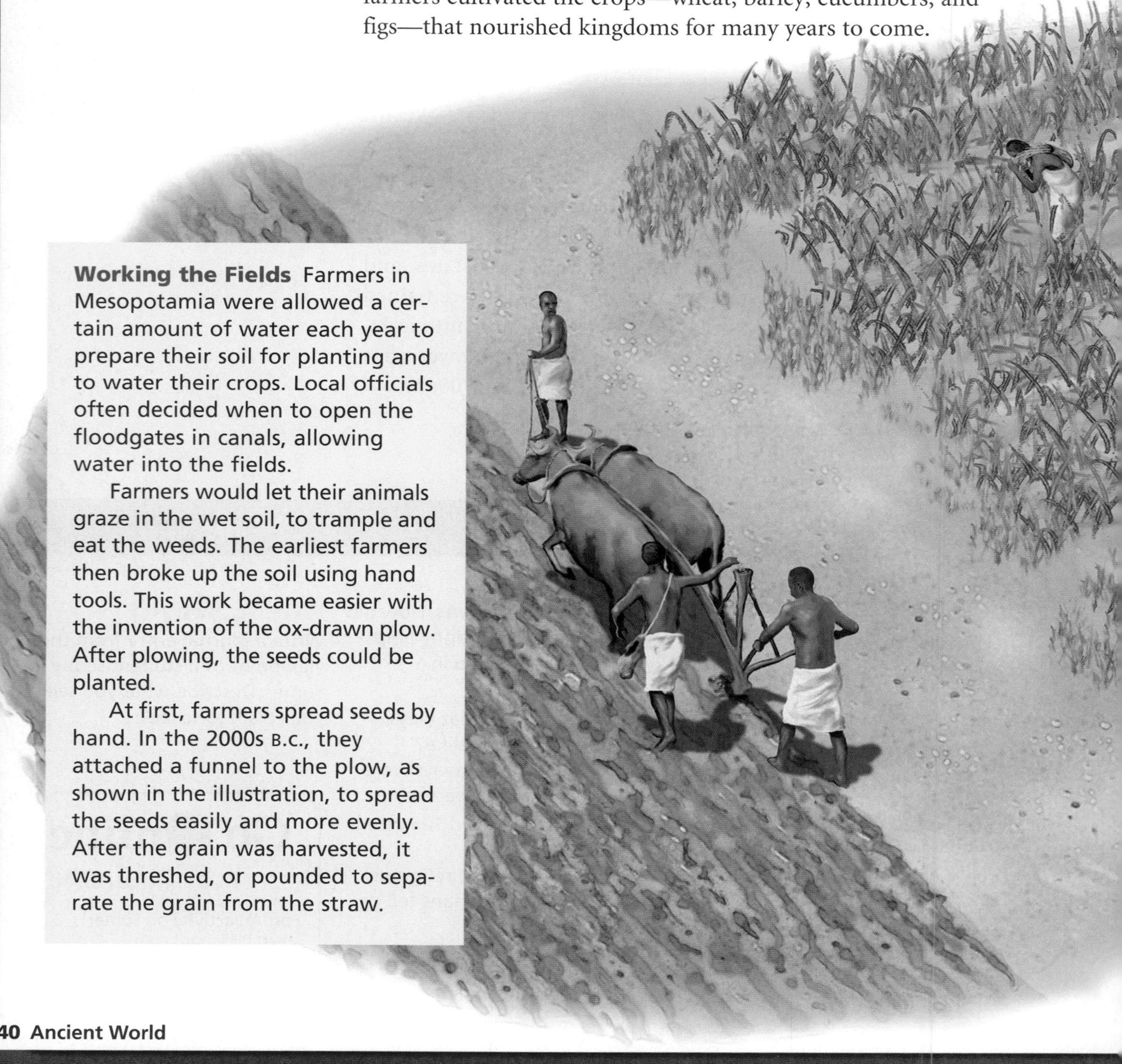

Working the Fields Farmers in Mesopotamia were allowed a certain amount of water each year to prepare their soil for planting and to water their crops. Local officials often decided when to open the floodgates in canals, allowing water into the fields.

Farmers would let their animals graze in the wet soil, to trample and eat the weeds. The earliest farmers then broke up the soil using hand tools. This work became easier with the invention of the ox-drawn plow. After plowing, the seeds could be planted.

At first, farmers spread seeds by hand. In the 2000s B.C., they attached a funnel to the plow, as shown in the illustration, to spread the seeds easily and more evenly. After the grain was harvested, it was threshed, or pounded to separate the grain from the straw.

Farming Tools

Early farmers in Mesopotamia first used simple tools—sticks for plowing and stone-bladed sickles, like the one shown here, for harvesting grain. In time, more efficient tools were invented.

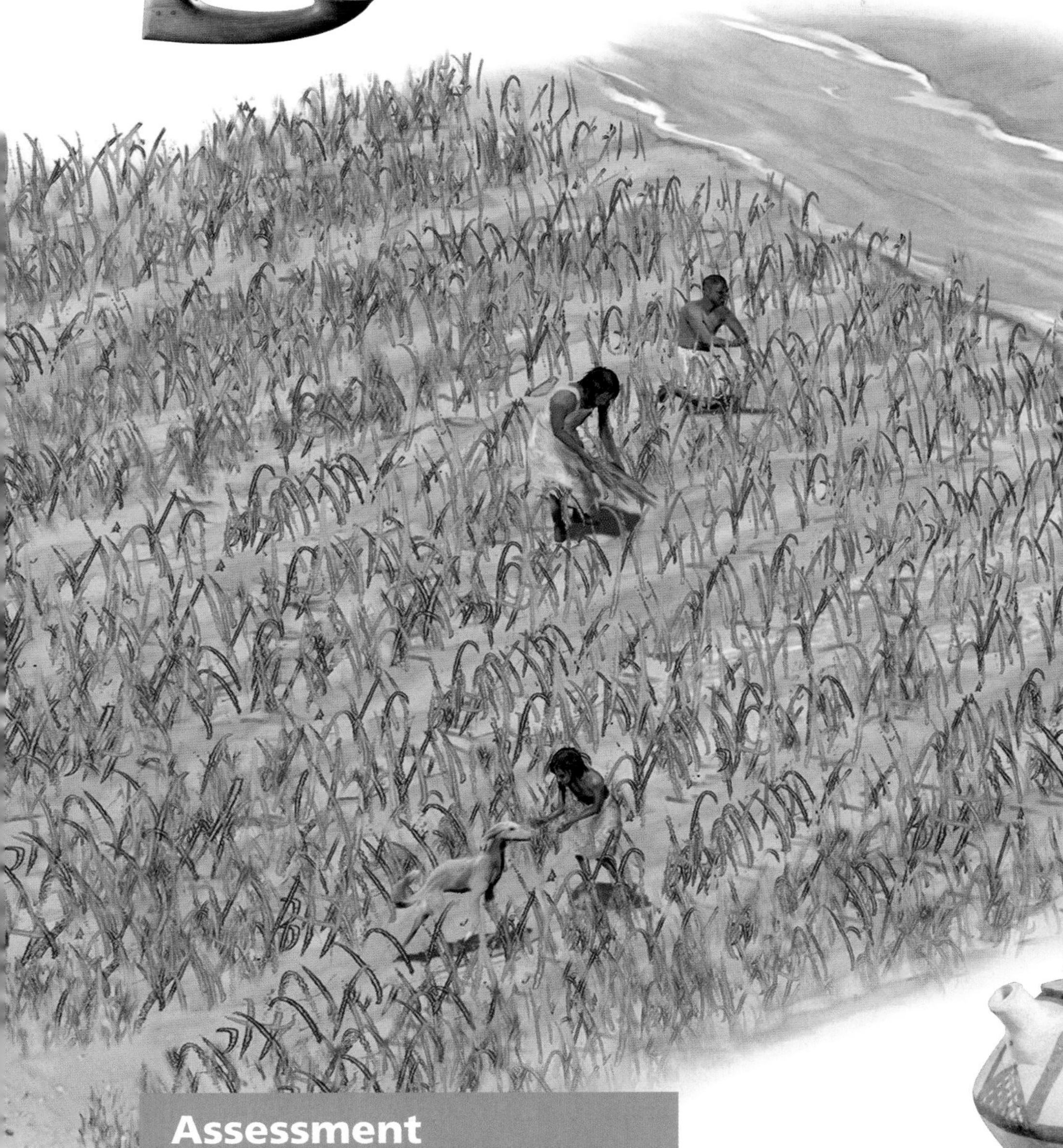

Assessment

Analyze Information Describe how farmers in Mesopotamia prepared the soil and planted their crops.

Draw Conclusions How did Mesopotamians improve their farming methods over time?

Pottery

The pottery made by Mesopotamians had many uses. The spouted vessel above, from about 3000 B.C., was found in Iraq. It may have been used to carry water. The cup, dated to 2200–1900 B.C., was found in Israel. It was probably used to measure grain.

Fertile Crescent Empires

Prepare to Read

Objectives

In this section you will
1. Learn about the three most important empires of the Fertile Crescent.
2. Find out what characterized the Babylonian and Assyrian empires.
3. Investigate the achievements of the Persian Empire.

Taking Notes

As you read, note the similarities and the differences between Babylonia and Assyria. Copy the Venn diagram below, and record your findings in it.

Mesopotamian Empires

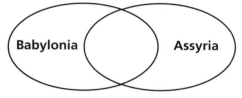

Babylonia   Assyria

Target Reading Skill

Paraphrase When you paraphrase, you restate what you have read in your own words. You could paraphrase the first paragraph of this section this way: "King Sargon II of Assyria learned that two kingdoms were joining together to resist him. In 714 B.C., he attacked the weaker forces of Urartu and Zikirtu."

As you read, paraphrase or "say back" the information following each red or blue heading.

Key Terms

- **empire** (EM pyr) *n.* many territories and peoples controlled by one government
- **Babylon** (BAB uh lahn) *n.* the capital of Babylonia; a city of great wealth and luxury
- **caravan** (KA ruh van) *n.* a group of travelers journeying together
- **bazaar** (buh ZAHR) *n.* a market selling different kinds of goods
- **Zoroastrianism** (zoh roh AS tree un iz um) *n.* a religion that developed in ancient Persia

King Sargon II of Assyria (center) and two officials

King Sargon II of Assyria (uh SEER ee uh) heard the news: Assyria had attacked the nearby kingdoms of Urartu and Zikirtu as planned. But the two kingdoms had then joined forces against him. How dare they resist the most powerful monarch in the world? In the summer of 714 B.C., King Sargon II set out to confront his enemies.

The two kingdoms were no match for the powerful Assyrian ruler. His armies quickly overcame the forces of Urartu and killed all who resisted. The Assyrians howled with laughter when they saw the king of Urartu fleeing on an old horse. Sargon II let him go. He knew that the defeated king would serve as a warning to others who might later be tempted to challenge the mighty Assyrians. Sargon II was one of many kings who ruled the Fertile Crescent after the fall of Sumer.

The Babylonian Empire

A ruler who conquered all of Mesopotamia created an **empire**, or an area of many territories and peoples that is controlled by one government. Rulers of empires gained great wealth from trade and agriculture. Hammurabi (hah muh RAH bee) created the Babylonian Empire in 1787 B.C. by conquering cities in Sumer. Then he conquered lands far to the north. The beautiful city of **Babylon** was the center of the Babylonian empire. Find the boundaries of the empire on the map below.

The Babylonians built roads throughout the empire. The roads made travel easier, which encouraged trade. Babylon's location made it a crossroads of trade. **Caravans,** or groups of travelers, stopped in Babylon on their way between Sumer to the south and Assyria to the north. In the city's **bazaars,** or markets, shoppers could buy cotton cloth from India and spices from Egypt.

Trade made Babylon rich. But all the wealth that Babylon had gathered could not save it from conquest. The empire that Hammurabi had conquered shrank and was finally destroyed by invaders in the early 1500s B.C.

√ **Reading Check** **Who was Hammurabi, and what did he accomplish?**

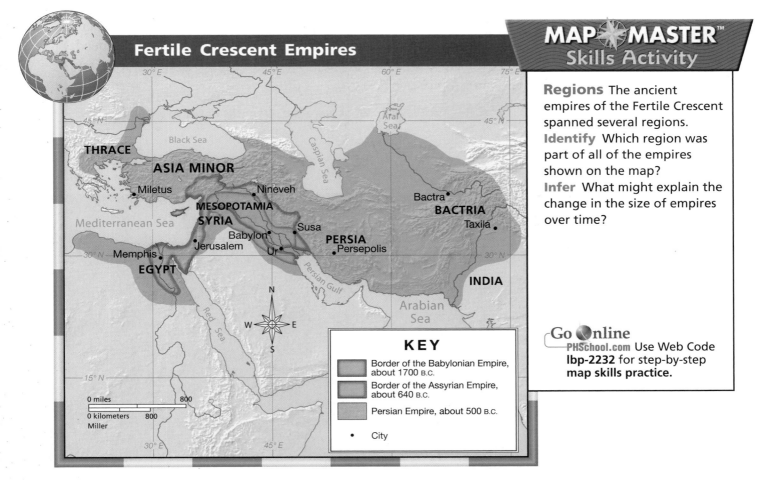

Fertile Crescent Empires

THRACE
Black Sea
ASIA MINOR
Miletus
Nineveh
Aral Sea
Caspian Sea
MESOPOTAMIA
SYRIA
Mediterranean Sea
Babylon
Susa
Bactra
BACTRIA
Taxila
Jerusalem
Ur
PERSIA
Persepolis
Memphis
EGYPT
Persian Gulf
INDIA
Arabian Sea
Red Sea

N W E S

0 miles 800
0 kilometers 800
Miller

KEY
Border of the Babylonian Empire, about 1700 B.C.
Border of the Assyrian Empire, about 640 B.C.
Persian Empire, about 500 B.C.
• City

MAP MASTER™
Skills Activity

Regions The ancient empires of the Fertile Crescent spanned several regions. **Identify** Which region was part of all of the empires shown on the map? **Infer** What might explain the change in the size of empires over time?

Go Online
PHSchool.com Use Web Code **lbp-2232** for step-by-step **map skills practice.**

The Empire of the Assyrians

The kingdom of Assyria lay in open land, making it easy for other peoples to invade. Since they were constantly defending themselves, the Assyrians became skilled warriors. About 1365 B.C., they decided the best method of defense was to attack. By 650 B.C., Assyria had conquered a large empire. It stretched across the Fertile Crescent, from the Nile River to the Persian Gulf.

Assyria's Contributions The Assyrians were clever when it came to waging war. They invented the battering ram, a powerful weapon having a wooden beam mounted on wheels. Battering rams pounded city walls to rubble. Warriors used slings to hurl stones at the enemy. Expert archers were protected with helmets and armor. But most feared were the armed charioteers who slashed their way through the enemy troops.

As the empire grew, Assyria's capital of Nineveh (NIN uh vuh) became a city of great learning. It had a remarkable library that held thousands of clay tablets with writings from Sumer and Babylon. Because the Assyrians kept these records, we now know a great deal about life in early Mesopotamia.

Assyria Overthrown The Assyrians had few friends in the lands that they ruled. Conquered peoples attempted a number of revolts against Assyrian rule. Two groups, the Medes (meedz) and Chaldeans (kal DEE unz), joined together to defeat the Assyrian Empire in 612 B.C.

✓ **Reading Check** What were the strengths of the Assyrian Empire?

Assyrian warriors carry off goods from a defeated enemy.

Paraphrase
Paraphrase the paragraph that follows the heading Assyria's Contributions.

Babylonia Rises Again

Under the Chaldeans, Babylon rose again to even greater splendor. It became the center of the New Babylonian Empire. The New Babylonian Empire controlled the entire Fertile Crescent.

Nebuchadnezzar, King of Babylon   King Nebuchadnezzar II (neb you kud NEZ ur) rebuilt the city of Babylon, which the Assyrians had destroyed. He put up massive walls around the city for protection. He also built a gigantic palace, decorated with colored tiles. Nebuchadnezzar's royal palace was built on several terraces that rose to the height of some 350 feet (110 meters). It had a dazzling landscape of trees and gardens. According to legends, he built the towering palace and gardens for his wife, who hated the dry plains of Mesopotamia.

Advances in Learning   Under the rule of the Chaldeans, Babylon again became a center of learning and science. Building on earlier Babylonian knowledge of mathematics, Chaldean astronomers charted the paths of the stars and measured the length of a year. Their measurement was only a few minutes different from the length modern scientists have found. And Chaldean farmers raised "the flies that collect honey"—honey bees.

Like other Mesopotamian empires, the Chaldeans were open to attack by powerful neighbors. In 539 B.C., the New Babylonian Empire fell to the Persians, led by Cyrus the Great. But the city of Babylon was spared.

✓ **Reading Check**   **Who was Nebuchadnezzar II?**

Assyrian and Arab Troops in Battle
This stone panel shows Assyrian soldiers fighting Arabs mounted on camels.
❶ Sturdy shields protected the Assyrian soldiers.
❷ The Arab archers fought from swift camels.
❸ The Assyrians fought from horseback and from chariots.
❹ The Assyrian army was well armed and highly trained.
Predict *Judging by what you have read about the Assyrian army, who is likely to have won the battle shown on this carving?*

The Persian Empire

Just to the east of the plains of Mesopotamia is a region of mountains, valleys, and deserts that is today the nation of Iran. This region was the homeland of the Persians who conquered Babylon in 539 B.C. The Persians built the largest empire that the Fertile Crescent had ever known. By 490 B.C, their empire stretched from Greece in the west to India in the east.

A Rich and Tolerant Culture Persian culture included **Zoroastrianism,** an ancient Persian religion. Zoroastrians originally worshiped one god, unlike their neighbors, who worshiped many. To rule their giant empire, the Persians developed a bureaucracy, or a complex structure of government offices. The Persians also built a road network across their vast empire, which promoted trade with neighboring civilizations.

The Persians tolerated the civilizations of conquered peoples. For example, they freed Jews who had been held against their will in Babylon. They also supported Babylonian science and mathematics.

Lasting Influences Through conquest and trade, the Persians spread their religion, their system of bureaucracy, and Babylonian science to neighboring peoples, including the Greeks of Europe. These Persian cultural achievements survived to help shape our modern civilization.

✓ Reading Check **How did the Persians promote trade?**

An Ancient Persian Earring
This golden earring shows the Zoroastrian god, Ahura Mazda. **Synthesize** What does this object show about Persian culture?

Section 2 Assessment

Key Terms
Review the key terms at the beginning of this section. Use each term in a sentence that explains its meaning.

Target Reading Skill
Paraphrase the last paragraph in this section.

Comprehension and Critical Thinking
1. (a) **Identify** Where was the city of Babylon located, and why was it important?

(b) **Analyze** How did the New Babylonian Empire build on the achievements of earlier empires?
2. (a) **Recall** How did the Assyrians build an empire?
(b) **Compare** How was the Assyrian empire similar to or different from other Fertile Crescent empires?
3. (a) **Identify** Where was the homeland of the Persians?
(b) **Synthesize** What were the main achievements of the Persians and what has been their lasting influence?

Writing Activity
Epitaphs are messages carved into tombstones. They praise and honor the deceased. Write an epitaph in remembrance of Nebuchadnezzar II.

> **Writing Tip** Keep your message short and to the point. To get started, summarize what you know about Nebuchadnezzar II.

The Legacy of Mesopotamia

Prepare to Read

Objectives

In this section you will
1. Learn about the importance of Hammurabi's Code.
2. Find out how the art of writing developed in Mesopotamia.

Taking Notes

As you read, look for details summarizing the achievements of Mesopotamian civilizations. Copy the table below, and record your findings in it.

The Legacy of Mesopotamia	
Hammurabi's Code	The Art of Writing

Target Reading Skill

Summarize You can better understand a text if you pause to restate the key points briefly in your own words. A good summary includes important events and details, notes the order in which the events occurred, and makes connections between the events or details.

Use the table at the left to help you summarize what you have read.

Key Terms

- **code** (kohd) *n.* an organized list of laws and rules
- **Hammurabi** (hah muh RAH bee) *n.* the king of Babylon from about 1792 to 1750 B.C.; creator of the Babylonian Empire
- **cuneiform** (kyoo NEE uh fawrm) *n.* groups of wedges and lines used to write several languages of the Fertile Crescent

Sometimes the customs and laws of other countries may seem strange to us. Imagine what it would be like to have to obey the laws set down by early civilizations.

> **❝If a man has destroyed the eye of a man of the class of gentlemen, they shall destroy his eye. If he has broken a gentleman's bone, they shall break his bone. If he has destroyed the eye of a commoner or broken a bone of a commoner, he shall pay one mina [measure of weight] of silver. If he has destroyed the eye of a gentleman's slave, or broken a bone of a gentleman's slave, he shall pay half [the slave's] price. If a gentleman's slave strikes the cheek of a gentleman, they shall cut off [the slave's] ear.❞**
>
> —*from Hammurabi's Code*

King Hammurabi standing before Shamash, the sun god and the god of justice

Hammurabi's Code

What kind of justice system do you think we would have if our laws were not written down? What would happen if a judge were free to make any law he or she wanted, or if the judge could give any punishment? Would people think that the laws were fair? A written **code,** or organized list of laws, helps people know what is expected of them and what punishment they will receive if they disobey a law.

We live by the idea that all laws should be written down and applied fairly. The Babylonians held similar beliefs about law. **Hammurabi** ruled Babylonia from about 1792 to 1750 B.C. He set down rules for everyone in his empire to follow. These rules are known as Hammurabi's Code. The code told the people of Babylonia how to settle conflicts in all areas of life.

Hammurabi's Code, which was based partly on earlier Sumerian codes, contained 282 laws organized in different categories. These included trade, labor, property, and family. The code had laws for adopting children, practicing medicine, hiring wagons or boats, and controlling dangerous animals.

Summarize Summarize the paragraph at the right. Give the main point and two details.

Target Skill

This clay lion once stood guard at a Babylonian temple.

An Eye for an Eye Reread the first law from the quotation on page 47. Hammurabi's Code was based on the idea of "an eye for an eye." In other words, punishment should be similar to the crime committed. However, the code did not apply equally to all people. The harshness of the punishment depended on how important the victim and the lawbreaker were. The higher the class of the victim, the greater the penalty was. For example, an ox owner would pay half a mina of silver if the ox gored a noble. If the victim was a slave, however, the owner would pay only one third of a mina.

A person who accidentally broke a law was just as guilty as someone who meant to break the law. People who could not always control the outcome of their work, such as doctors, had to be very careful, as the following law shows:

> **❝If a surgeon performed a major operation on a citizen with a bronze lancet [knife] and has caused the death of this citizen . . . his hand shall be cut off. ❞**
>
> —from Hammurabi's Code

Laws for Everyone You probably know many rules. There are rules for taking tests, playing ball, and living in your home. People have followed—or broken—rules for thousands of years. What, then, was the importance of Hammurabi's Code?

The laws are important to us because they were written down. With written laws, everyone could know the rules—and the punishments. Hammurabi's punishments may seem harsh to us, but they improved upon previous laws. Hammurabi's laws were not the first attempt by a society to set up a code of laws. But his laws are the first organized, recorded set that we have found.

√ **Reading Check** What was Hammurabi's Code?

Hammurabi's Code

- If any one steal the minor son of another, he shall be put to death.
- If any one is committing a robbery and is caught, then he shall be put to death.
- If any one open his ditches to water his crop, but is careless, and the water flood the field of his neighbor, then he shall pay his neighbor corn for his loss.
- If a man adopt a child [as his] son, and rear him, this grown son cannot be demanded back again.
- If a son strike his father, his hands shall be hewn (cut) off.

■ | **Chart Skills**

The table above shows five of the nearly 300 laws that make up Hammurabi's Code. At the left is a detail of the stone pillar on which the laws were carved. **Identify** Which of the laws in the table deals with the crime of kidnapping? **Generalize** What do the laws shown above tell us about the Babylonians' ideas of justice?

The Art of Writing

Think how much more difficult life would be if no one knew how to read and write. But writing did not suddenly appear. It took a long time for the art of writing to be developed.

Ancient Scribes Writing first developed in Mesopotamia around 3100 B.C. Long before Hammurabi issued his code, the people of Sumer had developed a system of writing. Writing met the need Sumerians had to keep records. Record keepers were very important—and busy—people in Sumer. The Sumerians' earliest written documents are records of farm animals. Since only a few people could write, it was one of the most valuable skills in the ancient world. Scribes held positions of great respect in Mesopotamia.

The scribes of Sumer recorded sales and trades, tax payments, gifts for the gods, and marriages and deaths. Some scribes had special tasks. Military scribes calculated the amount of food and supplies that an army would need. Government scribes figured out the number of diggers needed to build a canal. Written orders then went out to local officials who had to provide these supplies or workers. None of these records were written on paper, however. Paper had not yet been invented. Instead, the scribes of Mespotamia kept their notes and records on clay.

Links Across Time

New Discoveries In 2000, archaeologists uncovered a small stone with an unfamiliar type of ancient writing inscribed upon it. Scientists estimate that the stone, found in the present-day country of Turkmenistan, dates back to about 2300 B.C. The stone and other findings in the area indicate the existence of an ancient culture that had been entirely unknown.

A Record in Clay The Tigris and the Euphrates rivers provided scribes with the clay they used to write on. Each spring, the rivers washed down clay from the mountains. Scribes shaped the soft, wet clay into smooth, flat surfaces called tablets. They marked their letters in the clay with sharp tools. When the clay dried, it was a permanent record.

The shape and size of a tablet depended on its purpose. Larger tablets were used for reference purposes. Like the heavy atlases and dictionaries in today's libraries, they stayed in one place. Smaller tablets, the size of letters or postcards, were used for personal messages. Even today, these personal tablets can be fun to read. They show that Mesopotamians used writing to express the ups and downs of everyday life:

> **❝This is really a fine way of behaving! The gardeners keep breaking into the date storehouse and taking dates. You yourselves cover it up and do not report it to me! Bring these men to me—after they have paid for the dates. ❞**
>
> *—from a Mesopotamian tablet*

Scribes sometimes enclosed a message (above) in an envelope (top) made from wet clay. As the envelope dried, it formed a seal around the tablet. A sharpened reed (below) is used to write cuneiform script on soft clay.

How Writing Was Invented Like most inventions, writing developed over time. Long before the Sumerians invented writing, they used shaped pieces of clay as tokens, or symbols. They used the clay tokens to keep records. Tokens could keep track of how many animals were bought and sold, or how much food had been grown. By around 3100 B.C., this form of record keeping had developed into writing.

At first, written words were symbols that represented specific objects. Grain, oxen, water, or stars—each important object had its own symbol. As people learned to record ideas as well as facts, the symbols changed. Eventually, scribes combined symbols to make groups of wedges and lines known as **cuneiform** (kyoo NEE uh fawrm). Cuneiform script could be used to represent different languages. This flexibility was highly useful in a land of many peoples.

The Development of Cuneiform

Word	Outline Character, About 3000 B.C.	Sumerian, About 2000 B.C.	Assyrian, About 700 B.C.	Chaldean, About 500 B.C.
Sun				
God or heaven				
Mountain				

Chart Skills

The table at the left shows how cuneiform changed over time.
Identify The simplest symbols came from which time period? **Generalize** How did the symbols for each word change over time?

Refer to the table above titled The Development of Cuneiform. Notice how the symbols developed over time. Scholars believe that the Sumerians developed their system of writing independently. That means that they did not borrow ideas from the writing systems of other civilizations. Working independently meant that they had many decisions to make. They decided that the symbols should be set in rows, that each row should be read from left to right, and that a page should be read from top to bottom. What other languages are written this way?

✓ **Reading Check** **When, where, and how did writing first develop?**

Section 3 Assessment

Key Terms
Review the key terms at the beginning of this section. Use each term in a sentence that explains its meaning.

Target Reading Skill
Summarize the information in the last paragraph of this section.

Comprehension and Critical Thinking
1. (a) Recall What was Hammurabi's Code, and what was its purpose in ancient Babylonia?

(b) Analyze What does the expression "an eye for an eye" mean in relation to the laws in Hammurabi's Code?
(c) Apply Information Hammurabi's Code was fair in some ways and unfair in other ways. Explain.
2. (a) Describe What were some uses of writing in Sumer?
(b) Contrast How do the early forms and methods of writing differ from the way we write today?
(c) Draw Inferences Why was the development of writing an important step in human history?

Writing Activity
Reread the quote on page 50 in which the writer complains about the gardeners. Write a law that applies to the gardeners who stole the dates. What do you think should happen to the people who didn't tell about the theft?

Go Online PHSchool.com

For: An activity on cuneiform writing
Visit: PHSchool.com
Web Code: lbd-2203

Mediterranean Civilizations

Prepare to Read

Objectives

In this section you will

1. Understand how the sea power of the Phoenicians helped spread civilization throughout the Mediterranean area.
2. Learn about the major events in the history of the Israelites.

Taking Notes

As you read, create an outline of the history of the Phoenicians and the Israelites. Copy the outline below, and record your findings in it.

> I. The Phoenicians
>   A. Sea-trading power
>   1.
>   2.
>   B. Phoenician alphabet
>   1.
>   2.
> II. The Israelites

Target Reading Skill

Read Ahead Reading ahead is a strategy that can help you to understand words and ideas in the text. If you do not understand a certain passage, read ahead, because a word or idea may be clarified later on. Use this strategy as you read this section.

Key Terms

- **alphabet** (AL fuh bet) *n.* a set of symbols that represent the sounds of a language
- **monotheism** (MAHN oh thee iz um) *n.* the belief in one god
- **famine** (FAM in) *n.* a time when there is so little food that many people starve
- **exile** (EK syl) *v.* to force someone to live in another country

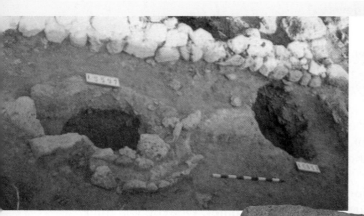

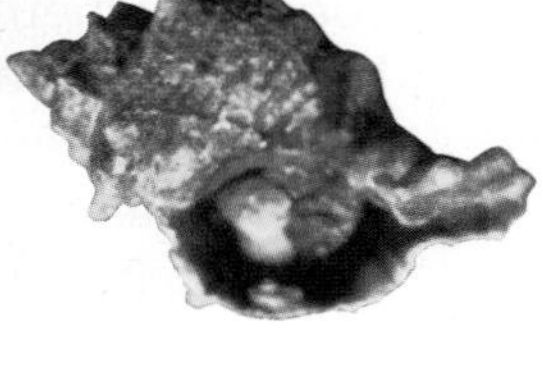

Above, ancient vats from a site in Tel Dor, Israel, once contained purple dye of the type used by the Phoenicians. The stained pottery piece in the middle probably came from a vessel that held the dye. The purple dye comes from the glands of the murex snail, shown at the right.

While the great empire of Hammurabi was rising and falling, the people of a city on the shores of the Mediterranean Sea were becoming rich by gathering snails.

The snails collected near the coastal city of Tyre (tyr) were not ordinary snails. These snails produced a rich purple dye. Cloth made purple with the dye was highly valued by wealthy people throughout the Mediterranean region. Ships from Tyre sold the purple cloth at extremely high prices. The profits helped make Tyre a wealthy city.

Phoenician Sea Power

Tyre was the major city in a region called Phoenicia (fuh NISH uh). Locate Phoenicia and its colonies on the map below. The Phoenicians' outlook was westward, toward the Mediterranean Sea and the cities that were growing around it.

Masters of Trade The Phoenicians had settled in a land that had limited, but very important, resources. Besides the snails used to dye cloth, Phoenicia had a great amount of dense cedar forests. The Phoenicians sold their dyed cloth and the wood from their forests to neighboring peoples.

As trade grew, the Phoenicians looked to the sea to increase their profits. In time, they controlled trade throughout much of the Mediterranean. From about 1100 to 800 B.C., Phoenicia was a great sea power. Phoenician ships sailed all over the Mediterranean Sea and into the stormy Atlantic Ocean. They came back from these trips with stories of horrible monsters that lived in the ocean depths. These stories helped keep other peoples from trying to compete for trade in the Atlantic.

A silver coin from Sidon showing a Phoenician galley, a ship powered by oars

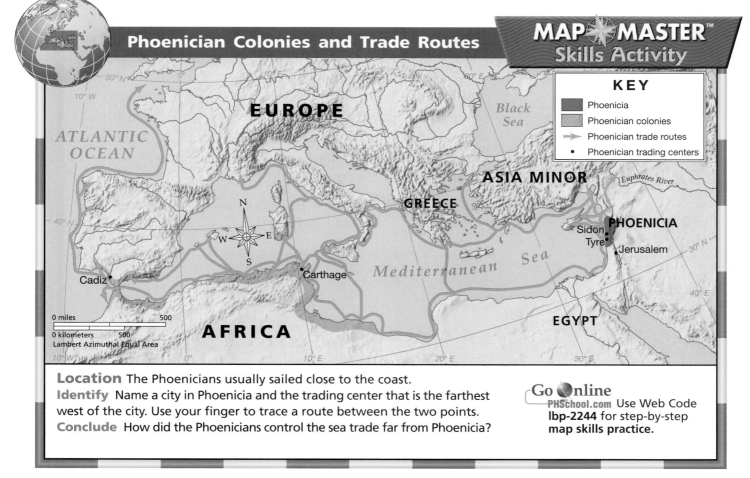

Phoenician Colonies and Trade Routes

MAP MASTER™ Skills Activity

KEY
- Phoenicia
- Phoenician colonies
- → Phoenician trade routes
- • Phoenician trading centers

Location The Phoenicians usually sailed close to the coast.
Identify Name a city in Phoenicia and the trading center that is the farthest west of the city. Use your finger to trace a route between the two points.
Conclude How did the Phoenicians control the sea trade far from Phoenicia?

Go Online
PHSchool.com Use Web Code **lbp-2244** for step-by-step map skills practice.

Exotic Marketplaces Trade brought valuable goods from lands around the Mediterranean Sea to the Phoenician cities of Tyre and Sidon (SY dun). Bazaars swelled with foods brought from faraway places. These foods included figs, olives, honey, and spices. In the bazaars, merchants sold strange animals, such as giraffes and warthogs from Africa and bears from Europe.

The overflowing markets of Tyre awed visitors. Here is one description of Tyre's bazaars:

> **When your wares came from the seas, you satisfied many peoples. With your great wealth and merchandise, you enriched the kings of the earth.**
>
> —the Bible

✓ Reading Check **What resources did the Phoenicians first use to build their wealth?**

The Phoenician Alphabet

The Phoenicians relied on writing to help them conduct trade. They developed a writing system that used just 22 symbols. This system was the Phoenician **alphabet,** a set of symbols that represents the sounds of the language. It forms the basis of the alphabet used in many languages today, including English. In the Phoenician alphabet, however, each letter stood for one consonant sound.

The simple Phoenician alphabet was far easier to learn than cuneiform. Before the alphabet, only highly educated scribes were skilled in writing. Now many more people could write using the new alphabet. The alphabet simplified trade between people who spoke different languages. The Phoenician sea trade, in turn, helped the alphabet to spread.

✓ Reading Check **How did the Phoenician alphabet differ from cuneiform script?**

The Phoenician Alphabet

A	⪤	N	4
B	⅃	O	○
C	↑	P	7
D	◿	Q	ⵁ
E	⧧	R	⅁
F	Y	S	W
G	↑	T	+
H	⊟	U	Y
I	2	V	Y
J	2	W	Y
K	↓	X	⹦
L	∤	Y	�252
M	⋌⋌	Z	⼯

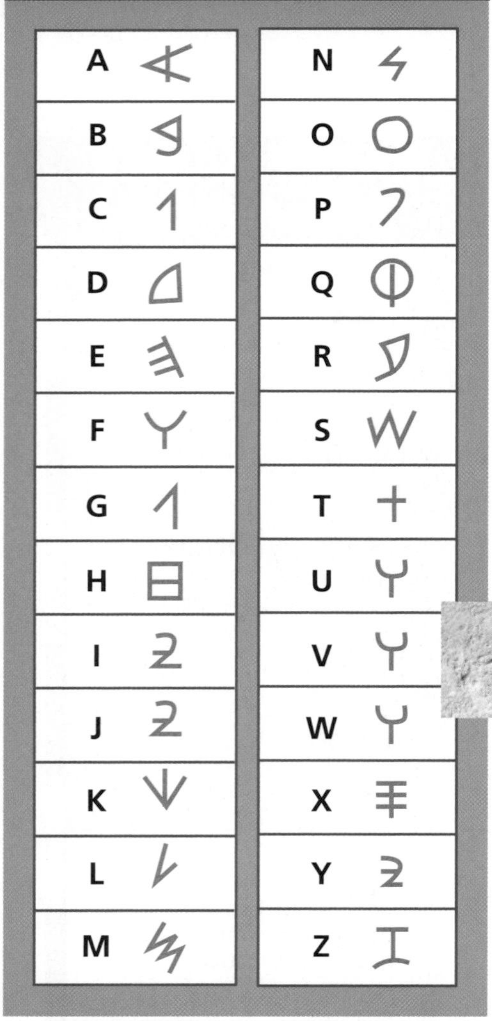

▪ Chart Skills

The chart at the left shows the Phoenician letters that correspond to our alphabet. The symbols for A, E, I, O, and U originally represented consonant sounds. The Greeks later used the symbols to represent vowel sounds. The Phoenician stone inscription above dates to about 391 B.C. **Identify** Which letters in the Phoenician alphabet seem similar to the letters in our alphabet? **Identify Effects** How did the Phoenician alphabet affect other civilizations?

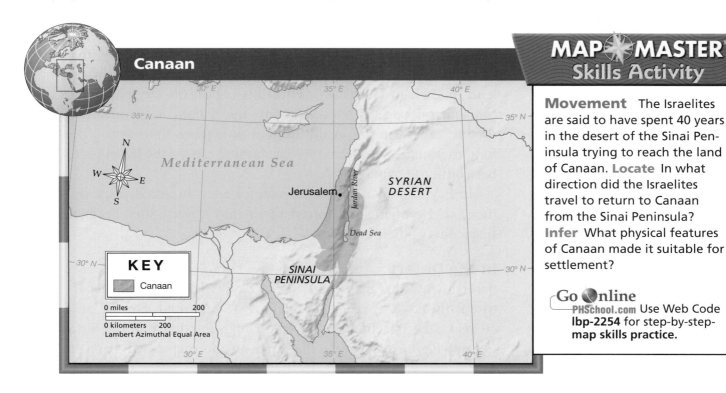

MAP MASTER™
Skills Activity

Movement The Israelites are said to have spent 40 years in the desert of the Sinai Peninsula trying to reach the land of Canaan. **Locate** In what direction did the Israelites travel to return to Canaan from the Sinai Peninsula? **Infer** What physical features of Canaan made it suitable for settlement?

Go **Online**
PHSchool.com Use Web Code **lbp-2254** for step-by-step-map skills practice.

KEY

Canaan

0 miles   200
0 kilometers   200
Lambert Azimuthal Equal Area

Mediterranean Sea

Jerusalem

Jordan River

SYRIAN DESERT

Dead Sea

SINAI PENINSULA

The Rise of the Israelites

South of Phoenicia, a small band of people settled in the hills around the Jordan River valley. Called Hebrews at first, they later became known as Israelites. Although the Israelites never built a large empire, they had a great influence on our civilization.

Much of what is known about the early history of the Israelites comes from stories told in the Torah (TOH ruh), the Israelites' most sacred text. Historians compare biblical and other religious stories with archaeological evidence to piece together events from the past. In this way they have determined that Abraham, whose story follows, may have lived around 2000 B.C.

Abraham the Leader The Israelites traced their beginnings to Mesopotamia. For hundreds of years, they lived as shepherds and merchants who grazed their flocks outside Sumerian cities.

According to the Torah, a leader named Abraham taught his people to practice monotheism, a belief in one god. *Mono-* is the Greek prefix for "one." The Torah says that God told Abraham to leave Mesopotamia and settle elsewhere:

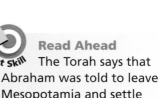

Read Ahead
The Torah says that Abraham was told to leave Mesopotamia and settle elsewhere. Keep reading to see what that means.

❝Get you out of your country, and from your kindred [relatives], and from your father's house, to the land that I will show you. And I will make of you a great nation.❞

—*Genesis 12: 1–2*

From Canaan to Egypt The Torah goes on to say that Abraham led the Israelites from Mesopotamia to settle in the land of Canaan (KAY nun). Find this region on the map titled Canaan, on page 55. According to the Torah, a famine then spread across Canaan. A **famine** is a time when there is so little food that many people starve. The famine caused the Israelites to flee south to Egypt.

In Egypt, the Israelites lived well for a few hundred years. But then, an Egyptian king forced them into slavery after he grew suspicious of their power.

In the Desert According to the Torah, an Israelite leader named Moses led his people out of Egypt. The Israelites' departure from Egypt is called the Exodus (EKS uh dus). For the next 40 years, the Israelites wandered through the desert of the Sinai (SY ny) Peninsula. Locate the Sinai on the map titled Canaan. The Torah says that while in the desert, God gave the Israelites the Ten Commandments, a code of laws. Eventually, the Israelites returned to Canaan. There, over time, the Israelites moved from herding to farming and built their own cities.

Old and New Jerusalem
People have lived in Jerusalem since 1800 B.C. Today, centuries-old buildings stand near modern hospitals, apartments, and hotels. **Analyze Images** *Using clues from the photo, describe features that point to Jerusalem's ancient past.*

Settlement in Canaan As they moved farther north, the Israelites were able to settle in many parts of Canaan. They united under their first king, Saul, who defended them against their enemies. The next king, David, established his capital in the city of Jerusalem.

A Divided Kingdom After David died, his son, Solomon, inherited the kingdom. After Solomon's death, the country split into two kingdoms. The northern kingdom was called Israel. The southern kingdom took the name Judah. The divided kingdom was ripe for invasion. Its neighbor, Assyria, conquered the Israelites and gained control of Judah.

Sent Into Exile In 722 B.C., the Israelites resisted Assyrian rule. In response, the Assyrians exiled thousands of people to distant parts of their empire. To **exile** means to force people to live in another place or country. The Assyrians controlled Judah until 612 B.C., when Assyria was conquered by the Chaldeans. Judah then fell under control of the Chaldean Babylonians. Later, in 587 B.C., the King of Judah rebelled against the Chaldeans. King Nebuchadnezzar responded by destroying the capital city of Jerusalem. He exiled the people of Judah to Babylonia.

King Solomon

✓ Reading Check **Who were the Israelites?**

Section 4 Assessment

Key Terms
Review the key terms at the beginning of this section. Use each term in a sentence that explains its meaning.

Target Reading Skill
What word or idea were you able to clarify by reading ahead?

Comprehension and Critical Thinking
1. (a) Identify Who were the Phoenicians?
(b) Recall How did the Phoenicians gain their wealth and power?

2. (a) Explain What are some features of the Phoenician alphabet?
(b) Identify Effects Describe the importance of the Phoenician alphabet. How did it affect the Mediterranean world and later civilizations?

3. (a) Identify Sequence Briefly trace the history of the Israelites from the leadership of Abraham to King Solomon.
(b) Identify Central Issues What important events in the history of the Israelites were shaped by movement and by war?

Writing Activity
Reread the description of Tyre. Using what you have read, write a poetic verse about Tyre's markets. Or work with a partner to write song lyrics on the same subject.

Writing Tip Poetic verses and song lyrics don't have to rhyme, but they usually have rhythm. To supply rhythm to your verse or lyrics, it sometimes helps to think of a familiar song as you write. Match words and phrases in your verse to the beats and phrases of the music.

"That movie was really confusing," Brandon said to his friend Juan as they left the theater.

"The action was great, though," said Juan. "Can you believe how much that explorer had to go through to find the treasure?"

Juan's comment gave Brandon an idea. "I guess that was the whole point of the movie—to show all the adventures they had while they tried to find the lost treasure."

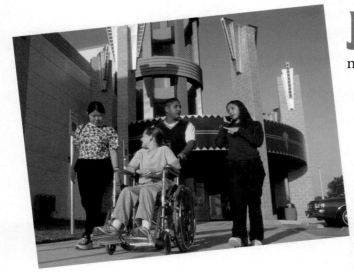

Juan and Brandon were right. To understand anything you read or see, you need to identify the main idea.

Learn the Skill

These steps will explain how to find the main idea in a written paragraph or in any kind of information that carries a message or a theme.

1. **Look for an idea that all the sentences in the paragraph have in common.** In a well-written paragraph, most of the sentences provide details that support or explain a particular idea.

2. **Identify the subject of the paragraph.** You may find the subject stated in several sentences. Or, you may find the subject in a topic sentence, one sentence that tells what the paragraph is about. The subject may also be stated in a title.

3. **State the main idea in your own words.** Write one or two versions of the main idea or topic. Then reread the passage to make sure that what you wrote accurately identifies the main idea.

Practice the Skill

Read the text in the box below, and then use the steps on page 58 to identify the main idea of the text.

 1 What idea do the sentences in the paragraph have in common?

2 This paragraph does not have a title, so you will need to find the sentence or sentences that state the main idea. Is there a topic sentence?

3 First, try to come up with a title for the paragraph. Then turn the title into a complete sentence that identifies the main idea.

In 1901, an archaeologist discovered a stone pillar with an ancient set of laws—Hammurabi's Code. The black stone is almost eight feet tall and more than seven feet around. At its top is a carving of Hammurabi receiving the code of laws from the Babylonian god of justice. About 3,500 lines of cuneiform characters are carved into the stone. These inscriptions are Hammurabi's Code.

Apply the Skill

Turn to page 48, and read the paragraph titled An Eye for an Eye. Follow the steps on page 58 to identify the main idea of the paragraph.

The stele, or stone pillar, on which Hammurabi's Code was written

Prepare to Read

Objectives

In this section you will

1. Learn about the basic beliefs of Judaism.
2. Find out about the effect that Judaism has had on other religions.

Taking Notes

As you read, list details that characterize Judaism. Copy the concept web below, and use it to help you summarize this section.

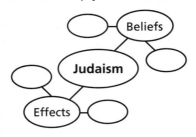

Target Reading Skill

Summarize When you summarize, you review and state, in the correct order, the main points you have read. Summarizing what you read is a good technique to help you comprehend and study. As you read, pause to summarize the main ideas about Judaism. The diagram you are using to take notes may help you to summarize.

Key Terms

- **covenant** (KUV uh nunt) *n.* a binding agreement
- **Moses** (MOH zuz) *n.* an Israelite leader whom the Torah credits with leading the Israelites from Egypt to Canaan
- **prophet** (PRAHF it) *n.* a religious teacher who is regarded as someone who speaks for God or for a god
- **diaspora** (dy AS pur uh) *n.* the scattering of people who have a common background or beliefs

Reading from the Torah

The Torah, the most sacred text of Judaism, says God made a promise to the Israelite leader Abraham:

> **❝I will make you exceedingly fruitful; and I will make nations of you, and kings shall come forth from you. And I will . . . be God to you and to your descendants. . . .❞**
>
> —*Genesis 17: 6–7*

The ancient Israelites viewed this promise as the beginning of a long relationship between themselves and God.

The early Israelites came to believe that God was taking part in their history. The Torah records events and laws important to the Israelites. It is made up of five books. They are called Genesis (JEN uh sis), Exodus, Leviticus (luh VIT ih kus), Numbers, and Deuteronomy (doo tur AHN uh mee). Later, Christians adopted these books as the first five books of the Old Testament. The promise that you just read is from the Book of Genesis. In Genesis, we learn of the very beginnings of Judaism, the world's first religion that was monotheistic. *Monotheistic* means "having only one god."

The Beliefs of Judaism

To the Israelites, history and religion were closely connected. Each event showed God's plan for the Israelite people. Over time, Israelite beliefs developed into the religion we know today as Judaism. You already know that Judaism was monotheistic from its beginning. It differed from the beliefs of nearby peoples in other ways as well.

A Promise to the Israelites Most ancient people thought of their gods as being connected to certain places or people. The Israelites, however, believed that God is present everywhere. They believed that God knows everything and has complete power.

According to the Torah, God promised Abraham that his people would become kings and build nations. God said to Abraham, "I will keep my promise to you and your descendants in future generations as an everlasting covenant." Because of this **covenant, or binding agreement,** the Israelites considered themselves God's "chosen people." This covenant was later renewed by **Moses,** an Israelite leader who lived sometime around 1200 B.C. He told the Israelites that God would lead them to Canaan, "the promised land." In return, the Israelites had to obey God faithfully.

The Dead Sea Scrolls
The Dead Sea Scrolls (above) were discovered in 1947 in jars like the one shown at the left. The scrolls helped historians reconstruct the early history of the Israelites.
Generalize *What is the importance of archaeological finds like the Dead Sea Scrolls?*

Summarize
Summarize the paragraph at the left. Be sure to include the key points and important details about God's promise to the Israelites.

Links Across
Time

Kosher In Judaism, laws require that certain foods be kosher (KOH shur), meaning "fit for use." These laws are based on passages from the Hebrew Bible. For seafood to be kosher, for example, it must have scales and fins. So, codfish is kosher, but clams are not. Other laws tell how animals meant for consumption should be slaughtered and how food must be prepared and eaten. Not all Jews follow these strict dietary laws today.

Before sunset on Friday evenings, Jewish women light white Shabbat candles and say a blessing.

The Ten Commandments At the heart of Judaism are the Ten Commandments. The Israelites believed that God delivered the Commandments to them through Moses. Some Commandments set out religious duties toward God. Others are rules for correct behavior. Here are some of the Commandments.

> **"I the Lord am your God who brought you out of the land of Egypt. . . . You shall have no other gods beside Me. . . . Honor your father and your mother, as the Lord your God has commanded. . . . You shall not murder. You shall not steal."**
>
> —the Ten Commandments

In addition to the Ten Commandments, the Torah set out many other laws. Some had to do with everyday matters, such as how food should be prepared. Others had to do with crimes. Like Hammurabi's Code, many of the Israelites' laws tried to match punishments to crimes. At the same time, religious teachers called on leaders to carry out the laws with justice and mercy.

Judaism and Women Some laws protected women. One of the Commandments, for example, requires that mothers be treated with respect. In fact, women enjoyed more rights under Judaism than under other religions of that time. A woman's rights and duties were different from those of men. Only a husband could seek a divorce. However, women had the right to avoid physical contact with their husbands.

Early in Israelite history a few women, such as the judge Deborah, won honor and respect as religious leaders. Later on, however, women were not allowed to take part in many religious leadership roles.

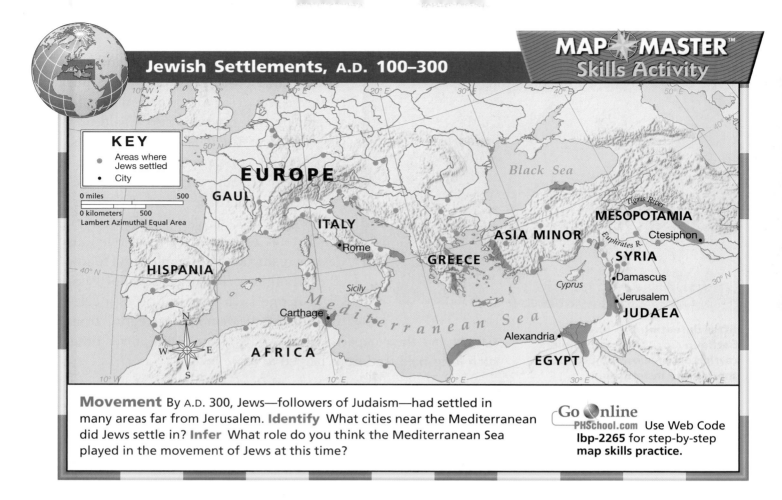

Jewish Settlements, A.D. 100–300

KEY
- Areas where Jews settled
- City

0 miles 500
0 kilometers 500
Lambert Azimuthal Equal Area

EUROPE

GAUL

Black Sea

Tigris River

MESOPOTAMIA

ITALY

ASIA MINOR

Euphrates R.

Ctesiphon

Rome

GREECE

SYRIA

HISPANIA

Damascus

Cyprus

Jerusalem

Sicily

JUDAEA

Carthage

Mediterranean Sea

Alexandria

AFRICA

EGYPT

N
W E
S

Movement By A.D. 300, Jews—followers of Judaism—had settled in many areas far from Jerusalem. **Identify** What cities near the Mediterranean did Jews settle in? **Infer** What role do you think the Mediterranean Sea played in the movement of Jews at this time?

Go Online
PHSchool.com Use Web Code **lbp-2265** for step-by-step **map skills practice.**

Justice and Morality   The history of the Israelites tells of **prophets,** or religious teachers who are regarded as speaking for God. The prophets told the Israelites how God wanted them to live. They warned the people not to disobey God's law. Disobedience could bring disaster.

Prophets preached a code of ethics, or moral behavior. They urged the Israelites to live good and decent lives. They also called on the rich and powerful to protect the poor and weak. All people, the prophets said, were equal before God. In many ancient societies, a ruler was seen as a god. To the Israelites, however, their leaders were human. Kings had to obey God's law just as shepherds and merchants did.

✓ Reading Check   **What did the prophets tell the Israelites?**

The Effects of Judaism

After their exile from Judah in 587 B.C., the Jews, or people who follow Judaism, saw their homeland controlled by various foreign powers, including the Romans. The Romans drove the Jews out of Jerusalem in A.D. 135. While some Jews remained in the region, others scattered to different parts of the world.

After defeating the Jews in battle in A.D. 70, Roman soldiers carried off precious objects from the temple in Jerusalem.

New Settlements The Romans carried on the Jewish **diaspora** (dy AS pur uh), the scattering of a group of people, begun by the Assyrians and Chaldeans. See the map titled Jewish Settlements, A.D. 100–300, on page 63.

Wherever they settled, the Jews preserved their heritage. They did so by living together in close communities. They took care to obey their religious laws, worship at their temples, and follow their traditions. The celebration of Passover is one such tradition. It is a celebration of the Israelites' freedom from slavery and their departure, or Exodus, from Egypt. Over time, such long-held traditions helped to unite Jews.

Effects on Later Religions Judaism had an important influence on two later religions, Christianity and Islam. Both religions have their beginnings in Judaism. Both faiths originated from the same geographical area. Both were monotheistic. Jews, Christians, and followers of Islam all honor Abraham, Moses, and the prophets. They also share the same moral point of view that the Israelites first developed.

✓ **Reading Check** How did the Jews preserve their heritage?

Section 5 Assessment

Key Terms
Review the key terms at the beginning of this section. Use each term in a sentence that explains its meaning.

Target Reading Skill
Write a summary of the last paragraph in this section.

Comprehension and Critical Thinking
1. (a) Identify What promise did the Israelites believe God made to Abraham?

(b) Explain What did God's covenant with Abraham require of the Israelites?
(c) Analyze Information Why did the Israelites believe that they were God's chosen people?
2. (a) Recall What religious laws did the Israelites follow?
(b) Compare and Contrast How does Judaism compare and contrast with the beliefs of other peoples in the ancient world?
(c) Draw Inferences What do the laws of Judaism say about the moral values of the Israelites?

Writing Activity
Suppose you have a friend who wants to learn more about Judaism. Write him or her a letter explaining the basic beliefs and history of Judaism.

> **Writing Tip** When writing a letter, remember to include the date, a salutation, or greeting, and a closing. It might help to have a specific friend in mind when you write your letter.

Review and Assessment

◆ Chapter Summary

Section 1: Land Between Two Rivers

- Mesopotamia's attractive location between two rivers drew people to settle there.
- Some of the earliest cities grew up in Sumer, in the region of Mesopotamia.
- Sumerians worshiped and honored many gods.

Cuneiform tablet

Section 2: Fertile Crescent Empires

- The Babylonian Empire included Sumer and lands reaching into Asia Minor.
- The Assyrians overthrew the Babylonians and created an even larger empire.
- The Assyrian Empire fell to the Chaldeans, who created the New Babylonian Empire under Nebuchadnezzar II.
- The Persians created the largest empire the Fertile Crescent had ever known and tolerated the cultures of conquered peoples.

Section 3: The Legacy of Mesopotamia

- The earliest existing set of written laws, known as Hammurabi's Code, established rules and punishments for Babylonians.
- Writing developed in Mesopotamia in about 3500 B.C., and was first used to keep records.

Section 4: Mediterranean Civilizations

- Phoenicia was a major sea power from 1100 to 800 B.C. Its wealth came from trade.
- The Phoenician alphabet forms the basis of alphabets used in English and other languages.
- The Israelites practiced monotheism and established a capital in the city of Jerusalem.

Section 5: Judaism

- The religion practiced by the Israelites was very different from other religions practiced in the ancient world.
- The Ten Commandments are the core beliefs of Judaism.
- Judaism has influenced other major religions of the world.

Babylonian statue

◆ Key Terms

Use each key term below in a sentence that shows the meaning of the term.

1. city-state
2. polytheism
3. myth
4. empire
5. caravan
6. bazaar
7. code
8. cuneiform
9. monotheism
10. famine
11. exile
12. covenant
13. prophet
14. diaspora

◆ Comprehension and Critical Thinking

15. (a) Identify What is the Fertile Crescent?
(b) Apply Information Explain the importance of the Tigris and the Euphrates rivers in the Fertile Crescent.
(c) Draw Conclusions How did the geography of the Fertile Crescent help the Sumerians to prosper?

16. (a) Recall Describe the Babylonian, Assyrian, New Babylonian, and Persian empires.
(b) Identify Cause and Effect Explain how the Fertile Crescent's location shaped the development of its civilizations.
(c) Find the Main Ideas What patterns do you see in the rise and fall of the many civilizations in the Fertile Crescent?

17. (a) Define What was Hammurabi's Code?
(b) Explain What was the purpose of Hammurabi's Code?
(c) Make Generalizations What effect did Hammurabi's Code have on future civilizations?

18. (a) Name Who were the Phoenicians?
(b) Explain Describe two cultural contributions of the Phoenicians and explain their importance.

(c) Compare and Contrast Compare and contrast cuneiform and the Phoenician alphabet.

19. (a) Recall Who were the Israelites and what did they believe?
(b) Explain Describe two major events in the history of the Israelites.
(c) Analyze Information Choose an event from the history of the Israelites and describe its importance.

◆ Skills Practice

Identifying Main Ideas In the Skills for Life Activity, you learned how to identify main ideas. You also learned how to summarize main ideas in a brief statement. Review the steps you followed to learn this skill. Then turn to page 49 and read the three paragraphs on that page under the heading The Art of Writing. Identify the main ideas and then summarize them in a few sentences.

◆ Writing Activity: Math

Turn to page 3 at the beginning of this book. According to the dates in the map key, how long did the civilization of ancient Mesopotamia last? Write a sentence explaining your answer.

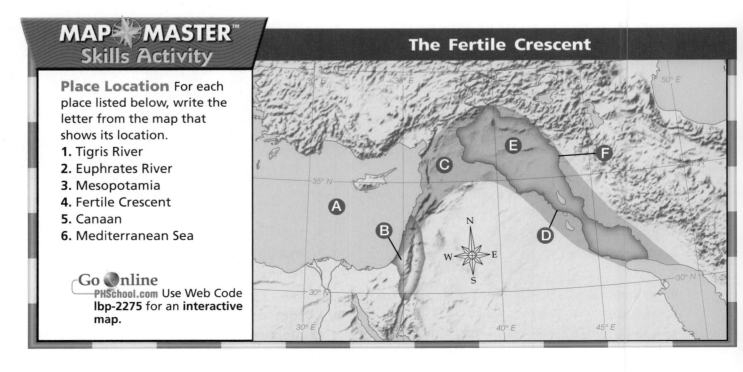

MAP✹MASTER™
Skills Activity

Place Location For each place listed below, write the letter from the map that shows its location.
1. Tigris River
2. Euphrates River
3. Mesopotamia
4. Fertile Crescent
5. Canaan
6. Mediterranean Sea

Go Online
PHSchool.com Use Web Code **lbp-2275** for an **interactive map.**

The Fertile Crescent

Standardized Test Prep

Test-Taking Tips

Some questions on standardized tests ask you to draw conclusions by analyzing a reading passage. Read the paragraph below. Then follow the tips to answer the sample question.

> Sumerian priests washed the statues of gods before and after each meal was offered. Music sounded and incense burned as huge plates of food were laid before them. In most ancient religions, the food was often eaten after it was presented to the gods. Perhaps the worshipers thought that by eating the offering, they would be taking in the qualities they admired in the gods.

TIP Reread if necessary before answering.

Pick the letter that best completes the statement.

TIP Use logic—or good reasoning—to choose your answer.

Which conclusion can you reach, based on the passage?

- A The Sumerians were not as intelligent as modern people.
- B Only priests were allowed into temples.
- C The Sumerians did not like to waste food.
- D Religious ceremonies were important to the Sumerians.

Think It Through You can rule out B. The passage does not say that only priests were allowed in the temples. The practices of the Sumerians may seem odd to us, but odd does not mean unintelligent. So A is not correct. The passage states that people possibly ate offerings to honor their gods. So C is not the best answer. The correct answer is D.

Practice Questions

Use the tips above and other tips in this book to help you answer the following questions.

1. Where was Mesopotamia located?
   - A along the Nile River
   - B between the Tigris and the Euphrates rivers
   - C in the Arabian Desert
   - D in present-day Egypt

2. Which civilization mastered seafaring?
   - A Phoenicia
   - B Sumer
   - C Assyria
   - D Babylonia

Read the passage below, and then answer the questions that follow.

The Assyrians invented the battering ram to tear down city walls. They trained people to hurl stones with slings, and they created special armor to protect their archers. They also perfected the skill of fighting while on horse-drawn chariots.

3. What can you conclude about the Assyrians from this passage?
   - A They were inexperienced warriors.
   - B They liked inventing new things.
   - C They disliked fighting.
   - D They had fought many wars.

4. Judaism differed from other early religions in that it
   - A was polytheistic.
   - B treated men and women equally.
   - C was monotheistic.
   - D developed in the Fertile Crescent.

Use Web Code lba-2205 for **Chapter 2 self-test.**

Ancient Egypt and Nubia

Chapter Preview

This chapter will introduce you to the civilizations of Ancient Egypt and Nubia.

Target Reading Skill

Context In this chapter you will focus on using context to help you understand unfamiliar words. The context of a word includes the words, phrases, and sentences surrounding the word.

▶ **A tomb painting of Egyptian fishermen, dating from about 1292 to 1225 B.C.**

MAP MASTER™
Skills Activity

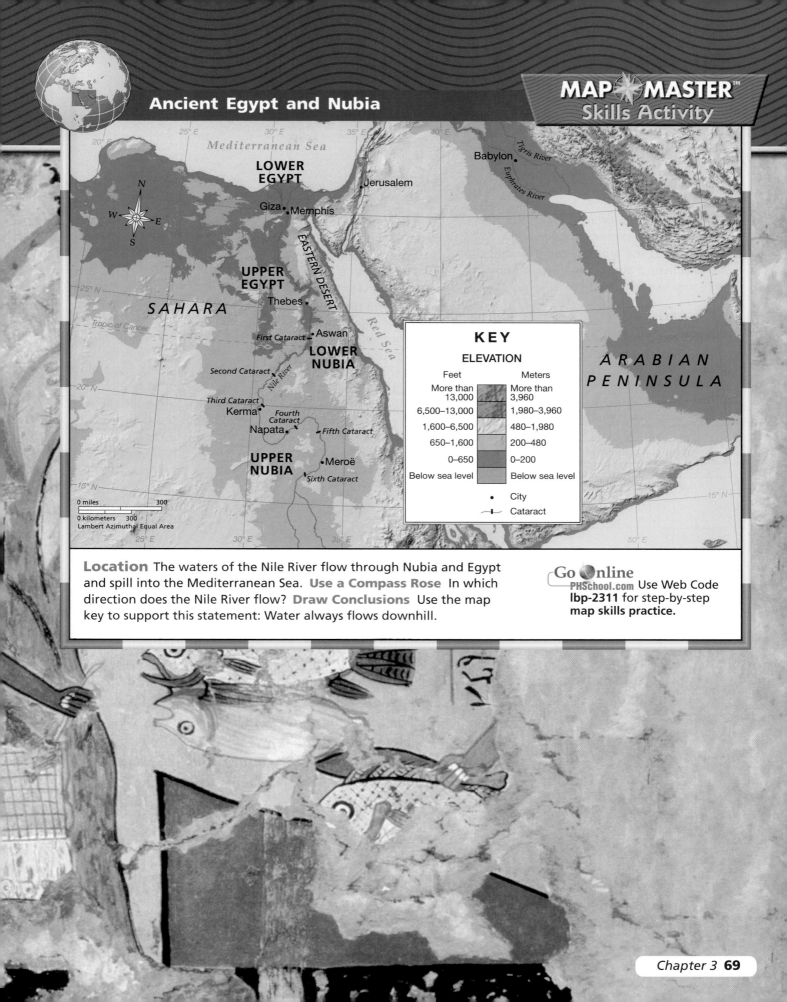

KEY
ELEVATION

Feet		Meters
More than 13,000		More than 3,960
6,500–13,000		1,980–3,960
1,600–6,500		480–1,980
650–1,600		200–480
0–650		0–200
Below sea level		Below sea level

• City
⌐ Cataract

Mediterranean Sea

LOWER EGYPT

Babylon

Jerusalem

Giza • Memphis

UPPER EGYPT

SAHARA

Thebes

Tropic of Cancer

First Cataract • Aswan

LOWER NUBIA

Second Cataract

Third Cataract

Kerma • Fourth Cataract

Napata • Fifth Cataract

UPPER NUBIA

• Meroë

Sixth Cataract

Nile River

Red Sea

Tigris River

Euphrates River

ARABIAN PENINSULA

0 miles 300
0 kilometers 300
Lambert Azimuthal Equal Area

Location The waters of the Nile River flow through Nubia and Egypt and spill into the Mediterranean Sea. **Use a Compass Rose** In which direction does the Nile River flow? **Draw Conclusions** Use the map key to support this statement: Water always flows downhill.

Go Online
PHSchool.com Use Web Code **lbp-2311** for step-by-step **map skills practice.**

The Geography of the Nile

Prepare to Read

Objectives

In this section you will
1. Find out how the geography of the Nile changes as the river runs its course.
2. Learn about the types of communities that first appeared along the Nile, and how the Nile was used for trade.

Taking Notes

As you read, note the effects the Nile had on the growth of communities and trade. Copy the chart below, and use it to record your findings.

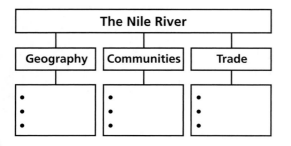

Target Reading Skill

Use Context Clues When reading, you may come across an unfamiliar word, or a word that is used in an unfamiliar way. Look for clues in the context—the surrounding words, sentences, and paragraphs—to help you understand the meaning. Look at the context for the word *sediment* on page 72 in the paragraph that begins with The Gifts of the Nile. What do you think *sediment* means?

Key Terms

- **Nubia** (NOO bee uh) *n.* an ancient region in the Nile River Valley, on the site of present-day southern Egypt and nothern Sudan
- **cataract** (KAT uh rakt) *n.* a large waterfall; any strong flood or rush of water
- **delta** (DEL tuh) *n.* a plain at the mouth of a river, formed when sediment is deposited by flowing water
- **silt** (silt) *n.* fine soil found on river bottoms

The Greek historian Herodotus (huh RAHD uh tus) wrote, "Egypt is the gift of the Nile." Herodotus explored Egypt in the 400s B.C. On his journey, he saw the life-giving waters of its great river. He traveled upriver until he was stopped by churning rapids of white water. Forced to turn back, he never found the source of the river.

Herodotus wrote down his observations of Egypt and other lands. His writings still make interesting reading today. Despite his failure to locate the source of the Nile, Herodotus had learned a basic truth: There would be no Egypt without the Nile.

River of Life
An Egyptian uses a throwstick, a sort of boomerang, to hunt for birds from his boat. **Analyze Images** *What gifts of the Nile are shown in this painting?*

The Course of the Nile River

The Nile River is the world's longest river. It flows north from its sources in East Africa to the Mediterranean Sea for more than 4,000 miles (6,400 kilometers). That is about the distance from New York to Alaska. The Nile has two main sources. The Blue Nile rises in the highlands of the present-day country of Ethiopia and races down to the desert in thundering torrents. The White Nile is calmer. It begins deep in East Africa and flows northward through swamps. The two rivers meet in the present-day country of Sudan. There, the Nile begins its journey through desert lands to the Mediterranean Sea.

The Nile Through Ancient Nubia   Just north of the point where the Blue Nile and White Nile meet, the Nile makes two huge bends. It forms an S shape 1,000 miles (1,600 kilometers) in length. The northern tip of the S is at the city of Aswan in Egypt. Along this stretch of the Nile was **Nubia,** an ancient region in the Nile River valley.

The Nubian section of the Nile contained six **cataracts,** or rock-filled rapids. Between the first and second cataracts was Lower Nubia. In that region, the desert and granite mountains lined the riverbanks, leaving very little land for farming. Because it rarely rained in Lower Nubia, people had to live close to the Nile for their water supply.

Farther south, between the second and sixth cataracts, lies the area that was known as Upper Nubia. In that region, rain does fall, so people could plant in the fall and then harvest in the spring. But the farmland was in a very narrow strip, no more than 2 miles (3 kilometers) wide on each side of the river.

Nubia's Resources
Nubian princes bring gifts of gold to an Egyptian ruler. **Infer** *How did geography help link the cultures of Egypt and Nubia?*

The Nile Through Ancient Egypt The Nile ran for about 700 miles (1,100 kilometers) through ancient Egypt, from the First Cataract at Aswan to the Mediterranean Sea. On its way, it passed through a narrow region called Upper Egypt. This fertile strip had an average width of around 6 miles (10 kilometers) on each side of the river. In the north, the Nile spread out to form a fertile, marshy area called Lower Egypt. Deserts stretched on each side of the river's green banks.

At the end of the Nile in the north, the river split into several streams that flowed to the Mediterranean Sea. These streams formed an area called the delta. A delta is a plain at the mouth of a river. The flowing water deposited mineral-rich sediment. Because of this, the Nile delta contained very fertile farmland.

The Gifts of the Nile Every spring, far away in the highlands of Africa, waters began to rush downstream. As they flowed, they brought a rich, fertile sediment called silt. Silt is fine soil found on river bottoms. By late summer, the Nile spilled over its banks all the way to the delta. The floodwaters deposited a thick layer of silt, making the land ideal for farming. In gratitude, the Egyptians praised Hapi (HAH pea), the god of the Nile:

> "Hail to you, O Nile, who flows from the Earth and comes to keep Egypt alive."
>
> —*ancient Egyptian prayer*

Target Skill

Using Context Clues In the paragraph at the right, sediment is described as being mineral rich and carried by water. If you read ahead, you will learn that silt is a kind of sediment What is the meaning of *sediment*?

Black Land and Red Land The ancient Egyptians called their land Kemet (KEH met), "the black land," because of the dark soil left by the Nile's floods. The timing of the floods and the height of the floodwaters might vary from year to year. But unlike the Mesopotamians, the Egyptians usually did not have to worry about flash floods. Dry years were rare in Egypt, but they could cause famine.

Beyond the fertile river banks lay the "red land," the vast desert. It spread out on either side of the river. Most of the Sahara lay to the west, and the part of the Sahara called the Eastern Desert lay to the east. These lands were not friendly to human life. They were useless for farming. Only those who knew the deserts well dared travel over this blistering-hot land.

Desert Protection The hot sands shielded Egypt and Nubia from foreign attacks. That was a protection Mesopotamia did not have. The land between the Tigris and Euphrates rivers was wide open to outsiders. The people of Mesopotamia often faced invasions. Over a period of 2,000 years, the people of ancient Egypt and Nubia faced few invasions. Yet they were not isolated. The Nile valley provided a path for trade with Central Africa. The Mediterranean Sea and the Red Sea provided access to Southwest Asia.

✓ Reading Check **How did the people of Nubia and Egypt benefit from the geography of the region?**

Geography and Civilization
In the large photo below, you can see the date palms and fields that line the Nile River near the city of Luxor. The small photo shows the desert landscape that surrounds the Nile.
Analyze Images *Compare the two photos. What are the challenges of living in the desert? What are the advantages of living along the Nile?*

The Growth of Communities and Trade Along the Nile

Settled hunting and fishing communities may have appeared in Nubia around 6000 B.C. Unlike the communities of the Fertile Crescent that settled after taking up agriculture, the Nubians formed settlements before they began to farm. Settled farming communities began to appear in both Egypt and Nubia sometime around 5000 B.C. As these communities grew, trade also expanded.

Living Along the Nile Egypt's early farming communities settled in the delta and valley regions of the Nile. The people of the delta built villages around the fertile river beds. Their homes were built of straw or of bricks made from a mix of mud and straw. To the south, in Upper Egypt, people built scattered farming villages along the banks of the Nile.

Nubia had less farmland along the Nile than Egypt. Because of the shortage of farmland, Nubians added to their diet by fishing in the Nile and hunting ducks and other birds along its banks.

Links Across Time

Saving Monuments To control flooding, the Egyptians built the Aswan High Dam on the Nile River in the 1960s. The water held back by the dam created Lake Nasser. During its creation, Lake Nasser threatened to flood ancient monuments that had been carved in the cliffs above the Nubian Nile. Egypt, with the help of about 50 nations, saved some of the monuments. At a site called Abu Simbel, the temple of Ramses II (below) was saved. Workers cut the temple into blocks. They moved the blocks to higher ground and then rebuilt the temple.

A Highway for Trade In Egypt, the Nile was used to transport goods. Ships could travel north on the Nile because it was moving downriver. But they could also sail upriver with the help of the winds that blew toward the south. Other trade links ran east across the desert to the Red Sea ports or to Mesopotamia. Caravans loaded with gold, silver, copper, and fine pottery traveled the overland trade routes. Valuable goods such as cedar from the eastern coast of the Mediterranean Sea and gold from Nubia were sold in the bazaars of Egypt's towns.

Routes Through Nubia Because of the cataracts, people could not travel through Nubia by river. Instead, the Nubians developed trade routes over land. The Nubians became famous traders of the ancient world. They carried goods from central Africa and Nubia into Egypt and southwestern Asia and brought other goods back.

One Nubian caravan that traveled into Egypt had 300 donkeys. The donkeys carried ebony wood, ivory from elephant tusks, ostrich feathers and eggs, and panther skins. Another popular object was a throwstick, a type of boomerang that Africans used for hunting.

✓ **Reading Check** How did the Nile operate as a "highway for trade"?

Nubians traded many valuable goods. This Nubian bronze mirror with a gilt silver handle, from about 700 B.C., was found in present-day Sudan.

Section 1 Assessment

Key Terms
Review the key terms at the beginning of this section. Use each term in a sentence that explains its meaning.

Target Reading Skill
Find the word *torrents* on page 71. Use context clues to find the meaning of *torrents*.

Comprehension and Critical Thinking
1. (a) Recall Describe the course of the Nile River from its source all the way to the delta.

(b) Identify Cause and Effect How did the Nile River affect the lives of the early Egyptians and Nubians?
(c) Predict If the Nile did not flood regularly, how might life along the river have been different in ancient times?
2. (a) List What kinds of trade goods passed through Nubia on their way to Egypt?
(b) Identify Effects How did the cataracts of the Nile River affect Nubian trade?
(c) Draw Conclusions How did the Nubians become famous as traders?

Writing Activity
Suppose that you are traveling along the Nile from its source to the Nile delta. Write a journal entry about the changes you notice in the river as you travel.

Go Online
PHSchool.com
For: An activity on the Nile River
Visit: PHSchool.com
Web Code: lbd-2301

Prepare to Read

Objectives

In this section you will

1. Learn about the history of kingship in ancient Egypt.
2. Find out about Egypt's accomplishments during each of the three kingdom periods.
3. Understand what characterized the rule of Egypt during the New Kingdom period.

Taking Notes

As you read, look for the main ideas about ancient Egyptian rulers. Copy the diagram below, and record your findings in it.

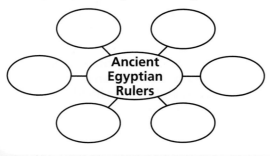

Ancient Egyptian Rulers

Target Reading Skill

Use Context Clues When you read an unfamiliar word, you can sometimes figure out its meaning from clues in the context. Sometimes the context will restate the word. The following phrase, for example, restates the meaning of *sphinx*: "a legendary creature with a lion's body and a human head." As you read, look at the context for the word *timber* on page 78. What do you think *timber* means?

Key Terms

- **pharaoh** (FEHR oh) *n.* the title of the kings of ancient Egypt
- **dynasty** (DY nus tee) *n.* a series of rulers from the same family or ethnic group
- **absolute power** (AB suh loot POW ur) *n.* complete control over someone or something
- **regent** (REE junt) *n.* someone who rules for a child until the child is old enough to rule

A sculpture of Queen Hatshepsut as a sphinx, a legendary creature with a lion's body and a human head

She seized control of Egypt's throne and made herself **pharaoh** (FEHR oh), the title used by the kings of Egypt. Hatshepsut (haht SHEP soot) was not the only woman to rule Egypt. But the title of pharaoh was traditionally held by men. Hatshepsut took on all the responsibilities of a pharaoh. Sometimes she even wore the false beard traditionally worn by pharaohs. Like all Egyptian pharaohs, Hatshepsut controlled the wealth and power of a great civilization.

Egyptian Kingship

Hatshepsut was one of many famous Egyptian pharaohs who ruled Egypt. Some, like her, were wise. Others were careless or cruel. Egypt's fortunes rested on the strength of its pharaohs.

From Dynasty to Dynasty The history of ancient Egypt is the history of each of its dynasties. **A dynasty** is a series of rulers from the same family or ethnic group. Egypt had 31 dynasties, from about 3100 B.C. until it was conquered in 332 B.C. Historians group Egypt's dynasties into three major time periods, called kingdoms. The earliest major time period is called the Old Kingdom. Next comes the Middle Kingdom. The latest time period is called the New Kingdom. The timeline titled Major Time Periods in Ancient Egypt on page 78 shows the approximate dates of each kingdom. Remember, these kingdoms are not places. They are time periods.

The gaps between the kingdoms were times of troubles—wars, invasions, or weak rulers. These in-between periods were rare, however. For most of ancient Egyptian history, rule was stable.

Egypt Is Unified According to legend, Egypt's first dynasty began when a king named Menes (MEE neez) united Upper and Lower Egypt. Menes built a city named Memphis near the present-day city of Cairo (KY roh). From there, he ruled over the Two Lands, the name the ancient Egyptians gave to Upper and Lower Egypt. Carvings from Menes' time show a pharaoh named Narmer wearing two crowns—the white crown of Upper Egypt and the red crown of Lower Egypt. Some historians believe that Menes and Narmer may have been the same man. The unification of Egypt was the beginning of one of the most stable civilizations in history.

All-Powerful Pharaohs The pharaohs had **absolute power,** or complete control over their people. For help in making decisions, they could turn to their advisors or appeal to Ma'at, the goddess of truth. In the end, whatever the pharaoh decided became law. For example, he decided when the fields would be planted. At harvest time, he demanded crops from the workers in the fields.

The Narmer Palette
This two-sided tablet honors the unification of Upper and Lower Egypt by a king named Narmer.

❶ Narmer wears symbols of Egyptian kingship: the cone-shaped crown of Upper Egypt and a false beard and tail. He prepares to strike the enemy.

❷ The falcon represents Horus, the god of kingship.

❸ Reed plants, which grow in the Nile delta, represent Lower Egypt.

❹ A royal sandal bearer carries Narmer's shoes. **Predict** *Narmer wears a different crown on the opposite side of the tablet. What crown do you think he wears?*

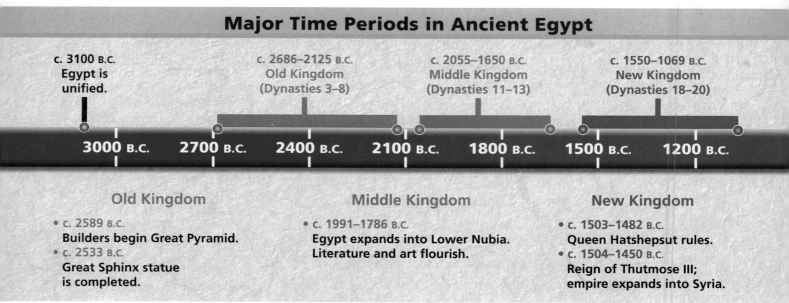

Major Time Periods in Ancient Egypt

c. 3100 B.C.
Egypt is
unified.

c. 2686–2125 B.C.
Old Kingdom
(Dynasties 3–8)

c. 2055–1650 B.C.
Middle Kingdom
(Dynasties 11–13)

c. 1550–1069 B.C.
New Kingdom
(Dynasties 18–20)

3000 B.C.   **2700** B.C.   **2400** B.C.   **2100** B.C.   **1800** B.C.   **1500** B.C.   **1200** B.C.

Old Kingdom
- **c. 2589 B.C.**
  Builders begin Great Pyramid.
- **c. 2533 B.C.**
  Great Sphinx statue
  is completed.

Middle Kingdom
- **c. 1991–1786 B.C.**
  Egypt expands into Lower Nubia.
  Literature and art flourish.

New Kingdom
- **c. 1503–1482 B.C.**
  Queen Hatshepsut rules.
- **c. 1504–1450 B.C.**
  Reign of Thutmose III;
  empire expands into Syria.

■ Timeline Skills

Notice the three time periods called kingdoms, as well as the number of years between the kingdoms. **Identify** How many dynasties ruled from 2686 to 2125 B.C.? How many ruled from 2125 to 2055 B.C.? **Infer** During which of those two time periods was Egypt most stable? Explain your answer.

Use Context Clues
If you do not know what timber is, look for context clues. Find a restatement of the word *timber*. Then reread what the Egyptians used timber for. What is timber?

Ancient Egyptians believed that their pharaohs were the earthly form of Horus, the falcon god. Over time, pharaohs came to be connected with other gods, including the sun god Re (ray). In this way, the pharaohs were god-kings. It was the pharaoh, Egyptians believed, who provided his people with the Nile's yearly floods and the harvests that followed.

> **He is the god Re whose beams enable us to see.
> He gives more light to the Two Lands than the sun's disc.
> He makes Earth more green than the Nile in flood.
> He has filled the Two Lands with strength and life.**
>
> —*an official of ancient Egypt*

✓ **Reading Check** **Who was Menes and what did he accomplish?**

The Three Kingdoms

Important events and achievements marked each of Egypt's three kingdoms. The Old Kingdom was noted for its well-run system of government.

The Old Kingdom The Old Kingdom pharaohs kept the peace and traded with Nubia, with only occasional conflicts. They sent merchants to the eastern coast of the Mediterranean to find timber, or trees used for building. The timber was used to make houses, boats, and furniture. Merchants may have traveled north across the Mediterranean in search of trade items.

Toward the end of the Old Kingdom, governors in the provinces began to challenge the power of the pharaohs' government. Egypt's unity crumbled, and the dynasties grew weak.

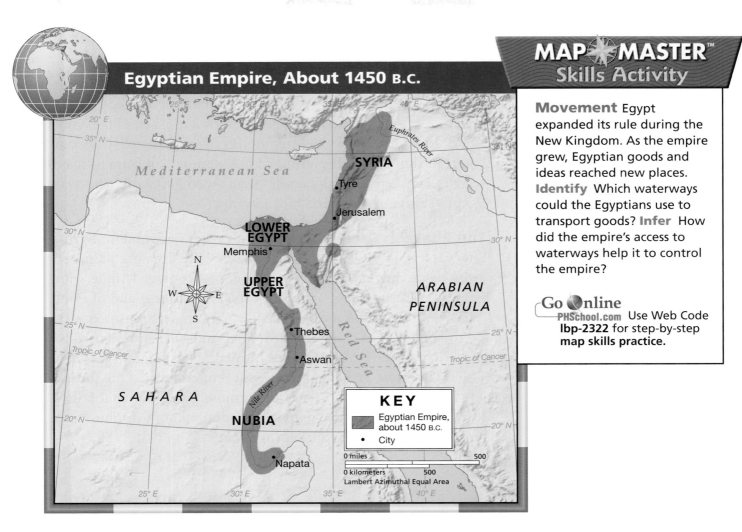

Egyptian Empire, About 1450 B.C.

MAP MASTER™
Skills Activity

Movement Egypt expanded its rule during the New Kingdom. As the empire grew, Egyptian goods and ideas reached new places. **Identify** Which waterways could the Egyptians use to transport goods? **Infer** How did the empire's access to waterways help it to control the empire?

Go Online
PHSchool.com Use Web Code **lbp-2322** for step-by-step map skills practice.

The Middle Kingdom The early rulers of the Middle Kingdom restored order and reunited the country. Pharaohs spent the nation's wealth on public works instead of on wars. For example, they constructed buildings and irrigation projects. Egypt grew even richer. However, weaker and less able rulers followed. In time, they lost control of the country to foreign invaders.

The New Kingdom Egyptian princes became strong enough to drive out the foreign invaders. This event marks the start of the New Kingdom, which began in 1567 B.C. The first pharaohs of the New Kingdom wanted to build an empire. They created huge armies of foot soldiers, mounted warriors, and charioteers. Bronze swords and body armor made the Egyptians nearly unbeatable. One New Kingdom pharaoh is of special interest to scholars. King Tutankhamen became ruler of Egypt while he was still a child. At about age 18 he died and was buried with many precious objects. An archaeologist discovered his tomb in 1922. Since then, studies of Tutankhamen's funeral treasures have taught us a great deal about the ancient Egyptians.

A gold portrait mask was one of the many treasures found in King Tutankhamen's tomb.

✓ Reading Check **What characterized each of the three kingdoms?**

Rule During the New Kingdom

In 1504 B.C., a child named Thutmose III (thoot MOH suh) began his reign. Because of his youth, his stepmother was appointed regent. A **regent** is someone who rules for a child until the child is old enough to rule. His stepmother was Hatshepsut, whom you read about at the beginning of this section. Not content to be regent, Hatshepsut had herself proclaimed pharaoh. She was Egypt's supreme ruler for about 15 years.

The Pharaoh Queen Hatshepsut's reign was good for Egypt. She was a bold leader who is most known for creating a time of great peace and economic success. She encouraged trade with faraway places, sending a famous expedition to the land of Punt on the east coast of Africa. Egyptian traders returned with shiploads of ivory, leopard skins, and special trees used to make incense, a substance burned for its fragrance. When Thutmose grew up, Hatshepsut refused to yield the throne to him. After her death, Thutmose became pharaoh and destroyed all her statues. We don't know if Thutmose played a part in Hatshepsut's death.

Deir el-Bahri, Thebes
This temple built by Queen Hatshepsut was set into a cliff on the west bank of the Nile River.
1 The lower court entrance was once planted with trees and vines.
2 Ramps lead visitors to the middle and upper levels.
3 Inside the colonnades are carvings honoring Hatshepsut's birth as well as a famous trade journey to Punt that she once sponsored. **Analyze** *What features of Hatshepsut's temple would have impressed its visitors in ancient Egypt?*

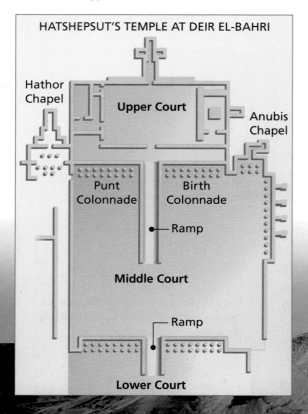

HATSHEPSUT'S TEMPLE AT DEIR EL-BAHRI

Hathor Chapel

Upper Court

Anubis Chapel

Punt Colonnade

Birth Colonnade

Ramp

Middle Court

Ramp

Lower Court

Thutmose III Rules Thutmose III became one of the greatest pharaohs of the New Kingdom. He led his army in wars against Syria and Phoenicia, in Southwest Asia. His troops advanced as far east as the Euphrates River and south into Nubia. Yet Thutmose was more than a conqueror. He was an educated man who loved to study plants. Unlike most rulers of his time, he treated those he defeated with mercy.

Thutmose III finally assumed the throne after the death of his stepmother, Hatshepsut.

Ancient Egypt After the New Kingdom Toward the end of the New Kingdom, Egypt declined. Civil war left Egypt weak and poorly defended. In 332 B.C., long after the end of the New Kingdom, Egypt fell to the famous conqueror Alexander the Great of Macedonia. The Macedonians continued to rule Egypt for about 300 years.

In 51 B.C., Queen Cleopatra VII became the last Macedonian to rule Egypt. She shared the throne with other members of her family until Egypt was conquered by the Romans. Egypt became part of the Roman Empire in 31 B.C. Cleopatra suspected that the Romans would parade her through Egypt to celebrate their victory. To avoid this humiliation, she committed suicide. Egypt would not govern itself again for almost 2,000 years.

✓ **Reading Check** What caused the decline of Egypt during the New Kingdom period?

Section 2 Assessment

Key Terms
Review the key terms at the beginning of this section. Use each term in a sentence that explains its meaning.

Target Reading Skill
Find the word *incense* on page 80. Use context to figure out its meaning. What clues helped you to understand the meaning of *incense*?

Comprehension and Critical Thinking
1. (a) Identify What unusual powers did Egyptians believe their kings had?

(b) Link Past and Present Explain why Egypt's rulers had more authority than most rulers have today.

2. (a) Recall Describe some of the accomplishments of each of the three Egyptian kingdoms.
(b) Compare What characteristics did all three kingdoms have in common?
3. (a) Generalize Describe the New Kingdom under Thutmose III and during its later decline.
(b) Analyze Information Why do you think the pharaohs of Egypt were so successful for so long? What factors led to the decline of Egypt?

Writing Activity
Write a paragraph explaining the following statement: "Ancient Egypt was strongest when its rulers were strong."

Writing Tip Before you write, reread Section 2. Pay special attention to the parts of the text that describe Egypt's strongest pharaohs. Use the statement above as your topic sentence, the sentence that begins your paragraph.

Prepare to Read

Objectives

In this section you will
1. Learn about Egyptian gods and goddesses.
2. Find out about the Egyptians' belief in the afterlife.
3. Discover how and why the pharaohs' tombs were built.

Taking Notes

As you read, take notes to summarize the religious beliefs and practices of the ancient Egyptians. Copy the chart below, and use it to record your notes.

```
            Egyptian Religion
      ┌──────────┬──────────┬──────────┐
   Beliefs     Practices    Pyramids
    •            •            •
    •            •            •
    •            •            •
```

 Target Reading Skill

Use Context Clues When reading, you may find a word that is unfamiliar or even a word you know that is used in an unfamiliar way. Look for clues in the surrounding words and sentences, to help you understand the meaning of the word. For example, look at the context for the word *linen* in the second paragraph on this page. Find the explanation of how linen was used in mummification. What do you think *linen* means?

Key Terms

- **afterlife** (AF tur lyf) *n.* a life after death
- **mummy** (MUM ee) *n.* a dead body preserved in lifelike condition
- **pyramid** (PIH ruh mid) *n.* a huge building with four sloping triangle-shaped sides; built as royal tombs in Egypt
- **Giza** (GEE zuh) *n.* an ancient Egyptian city; the site of the Great Pyramid

Anubis, god of the dead, tends a dead pharaoh. According to Egyptian myth, Anubis invented mummification.

As the royal family wept over the pharaoh's body, the priest chanted:

> **"You will live again. You will live forever. Behold, you will be young forever."**
>
> —*ancient Egyptian prayer*

One hundred days had passed since the pharaoh had died. During that time, the royal officials had been carefully preparing his body. Now, they wrapped the body in many strips of fine linen and placed it in a gold-covered coffin decorated to resemble the king in all of his royal glory.

The Egyptians believed in an **afterlife,** a life after death. They said prayers during the funeral, hoping to help the pharaoh's soul on its way to the afterlife. Then the nobles and royal family followed the body as it was carried to the royal tomb. Workers closed the tomb and the mourners went home. The pharaoh's journey to the afterlife had begun.

Egyptian Gods and Goddesses

Religion was an important part of daily life in ancient Egypt. The Egyptians believed that their gods and goddesses controlled the workings of nature. They built temples to honor their gods, and offered them food, gifts, and prayers.

Regional Differences   Early on, Egyptian towns had their own gods and goddesses with their own temples. These included gods who were often shown as humans with animal heads. All Egyptians also worshiped certain principal gods, such as the sun god, Re and the falcon god, Horus. Over time, however, all ancient Egyptians came to believe in several groups of gods.

Important Gods   The chief god of the ancient Egyptians was Amon-Re (ah mun RAY). He protected the rich and the poor alike. The Egyptians believed that Amon-Re was born each morning in the east with the sunrise. Each evening he died in the west with the setting sun. That is why the desert area to the west was believed to be the home of the dead.

Other powerful gods included Osiris (oh SY ris), the god of the living and the dead. The goddess Isis (EYE sis) was his wife. She was worshiped as the great mother who protected her children. The sky god, Horus, was their son.

√ Reading Check   **Who was Osiris?**

Egyptian Gods and Goddesses
The ancient Egyptians believed that their gods controlled life, death, and all of nature.
❶ Horus, the sky god and the god of kingship
❷ Osiris, the god of the afterlife
❸ Isis, the goddess of women
❹ Thoth, the god of wisdom and of writing
❺ Amon-Re, the sun god and god of creation

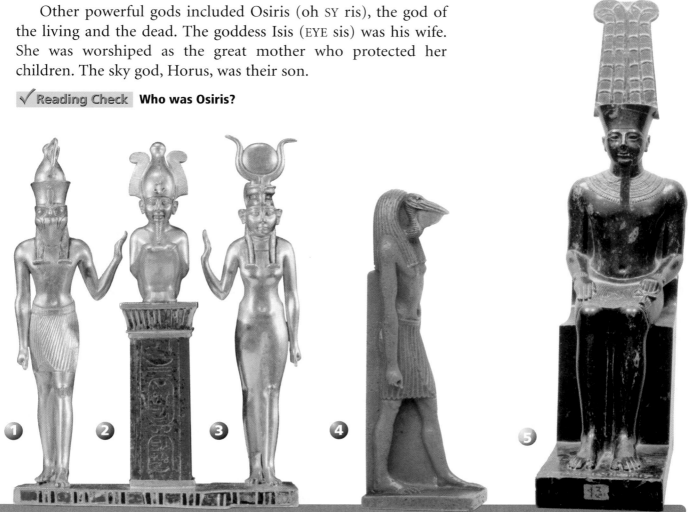

Links Across The World

A King With One God

Amenhotep IV (ah mun HOH tep) became pharaoh in 1352 B.C. Five years later, he changed his name to Akhenaton (ah keh NAH tun) to show his devotion to the god, Aton, the life-giving disk of the sun. Like the Israelites, Akhenaton worshiped only one god. He ordered workers to remove the names of other Egyptian gods from temples. Most Egyptians rejected the practice of monotheism. After the king's death, they went back to worshiping many gods.

Burials, rich and poor
The decorative coffin on the right held the expensively preserved internal organs of King Tutankhamen. The reed coffin tied with rope (above), from about 1450 B.C., holds the naturally preserved body of a baby. **Infer** *According to ancient Egyptian religious beliefs, which of the two souls would enjoy a more comfortable afterlife? Explain.*

Belief in an Afterlife

Like the people of many civilizations, the ancient Egyptians believed in life after death. Evidence of this belief is often found in the art and artifacts they left behind.

Journey to the Afterlife   The ancient Egyptians believed the spirits of the dead made their way to the afterlife in heavenly boats. If they had pleased the gods in this world, they joined Osiris and lived a life of ease and pleasure. They spent their days eating, drinking, and visiting with friends and family members who had died. Because the souls of the dead could not survive without food, clothing, and other items from this life, their possessions were buried with them.

During the Old Kingdom, the afterlife was thought to be only for kings and their associates. But beginning in the Middle Kingdom, people of all classes looked forward to an afterlife.

Preparing the Dead   Before the building of pyramids, most Egyptians were buried in the desert in shallow pits. Egypt's climate dried out a person's remains, creating a **mummy,** the preserved body of a dead person. According to religious beliefs, the soul would leave the mummy, but return to it to receive food offerings. The preserved appearance of the body allowed it to be recognized by the person's spirit. By the time of the Fourth Dynasty, the Egyptians had begun to practice mummification, artificially preserving the bodies before burial.

Mummification was expensive and took two or three months. Workers carefully removed the organs. The body was then filled with a natural salt and stored for about 40 days. During that time, it completely dried out. Once dry, the body was cleaned and bathed in spices. It was then wrapped with long linen bandages.

While workers were preparing the mummy, artisans were busy carving the coffin. Pharaohs actually had three or four coffins. The coffins nested one inside another like boxes. The innermost coffin was usually shaped like a human body, with the dead person's face painted on the cover.

✓ **Reading Check**   **Why did ancient Egyptians bury their dead with food and other possessions?**

The Great Pyramid

For more than 4,000 years, the Great Pyramid at Giza stood taller than any other human-made structure in the world. About 480 feet (147 meters) high, it still stands today. It has four triangle-shaped sides and a square base.

These stones spread the weight of the pyramid above, preventing the whole structure from collapsing.

Graffiti carved into these slabs records the names of the workers who built the chamber.

The pharaoh's outer coffin is larger than the entrance to the chamber, meaning that the pyramid was built around it.

Inside the Grand Gallery
In the 1800s, Napoleon Bonaparte of France ordered a study of the pyramids. His scientists made drawings as they passed through the Grand Gallery to the King's Chamber.

Building the King's Chamber
The King's Chamber was hidden away at the heart of the Great Pyramid. The pharaoh's mummy was sealed into the chamber and lay undisturbed until grave robbers stole it.

The pharaoh's body was carried to the burial chamber through secret tunnels. Some tunnels were false, leading to dead ends.

Granite blocks sealed off the Grand Gallery route to the King's Chamber.

The King's Chamber lay at the center of the pyramid.

A temple held the pharaoh's body before burial.

ANALYZE IMAGES
What did the builders of the Great Pyramid at Giza do to keep out grave robbers?

The Pharaohs' Tombs

The planning for a pharaoh's tomb began soon after he was crowned. The earliest royal tombs were made of mud brick. As time went on, however, tomb building became a complex art.

The Pyramids The pharaohs of the Fourth Dynasty built the largest and most famous tombs. These were the **pyramids,** huge buildings with four sloping triangle-shaped sides. Most of the pyramids were built during the Old Kingdom. The largest is called the Great Pyramid, built for Khufu (KOO foo), the second king of the Fourth Dynasty. The Great Pyramid was built in the ancient city of **Giza.** Find Giza on the map at the beginning of this chapter.

The Building Process Building the pyramids required a great deal of organization. The Great Pyramid is made up of more than 2 million stones. The average weight of each stone is 5,000 pounds (2,270 kilograms). Each stone had to be hauled up the side of the pyramid and put into its proper place.

Using Context Clues
What does *hauled* mean? Look for an explanation in the text under the heading The Building Process.

The Great Sphinx is a portrait of King Kafre with the body of a lion. Kafre's pyramid is behind and to the right of the Sphinx.

A pyramid could take more than 20 years to build. The project began with the selection of a site on the west bank of the Nile. Remember that the west was thought to be the land of the dead. Once the site was chosen, workers cleared the ground. Engineers set the pyramid square so that the sides faced the main points of the compass—north, south, east, and west.

Workers then cut the building blocks. Stone for the inside of the pyramid came from nearby quarries. But fine stone for the outside came from farther away. Some stone came all the way from Nubia. It had to be loaded onto barges and carried to the building site either along the Nile or along canals near the Nile.

Carpenters at work, from a painting in an official's tomb

Teamwork To get the blocks of stone into place, workers used sleds, wooden rollers, and levers. They dragged and pushed the huge blocks up ramps of packed rubble to the level they were working on.

Building pyramids was dangerous work. Each year, men lost their lives, crushed by falling blocks. Modern archaeologists believe that the pyramid workers were not slaves but rather peasants from throughout Egypt. The peasants were forced to work for a few months at a time under the supervision of skilled craftsmen.

✓ **Reading Check** **Why did the Egyptians build pyramids?**

Section 3 Assessment

Key Terms
Review the key terms at the beginning of this section. Use each term in a sentence that explains its meaning.

Target Reading Skill
Find the word *quarries* in the second paragraph of this page. What do you think it means?

Comprehension and Critical Thinking
1. (a) Identify What were the religious beliefs of the ancient Egyptians?

(b) Describe In what ways did the ancient Egyptians use religion to understand nature?

2. (a) Explain Why did the Egyptians mummify their dead?

(b) Analyze How do we know that the afterlife was important to the ancient Egyptians?

3. (a) Recall Why were the pharaohs concerned about the condition of their tombs?

(b) Sequence Describe how the ancient Egyptians organized the building of the pyramids.

Writing Activity
Suppose the pharaoh invites you to go with him to inspect his pyramid as it is being built. Write a journal entry describing what you see on your visit.

Go Online
PHSchool.com

For: An activity on the religion of the ancient Egyptians
Visit: PHSchool.com
Web Code: lbd-2303

In the shadow of the three pyramids at Giza, archaeologists are uncovering a lost city. It is the workers' city, a sprawling site on which as many as 20,000 men and women lived and worked about 4,500 years ago. The workers came from all over Egypt. They included pyramid builders and their bosses, administrators, priests, cooks, doctors, metalworkers, masons, weavers, and gravediggers. Laborers could be forced to work, but some probably volunteered to build the sacred tombs.

Preheating
Pot tops warm up over an open fire.

Baking
Pots filled with dough are set in hot ashes and topped with the preheated pots.

Copper Smelting
This carving shows workers blowing on flames to smelt copper, a process in which heat was used to remove impurities from the metal. Copper tools like the one shown at the top of this page were pounded into wedges to split rock.

An Ancient Bakery Without bread to feed the workers, the pyramids could not have been built. In the workers' city, bakers ground barley and wheat into flour for the bread dough. Wild airborne yeast helped the dough to rise. (The Egyptians, however, believed it rose by the power of the gods.) Workers set covered pots of dough onto a bed of hot ashes for baking. The finished loaves were heavy and filling—enough to feed a hungry pyramid builder.

The workers' site also included buildings for preparing meat and fish, to complete the workers' diet. There was one drawback to the bread-making process. Tiny pieces of the grain-grinding stones often wound up in the loaves, creating life-threatening dental diseases for the Egyptians.

Cooling Bread
After the bread bakes, it cools.

Making Bread Dough
Flour and water are mixed in a large terra-cotta vat.

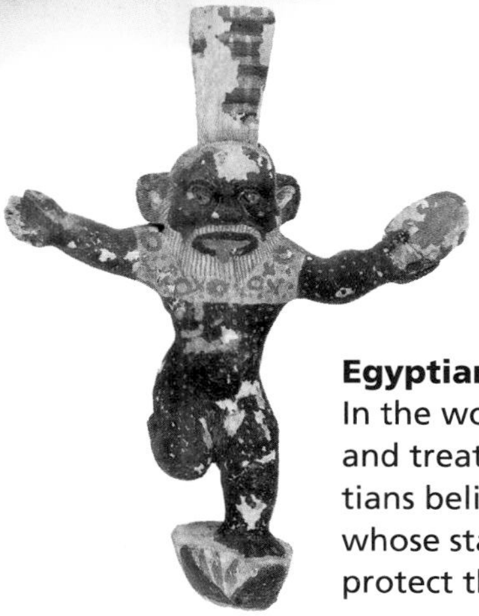

Egyptian Medicine
In the workers' city, doctors set bones and treated a variety of ailments. Egyptians believed the household god Bes, whose statue is shown at the left, could protect them from danger.

Assessment

Identify Who were the people who lived in the lost city near the pyramids at Giza?

Infer Why was a city of workers needed to build the pyramids?

Section 4

Ancient Egyptian Culture

Prepare to Read

Objectives

In this section you will
1. Find out about the everyday life of the ancient Egyptians.
2. Learn about writing in ancient Egypt.
3. Discover advances made by the Egyptians in science and medicine.

Taking Notes

As you read, look for details about ancient Egyptian culture. Copy the flowchart below and record your findings in it.

Egyptian Culture	
Everyday Life	**Achievements**
•	•
•	•
•	•

🎯 Target Reading Skill

Use Context Clues Cause-and-effect clues can help you understand the meaning of an unfamiliar word. In the following sentence, a cause-and-effect clue points to the meaning of *scattered:* When the farmer scattered the seeds, he caused them to fly and land in many directions. What do you think *scattered* means?

Key Terms

- **hieroglyphs** (HY ur oh glifs) *n.* pictures and other written symbols that stand for ideas, things, or sounds
- **papyrus** (puh PY rus) *n.* an early form of paper made from a reed plant found in the marshy areas of the Nile delta; the plant used to make this paper
- **astronomer** (uh STRAHN uh mur) *n.* a scientist who studies the stars and other objects in the sky

A high official of ancient Egypt and his wife

Uni was a high-ranking Egyptian of the Old Kingdom. His life story—a success story—is recorded in his tomb.

Uni began his career in a simple way—running a storehouse. Later, he was promoted to groundskeeper of the royal pyramid. In his job, he oversaw the delivery of stone from the quarry, the site where stone was cut, to the pyramid. Uni must have worked hard, because later he was made a general. Then, he became Governor of Upper Egypt, in charge of goods and taxes for half the kingdom. By the time of his death, Uni had become royal tutor at the palace and an honored companion of the pharaoh. Uni and many other people like him were part of everyday life in ancient Egypt.

The Lives of the Egyptians

Most of what we know about the everyday life of the Egyptians is based on paintings that cover the walls of tombs and temples. Written records also tell us much about their lives.

Social Classes Historians often turn to Egyptian art to learn about the social classes of ancient Egypt. Egyptian paintings and carvings show royalty and ordinary people involved in all aspects of life. Like Uni, most Egyptians were busy and hard-working people. They also had a sense of fun and a love of beauty.

Egyptian society itself resembled a pyramid. At the very top stood the pharaoh. Beneath him was a small upper class. This group included priests, members of the pharaoh's court, and nobles who held the largest estates. The next level was the middle class, made up of merchants and skilled workers. At the base of the pyramid was by far the largest class, the peasants. Mostly, the peasants did farm labor. But they also did other kinds of labor, such as building roads and temples. A person could rise to a higher class. Generally, the way to rise was through service to the pharaoh, as Uni did.

Slavery Prisoners captured in wars were made slaves. Slaves formed a separate class, which was never very large. Egyptian society was flexible, however. Even slaves had rights. They could own personal items and inherit land from their masters. They could also be set free.

Working in Egypt
Models showing scenes from everyday life were often placed in tombs. This wood model shows workers in a bakery. **Infer** *Why do you think such scenes are useful to archaeologists?*

Lives of the Peasants Although peasants could own land, most worked the land of wealthier people. During the flood season, the peasants worked on roads, temples, and other buildings. As soon as the waters left the land, they had to plant the fields. The work had to be done quickly while the soil was still moist. One farmer plowed the black earth with a team of oxen while another followed behind, scattering the seeds.

The harvest was the busiest season for Egypt's peasants. All men, women, and older children went into the fields to gather the crops of wheat or barley. Work went on from sunrise to sunset. Once the crops were gathered, the villagers feasted. They offered food and drink to the gods in thanks for their help.

Women of Egypt Egyptian women were looked upon as living models of Isis, the wife of the god Osiris. They had most of the rights that men had. They could own property, run businesses, and enter into legal contracts. For the most part, women traveled about freely. Egyptian paintings often show them supervising farm work or hunting. And women performed many roles—from priestess to dancer.

Noble women held a special position in Egyptian society. Sometimes they were in charge of temples and religious rites. They could also use their position to influence the pharaoh. Some women acted as regents until the pharaoh was old enough to rule on his own.

✓ **Reading Check** **How was Egyptian society organized?**

Women's Lives
The women shown above are wearing scented wax cones on their heads. The wax melted in the heat, surrounding the women with perfume. At the right, a woman works in a field with her husband. **Conclude** *Which social classes do you think the women in the paintings belonged to? Explain your answer.*

Hieroglyphs

A	𓅃	P	◻
AH		F	
AY		M	or
EE		N	
U		L	
B		H	◻
H		Q	◺
S		K	
SH		T	◠

Writing in Ancient Egypt

The records and writings left by the ancient Egyptians allow us to learn more about their culture. From these records, we know that they possessed an amazing amount of knowledge.

A New System of Writing In ancient Egypt, as in Mesopotamia, ideas were written down in picturelike symbols called **hieroglyphs** (HY ur oh glifs). In this script, some pictures stand for ideas or things. For example, a picture of two legs means "go." Other pictures stand for sounds. For example, a drawing of an owl stands for the "m" sound.

The Egyptians began to use hieroglyphs because they needed a way to keep track of the kingdom's growing wealth. As the Egyptian empire grew, it became necessary to create more pictures for more complicated ideas.

Writing Materials At first, the Egyptians wrote on clay and stone, as the Sumerians did. But they needed a more convenient writing surface. They found it in **papyrus** (puh py ruhs), an early form of paper made from a reed found in the marshy areas of the Nile delta. The plant used to make this paper is also called papyrus. To make the paper, the inner stalks of the plant were cut into narrow strips. The strips were cut to the same length and placed side by side by side in one layer. Another layer of strips was placed crosswise on top to form a sheet. Papyrus makers wet the sheet, pressed it flat, and dried it in the sun. Sap from the plant glued the strips together. Pasted side by side, the sheets formed a long strip that could be rolled up.

■ Chart Skills

The text of the *Book of the Dead* (top left) was meant to guide the dead on their journey to the afterlife. The book's hieroglyphs are written on papyrus. The table (above) shows some hieroglyphs and the sounds they stood for. **Identify** What is the hieroglyph for the "p" sound? **Analyze Images** What are some English words you could spell using the hieroglyphs in the chart?

Use Context Clues What does *sap* mean? Look for cause-and-effect clues in the text. Sap from the plant glues the strips of papyrus together. What does that tell you about sap?

Unlocking a Mystery The meaning of ancient Egypt's hieroglyphic writing was lost after the A.D. 400s. Scholars could not read the mysterious pictures. It wasn't until about 200 years ago, in 1799, that an important find took place. A soldier digging a fort near the Nile found a large black stone with three different types of writing on it. The upper part showed hieroglyphs, the middle part showed a later Egyptian script called demotic, and the lower part showed Greek letters. The stone was named the Rosetta Stone because it was found near Rosetta, a city in the Nile delta near the Mediterranean Sea.

The three texts on the stone held the same meaning. Therefore, many scholars tried to use the Greek letters on the Rosetta Stone to figure out the meaning of the hieroglyphs. But it was not an easy task. Then, in the 1820s, a young French scholar named Jean François Champollion (zhahn frahn SWAH shahm poh LYOHN) finally figured it out. When Champollion published his results, a new window onto the world of ancient Egypt opened.

✓ **Reading Check** What was the significance of the Rosetta Stone?

Clues to the Past
The circled hieroglyphs on the Rosetta Stone (above left) spell the name of King Ptolemy V. Jean François Champollion (above right) realized that hieroglyphs stood for sounds in the Egyptian language and was able to decipher the hieroglyphs used to spell Ptolemy's name.
Generalize *Why was the translation of hieroglyphs an important discovery in the study of Egyptian history?*

Science and Medicine

In addition to their developments in writing, the ancient Egyptians made important advances in such fields as astronomy and medicine. Among the people of the ancient world, Egypt was known as a land of great learning.

Keeping Track of Time Because they were an agricultural people, the Egyptians needed to be able to predict when the Nile would flood. Astronomers noticed that the Nile appeared to rise rapidly about the same time that they could see Sirius (SIHR ee us), the Dog Star, in the sky shortly before sunrise. **Astronomers are scientists who study the stars and other objects in the sky.** They worked out the average time between the appearances of the star. They found that it came to about 365 days. This became the length of their year.

Mathematics The Egyptians used basic mathematics in finding solutions to problems they faced every day. We know they could add, subtract, multiply, and divide. We also know they used simple fractions. Mathematics helped Egyptians measure stone so that it could be cut to the proper size to build pyramids. They used geometry to measure area so that they could figure out the amount of taxes for a plot of land.

Medicine Religion and medicine were closely related in ancient Egypt. Doctors were specially trained priests who used religious practices and their knowledge of illnesses to try to heal the sick. Probably because of their work on mummies, the ancient Egyptians knew a great deal about the body. By studying the body, they learned to perform surgery. They could set broken bones and treat many minor injuries.

The Egyptians also understood herbalism, the practice of creating medicines from plants. They used these natural remedies to help ease everyday illnesses such as stomachaches and headaches. Mothers prepared their own home remedies, or cures, to reduce children's fevers. The Egyptians wrote much of their medical knowledge down on papyrus. Centuries later, the ancient Greeks and Romans used these records.

√ **Reading Check** **Why was it important for the Egyptians to figure out the length of their year?**

Links to **Math**

Measurement Some units of measurement used by the Egyptians were based on the human body. The cubit was the distance from an elbow to the tip of the fingers. Of course, this length varied from person to person, so the Egyptians made a standard cubit out of black granite. Other cubits, such as the one below, could then be modeled from the standard. The Egyptians used their accurate measuring system to build the Great Pyramid.

Section 4 Assessment

Key Terms
Review the key terms at the beginning of this section. Use each term in a sentence that explains its meaning.

Target Reading Skill
Find the word *remedies* in the last paragraph in this section. Use cause-and-effect clues to figure out its meaning.

Comprehension and Critical Thinking
1. (a) Describe How were the lives of Egypt's peasants ruled by the seasons?

(b) Draw Conclusions How did the seasons affect all of Egyptian society?
2. (a) Recall Describe how the Egyptians used hieroglyphs to communicate.
(b) Analyze Information What was the importance of writing in Egyptian society?
3. (a) List What areas of science and medicine did the ancient Egyptians study?
(b) Link Past and Present How did the learning achievements of the Egyptians affect later civilizations?

Writing Activity
Suppose you are an Egyptian scribe. Write a description that shows how you use your skill in the service of the pharaoh. Then, use the table of hieroglyphs in this section to create a word.

Writing Tip Scribes kept records and accounts for the pharaohs. They also wrote prayers on the wall paintings of tombs. Think about some other work a scribe might perform for a pharaoh. Then write your description from the scribe's point of view.

The leader of the caravan turned and saw the storm approaching in the distance. Then he looked ahead, straining to see some glimpse of Assur. The caravan had been traveling for many days, carrying goods from Giza. Although his men were tired, the leader signaled for them to move faster. He wanted to reach the city before the storm came.

For years, the caravan leader had brought goods from Lower Egypt to Syria and Sumer. This particular road, however, was new to him. He hoped that they would reach Assur soon.

A silver jug from ancient Egypt

The leader of the caravan might have found a route map useful. Although maps did exist in ancient times, most people's knowledge of roads was passed along by word of mouth. Today, most road travel is fairly easy. You just need to know how to read a route map.

Learn the Skill

Use the following steps to read a route map.

 Read the title of the map, and become familiar with the map's features. What is the purpose of the map? What type of map is it—physical or political, modern or historical, or a standard road map?

A camel caravan in the Sahara

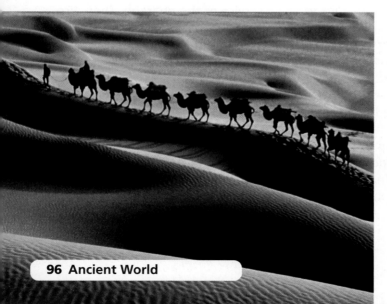

2 Study the key to understand its symbols. Colors are generally used on route maps to show different routes or different types of roads.

3 Trace routes on the map. Using the scale of miles, you can calculate distances. A physical map will show the geographic features of a route.

4 Interpret the map. Draw conclusions about which routes would be fastest, safest, most scenic, or the easiest to follow.

Practice the Skill

Use the steps on page 96 and the map at the right to gather and interpret information about ancient trade routes.

1. Write down the purpose of the map. What does the map show?

2. Look at the key to see information about Egyptian trade routes. Identify the purple region on the map. Find routes that travel over land and water. Identify the landmarks indicated in the map key.

3. Using the compass rose, note the general direction of the trade routes. Identify the geographic features of the routes. Look for geographic features that the routes seem to avoid.

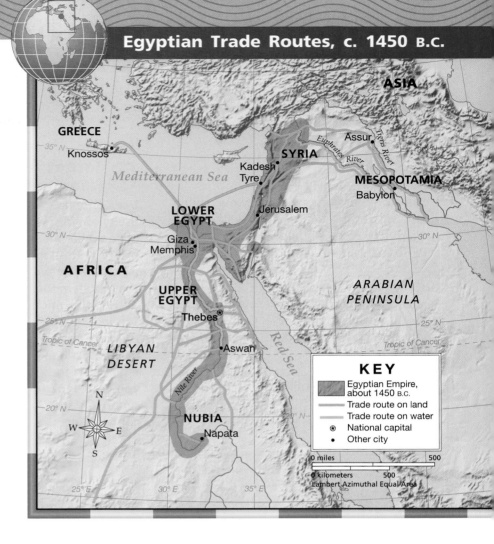

Egyptian Trade Routes, c. 1450 B.C.

KEY

Egyptian Empire, about 1450 B.C.
Trade route on land
Trade route on water
⊛ National capital
• Other city

0 miles 500
0 kilometers 500
Lambert Azimuthal Equal Area

4. Write a paragraph that draws conclusions about Egyptian trade routes. Answering these questions might help you: Why did most of the trade routes run through the purple area? How did geography influence the paths that traders took? Why does the map show no direct road connecting the major Egyptian cities of Thebes and Giza?

Apply the Skill

Draw a map showing the route you take from your home to your school. Add a scale and a compass rose. Mark the location of your school and your home with symbols. Explain the symbols in a map key.

When you are finished, exchange maps with a classmate. Identify the symbols used in the map key. Determine the distance from your classmate's home to school.

The Cultures of Nubia

Prepare to Read

Objectives

In this section you will
1. Examine the relationship between Nubia and Egypt.
2. Learn about the Nubian kingdoms centered in Kerma, Napata, and Meroë.

Taking Notes

As you read, find details on the resources and culture of ancient Nubia. Copy the table below, and fill in the columns to record your findings.

Nubia			
Relations With Egypt	Kerma	Napata	Meroë
• •	• •	• •	• •

Target Reading Skill

Use Context Clues You can use synonyms, words that have similar meanings, to figure out the meaning of an unfamiliar word. Find the synonym for *ultimate* in the following sentence: Taharka received the *ultimate* prize, the greatest honor possible. *Greatest* is a synonym for *ultimate*. As you read, look for synonyms and other context clues.

Key Terms

- **ore** (awr) *n.* a mineral or a combination of minerals mined for the production of metals
- **Lower Nubia** (LOH ur NOO bee uh) *n.* the region of ancient Nubia between the first and second Nile cataracts
- **Upper Nubia** (UP ur NOO bee uh) *n.* the region of ancient Nubia between the second and sixth Nile cataracts
- **artisan** (AHR tuh zun) *n.* a worker who is skilled in crafting goods by hand

This Egyptian bronze statue shows Pharaoh Taharka making an offering to the falcon god.

Prince Taharka of Nubia loved a good contest. He once held a 5-hour, 30-mile race across the desert. The athletes, Taharka's soldiers, ran at night to avoid the blazing heat. In the end, he gave prizes to the winners and losers alike.

In 690 B.C., Taharka himself would receive the ultimate prize: He was to be crowned king of both Nubia and Egypt. He would become the greatest ruler of his dynasty. Taharka's mother traveled 1,200 miles from Nubia north to Memphis to see her son made king. Their homeland of Nubia gave birth to some of the world's oldest cultures.

Nubia and Egypt

Archaeologists have found pottery, weapons, and jewelry at Nubian burial sites. Some of these items date to about 6000 B.C. Findings also show that trade existed among these early peoples. From about 3100 B.C., many Nubian kingdoms arose, only to die out as their rulers lost power.

Land of the Bow Recall that the region of Nubia was located south of ancient Egypt, beyond the first cataract of the Nile River. For most of their long history, Nubia and Egypt were peaceful, friendly neighbors. The Egyptians called Nubia Ta Sety (tah SEHT ee), the "land of the bow." They were probably referring to the Nubians' skill as archers. The Nubian archers were so skilled that Egypt hired many of them for its armies.

Valuable Resources Egypt valued Nubia for its rich mineral resources, such as gold, copper, and iron ore. An **ore** is a mineral or a combination of minerals mined for the production of metals. Because of its location, Nubia became a bridge for goods traveling between central Africa and Egypt. Early in its history, Egypt benefited from goods that came from **Lower Nubia,** the region between the first and second Nile cataracts. Later, powerful kingdoms began to rise to the south, in **Upper Nubia,** the region between the second and sixth Nile cataracts. These kingdoms rivaled Egypt for control of land. The most powerful of these kingdoms were in the cities of Kerma (KUR muh), Napata (nuh PAY tuh), and Meroë (MEHR oh ee). Find these cities on the map on page 100. These kingdoms were ruled by Kushites, people who lived in southern Nubia.

✓ **Reading Check** Why did Nubia and Egypt become rivals?

Links to
Science

Nubia and Egypt A recent discovery of a Nubian incense burner has some scientists thinking about Nubia's early relationship with Egypt. Some scientists think the object was made around 3100 B.C., or even earlier. Carved on its side are a seated king and other figures that later became the symbols of Egyptian pharaohs. Scholars are debating whether Nubia or Egypt had the first kings.

Nubian Archers
A model shows an army of Nubian archers. The Egyptians admired the Nubians' skill in archery. **Conclude** *Why was Nubia called the "land of the bow"?*

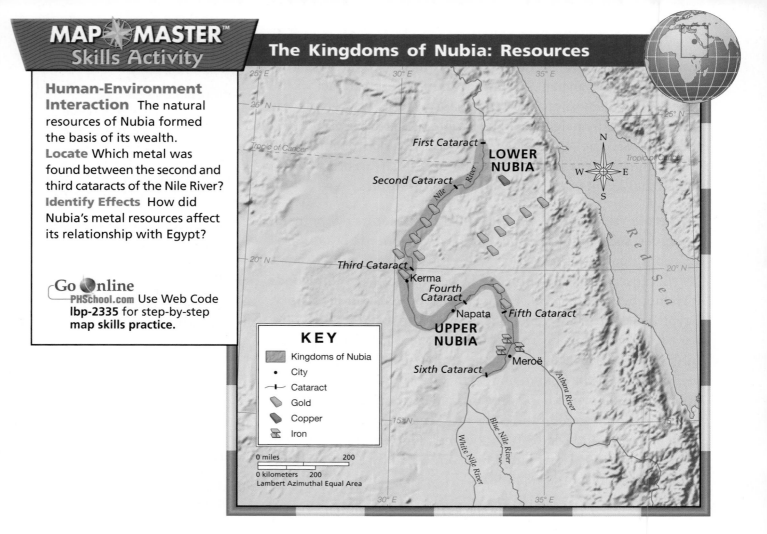

Human-Environment Interaction The natural resources of Nubia formed the basis of its wealth. **Locate** Which metal was found between the second and third cataracts of the Nile River? **Identify Effects** How did Nubia's metal resources affect its relationship with Egypt?

Go Online
PHSchool.com Use Web Code **lbp-2335** for step-by-step map skills practice.

KEY

Kingdoms of Nubia
• City
⊢ Cataract
Gold
Copper
Iron

0 miles 200
0 kilometers 200
Lambert Azimuthal Equal Area

The Kerma Culture

The Kushites came to power at a time when Egypt was weakening. By about 1600 B.C., the Kushite kingdom had expanded from the city of Kerma into parts of southern Egypt. These Nubians are known as the Kerma culture. Their kingdom lasted from about 2000 to 1500 B.C.

Kerma's Wealth Kerma had gained not only power but wealth, mainly from controlling the trade between Central Africa and Egypt. It was noted for its **artisans,** or workers skilled at crafting items by hand. They made highly prized, delicate pottery. Items made by Kerma artisans have been found in the tombs of pharaohs.

Like the Egyptians, the people of Kerma devoted a great deal of energy and resources to royal burials. They buried their kings in mounds of earth as large as football fields. Inside their tombs, the kings' bodies rested on top of gold-covered beds surrounded by jewelry, gold, and ivory.

A Kerma pottery bowl

Conflict With Egypt Around the 1500s B.C., Egypt began to recover its strength and to reclaim control of the area. Pharaoh Thutmose I sent his armies into Nubia. After a war that lasted about 50 years, the Egyptians took control of Nubia as far south as the fourth cataract. Egypt ruled Nubia for about the next 700 years.

During this period, the Nubians adopted many Egyptian ways. They even began to worship Egyptian gods along with their own. Throughout these times of conflict and peace, people and goods continued to pass between Nubia and Egypt. The two cultures became mixed.

✓ **Reading Check** **What were some characteristics of Kerma?**

Napata and Meroë

South of Kerma lay the Nubian cities of Napata and Meroë, in the ancient land called Kush. After centuries of Egyptian rule, the Kushites rose again to power. Their kingdom was centered in the Nubian city of Napata and then later in Meroë.

The Capital of Napata In the late 700s B.C., Egypt was once again weak and divided. From their capital in Napata, the Kushites expanded their power into Egypt.

The Napatan kings gradually took control of more of Egypt. They moved their capital city first to Thebes and then to Memphis. By the time of Taharka, whose coronation you read about earlier, the Nubians controlled all of Egypt. The pharaohs of Egypt's Twenty-fifth Dynasty were Nubians.

The Napatan kings admired Egyptian culture. They brought back many old Egyptian ways and preserved them. They even began building pyramids in which to bury their kings. The ruins of these small Nubian pyramids can still be seen today.

The rule of the Napatan kings did not last very long. About 660 B.C., they were forced back into Nubia. They retreated to Napata and then gradually moved their capital south to Meroë. The Nubians never again controlled Egyptian land.

Use Context Clues Do you know what *recover* means? Find a synonym for *recover* later in the same sentence. What does it mean?

Monuments of Napata
The pyramids of Napata (top) and a ram statue (bottom) from the entrance to the Great Amum Temple at Napata reflect the ties between Nubian culture and Egyptian culture. **Contrast** *How do the Nubian pyramids differ from the Egyptian pyramids shown in the photo on page 86?*

The Women of Nubia
Women held very high status in Nubian society. Most often, the children of the ruler's sister would be next in line for the throne. Compared to Egypt, Nubia had many more women as rulers. In ancient artwork, the queens of Meroë have large and powerful figures. The queens were considered ideal beauties, and their weight reflected their wealth and rank.

The Capital of Meroë After moving south of Egypt's reach, the Nubians founded a royal court in the ancient city of Meroë. This city was located on the Nile between the fifth and sixth cataracts. It became the center of an empire that included much of Nubia. It also stretched south into central Africa.

The rocky desert east of Meroë held large deposits of iron ore. The Nubians used the ore to make iron weapons and tools. Iron plows allowed them to produce generous supplies of food. Iron weapons allowed them to control trade routes that ran all the way to the Red Sea. There they traded goods from central Africa for articles from India, the Arabian Peninsula, and Rome. Meroë grew rich from this trade.

Today, Meroë remains largely a mystery. The Nubians of Meroë created their own system of hieroglyphic writing. Scholars have so far been unable to fully understand these hieroglyphics, which are found on the temples and tombs of the kingdom.

Meroë began to weaken in the A.D. 200s, and it fell to the African kingdom of Axum in the next century. Features of Nubian culture, however, have lasted for 3,500 years. To this day, Nubian styles of pottery, furniture, jewelry, braided hairstyles, and clothing survive among people of the modern-day African country of Sudan.

✓ **Reading Check** **How did the people of Meroë use iron ore?**

Section 5 Assessment

Key Terms
Review the key terms at the beginning of this section. Use each term in a sentence that explains its meaning.

Target Reading Skill
Find *articles* in the second paragraph on this page. If it is used in an unfamiliar way, find a synonym to understand its meaning.

Comprehension and Critical Thinking
1. (a) Explain What was the relationship between Egypt and Nubia?

(b) Apply Information How did the Nubians and the Egyptians borrow from each other's cultures?
2. (a) Recall What were the resources of Kerma?
(b) Identify the Main Idea What part did Kerma's wealth play in its conflict with Egypt?
3. (a) Explain How are the histories of Napata and Meroë tied to Egypt?
(b) Link Past and Present What signs of Nubian culture exist in Africa today? Do you think present-day Africans are likely to be interested in Nubian culture? Explain why or why not.

Writing Activity
List the names of the three major Nubian cities you learned about in this section. Write a brief description of each of the cities, and include its importance in the history of Nubia.

Writing Tip Before you begin, reread Section 5. As you read, look for important details about each city of Nubia. Your list should include the most important and most interesting details. Refer to the list when you write your description.

Review and Assessment

◆ Chapter Summary

Section 1: The Geography of the Nile
- Beginning from two sources, the Nile flows northward in a varied course until it reaches the Mediterranean Sea.
- The Nile provided the ancient Egyptian and Nubian peoples with water, food, and fertile soil.
- The Nile River and its valley were central trade routes for the ancient Egyptians and Nubians.

Section 2: The Rulers of Egypt
- Egyptian kings had absolute power and were thought to be gods.
- Ancient Egypt prospered during three major time periods, the Old Kingdom, the Middle Kingdom, and the New Kingdom.
- After Hatshepsut died, Thutmose III rose to power and became one of the greatest pharaohs of the New Kingdom.

Section 3: Egyptian Religion
- Egyptians were deeply religious and believed in several gods and goddesses.
- Egyptians believed in life after death and carefully prepared their dead for the afterlife.
- Pharaohs began the long, difficult process of building their tombs as soon as they came into power.

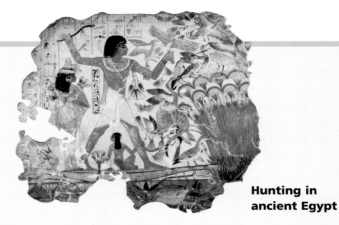

Hunting in ancient Egypt

Section 4: Ancient Egyptian Culture
- The Egyptian social order resembled a pyramid, with the pharaoh at the top, and the largest class, the peasants, at the base.
- The ancient Egyptians used a pictorial writing system similar to that used in Mesopotamian civilization.
- Egyptians also studied the stars and practiced medicine.

Section 5: The Cultures of Nubia
- Throughout its history, Nubia was both a friend and a rival of Egypt.
- The Nubian kingdom of Kerma was known for its skilled artisans.
- The people of Meroë were the first Africans to work with iron.

Nubian Pharaoh and falcon god

◆ Key Terms

Match the definitions in Column I with the key terms in Column II.

Column I
1. a strong rush of water
2. a skilled worker
3. a series of rulers from the same family
4. a picturelike symbol
5. a building with four triangle-shaped sides
6. minerals mined for the production of metal
7. fertile soil deposited by flooding rivers

Column II

A ore

B dynasty

C pyramid

D artisan

E hieroglyph

F cataract

G silt

◆ Comprehension and Critical Thinking

8. Recall Describe the geography of the Nile River and the lands that surround it.
(a) Explain Why did the people of Egypt and Nubia consider their deserts to be a blessing?
(b) Identify Effects In what ways did the Nile river affect ancient civilizations?

9. (a) List Name and describe the three major periods in ancient Egyptian history.
(b) Describe What was the role of the pharaoh in Egyptian government and society?
(c) Compare and Contrast Compare the pharaohs' rule of Egypt with Hammurabi's rule of Babylonia. How are the rulers similar or different?

10. (a) Identify What was the purpose of the pyramids in ancient Egypt?
(b) Generalize Why was religion so important to the people of ancient Egypt?
(c) Analyze Why did the idea of the afterlife appeal to the ancient Egyptians?

11. (a) Recall List the accomplishments of the ancient Egyptians.
(b) Conclude Choose one accomplishment of the ancient Egyptian civilization and describe its importance.

12. (a) Explain Why was it in the interests of Egypt and Nubia to maintain friendly relations?
(b) Compare and Contrast Compare the length of time Egypt's and Nubia's civilizations lasted with that of the Assyrians and the Babylonians. How do you account for the differences?

◆ Skills Practice

Using Route Maps In the Skills for Life lesson in this chapter, you learned how to analyze and interpret route maps. You also learned how to create your own route map.

Review the steps for this skill. Using your route map, complete the following: (a) Add another route between your home and your school. It could be a shortcut, or a longer route. (b) Explain the advantages and disadvantages of your alternate route.

◆ Writing Activity: Language Arts

Think about the Nile River and how important it was to the ancient Egyptians and Nubians. Then write a poem about the Nile, from the point of view of an ancient Egyptian or Nubian.

The poem can be in any form, rhyming or unrhyming. Be sure to include details that show the importance of the river. Reread Section 1 to refresh your memory on the geography of the Nile.

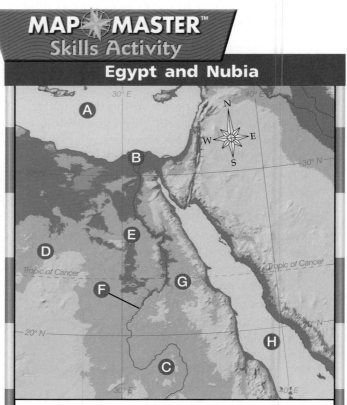

MAP MASTER™
Skills Activity

Egypt and Nubia

Place Location For each place listed below, write the letter from the map that shows its location.

1. Nile River
2. Mediterranean Sea
3. Red Sea
4. Upper Nubia
5. Lower Nubia
6. Sahara
7. Upper Egypt
8. Lower Egypt

Go **Online**
PHSchool.com Use Web Code **lbp-2345** for an **interactive map**.

Standardized Test Prep

Test-Taking Tips

Some questions on standardized tests ask you to draw conclusions by analyzing a table. Study the table below. Then follow the tips to answer the sample question.

BUILDING THE GREAT PYRAMID

Number of blocks	2 million
Weight of each block	5,000 pounds
Height of pyramid	450 feet
Time to build	about 20 years

Pick the letter that best completes the statement.

The information in the table could be used to show the

A ~~importance of the Nile River in Egypt.~~

B division of Egyptian society into classes.

C ~~cruelty of the Egyptian pharaohs.~~

D organization and skills of the Egyptians.

Think It Through All of the information in the table has to do with the construction of the pyramids. You can rule out answer A, because it has to do with the river. You can eliminate C, because it has to do with the characteristics of the pharaohs. Of B and D, which answer has the most to do with the construction of the pyramids? The answer is D. It states correctly that the pyramids show the organization and skill of the Egyptians.

TIP Preview the question first and think about it as you study the table.

TIP Eliminate answer choices that don't make sense. Then decide which remaining choice is BEST.

Practice Questions

Use the tips above and other tips in this book to help you answer the following questions.

1. Why did the Nubians develop trade routes over land?

   A Cataracts on the Nile River limited travel.

   B The Egyptians tended to attack by boat.

   C Nubians had no ship-building skills.

   D Travel in the desert was easy.

Study the table below, and then answer the question that follows.

Ancient Civilizations

Location	Time Span
Ancient Mesopotamia	About 3300 – 539 B.C.
Ancient Egypt	About 3100 – 31 B.C.
Ancient Nubia	About 3100 B.C. – A.D. 350

2. Which sentence accurately describes the information in the table?

   A All ancient civilizations ended before A.D. 1.

   B The civilizations of Mesopotamia began after those of Egypt and Nubia.

   C The civilizations of ancient Egypt and Nubia both lasted about 1,000 years.

   D Several ancient civilizations lasted thousands of years.

3. Egyptian society was pyramid-shaped, with

   A the pharaoh at the top and peasants at the bottom.

   B the pharaoh at the top and priests at the bottom.

   C priests at the top and no peasants.

   D priests and peasants at the top.

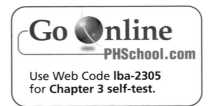

Use Web Code lba-2305 for **Chapter 3** self-test.

4 Ancient India

Chapter Preview

This chapter will introduce you to the geography and civilizations of ancient India.

Target Reading Skill

Cause and Effect In this chapter you will learn how to focus on identifying the cause-and-effect relationships in your text. Identifying causes and effects will give you a deeper understanding of the text.

► Somnath Temple, Gujarat, India

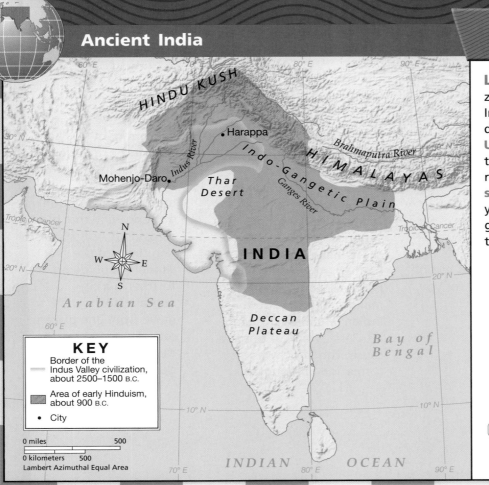

MAP MASTER™
Skills Activity

Location Like other civilizations you have read about, India's earliest civilizations developed near large rivers. **Using a Map Key** What do the shaded areas on the map represent? **Draw Conclusions** What conclusions can you draw about the effect of geography on the civilizations of ancient India?

Go Online
PHSchool.com Use Web Code **lbp-2411** for step-by-step **map skills practice.**

KEY
— Border of the Indus Valley civilization, about 2500–1500 B.C.

■ Area of early Hinduism, about 900 B.C.

• City

0 miles 500
0 kilometers 500
Lambert Azimuthal Equal Area

The Indus and Ganges River Valleys

Prepare to Read

Objectives

In this section you will
1. Learn about India's geographic setting.
2. Find out about life in an ancient city of the Indus River valley.
3. Examine the rise of a new culture in the Indus and Ganges river valleys.

Taking Notes

As you read, create an outline of this section. The outline below has been started for you.

```
I. India's geographic setting
   A. Monsoon climate
      1.
      2.
   B.
      1.
      2.
II. Life in the Indus River valley
```

Target Reading Skill

Identify Causes and Effects Determining causes and effects can help you understand the relationships among situations or events. A cause makes something happen. An effect is what happens. For example, millions of years ago the Indian landmass crashed into Asia. Think of this as a cause. The effect was the formation of mountains.

Key Terms

- **subcontinent** (SUB kahn tih nunt) *n.* a large landmass that juts out from a continent
- **monsoon** (mahn SOON) *n.* a strong wind that blows across East Asia at certain times of the year
- **citadel** (SIT uh del) *n.* a fortress in a city
- **migrate** (MY grayt) *v.* to move from one place to settle in another area
- **caste** (kast) *n.* a social class of people

The land of India is separated from the rest of the world by a great wall. Rising along India's northern border, the wall is more than 1,500 miles (2,400 kilometers) long and nearly 5 miles (8 kilometers) high. The wall is not made of stone or bricks. It is a wall of snow-capped peaks and icy glaciers. This great barrier is the Himalayas, the highest mountain range in the world.

The Himalayas

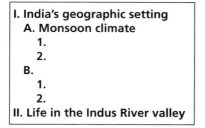

India's Geographic Setting

Stretching south from the Himalayas, the kite-shaped land of India juts out from Asia into the Indian Ocean. Geographers call this land a **subcontinent,** or a large landmass that juts out from a continent. Historians refer to the entire subcontinent as India, although today it is divided into several countries, including India, Pakistan, and Bangladesh.

For centuries, geography limited the contact the people of the Indian subcontinent had with the rest of the world. Turn to the map titled Ancient India on page 107. Notice how the Himalaya and the Hindu Kush mountain ranges separate India from the rest of Asia. Like these mountains, the bodies of water around India separated it from surrounding regions.

A Climate of Monsoons India's climate is dominated by the **monsoons,** strong winds that blow across the region at certain times of the year. Look at the map below titled India: Monsoons. From October to May, the winter monsoon blows from the northeast, spreading dry air across the country. Then, in the middle of June, the wind blows in from the Indian Ocean. This summer monsoon picks up moisture from the ocean. It carries rains that drench the plains and river valleys daily.

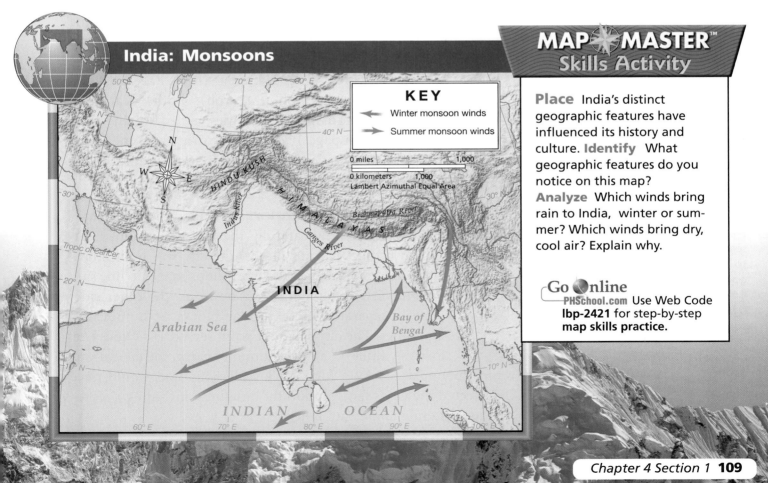

India: Monsoons

KEY
← Winter monsoon winds
→ Summer monsoon winds

0 miles 1,000
0 kilometers 1,000
Lambert Azimuthal Equal Area

MAP MASTER™
Skills Activity

Place India's distinct geographic features have influenced its history and culture. **Identify** What geographic features do you notice on this map? **Analyze** Which winds bring rain to India, winter or summer? Which winds bring dry, cool air? Explain why.

Go Online
PHSchool.com Use Web Code **lbp-2421** for step-by-step **map skills practice.**

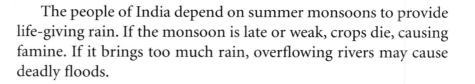

Identify Causes and Effects

What cause-and-effect relationships are described in the paragraph at the right?

The people of India depend on summer monsoons to provide life-giving rain. If the monsoon is late or weak, crops die, causing famine. If it brings too much rain, overflowing rivers may cause deadly floods.

Barriers and Pathways   Although the mountains separate India from other lands, they do have openings. For thousands of years, passes through the Hindu Kush mountain range have served as highways for migration and invasion. The earliest people of northern India probably entered the Indus River valley through these pathways.

Great rivers begin in the mountains. The Indus (IN dus) River crosses the Himalayas and empties into the Arabian Sea. The Ganges (GAN jeez) River flows from the Himalayas into the Bay of Bengal. Fed by melting snow and rain, the Indus and Ganges rivers cut through the mountains. They flow across northern India and make farming possible in the river valleys.

✓ **Reading Check**   **How do winter monsoons differ from summer monsoons?**

Life in the Indus River Valley

From the rich soil of the Indus valley, early farmers harvested a surplus of wheat and other grains. With a surplus of food, the population grew. Some villages grew to become cities. From around 2500 to 1500 B.C., well-planned cities flourished in the valley. Two such cities were Harappa (huh RAP uh) and Mohenjo-Daro (moh HEN joh DAH roh), both located in present-day Pakistan. To find these cities, return to the map titled Ancient India on page 107. Mohenjo-Daro was the larger of the two cities, and it lay along the banks of the Indus River.

Stone Seals
Merchants of Mohenjo-Daro may have used seals like these to identify their goods.
Compare How do these seals compare to the ways that present-day merchants identify their goods?

Ancient City Planners   The ruins of Mohenjo-Daro show how carefully the city was planned. To help protect it from floods, the city was built above ground level. Homes and workshops made up one side of the city. Public buildings stood on the other side. Streets separated these regular blocks of homes and buildings. The city's highest point served as a **citadel,** or fortress. Built on a high mound of earth, the citadel was probably enclosed by a high brick wall. This wall would have protected the city's most important buildings, including a storehouse for grain and a bath house.

Unlike most other cities of the time, Mohenjo-Daro had a drainage system. Clay pipes ran under the brick streets. They carried waste from homes and public buildings away from the city. Outside the city, canals ran along the Indus River, which often flooded. The canals helped to control flooding by catching overflow from the river. The water was then directed where it was most needed.

A mythical animal on a stone seal

Life in Mohenjo-Daro In Mohenjo-Daro, merchants and artisans sold their wares from shops that lined the streets. Carts loaded with grain rolled through the city. Traders came from as far away as Mesopotamia to buy and sell precious goods. The citizens of Mohenjo-Daro lived in homes that opened onto courtyards. Children played with toys and pets. Adults enjoyed games and music. Artisans fashioned jewelry and bright cotton clothing for the people to wear.

The language of the people is still a mystery. Their writings appear on square seals, but experts have not yet been able to figure out what the symbols mean. The form of government and the religion of Mohenjo-Daro are also unknown. No royal tombs or great temples have been found. But evidence found in the city's ruins suggests that the people had a number of gods.

Ancient City
The baked-brick ruins of Mohenjo-Daro are in the present-day country of Pakistan. **Analyze Images** *How does the photograph below suggest that Mohenjo-Daro was probably a crowded city?*

Farming the Indus Valley
In Ladakh, India, farming is part of an ancient tradition. **Generalize** *How did farmers help make civilization possible in the Indus valley?*

A Mysterious Decline   Around 2000 B.C., Indus valley farmers began to abandon their land. The climate may have changed, turning the fertile soil into desert. Or great earthquakes may have caused floods that destroyed the canals. Without enough food, people began to leave the cities of the Indus valley. Between 2000 and 1500 B.C., newcomers from the north entered the valley. These newcomers eventually gained power throughout the region.

✓ Reading Check   **When did the Indus valley civilization begin to decline?**

A New Culture Arises

The newcomers called themselves Aryans (AYR ee unz), which in their language meant "noble" or "highborn." They **migrated, or moved,** from their homelands in central Asia. For several centuries, waves of these nomadic herders swept into India.

The Aryans drove horse-drawn chariots that helped them gain power. The chariots overwhelmed the enemy's slow-moving foot soldiers and settled populations. In time, local people adopted the language and some of the beliefs of the Aryans. Gradually, a new Aryan culture developed. This culture combined the traditions of the original inhabitants with ideas and beliefs brought by the newcomers. Marriages between members of the two groups created a mixed population.

Aryan Culture Spreads   This new culture first developed in the northern Indus valley. Gradually, it spread into the Ganges valley to the east, where people also adopted the Aryan language. By about 800 B.C., the people of northern India had learned to make tools and weapons out of iron. With iron axes, these people cleared areas of the thick rain forests of the northeast. There they built farms, villages, and even cities.

Aryan Life Most of what we know of early Aryan life comes from religious books called Vedas, which means "knowledge." The Vedas tell us that the earliest Aryans were herders and warriors who lived in temporary villages. Often on the move, these people did not at first build cities or spacious homes.

The Aryans organized their society around three classes. Aryan priests, called Brahmans, performed religious services and composed hymns and prayers. Ranked below them was a class of warriors and nobles. Next came the artisans and merchants. Gradually, a low-ranking fourth class was formed. It was made up of farm workers, laborers, and servants.

The Social Order By 500 B.C., there was a strict division of classes. Europeans later called it the caste system. At first, each caste, or class, performed special duties. Under the caste system, people always had to stay in the caste of their parents. Over time, the caste system became more complicated. The main castes divided into hundreds of different groups, in which each person had the same occupation. Since people could not leave their caste, they did the same work that their parents and other group members did.

The caste system still exists in present-day India, but it is much less rigid. For example, people of different castes interact more freely. Also, many modern professions have no caste ranking.

✓ **Reading Check** How was Aryan society organized?

Indian Society
In the caste system, a weaver's son would be a weaver. A barber's daughter would marry a barber. The manuscript page above shows workmen building a royal city.
Summarize *How did the caste system develop in India?*

Section 1 Assessment

Key Terms
Review the key terms at the beginning of this section. Use each term in a sentence that explains its meaning.

Target Reading Skill
What may have caused the decline of Indus valley civilizations around 2000 B.C.? What was the effect of this decline?

Comprehension and Critical Thinking
1. (a) Recall Describe the geography of the Indus and Ganges river valleys.

(b) Identify Effects How do the monsoons affect India and its climate?
2. (a) Explain How did geography influence the building of Mohenjo-Daro?
(b) Draw Conclusions How was Mohenjo-Daro similar to modern cities?
3. (a) Identify Who were the Aryans?
(b) Analyze Information How was it possible for the Aryans to spread their influence over the Indus and Ganges river valleys so successfully?

Writing Activity
List some words that describe the city and the people of Mohenjo-Daro. Use these words to write a paragraph about life in that city.

> **Writing Tip** Use vivid language when writing a description. Reread the text on Mohenjo-Daro to see what life was like in the ancient city. When you write your description, carefully choose adjectives that will bring Mohenjo-Daro to life.

Focus On
Mohenjo-Daro

The advertisement shown below is fiction, of course, but the details are quite true. While villagers in ancient Mesopotamia and Egypt were living in mud huts, Indus valley dwellers lived in relatively high style—especially in the two large cities of Harappa and Mohenjo-Daro. Discovered by archaeologists in 1922, Mohenjo-Daro was a feat of engineering, architecture, design, mathematics, and social organization.

Homes available in fashionable Mohenjo-Daro! Houses feature from 1 to 24 rooms in cool, brick buildings, some with courtyards. Good security. Indoor baths and well water in most units. Close to the Indus River and to downtown area. Dogs, cats, chickens, pigs, goats, mules, and sheep welcome.

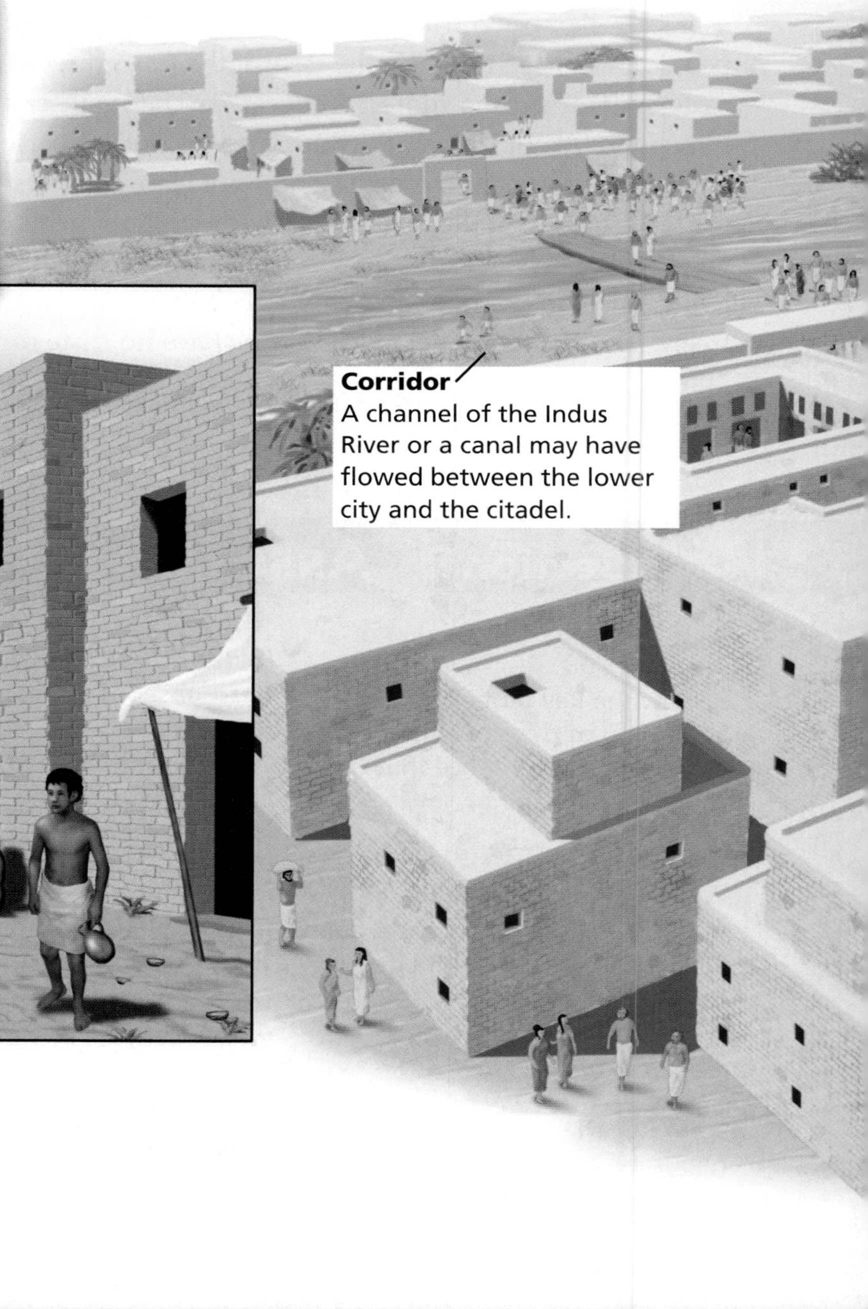
Corridor
A channel of the Indus River or a canal may have flowed between the lower city and the citadel.

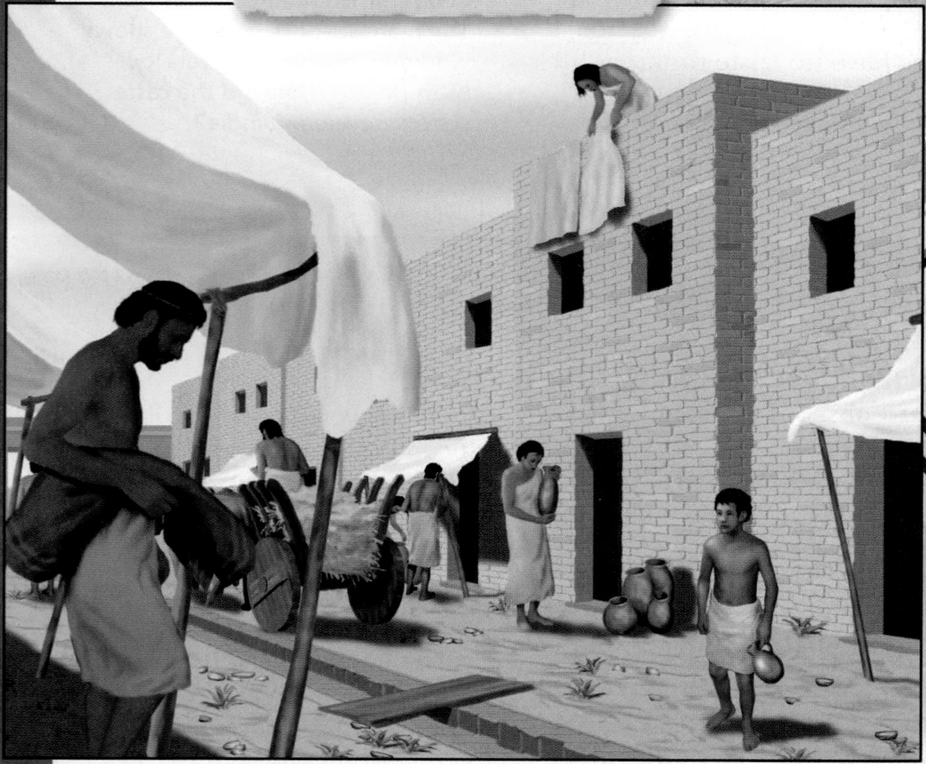

A street scene from the lower city

A lamp found in the ruins of Mohenjo-Daro

City Life From its beginnings in around 2500 B.C., Mohenjo-Daro was a booming city where more than 35,000 people lived and worked. Planners divided the city into two sections: a western side for public facilities, known as the citadel, and a residential east side, known as the lower city. Built on mud-brick platforms to protect it from floods, Mohenjo-Daro was laid out with mathematical precision on one square mile.

Artisans of Mohenjo-Daro created jewelry, crafted copper and bronze objects, and found a way to mass-produce pottery. Cotton fabric found in the city's ruins is the earliest evidence of a textile industry for which India would later become famous. Yet despite these signs of success, we find no great tombs of kings or priests. Few clues remain as to who built this city and extended its influence for thousands of miles.

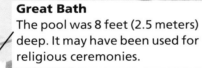

Lower City
Homes and shops

Citadel
Public buildings

Great Bath
The pool was 8 feet (2.5 meters) deep. It may have been used for religious ceremonies.

Granary
Vents in the building kept the grain from spoiling.

Assessment

Identify Describe the citadel and the lower-city sections of Mohenjo-Daro.

Draw Conclusions What do the features of Mohenjo-Daro tell us about the people who lived there?

Hinduism in Ancient India

Prepare to Read

Objectives

In this section you will
1. Find out about the beginning of Hinduism.
2. Learn about the teachings of Hinduism.
3. Examine the practice of Hinduism.

Taking Notes

As you read, find details about the basic beliefs of Hinduism. Copy the concept web below, and record your findings in it.

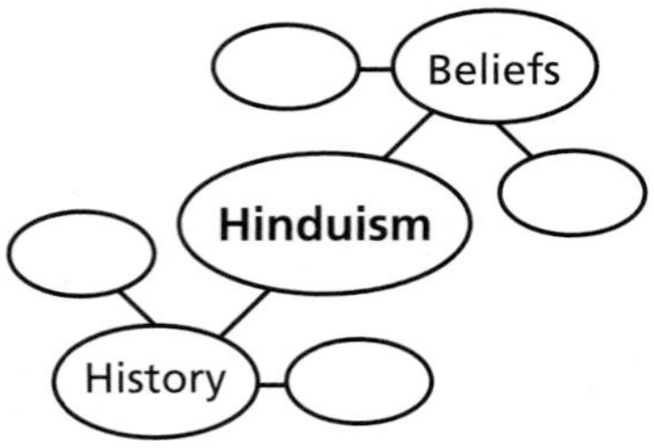

Beliefs

Hinduism

History

🎯 Target Reading Skill

Recognize Cause-and-Effect Signal Words
Sometimes certain words, such as *affect, from,* and *as a result,* signal a cause or an effect. In the following sentence, *from* signals both a cause and an effect: "*From* this blending of ideas and beliefs came one of the world's oldest living religions, Hinduism." The cause is a blend of ideas and beliefs, and the effect is Hinduism. As you read, look for signals announcing other causes and effects.

Key Terms

- **brahman** (BRAH mun) *n.* a single spiritual power that Hindus believe lives in everything
- **avatar** (av uh TAHR) *n.* a representation of a Hindu god or goddess in human or animal form
- **reincarnation** (ree in kahr NAY shun) *n.* the rebirth of the soul in the body of another living being
- **dharma** (DAHR muh) *n.* the religious and moral duties of Hindus
- **ahimsa** (uh HIM sah) *n.* the Hindu idea of non-violence

Shiva, one of the most important Hindu gods

The following prayer was part of one of the early Aryan Vedas:

    ❝O Lord of the storm gods, . . . [d]o not hide the sun from our sight. O Rudra, protect our horseman from injury. . . . Your glory is unbounded, your strength unmatched among all living creatures, O Rudra, wielder [handler] of the thunderbolt. Guide us safely to the far shore of existence where there is no sorrow.❞

—*Aryan Vedas*

The prayer praises Rudra and other gods of nature. What parts of the prayer ask the gods for their protection?

The Beginnings of Hinduism

Aryan prayers were passed down through generations. As Aryan culture mixed with India's existing cultures, new ideas and beliefs became part of the Vedas. From this blending of ideas and beliefs came one of the world's oldest living religions, Hinduism.

A Blend of Religions As Hinduism developed over 3,500 years, it absorbed many beliefs from other religions. Hinduism became very complex over time, with many different practices existing side by side. Hindus believe that since people are different, they need many different ways of approaching god.

Hinduism is one of the world's major religions, and a way of life for more than 850 million people in India today. Its beliefs have influenced people of many other religions. Yet Hinduism is unlike other major world religions.

Hinduism has no one single founder, but Hindus have many great religious thinkers. Hindus worship many gods and goddesses. However, they believe in one single spiritual power called brahman, which lives in everything. Hindus believe that there is more than one path to the truth.

Hindu Gods and Goddesses The gods and goddesses of Hinduism stand for different parts of brahman. An ancient Hindu saying expresses this idea: "God is one, but wise people know it by many names." The most important Hindu gods are Brahma, the Creator; Vishnu, the Preserver; and Shiva, the Destroyer.

Hindu gods take many different forms, called avatars. An avatar is the representation of a Hindu god or goddess in human or animal form.

Hindu teachings say that the god Brahma was born from a golden egg. He created Earth and everything on it. However, he is not as widely worshiped as Vishnu and Shiva.

Bathing in the Ganges
People practice the ancient ritual of cleansing in the Ganges River. Hindus believe the waters of the Ganges to be sacred. **Infer** *Why do you think Hindus believe the Ganges to be sacred?*

The Hindu temple of Kandarya Mahadeva was built in central India around A.D. 1000. The temple is covered with carvings of Hindu gods. **Synthesize** *In what ways are the gods of Hinduism complex, or many-sided?*

Hindus believe that Vishnu is a kindly god who is concerned with the welfare of human beings. Vishnu visits Earth from time to time in different forms. He does this to guide humans or to protect them from disaster.

Unlike Vishnu, Shiva is not concerned with human matters. He is very powerful. Shiva is responsible for both the creative and the destructive forces of the universe. Shiva developed from the god Rudra, the "wielder of the thunderbolt" in the prayer at the beginning of this section.

Hindu gods have their own families. Many Hindus, for example, worship Shiva's wife, the goddess Shakti. Hindus believe Shakti plays a role in human life. Like her husband, she is both a destroyer and a creator. She is both kind and cruel.

✓ Reading Check **What are the three main Hindu gods?**

The Teachings of Hinduism

All Hindus share certain central beliefs that are contained in religious writings or sacred texts.

The Upanishads One of the Hindu religious texts is the Upanishads (oo PAN uh shadz). *Upanishad* means "sitting near a teacher." Much of the Upanishads is in the form of questions by pupils and responses by teachers. For example, a pupil asks, "Who created the world?" The teacher replies, "Brahman is the creator, the universal soul." When asked to describe brahman, the teacher explains that it is too complicated for humans to understand. Brahman has no physical form.

Reincarnation One important idea in the Upanishads is **reincarnation,** or rebirth of the soul. Hindus believe that when a person dies, the soul is reborn in the body of another living thing. Hindus believe that every living thing has a soul. This idea is an important part of other Asian beliefs as well.

According to Hindu belief, the actions of a person in this life affect his or her fate in the next. Good behavior is always rewarded. Bad behavior is always punished. Faithful followers of Hinduism will be reborn into a higher position. Those whose acts have been bad may be born into a lower caste, or may even return as animals. If a person leads a perfect life, he or she may be freed from this cycle of death and rebirth. As a result, the person's soul becomes one with brahman.

A Hindu's Duties To become united with the one spirit and escape the cycle of death and rebirth, a person must obey his or her dharma (DAHR muh). **Dharma** is the religious and moral duties of each person. These duties depend on such factors as a person's class, age, and occupation. In Hinduism, it is a man's duty to protect the women in his family, and it is a ruler's duty to protect his subjects. Another important idea of Hinduism is **ahimsa** (uh HIM sah), or nonviolence. To Hindus, people and living things are part of brahman and therefore must be treated with respect. For that reason, many Hindus do not eat meat and try to avoid harming living things.

✓ **Reading Check** **According to Hindu belief, what happens to a person's soul after death?**

Links to

Language Arts

Common Roots The Hindu sacred books were written in a language called Sanskrit. It is one of the oldest known languages. Sanskrit is related to many other languages in the world, such as Greek and Latin. Modern languages, including Spanish, German, and English, also have roots in common with ancient Sanskrit. The page shown below is from an ancient Indian book written in Sanskrit.

Target Skill **Recognize Cause-and-Effect Signal Words** What does *as a result* signal?

The Practice of Hinduism

As you have read, Hinduism teaches that there is more than one path to the truth. Because of this view, Hinduism allows its followers to worship in various ways.

The Yogas   Many non-Hindus know yoga (YOH guh) as a physical activity, a system of special exercises and breathing. Hindus believe yoga exercises help free the soul from the cares of the world. In this way, the soul may unite with brahman. In fact, the word *yoga* means "union." For Hindus, there are many yogas that may be used as paths to brahman. Physical activity is one yoga. Another is the yoga of selfless deeds, such as giving to the poor. By learning the sacred writings, a Hindu practices the yoga of knowledge. And by honoring a personal god, a Hindu follows the yoga of devotion.

Private Devotion   Hindus worship in public by praying and performing rituals in temples. They also show devotion privately at home. It is common for Hindus to choose a personal god, and to honor that god by offering food, gifts, and prayers at a home altar. A Hindu's devotion to the god brings the soul closer to brahman.

✓ **Reading Check**   How is yoga practiced by Hindus?

Home Altar
Many Hindus, like the woman shown above, worship before altars in their homes. **Contrast** *What are some differences between public and private worship for Hindus?*

Section 2 Assessment

Key Terms
Review the key terms at the beginning of this section. Use each term in a sentence that explains its meaning.

Target Reading Skill
Return to the fourth paragraph on page 119 and find the signal word *affect*. What cause-and-effect relationships are described in the two sentences that follow?

Comprehension and Critical Thinking
1. (a) **Explain**   How did the early Aryan religion grow into Hinduism?

(b) **Compare and Contrast**
How is Hinduism different from other religions you have learned about? How is it similar?
2. (a) **Analyze Information**
What is the relationship between good and bad behavior and the Hindu idea of reincarnation?
(b) **Find the Main Idea**   What does "escaping the cycle of birth and death" mean to Hindus?
3. (a) **Describe**   In what ways do Hindus practice their faith?
(b) **Draw Conclusions**   How do you think the yogas bring Hindus closer to brahman?

Writing Activity
Hindu teachers often instruct their students through questions and answers. Write a dialogue in which a student asks questions about Hindu beliefs and the teacher responds.

> **Writing Tip**   A dialogue is similar to a script for a play. When you write your dialogue, make it clear that either the student or the teacher is speaking. Try to make the dialogue sound like a conversation.

The Beginnings of Buddhism

Prepare to Read

Objectives

In this section you will
1. Learn about the Buddha and his teachings.
2. Find out how Buddhism was received inside and outside India.

Taking Notes

As you read, find details on the beginnings of Buddhism. Copy the flowchart below, and record your findings in it.

Beginnings of Buddhism

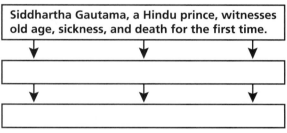

Target Reading Skill

Recognize Multiple Causes A cause is what makes something happen. An effect is what happens. Sometimes an effect can have more than one cause. For example, in the story that begins this section, Siddhartha Gautama witnesses three events that cause him to change the direction of his life. Can you identify the three causes? As you read, look for effects that have multiple causes.

Key Terms

- **meditate** (MED uh tayt) *v.* to focus the mind inward in order to find spiritual awareness or relaxation
- **nirvana** (nur VAH nuh) *n.* the lasting peace that Buddhists seek by giving up selfish desires
- **missionary** (MISH un ehr ee) *n.* a person who spreads his or her religious beliefs to others

According to Buddhist tradition, a young Hindu prince once lived a life of luxury in his palace in northern India. The prince was surrounded by beauty and youth. He had never witnessed old age, sickness, or death.

Then, around the age of 30, the prince traveled outside the palace walls. What he saw changed his life. He met a bent and tired old man. Then he saw a man who was very sick. Finally, he saw a corpse, or dead body, as it was carried to a funeral.

This suffering and death troubled the young man greatly. He wondered why there was so much misery and pain in the world. He decided he must change his life to find the answer. He gave up his wealth, his family, and his life of ease in order to find the causes of human suffering. The young man was named Siddhartha Gautama (sih DAHR tuh GOW tuh muh). What he discovered after seven years of wandering led to the beginnings of a major world religion: Buddhism.

Indian statue of the young Buddha

The Buddha and His Teachings

As Gautama traveled in the 500s B.C., he sought answers to his questions about the meaning of life. At first, Gautama studied with Hindu philosophers, but their ideas did not satisfy him. He could not accept the Hindu belief that only priests could pass on knowledge.

The Search for Understanding Gautama decided to stop looking outwardly for the cause of suffering. Instead, he tried to find understanding within his own mind. To do this, he decided to **meditate,** to focus the mind inward in order to find spiritual awareness. Meditation was an ancient Hindu practice used by Indus valley civilizations. Buddhist tradition says that Gautama fasted and meditated under a fig tree. After 49 days, he found the answers he sought. He believed he finally understood the roots of suffering.

For the next 45 years, Gautama traveled across India and shared his knowledge. Over the years, he attracted many followers. His followers called him the Buddha (BOO duh), or "Enlightened One." His teachings became known as Buddhism.

The Middle Way Buddhism teaches people to follow the Eightfold Path, also called the Middle Way. By following this path, a person avoids a life of extreme pleasure or extreme unhappiness.

The Buddha believed that selfish desires for power, wealth, and pleasure cause humans to suffer. By giving up selfish pleasures, a person can become free from suffering. He taught that the way to end human suffering is by following the Eightfold Path. To overcome selfish desires, Buddhists must learn to be wise, to behave correctly, and to develop their minds.

The Practice of Buddhism: The Eightfold Path

1. Right Understanding
Having faith in the Buddhist view of the universe

2. Right Intention
Making a commitment to practice Buddhism

3. Right Speech
Avoiding lies and mean or abusive speech

4. Right Action
Not taking life, not stealing, and not hurting others

5. Right Livelihood
Rejecting jobs and occupations that conflict with Buddhist ideals

6. Right Effort
Avoiding bad attitudes and developing good ones

7. Right Mindfulness
Being aware of one's own body, feelings, and thoughts

8. Right Concentration
Thinking deeply to find answers to problems

SOURCE: *Encyclopaedia Britannica*

The Eightfold Path
The Eightfold Path outlines the steps a person should take to lead a balanced life.
Analyze *Which steps direct followers to lead a moral life?*

Release From Reincarnation To find this Middle Way, the Buddha taught, people must act unselfishly toward others and treat people fairly. They must tell the truth at all times. People should also avoid violence and the killing of any living thing. If people follow the Buddha's path, their suffering will end. They will eventually find **nirvana,** or lasting peace. By reaching nirvana, people will be released from the cycle of reincarnation.

Followers of Buddhism Buddhism also taught that all people are equal. Anyone, the Buddha declared, could follow the path to nirvana, regardless of his or her social class. This idea appealed to many people living under the caste system.

Like other religions, Buddhism has priests. Although monastery life is difficult, people of any social class can work to become a Buddhist priest or monk. The Buddha encouraged his followers to establish monasteries. There they would learn, meditate, and teach. He also urged monks to become **missionaries,** or people who spread their religious beliefs to others.

✓ Reading Check **Why do Buddhists try to follow the Middle Way?**

Target Skill

Recognizing Multiple Causes
Which factors in the paragraph at the left affect a Buddhist's ability to reach nirvana?

Reclining Buddha
Like many statues of the Buddha, this sculpture in Vientiane, Laos, located in Southeast Asia, shows the Buddha lying down. The pose may be linked to one of the great events of the Buddha's life, his reaching nirvana.
Analyze *Describe the importance of nirvana.*

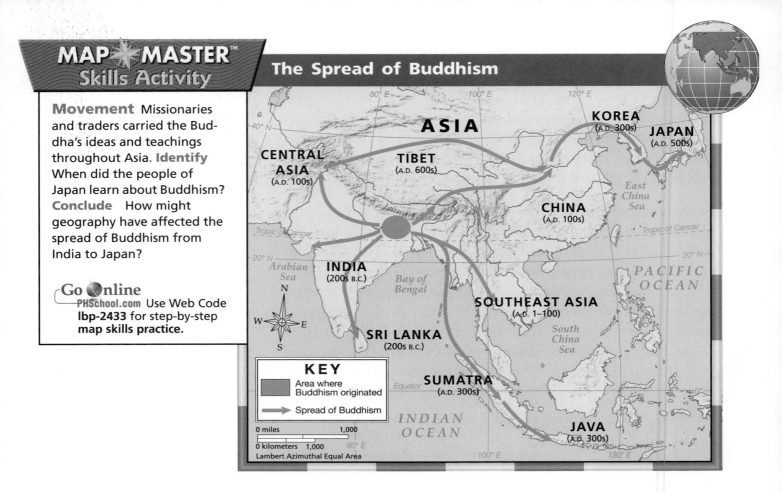

The Spread of Buddhism

Movement Missionaries and traders carried the Buddha's ideas and teachings throughout Asia. **Identify** When did the people of Japan learn about Buddhism? **Conclude** How might geography have affected the spread of Buddhism from India to Japan?

Go Online
PHSchool.com Use Web Code **lbp-2433** for step-by-step map skills practice.

ASIA

CENTRAL ASIA
(A.D. 100s)

TIBET
(A.D. 600s)

KOREA
(A.D. 300s)

JAPAN
(A.D. 500s)

East China Sea

CHINA
(A.D. 100s)

Tropic of Cancer

INDIA
(200s B.C.)

Arabian Sea

Bay of Bengal

SOUTHEAST ASIA
(A.D. 1–100)

PACIFIC OCEAN

SRI LANKA
(200s B.C.)

South China Sea

SUMATRA
(A.D. 300s)

Equator

JAVA
(A.D. 300s)

INDIAN OCEAN

KEY

■ Area where Buddhism originated

→ Spread of Buddhism

0 miles 1,000
0 kilometers 1,000
Lambert Azimuthal Equal Area

Buddhism Inside and Outside India

After the Buddha's death, his teachings spread all over India. But the Buddha's teachings did not last in the land of his birth. Hinduism gradually regained favor among those in power. Meantime, Hinduism had developed in ways that made it more appealing to the lower castes. Over time, Buddhism died out almost completely in India. But for many years, Buddhism and Hinduism existed side by side.

Some Hindus believed that the Buddha was the reincarnation of the god Vishnu, shown at the center of the bronze altar piece below.

Hindus and Buddhists: Shared Beliefs

When Hinduism and Buddhism coexisted in India, a number of basic ideas came to be shared by both. Both Hindus and Buddhists accept the idea that it is wrong to harm other living creatures. Both value nonviolence and believe in dharma and the cycle of rebirth. Some Hindus came to honor the Buddha as a reincarnation of the god Vishnu. But because Buddhists do not embrace the sacred texts of Hinduism, most Hindus do not worship the Buddha as an avatar.

Buddhism Spreads to Other Countries Buddhism was accepted by millions of people in other lands. Missionaries and traders carried the Buddha's message throughout Asia. It took root first in China, where the ideas of the Buddha became mixed with those of earlier Chinese thinkers. Millions of Chinese became Buddhists, and Buddhist monastaries in China became centers of religious thought. From China, Buddhism spread to Korea and Japan. Today, Buddhism is part of the cultures of such countries as Japan, the Koreas, China, Tibet (part of China), and Vietnam.

Boy Monks
Young novice monks study Buddhism in Sri Lanka, an island nation off the southeast coast of India. **Generalize** *How did Buddhism spread to Sri Lanka and other parts of Asia?*

✓ Reading Check **What other countries has Buddhism spread to?**

Section 3 Assessment

Key Terms
Review the key terms at the beginning of this section. Use each term in a sentence that explains its meaning.

Target Reading Skill
What are the three events witnessed by Siddhartha Gautama that caused him to change his life?

Comprehension and Critical Thinking
1. (a) Identify Who was Siddhartha Gautama?

(b) Infer Why did Siddhartha Gautama look for the cause of human suffering?
(c) Identify Cause and Effect According to Buddhism, how is human suffering connected to human desires?
2. (a) Explain What happened to the Buddha's teachings in India after he died?
(b) Compare What is the relationship between Buddhist and Hindu beliefs?
(c) Analyze Why do you think that Buddhism was accepted in so many countries outside of India?

Writing Activity
Turn to page 121 and reread the passage about Siddhartha Gautama's journey outside the palace. Write a description of his journey from the point of view of a servant who has followed him from the palace.

For: An activity on Buddhism
Visit: PHSchool.com
Web Code: lbd-2403

Ms. Bell's world studies class was working on a project. They had thought of a plan to help fight world hunger.

"We are going to sell candles and donate the money to a children's nutrition organization," said Indira.

"The group provides food and clean water for kids in poor countries," Troy explained.

"Look, Ms. Bell, we've already made a table to keep track of the orders we get," added Elizabeth.

A food relief program in Damana, India

 table displays information in vertical columns and horizontal rows. Look at the table on page 127 titled Candle Orders for Fundraiser. The numbers shown in the table are data, factual information collected and organized for a particular purpose. Making the table will help the class place an accurate order with the candle company.

Learn the Skill

To learn how to read a table, refer to the example of Ms. Bell's students and their fundraiser, as you follow the steps below.

1 **Read the title and then the column and row headings.** Reading the title and headings will help you determine the purpose of the table.

2 **Locate the information in the table.** Place one finger at the beginning of one row and another finger at the top of one column. Then look at the cell where the row and column meet. What does the number in each cell represent?

3 **Analyze information from the table.** Tables are helpful for summarizing and comparing data. The class can add the numbers in each column to find out how many of each color candle to buy from the manufacturer.

Practice the Skill

In this text, you are learning about some of the world's major religions. Read the table at the right to find out more about those religions.

 Study the kinds of information shown in the table.

 Suppose you want to locate information on where Judaism was founded. Under which column heading would you look? Which row has the information you want?

 Use the table to answer these questions: Which religion was founded most recently? Which religions were founded in India? How might this information be useful to you when reading about ancient history?

Major World Religions

Religion	Date Founded	Place of Origin
Buddhism	c. 525 B.C.	India
Christianity	c. A.D. 30	Southwest Asia
Hinduism	c. 1500 B.C.	India
Islam	c. A.D. 622	Southwest Asia
Judaism	c. 1800 B.C.	Southwest Asia

Candle Orders for Fundraiser

Seller	Green	Red	Blue
Katelyn			
Troy	2		5
Rashid			
Madelyn		3	
Indira	6		
Michael			
Elizabeth			

Apply the Skill

Now try making a table yourself. Interview at least four of your classmates to find out each person's favorite food, movie, and sport. Create a table to show the results.

Exchange tables with a classmate. Analyze the information in your classmate's table.

4 Empires of Ancient India

Prepare to Read

Objectives

In this section you will
1. Learn about the rise of the Maurya Empire.
2. Study Asoka's leadership.
3. Investigate the Gupta Empire.

Taking Notes

As you read, compare and contrast the rulers of the Maurya Empire. Copy the Venn diagram below. Write similarities in the overlapping space and differences in the outside ovals.

Rulers of Maurya

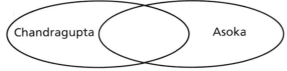

Chandragupta · Asoka

🎯 Target Reading Skill

Understand Effects Sometimes one cause may produce several effects. Turn to page 129 and read the paragraph after the heading Chandragupta's Legacy. What were the effects of wealth on the Maurya Empire?

Key Terms

- **Maurya Empire** (MOWR yuh EM pyr) *n.* Indian empire founded by Chandragupta, beginning with his kingdom in northeastern India and spreading to most of northern and central India
- **convert** (kun VURT) *v.* to change one's beliefs; in particular, to change from one religion to another
- **tolerance** (TAHL ur uns) *n.* freedom from prejudice

Around 321 B.C., a new ruler came to the throne of a kingdom in northeastern India. Within 35 years, the tiny kingdom had grown into the giant Maurya (MOWR yuh) Empire. Chandragupta (chun druh GUP tuh) Maurya founded India's **Maurya Empire.**

Chandragupta had been born to a poor family and sold into slavery at a young age. But later, when he became king, Chandragupta enjoyed luxuries from all parts of Asia. When he appeared before his subjects, he was often seated in a golden chair carried on his servants' shoulders. Sometimes he rode on an elephant covered with jewels.

The Rise of the Maurya Empire

India was made up of a number of warring states before Chandragupta came to power. Strong and ruthless, Chandragupta's armies overthrew kingdoms along the Ganges River. Turning west, the armies advanced into the Indus River valley. In only a few years, Chandragupta's power extended over most of northern and central India.

Terra-cotta figure of a mother goddess worshiped in India, 200s B.C.

Absolute Rule Chandragupta was guided by the basic belief that a ruler must have absolute power. According to legend, one of Chandragupta's advisors gave him a book of advice called *Arthasastra*. The book urged kings to maintain control of their subjects and to establish an army of spies to inform on them.

Chandragupta commanded a huge army. Thousands of foot soldiers and mounted troops were ready to enforce the law and to crush any revolts. The army also had a herd of 9,000 war elephants, which struck fear into the hearts of opponents.

Under Chandragupta, the empire enjoyed great economic success. Most of its wealth came from farming. The Maurya Empire also built up trade with such faraway places as Greece, Rome, and China.

However, as his rule continued, Chandragupta became fearful for his life. Afraid of being poisoned, he made servants taste his food. He slept in a different room every night to ward off assassins, or people who murder rulers or political figures. One story says that near the end of his life, Chandragupta left the throne to his son and became a monk in southern India. Fasting and praying, he starved himself to death.

Chandragupta's Legacy Chandragupta did not gain wealth for himself only. Although his rule was harsh, he used his wealth to improve his empire. New irrigation systems brought water to farmers. Forests were cleared, and more food was produced. Government officials promoted crafts and mining. A vast network of roads made it easier for Maurya traders to exchange goods with foreign lands. Chandragupta's leadership brought order and peace to his people.

✓ Reading Check **What kind of ruler was Chandragupta?**

Links to
Economics

The Emperor's Guidebook
Both Chandragupta and his grandson Asoka benefited from a book titled *Arthasastra*. *Artha* means "property and economics." Chandragupta used the book's advice on government as his guide to building an empire. Kautilya, the book's author, also served as an advisor to Chandragupta. Although Kautilya wrote about ways to achieve material success, he did not live in great luxury himself.

Fighting for Empire
Chandragupta's army rode elephants into war, causing fear and panic. This painting from the 1600s shows an elephant charging toward the enemy. **Evaluate** *How did Chandragupta use his army to create an empire?*

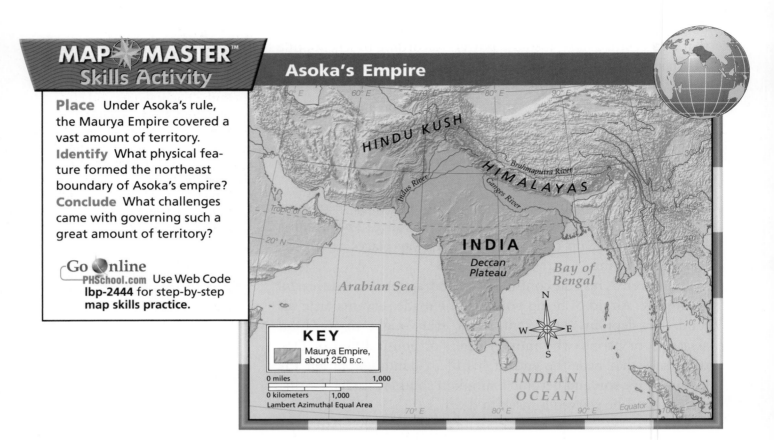

Place Under Asoka's rule, the Maurya Empire covered a vast amount of territory.
Identify What physical feature formed the northeast boundary of Asoka's empire?
Conclude What challenges came with governing such a great amount of territory?

Go Online
PHSchool.com Use Web Code **lbp-2444** for step-by-step **map skills practice.**

Understand Effects What effects did the Battle of Kalinga have on Asoka's life?

Asoka's Leadership

Chandragupta passed the leadership of the Maurya Empire on to his son. After the son died in 273 B.C., Chandragupta's grandson, Asoka, gained power. Asoka, whose name means "without sorrow," further expanded Chandragupta's empire. By the end of his lengthy rule in 232 B.C., Asoka had built the greatest empire India had ever seen.

The Battle of Kalinga For more than 35 years, Asoka ruled an empire that included much of the Indian subcontinent. During the first years of his rule, Asoka was as warlike as his grandfather had been. He conquered new territories which were not yet part of the empire.

Early in his rule, Asoka led his army south into the state of Kalinga. In about 261 B.C., he won a bloody battle in which thousands and thousands of people were injured or died. The great slaughter at Kalinga was a turning point in Asoka's life. He was filled with sorrow over the bloodshed. He gave up war and violence. He freed his prisoners and restored their land. Later, he chose to **convert,** or change his beliefs, to Buddhism. Asoka also spread the message of Buddhism to the people of his empire.

The Buddhist Ruler Asoka practiced and preached the teachings of the Buddha. He did not allow the use of animals for sacrifices. He gave up hunting, the traditional sport of Indian kings.

Asoka thought of his people as his children and was concerned about their well-being. He had hospitals built throughout his kingdom. He even had wells dug every mile beside the roads so that travelers and animals would not go thirsty.

Asoka was also concerned with his people's moral and spiritual life. To carry the Buddha's message throughout his vast empire, Asoka issued writings of moral advice. Some writings urged people to honor their parents. Others asked people not to kill animals. Still others encouraged people to behave with truthfulness and **tolerance,** or freedom from prejudice. Asoka practiced religious tolerance toward the Hindus.

Still, Buddhism grew under Asoka. He sent missionaries far and wide to spread its message. Buddhist missionaries spread the religion to Sri Lanka, China, Southeast Asia, and eventually to Korea and Japan.

√ Reading Check   **How did Asoka spread Buddhism?**

Honoring the Buddha
This stupa, or Buddhist monument, was built sometime between 100 B.C. and A.D. 100, in Sanchi, India. The umbrella at the very top represents protection. **Transferring Information** *How did Asoka's rulings reflect the teachings of the Buddha?*

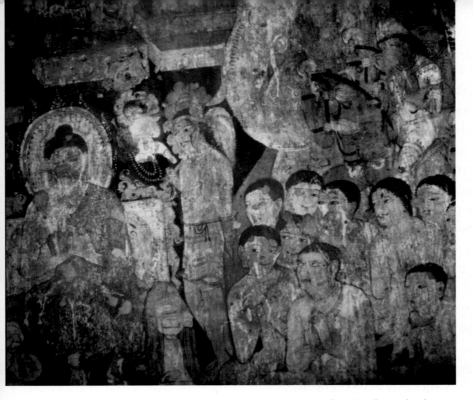

Indian Temple Painting
This painting comes from a temple carved into the Ajanta Caves during the Gupta Period. **Infer** *What details suggest that this is a religious painting?*

The Gupta Empire

After Asoka died, the Maurya Empire weakened and eventually split apart. For centuries, India suffered a series of conflicts among a patchwork of small states and foreign invaders.

However, in A.D. 320, the Gupta dynasty rose to power. By 400, the Guptas had built an empire across northern India. Invasions from Central Asia weakened the Gupta Empire. After 540, India again split into small states.

Under the Guptas, India enjoyed a rich culture. Indians invented the technique of printing cloth in this period. Hindu scholars and students gathered in colleges where they developed advanced schools of philosophy. Kalidasa (kah lee DAH suh), one of the greatest Indian writers of all time, wrote poems and plays. Indian mathematicians invented the decimal point and the system of numbers that we use today.

✓ **Reading Check** **How did learning advance under the Guptas?**

Section 4 Assessment

Key Terms
Review the key terms at the beginning of this section. Use each term in a sentence that explains its meaning.

Target Reading Skill
Reread Chandragupta's Legacy on page 129. What were the effects of wealth on the Maurya Empire?

Comprehension and Critical Thinking
1. (a) **Recall** How was India governed before the Maurya Empire?
(b) **Evaluate** What were some of the costs and benefits of Chandragupta's rule for Indians?

2. (a) **Describe** What were some of Asoka's accomplishments?
(b) **Identify Cause and Effect** How did Buddhism influence Asoka's rule of the empire?
3. (a) **Identify** What part of India did the Guptas control?
(b) **Explain** Why have some historians called the Gupta period a golden age?
(c) **Draw Conclusions** What Indian inventions under the Gupta have had a lasting impact?

Writing Activity
Asoka wrote many rules of conduct for himself and for others to follow. Write a list of rules of conduct that you would like to see today's leaders follow.

Go Online
PHSchool.com
For: An activity on Asoka
Visit: PHSchool.com
Web Code: lbd-2404

Review and Assessment

◆ Chapter Summary

Section 1: The Indus and Ganges River Valleys

Mohenjo-Daro seal

- India's geographic setting limited the contact the ancient peoples of the Indian subcontinent had with the rest of the world.
- Well-planned cities, such as Mohenjo-Daro, flourished along the banks of the Indus River.
- Aryans migrated in great waves from central Asia into India, influencing Indian life and culture.

Sanskrit

Section 2: Hinduism in Ancient India

- Hinduism is a complex religion that developed over a span of about 3,500 years.
- Hindus believe in nonviolence, and that good behavior will be rewarded and bad behavior will be punished.
- Hindus take many paths in their search for truth.

Sections 3: The Beginnings of Buddhism

- Buddhism was founded by a Hindu prince who preached nonviolence and unselfish behavior.
- Buddhism flourished in India, along with Hinduism, but it eventually declined there. Missionaries carried the Buddha's message to cultures throughout Asia.

Section 4: Empires of Ancient India

- Chandragupta's Maurya Empire extended over northern and central India.
- Chandragupta's grandson, Asoka, greatly expanded the Maurya Empire and embraced Buddhism.
- Under the Guptas, India made progress in textiles, philosophy, literature, and mathematics.

Indian warriors

◆ Reviewing Key Terms

Circle the underlined key term that best completes the sentence.

1. A <u>citadel, subcontinent</u> is a large landmass that juts out from a continent.

2. <u>Dharma, Nirvana</u> is the religious and moral duties of a Hindu.

3. To <u>meditate, migrate</u> is to move from one place to settle in another area.

4. Hindus and Buddhists believe in <u>ahimsa, reincarnation</u>, which is the rebirth of the soul.

5. Under the <u>caste, avatar</u> system, a weaver's son always became a weaver and a barber's daughter always married a barber.

6. Buddhism spread to other countries with the help of <u>monsoons, missionaries</u>.

7. Asoka encouraged his people to behave with <u>tolerance, dharma</u>, or freedom from prejudice.

◆ Comprehension and Critical Thinking

8. (a) Describe What were the geography and climate of ancient India?
(b) Identify Effects How did India's geography and climate affect the people of Mohenjo-Daro?
(c) Infer How do we know that the people of Mohenjo-Daro created a highly organized civilization?

9. (a) Identify Who were the Aryans?
(b) Explain What were some characteristics of Aryan culture?
(c) Summarize What influence did the Aryans have on the people of the Indus valley?

10. (a) Recall Describe the beginnings of ancient Hinduism.
(b) Summarize What are some of the basic beliefs of Hinduism?
(c) Evaluate Information Why is Hinduism considered to be a complex religion?

11. (a) Identify Who was the Buddha?
(b) Explain What is the central idea of Buddhism, and why did the religion appeal to so many people?
(c) Draw Inferences Buddhism and Hinduism were able to coexist in India for some time. Why do you think this was possible?

12. (a) Recall List Asoka's achievements as ruler of the Maurya Empire.
(b) Explain How did Asoka's actions show that he was a Buddhist?
(c) Compare How did Siddhartha Gautama's life-changing experience with suffering compare to Asoka's?

◆ Skills Practice

Reading Tables In the Skills for Life activity, you learned how to read tables and how to create your own table.

Review the steps you follow to do this skill. Return to the concept web you created to take notes on Section 2 of this chapter. Organize that same information into a table. Then, write a brief explanation of how a table makes comparing information from the section easy.

◆ Writing Activity: Language Arts

Asoka helped spread the Buddha's message by having his teachings carved into stone pillars. Turn to page 131 and reread the quote from one of Asoka's pillars. Next, turn to page 119 and reread The Teachings of Hinduism. Finally, write similar messages that could teach people about Hinduism.

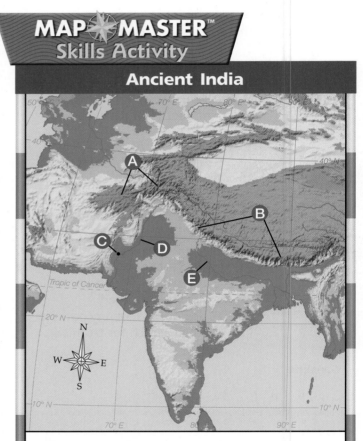

MAP MASTER™ Skills Activity

Ancient India

Place Location For each place listed below, write the letter from the map that shows its location.

1. Himalayas
2. Hindu Kush
3. Indus River
4. Ganges River
5. Mohenjo-Daro

Go Online
PHSchool.com Use Web Code **lbp-2454** for an **interactive map.**

Standardized Test Prep

Test-Taking Tips

Some questions on standardized tests ask you to analyze a reading selection for the main ideas. Read the passage below. Then follow the tips to answer the sample question.

> Buddhist missionaries spread their religion throughout Asia. Buddhism took root in China and grew there. Millions of Chinese became Buddhists. Gradually, Buddhist ideas mixed with earlier Chinese teaching. Buddhism then spread from China to Korea and Japan.

Pick the letter that best answers the question.

Which topic sentence is missing from this paragraph?

  A Buddhism died out in Turkey but took root in many parts of Asia.

  B Buddhist monasteries became centers of thought in China.

  C Buddhism died out in India but took root in many parts of Asia.

  D Today, Buddhism is a part of many Asian cultures.

Think It Through Start with the main idea of the paragraph. Each sentence tells about the spread of Buddhism. You can rule out answer B because the paragraph is not about monasteries. Nor is the paragraph about Buddhism today, so you can rule out D. That leaves A and C. Did Buddhism spread from Turkey or from India? The answer is India. Even if you were not sure, you might guess that India is much closer to China and the eastern part of Asia. Therefore, the best answer is C.

TIP Some paragraphs have a topic sentence that states the main idea. All sentences in the paragraph support this idea.

TIP Read all of the answer choices before making a final pick. You can't be sure you have the best answer until you have read every one.

Practice Questions

Use the tips above and other tips in this book to help you answer the following questions.

1. The Vedas are

  A a mountain range in northern India.

  B Aryan religious books.

  C nomadic herders who moved into the Indus River valley.

  D early inhabitants of the Indus River valley.

Read the passage below, and then answer the questions that follow.

Under Chandragupta, the Maurya Empire prospered. Asoka expanded and strengthened the empire. He encouraged the spread of Buddhism and united the various Indian states.

2. Which of the following would serve as the best topic sentence for this passage?

  A Asoka was the "Father of Buddhism."

  B The Maurya Empire grew and prospered under two leaders, Chandragupta and Asoka.

  C Chandragupta believed in absolute power.

  D Asoka converted to Buddhism.

3. Unlike other major world religions, Hinduism

  A had no single founder.

  B has had no influence on other religions.

  C has no sacred texts.

  D has no great thinkers.

Use Web Code **lba-2404** for a **Chapter 4 self-test.**

Chapter 5

Ancient China

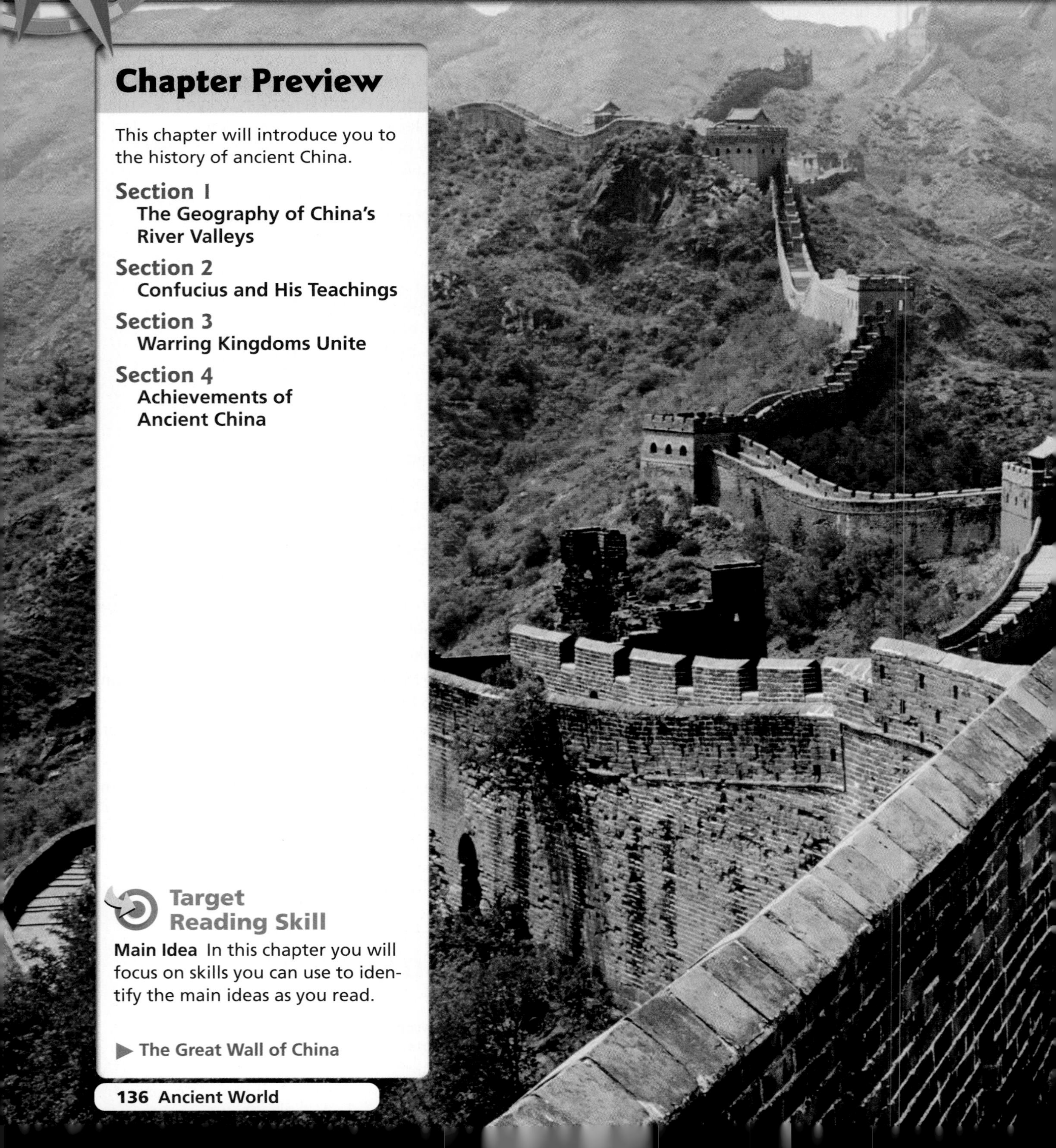

Chapter Preview

This chapter will introduce you to the history of ancient China.

Section 1
The Geography of China's River Valleys

Section 2
Confucius and His Teachings

Section 3
Warring Kingdoms Unite

Section 4
Achievements of Ancient China

Target Reading Skill

Main Idea In this chapter you will focus on skills you can use to identify the main ideas as you read.

▶ The Great Wall of China

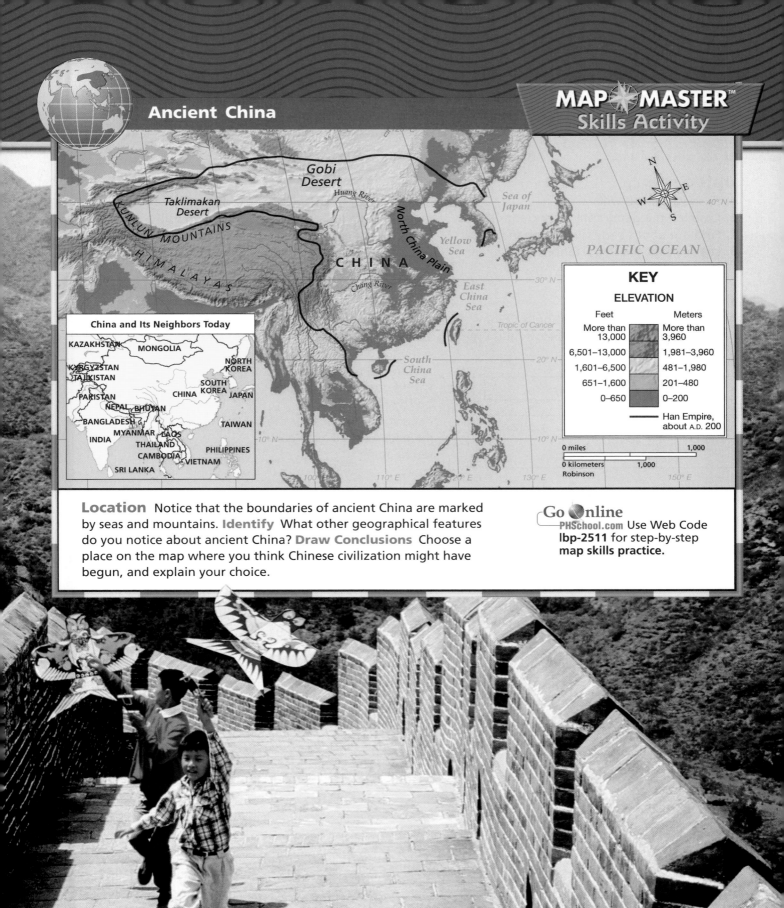

MAP MASTER™
Skills Activity

KEY

ELEVATION

Feet	Meters
More than 13,000	More than 3,960
6,501–13,000	1,981–3,960
1,601–6,500	481–1,980
651–1,600	201–480
0–650	0–200

—— Han Empire, about A.D. 200

0 miles 1,000
0 kilometers 1,000
Robinson

China and Its Neighbors Today

KAZAKHSTAN
MONGOLIA
KYRGYZSTAN
TAJIKISTAN
NORTH KOREA
PAKISTAN
SOUTH KOREA
CHINA
JAPAN
NEPAL BHUTAN
BANGLADESH
MYANMAR LAOS
INDIA
THAILAND
CAMBODIA
VIETNAM
SRI LANKA
TAIWAN
PHILIPPINES

Location Notice that the boundaries of ancient China are marked by seas and mountains. **Identify** What other geographical features do you notice about ancient China? **Draw Conclusions** Choose a place on the map where you think Chinese civilization might have begun, and explain your choice.

Go Online
PHSchool.com Use Web Code **lbp-2511** for step-by-step **map skills practice.**

The Geography of China's River Valleys

Prepare to Read

Objectives

In this section you will
1. Examine the geography of ancient China.
2. Find out about early civilization in China.
3. Learn about the importance of family ties in early Chinese society.

Taking Notes

As you read, look for details about China's river valleys. Copy the chart below, and use it to record your findings.

```
           China's River Valleys
    ┌──────────────┬──────────────┐
Geography      Civilization      Families
  •               •                •
  •               •                •
```

Target Reading Skill

Identify Main Ideas
The main idea is the most important point in a section of text. On page 139, the main idea for the section titled The Geography of Ancient China is stated in this sentence: "The climate, soil, landforms, and waterways varied greatly, depending on the region."

As you read, look for the main idea stated after each red heading.

Key Terms

- **loess** (LOH es) *n.* yellow-brown soil
- **dike** (dyk) *n.* a protective wall that controls or holds back water
- **extended family** (ek STEN did FAM uh lee) *n.* closely related people of several generations

A sculpture of a Chinese dragon

What words would you use to describe dragons? You might think of these imaginary beasts as being fierce and scary. People of some cultures would agree with you. But to the ancient Chinese people, the dragon was a respected spirit, not a terrible monster. In ancient China, dragons were friendly beasts that brought good luck. Dragon gods were believed to be responsible for the rains that made the fields fertile. In China, dragon rain ceremonies date as far back as the 500s B.C.

The Chinese also used the image of this respected spirit to show the importance of their rivers. They traditionally described their rivers as dragons. The dragon's limbs were the smaller streams. They flowed into the dragon's body, or main river. The dragon's mouth was the delta, where the river flowed into the sea. Rivers were important to the development of civilization in China. Other landforms and climate played an important role as well.

The Geography of Ancient China

Ancient China covered a large area. The climate, soil, landforms, and waterways varied greatly, depending on the region. Turn to the map on page 137 to study the geography of ancient China.

Contrasting Climate and Landforms The North China Plain is located in East Asia. It is built up of soil deposits from the Huang (hwahng) River.

The North China Plain and its surrounding highlands, as well as far northern China, have only a brief, but intense, summer rainy season caused by monsoon winds. However, the region doesn't get much rain the rest of the year. As a result, the climate is very dry.

The climate in the south, in contrast, is warm and wet. Monsoons from the South China Sea bring heavy rains to southern China from March to September. Light rain falls the rest of the year.

A painting of a river voyage in China

Effects on Civilization Geographic barriers such as mountains and seas separated China from other lands. As a result, the Chinese had little knowledge of the civilizations of Egypt, India, Greece, and Rome. They were so sure that they lived at the center of the world that they called themselves the Middle Kingdom.

China's rivers overflowed their banks each spring, bringing fresh, fertile topsoil to the land. For that reason, China's first farming villages developed along its rivers. Civilization began along the Huang River and later spread south to wetter land along the Chang, China's longest river.

Terrace Farming
A man grows a crop of millet in northern China. **Apply Information** *Why does it make sense to grow crops on terraces in this part of China?*

A woman collects water from the Huang River. ▶

Yellow River   The Huang is the second-longest river in China. The word *huang* means "yellow" in Chinese. It is called the "yellow river" because of the **loess** (LOH es), or yellow-brown soil, that its waters carry along. When the Huang floods, it deposits loess on the surrounding plain. Over many years, the Huang has carpeted the North China Plain with a thick layer of fertile soil. There, the Chinese grow a grain called millet. Millet has been an important part of the Chinese diet for thousands of years.

China's Sorrow   The Chinese people also called the Huang China's Sorrow. It brought life to the land, but it also took life away. Destructive floods could come without warning, sometimes as often as every two years. Some floods drowned thousands of people. At times, the floodwaters ran with such force that they cut an entirely new path over the land. As a result, the course of the river could change by hundreds of miles.

Flood Control   To help control the flooding, early Chinese people built dikes along the banks of the Huang. A **dike** is a protective wall that holds back the waters. As more loess settled to the bottom of the river, the level of the river rose. Eventually, the river rose high enough to overflow the dikes, causing even more deadly floods. Despite such dangers, the early Chinese people continued to settle along the banks of the Huang.

The Yellow River
You can see from this photograph why the Huang's Chinese name means "yellow river." **Analyze Images** *How is the land near the river used?*

✔ Reading Check   **What did the Chinese do to control flooding?**

Early Civilization in China

Early farmers of the North China Plain probably were once nomads who moved from place to place to hunt and gather food. Historians do not know exactly when the first farming settlements developed in the Huang Valley. Some think it was as early as 5000 B.C. These early farming societies grew into civilizations that controlled parts of the Huang Valley.

The Shang Dynasty The Shang dynasty was the first civilization in China. It probably arose sometime around 1760 B.C. The Shang people built China's first cities. Among their many accomplishments was the production of some of the finest bronze work of ancient China.

The Shang people also produced the first Chinese writing system. Like Mesopotamia's cuneiform and our own alphabet, the Chinese writing system could be used for different languages. This was helpful for communication, because China had many regional languages.

About 600 years after the founding of the Shang dynasty, a new group emerged. This group, known as the Zhou (joh) people, lived in the Wei Valley to the west of the Shang people.

The Zhou Dynasty The territory of the Zhou people partly bordered the Shang territory. Sometimes these two neighbors lived peacefully side by side. At other times, they fought over territory. Finally, the Zhou conquered the Shang in about 1122 B.C. The Zhou dynasty ruled over ancient China for almost 1,000 years. This long period is divided into two parts—the earlier Western Zhou dynasty and the later Eastern Zhou dynasty. It was near the end of the Eastern Zhou dynasty that a period known as the Warring States began. During that time, small kingdoms fought for control over one another until a new dynasty—the Qin (chin)— finally emerged.

Mandate of Heaven Sometimes Chinese rulers inherited the throne. At other times, they fought for the right to rule. In either instance, the Chinese believed that rulers came to power because it was their destiny, or fate. This idea was called the Mandate of Heaven. A mandate is a law, or an order. The Mandate of Heaven supported a leader's right to rule his people. It also gave a father authority over his family.

√ Reading Check **What was the Mandate of Heaven?**

Identify Main Ideas Which sentence states the main idea under the heading Early Civilization in China?

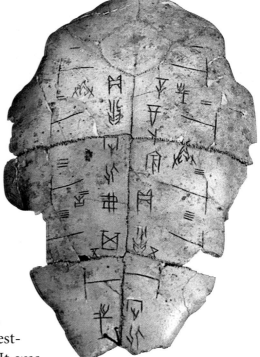

A Shang dynasty turtle shell shows one of the earliest examples of Chinese writing.

A Chinese Family
Wealthy Chinese families could afford to have their portraits painted, like this one dating from the late 1700s. **Analyze Images** *How do we know that the family members in this portrait are probably part of an extended family?*

Bronze statue of a Chinese girl with a lamp, around 100 B.C. ▶

Importance of the Family

The family was the center of early Chinese society. It was considered to be of far more importance than the individual or the nation. A person's first responsibility was always to the family. The family, in turn, was each person's chief source of well-being.

Traditional Families A household in ancient China might contain as many as five generations living together. This meant that small children lived with their great-great-grandparents as well as their parents, uncles and aunts, cousins, brothers and sisters, and so on. These closely related people are called an **extended family.** In rich families, the members might live together in one big home. But most of China's people were poor. In farming villages, members of the extended family might live in separate one-room cottages. The cottages were within easy walking distance from one another.

Family Authority The status of each person in a Chinese extended family depended on his or her age and sex. The center of authority was usually the oldest man. He had the most privileges and the most power in the family. He decided who his children and grandchildren would marry. When children were disrespectful, he punished them severely. After the oldest male died, by tradition all his lands were divided among his sons. Each son then started his own household.

Women's Roles Women were considered to be of lower status than men. According to tradition, women were bound by what were called the three obediences: to obey their fathers in youth, their husbands after their marriage, and their sons in widowhood. Four virtues also guided women's behavior in ancient China: morality, modesty, proper speech, and domestic skills. When a woman married, she left her household and became part of her husband's family. In her new household, she was expected to obey her husband and respect the wishes of her mother-in-law.

Family Names In the 300s B.C., Chinese established the practice of using inherited family names along with a personal name. The inherited name was passed down from father to child. The other was for the individual. Examples of present-day family names include Mao, Chan, and Lu. Of course, people in the United States also use two names. In Chinese society, however, the family name comes first. If this system were used in American society, you would know the first President of the United States as Washington George, not George Washington. Think of other famous people in American history. What would their names be in the Chinese naming style?

The tradition of using family names first dates back to China's earliest times. It showed how important the family was in China. Centuries later, a great philosopher, or thinker, called Confucius (kun FYOO shus) had ideas about the role of the family in Chinese society. These ideas would have a great effect on the Chinese people.

Royal Seals
Emperors used seals, like the decorated cube above, to mark their names in ink. The characters shown at the top left representing the emperor's name are carved into the bottom face of the cube. **Infer** *Why do you think the ancient Chinese began using family names in addition to personal names?*

✓ Reading Check **What factors determined a person's status within early Chinese families?**

Section 1 Assessment

Key Terms
Review the key terms at the beginning of this section. Use each term in a sentence that explains its meaning.

Target Reading Skill
State the main ideas of each of the red headings in Section 1.

Comprehension and Critical Thinking
1. (a) Identify Effects How did the Huang River affect ancient Chinese civilization?
(b) Compare What do you think ancient China had in common with the ancient civilizations of Mesopotamia, Egypt, and India?

2. (a) Recall What was the first known civilization in China?
(b) Draw Conclusions Describe the importance of China's first civilization. What effect do you think it had on later civilizations in ancient China?
3. (a) Recall Describe the importance of family in early China.
(b) Apply Information In ancient China, members of an extended family often lived together in one home. How do you think the ancient Chinese benefited from their family structure?

Writing Activity
Suppose you were a member of an ancient Chinese family. Write a description of what your life would have been like.

Writing Tip Specific details will bring your description to life. First focus on one important aspect of life in ancient China that you want to describe. Then choose two or three interesting details to make your description more colorful.

Sometimes people make broad generalizations that are not really true.
"People who like to read a lot are not interested in sports."
"Dog owners do not like cats."

A broad statement about a group of people is called a stereotype. A stereotype is not based on factual knowledge, and it is often untrue and unfair.

To avoid using stereotypes, be careful when you make a generalization. Some generalizations are valid—that is, they have value or worth. They are probably true, because they are based on specific facts. Other generalizations are not valid. They might be based on rumors or impressions instead of on facts. A stereotype is a generalization that may not be valid.

Learn the Skill

To make a valid generalization, follow these steps:

1 **Identify the specific facts that are contained within a source.** Become familiar with the facts in a piece of text, a table, or some other source.

2 **State what the facts have in common, and look for patterns.** Do any of the facts fit together in a way that makes a point about a broad subject? Do the data in a table or a graph point toward some kind of general statement?

3 **Make a generalization, or broad conclusion, about the facts.** Write your generalization as a sentence or paragraph.

4 **Test the generalization, and revise it if necessary.** You can test the validity of a generalization by using the guidelines in the box at left.

Testing a Generalization

- Are there enough facts in your source to support the generalization?
- Do any other facts support the generalization?
- Which are stronger, the examples of the generalization or the exceptions to it?
- Does the statement generalize too broadly or stereotype a group of people? Look for words such as *all, always,* or *every,* which can make a generalization invalid.
- Words such as *some, many, most,* and *often* help prevent a statement from being too general.

Practice the Skill

Turn to page 139, and reread the second paragraph that follows the title Effects on Civilization.

 The title of the text will help you understand the topic. Find and write down at least three facts that relate to that topic.

 From reading these facts, what major ideas can you learn about the topic? Do the facts suggest any ideas about China's rivers that are not specifically stated in the text?

 Make a generalization about China's rivers and how they affected the growth of Chinese civilization. Make sure the facts support your statement.

 If your statement does not meet the test for a valid generalization, try making it valid by rewriting it so that it is more limited.

The Huang River, China

Apply the Skill

We generalize in everyday speech: "Everybody loves the summer." "Most kids I know are into sports." "Nobody rents videos anymore. They rent DVDs." Find and write down three valid generalizations, and explain why they are valid. You can use generalizations that you find in your textbook, or you can write your own based on facts you know. Write down the facts that support each generalization.

Prepare to Read

Objectives

In this section you will
1. Learn about the life of Confucius.
2. Find out about the teachings of Confucius.
3. Understand the influence Confucianism had on Chinese society.

Taking Notes

As you read, summarize the teachings of Confucius and the influence they had on China. Copy the chart below, and use it to record your findings.

Confucius

Life		Teachings		Effects
•	→	•	→	•
•		•		•
•		•		•
•		•		•

Target Reading Skill

Identify Supporting Details The main idea of a section of text is supported by details. These details may explain the main idea or give examples. On page 147, the main idea for the text under the heading The Life of Confucius is stated in this sentence: "Confucius was the most famous—and important— of the early Chinese thinkers."

As you read, note the details following each of the blue headings that tell more about the life of Confucius.

Key Terms

• **Confucius** (kun FYOO shus) *n.* (551–479 B.C.) a Chinese philosopher and teacher whose beliefs had a great influence on Chinese life
• **philosophy** (fih LAHS uh fee) *n.* a system of beliefs and values
• **civil service** (SIV ul SUR vis) *n.* the group of people whose job it is to carry out the work of the government

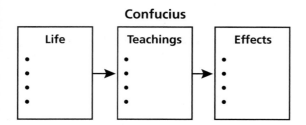

One day, the Chinese teacher and philosopher **Confucius** and his students were walking through the countryside. In the distance, they heard a woman crying. As they came around a bend in the road, they saw the woman kneeling at a grave. "Why are you crying?" they asked her. "Because," she answered, "a tiger killed my husband's father. Later, the tiger also killed my husband. Now, the tiger has killed my son as well."

They then asked the woman, "Why do you stay in this place after these terrible things have happened?" The woman answered, "Because there are no cruel rulers here." Confucius turned to his students and said, "Remember this. A cruel ruler is fiercer and more feared than a tiger."

After the death of Confucius, people told many stories about him. Like the story of the woman and the tiger, most stories contained an important lesson.

Confucius, c. 551–479 B.C.

The Life of Confucius

Confucius was the most famous—and important—of the early Chinese thinkers. The Chinese called him Kong Fu Zi (kong foo dzih), or "Master Kong." *Confucius* is the Latinized version of this name.

The Early Years Confucius was born in 551 B.C. to a noble but poor family of the North China Plain. He loved learning and was mostly self-taught. He hoped to advance to an important government office, but he never succeeded in that way. Instead, he decided to try teaching.

A Pioneer Teacher Many historians think that Confucius was China's first professional teacher. Confucius charged students a fee to take classes. He taught the students his views of life and government. He was a dedicated teacher:

> **❝From the very poorest upward . . . none has ever come to me without receiving instruction. I instruct only a student who bursts with eagerness.❞**
>
> —*Confucius*

Later in his life, Confucius searched for a ruler who would follow his teachings, but he could find no such ruler. He died in 479 B.C. at age 73. By the time of his death, he believed his life had been a failure. He had no way of knowing that his teachings would be followed for many centuries.

 Reading Check **What kind of students did Confucius like to teach?**

A Royal Welcome
A drawing shows Confucius meeting with leaders from various Chinese kingdoms. **Infer** *In what ways does the artist suggest the importance of Confucius?*

Identify Supporting Details
What detail in the paragraph at the left supports the idea that Confucius was an important Chinese thinker?

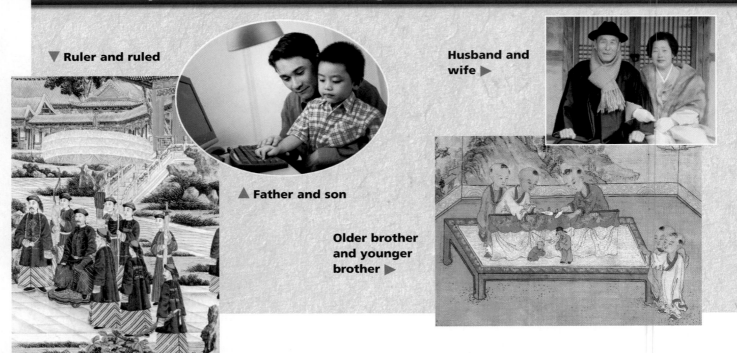

▼ **Ruler and ruled**

▲ **Father and son**

Husband and wife ▶

Older brother and younger brother ▶

Five Human Relationships
Confucius believed that Chinese society was built upon the five relationships shown above. **Conclude** *According to Confucius, how does a fair and just ruler benefit society?*

Confucius' ideas were studied in books like this one.

The Teachings of Confucius

Confucius did not claim to be an original thinker. He felt that his role was to pass on the forgotten teachings of wise people from an earlier age. In many of his teachings he tried to persuade rulers to reform. He also hoped to bring peace, stability, and prosperity to China's kingdoms.

Confucianism Confucius himself never wrote down his teachings. Instead, his students gathered a collection of his sayings after his death. Together, these writings made up a system of beliefs and values, or a **philosophy**. That philosophy became known as Confucianism. Confucianism was one of several important philosophies of ancient China. Over time, it began to govern many aspects of life there.

Bringing Order to Society Confucius lived during a time of frequent warfare in China. Powerful rulers of several Chinese states, or kingdoms, fought one another for the control of land. They seemed more interested in gaining power than in ruling wisely. Confucius hoped to persuade these rulers to change their ways and bring peace and order to China.

The goal of Confucius was to bring order to society. He believed that if people could be taught to behave properly toward one another, order and peace would result. Society would prosper.

▼ Friend and friend

Respecting Others Confucius said that people should know their place in the family and in society. They ought to respect the people above and below them and treat others justly. He described five human relationships: ruler and ruled; father and son; husband and wife; older brother and younger brother; and friend and friend. Then he explained how people should behave in each of these relationships. Confucius said that people in authority—princes or parents—must set good examples. For example, if a ruler was fair, his people would follow his example and treat one another fairly, too. Confucius summarized his ideas about relationships in a simple way. It is similar to what Christians and Jews call the Golden Rule: "Do not do to others what you would not want done to yourself."

Religious Traditions Although Confucianism is a philosophy, it has also functioned as a religion for many people. Like Hindus or Buddhists, those who practice Confucianism are part of a moral community. The teachings of Confucius helped guide many of the ancient Chinese in how to behave. But many ancient Chinese also practiced Confucianism alongside their existing religious traditions.

Ancient China was home to many kinds of religious beliefs and practices: the worship of ancestors, the honoring of gods, and the belief in spirits. Most Chinese believed that life should be lived in harmony with nature. Happiness came from living a balanced life. A religious philosophy known as Taoism (DOW iz um) supported these ideas. Taoism was based on the writings of Laozi (LOW dzuh), a Chinese thinker who lived in the 500s B.C. The Taoists loved nature, and they believed in leading simple and selfless lives.

At times, Taoism would rival Confucianism for popularity in China. But overall, the teachings of Confucius would remain the most widely studied of Chinese philosophies.

A painting of Laozi riding a buffalo, attended by a servant

✓ Reading Check **Describe the religious traditions of ancient China.**

A Chinese emperor oversees students at a civil service exam.

The Influence of Confucius

The teachings of Confucius came to have a major effect on Chinese government. They became part of the basic training for members of the civil service. The **civil service** is the group of people who carry out the work of government.

A Merit System Before the ideas of Confucius took hold, government posts were generally given to the sons of powerful people. Afterward, any man could hold a government post based on merit—that is, on how qualified he was or how well he did his job. Candidates for government jobs had to pass official examinations. These exams were based on the teachings of Confucius.

Rising to High Positions The examination system did not open government jobs to everyone. Candidates still had to know how to read. This rule made it difficult for a poor man to enter the government. But it was not impossible. Many talented but poor young men learned to read and rose to high government positions.

Confucius would have been surprised at the influence he had on China. He did not consider himself particularly wise or good. But he left a lasting mark on Chinese life.

✓ **Reading Check** Why was it difficult for poor men to work in the civil service?

Section 2 Assessment

Key Terms
Review the key terms at the beginning of this section. Use each term in a sentence that explains its meaning.

Target Reading Skill
State the details that support the main idea on page 147.

Comprehension and Critical Thinking
1. (a) Recall How did Confucius become a teacher?
(b) Transfer Information Confucius would teach only those students who wanted to learn. How does his rule apply to your experience as a student?

2. (a) List What were the basic teachings of Confucius?
(b) Explain Why did Confucius think it was important to teach rulers how to behave?
3. (a) Describe How did the ideas of Confucius change the way civil servants were chosen in ancient China?
(b) Predict Confucius hoped to become a government worker, but he became a teacher instead. Do you think his influence on Chinese society would have been different if he had gotten his wish? Explain your answer.

Writing Activity
Suppose that you are a government official in a small state in northern China. One day, a wandering teacher named Confucius arrives. Write a journal entry that describes what Confucius says and how your ruler reacts to him.

For: An activity on Confucius
Visit: PHSchool.com
Web Code: lbd-2502

Warring Kingdoms Unite

Prepare to Read

Objectives

In this section, you will
1. Learn about the rise of the Qin dynasty.
2. Find out how Emperor Shi Huangdi attempted to unify the economy and culture of China.
3. Examine the actions of the Han dynasty's leaders.

Taking Notes

As you read, find details about Chinese rulers and life in China during the Qin and the Han dynasties. Copy the table below, and use it to record your findings.

Qin Dynasty	Han Dynasty
•	•
•	•
•	•

Target Reading Skill

Identify Implied Main Ideas Sometimes main ideas are not stated directly. However, all the details in a section of text add up to a main idea. For example, after reading and adding up all the details on page 152 following the heading The Qin Dynasty, you could state the main idea this way: "China was unified and strengthened by its first emperor, Shi Huangdi."

Carefully read the details in the paragraphs below. Then state the main idea.

Key Terms

- **Shi Huangdi** (shur hwahng DEE) *n.* founder of the Qin dynasty and China's first emperor
- **currency** (KUR un see) *n.* the type of money used by a group or a nation
- **Liu Bang** (LYOH bahng) *n.* the founder of the Han dynasty
- **Wudi** (woo dee) *n.* Chinese emperor who brought the Han dynasty to its greatest strength
- **warlord** (WAWR lawrd) *n.* a local leader of an armed group

In 1974, several farmers were digging a well in a grove of trees in northern China. Six feet down, they found some terra cotta, a reddish type of pottery. Another five feet down, they unearthed the terra-cotta head of a man. Archaeologists took over and began digging. They discovered more than 6,000 life-sized statues of soldiers and horses, along with wood and bronze chariots and metal weapons. It was a terra-cotta army. For more than 2,000 years, these buried soldiers had kept watch at the tomb of China's first emperor, **Shi Huangdi** (shur hwahng DEE).

With his underground army, Shi Huangdi had planned to rule a second empire in the afterlife. He had also made grand plans for the real-life empire he created in China. His dynasty, he boasted, would last for 10,000 generations.

These terra-cotta warriors guarded Shi Huangdi's tomb in the ancient city of Chang'an, China.

The Great Wall of China
The Great Wall winds its way across the mountains and plains of northern China. **Infer** *What does the size of the wall tell you about Shi Huangdi's enemies?*

The Qin Dynasty

Shi Huangdi's dynasty lasted only two generations, but that was still a huge accomplishment. Before that time, China was divided into seven warring kingdoms. Shi Huangdi conquered these kingdoms to unify China.

China's First Emperor Shi Huangdi's original name was Zhao Zheng (jow jeng). He ruled the Qin (chin) people, who lived along China's western border. By 221 B.C., Zheng had extended his rule over most of the land that makes up modern-day China. When Zheng established the Qin dynasty, he took the name Shi Huangdi, meaning "First Emperor." Because Qin is sometimes spelled *Ch'in*, the name China comes from the Qin dynasty.

Strengthening the Empire Shi Huangdi sought to strengthen China through strong and harsh rule. One of his first tasks was to protect the new empire from its enemies.

Throughout history, nomads had attacked China along its vast northern border. Shi Huangdi had a plan to end these border wars. He ordered what became the largest construction project in Chinese history. It is now called the Great Wall of China. Turn to page 154 and locate the wall on the map titled Qin and Han Empires.

Previous rulers had built walls along the border. Shi Huangdi decided to connect them. He ordered farmers from their fields and merchants from their stores to form an army of hundreds of thousands of workers. Shi Huangdi's wall took about ten years to construct. After Shi Huangdi died, the wall fell into disrepair. Over time, other emperors repaired the wall and added new sections to it. Because some sections overlap, the Great Wall is really a system of walls. In all, the Great Wall stretches about 4,500 miles (7,200 kilometers) in length.

Organizing the Government To help put down rebellions within the empire, Shi Huangdi put thousands of farmers to work building roads. The new roads enabled his armies to rush to the scene of any uprisings. The emperor killed or imprisoned any local rulers who opposed him. Shi Huangdi divided all of China into areas called districts. Each district had a government run by the emperor's trusted officials.

✓ **Reading Check** **How was China's Great Wall built?**

Unifying Economy and Culture

Shi Huangdi was not content to unify the government of China. He also wanted the many peoples of his united kingdom to have one economy and one culture.

Economic and Cultural Improvements Shi Huangdi declared that one **currency,** or type of money, be used throughout China. The new currency was a round coin with a square hole in the middle. A common currency made it easier for one region of China to trade goods with another. Shi Huangdi also ordered the creation of common weights and measures, an improved system of writing, and a law code.

Restricting Freedoms Shi Huangdi also tried to control the thoughts of his people. In 213 B.C., he outlawed the ideas of Confucius and other important thinkers. Instead, he required that people learn the philosophies of Qin scholars.

The Qin believed in legalism, the idea that people should be punished for bad behavior and rewarded for good behavior. Legalists thought that the people of China should work to serve the government and the emperor. The Qin dynasty practiced a strict and sometimes brutal form of legalism. Shi Huangdi commanded that all the books in China be burned except those about medicine, technology, and farming. Hundreds of scholars protested the order. Shi Huangdi had them all killed.

The End of a Dynasty Shi Huangdi's death in 210 B.C. was followed by four years of chaos and civil war that ended in the murder of his son. Power then passed to Shi Huangdi's grandson, but he could not hold China together. Rebellions broke out. The dynasty that was supposed to last for 10,000 generations lasted for only 15 years.

✓ Reading Check **How did Shi Huangdi try to limit his people's freedoms?**

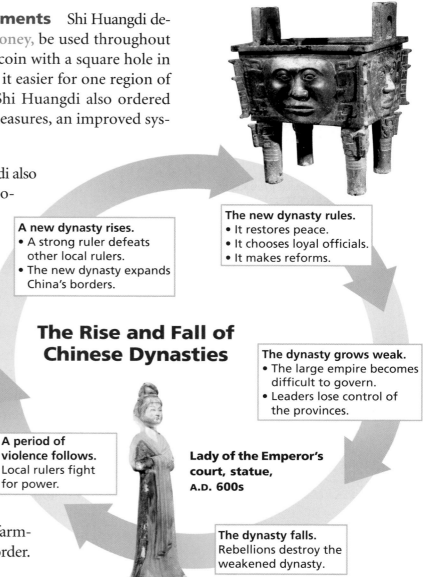

Bronze cooking pot, Shang dynasty

The Rise and Fall of Chinese Dynasties

A new dynasty rises.
• A strong ruler defeats other local rulers.
• The new dynasty expands China's borders.

The new dynasty rules.
• It restores peace.
• It chooses loyal officials.
• It makes reforms.

The dynasty grows weak.
• The large empire becomes difficult to govern.
• Leaders lose control of the provinces.

The dynasty falls.
Rebellions destroy the weakened dynasty.

A period of violence follows.
Local rulers fight for power.

Lady of the Emperor's court, statue, A.D. 600s

Diagram Skills

Although many different dynasties ruled China throughout its long history, each rose and fell in a similar pattern. **Describe** Why do dynasties fall? **Analyze Information** Why might a dynasty become weaker as it grows larger?

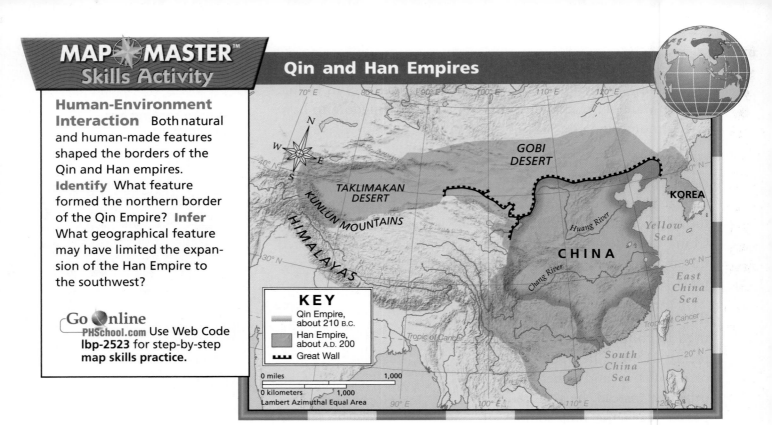

Human-Environment Interaction Both natural and human-made features shaped the borders of the Qin and Han empires. **Identify** What feature formed the northern border of the Qin Empire? **Infer** What geographical feature may have limited the expansion of the Han Empire to the southwest?

Go Online
PHSchool.com Use Web Code **lbp-2523** for step-by-step map skills practice.

KEY

Qin Empire, about 210 B.C.

Han Empire, about A.D. 200

Great Wall

0 miles 1,000
0 kilometers 1,000
Lambert Azimuthal Equal Area

The Han Dynasty

One of the rebels who helped overthrow the Qin dynasty was a talented ruler named Liu Bang (LYOH bahng). By 202 B.C., **Liu Bang** won out over his rivals and became emperor of China. Born a peasant, Liu Bang became the first emperor of a new dynasty: the Han (hahn). Liu Bang created a stable government, but one that was was less harsh than Shi Huangdi's.

Stable governments were a feature of the Han dynasty, which lasted for about 400 years. Han rulers realized that they needed educated people to work in the government. They set up the civil service system based on Confucianism to meet that need.

Wudi: The Warrior Emperor In 140 B.C., Liu Bang's great-grandson, Wudi, came to power. Under **Wudi** (woo dee), the Han dynasty reached its greatest power. About 15 years old when he took the throne, Wudi ruled for more than 50 years.

Wudi's main interests were war and military matters. In fact, his name means "Warrior Emperor." He made improvements to Shi Huangdi's Great Wall. He also strengthened the army. By the end of Wudi's reign, Chinese rule stretched west into Central Asia, east into present-day northern and central Korea, and south into present-day Vietnam. Locate the Han Empire on the map titled Qin and Han Empires.

Links to Art

Han Dynasty Bronze Work
Han dynasty artisans created beautiful objects of bronze, including finely made mirrors. On one side of the mirror, the metal was polished enough to show a reflection. The back was decorated with gems, animal symbols, and writing. Mirrors were important in China because they symbolized self-knowledge. At the right is the decorated side of a bronze mirror.

The End of the Han Empire The great emperor Wudi died in 87 B.C. China's stability and prosperity continued under later Han emperors. Many new ideas and technologies developed. But over time, the empire began to weaken. A series of very young emperors—one was only 100 days old—ruled the empire. People within the government struggled for power over these young emperors. While they struggled, no one paid attention to running the empire. Roads and canals fell into disrepair.

As the rule of the emperors weakened, **warlords,** local leaders of armed groups, gained power. The last Han emperor was kept in power by one such warlord, named Cao Pei. At first Cao Pei tried to control the empire through the emperor. In A.D. 220, he declared an end to the Han dynasty. In its place, he set up his own Wei dynasty. However, the Wei dynasty had control only over parts of northern China. It ended after about 50 years, and China broke up into a number of smaller kingdoms.

✓ **Reading Check** What happened in A.D. 220?

Target Skill **Identify Implied Main Ideas** In one sentence, state what all the details in the paragraph at the left imply.

This bronze statue of a man on horseback dates from the Han dynasty.

Section 3 Assessment

Key Terms
Review the key terms at the beginning of this section. Use each term in a sentence that explains its meaning.

Target Reading Skill
State the three main ideas in Section 3.

Comprehension and Critical Thinking
1. (a) Describe What measures did Shi Huangdi take to strengthen the empire and organize the government?
(b) Summarize Why is Shi Huangdi a major figure in Chinese history?

2. (a) Identify What measures did Shi Huangdi take to unite the economy and culture of China?
(b) Analyze Information How did all of Shi Huangdi's efforts strengthen the empire? How did his leadership hurt the empire?
3. (a) Recall What characterized the government of China during the Han dynasty?
(b) Compare and Contrast Compare the ways the emperors of the Qin dynasty and the emperors of the Han dynasty viewed the ideas of Confucius. How were their viewpoints similar or different?

Writing Activity
The farmers who discovered Shi Huangdi's terra-cotta army made one of the most important archaeological finds in history. Write a list of questions that you would like to ask them about their discovery.

Writing Tip Write your questions in a logical order. For instance, you could begin with a few general questions. Later, narrow your focus with more specific questions.

China's Western Frontier

Swooping down from the Mongolian plain, the legendary Xiongnu (shong noo) warriors came not to conquer, but to steal. They came on horseback, wild, dust-covered, and fierce. In attacks that terrorized Chinese border towns, the Xiongnu stole Chinese silks and other luxuries, galloping off with all they could carry. The great Han warrior emperor, Wudi, devoted his long half-century reign (140–87 B.C.) to taming China's frontier and exploring civilizations beyond the known world of his time.

The Expeditions Emperor Wudi chose Zhang Qian (jahng chyen) to lead a dangerous expedition to the western frontier. Zhang, an officer in Wudi's imperial guard, led the caravan (shown at the right) from the Han capital of Chang'an in 138 B.C. His mission was to befriend the Yuezhi (yooeh jur), enemies of the Xiongnu, and to rally them to war. Thirteen years later, Zhang returned—to tell Wudi not of war, but of unimagined wealth to be gained in trade with western societies. So Wudi sent him west again, in 119 B.C., to open government and economic ties with other lands.

During his travels, Zhang learned of swift horses owned by the people of the Fergana Valley. Wudi's forces later captured some of the Fergana horses (depicted in the bronze statue at the top of this page). Wudi's warriors ultimately drove the Xiongnu far from China's borders and opened a gateway to the west.

Han Bowl and Spoon
Everyday goods, such as this Han dynasty pottery, would have been useful on the expedition.

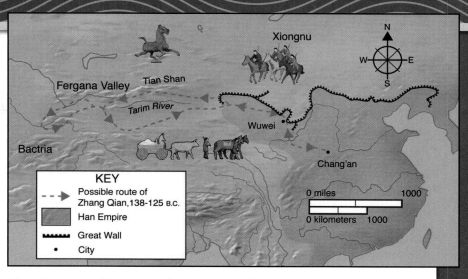

KEY
- - -→ Possible route of Zhang Qian,138-125 B.C.

▨ Han Empire

▰▰▰ Great Wall

• City

The First Expedition On their journey, Zhang and his men were captured by the Xiongnu. After ten years, they escaped. By the time Zhang met the Yuezhi, they were settled peacefully and had no appetite for war. Zhang continued west to gold-rich Bactria before heading home.

Assessment

Explain Why did Emperor Wudi send expeditions to China's western frontier?

Identify Effects How did these expeditions benefit China?

Achievements of Ancient China

Prepare to Read

Objectives

In this section you will
1. Learn about the Silk Road.
2. Find out about the Han dynasty's respect for tradition and learning.
3. Discover the important advances in technology that were made in China during the Han dynasty.

Taking Notes

As you read, create an outline of this section. Copy the outline below and use it to get started.

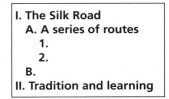

I. The Silk Road
   A. A series of routes
      1.
      2.
   B.
II. Tradition and learning

Target Reading Skill

Identify Supporting Details Details in a section of text may explain the main idea or give examples that support it. The main idea for the text on page 159 under the red heading The Silk Road, can be stated this way: "Both ideas and goods were exchanged along the Silk Road, a series of routes that connected the East to the West."

As you read, note the details following each of the blue headings that support the main idea.

Key Terms

- **Silk Road** (silk rohd) *n.* an ancient trade route between China and Europe
- **silk** (silk) *n.* a valuable cloth, originally made only in China from threads spun by caterpillars called silkworms
- **Sima Qian** (sih MAH chen) *n.* (c. 145–85 B.C.) a Chinese scholar, astronomer, and historian; author of the most important history of ancient China, *Historical Records*

The caravan slowly plods across the hot sand of the Taklimakan Desert. Weary travelers wearing long robes sway on top of camels. Riderless camels are heaped high with heavy loads.

Suddenly the camels stop, huddle together, and snarl viciously. An old man riding the lead camel turns around and shouts. No one can hear him because the screaming wind drowns out his words. The man jumps from his camel and quickly wraps a strip of felt around his own nose and mouth. The other travelers rush to dismount and cover their faces, too. Just then, the sandstorm hits with full force. The fine desert sand flies at the caravan, stinging man and beast with needle-sharp grit.

Then, as quickly as it came, the sandstorm is gone. The travelers wipe sand from their eyes and tend to their camels. They have survived just one of the many challenges of traveling on the **Silk Road,** an ancient trade route between China and Europe.

A camel caravan in Gansu Province, western China

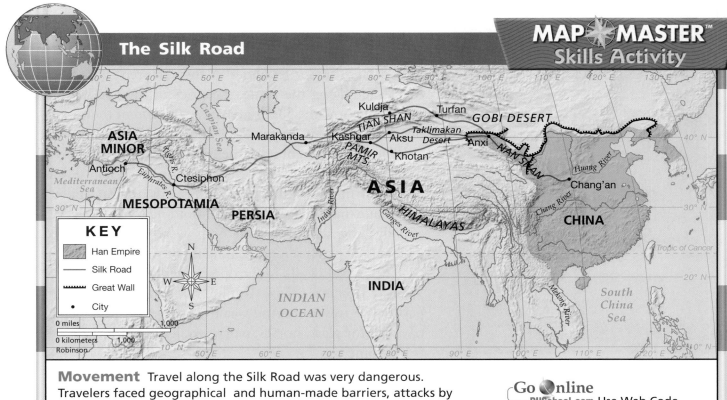

KEY
Han Empire
Silk Road
Great Wall
• City

0 miles 1,000
0 kilometers 1,000
Robinson

Movement Travel along the Silk Road was very dangerous. Travelers faced geographical and human-made barriers, attacks by robbers, and extreme weather conditions. **Note** Why did the Silk Road split into two routes in Central Asia? **Analyze Information** Judging from the map, what might have been the most difficult part of the route?

Go Online
PHSchool.com Use Web Code **lbp-2534** for step-by-step map skills practice.

The Silk Road

The Emperor Wudi's conquests in the west brought the Chinese into contact with the people of Central Asia. Trade with these people introduced the Chinese to such new foods as grapes, walnuts, and garlic. In turn, Chinese goods and ideas passed to the peoples living to the West. This exchange of goods gave rise to a major trade route—the Silk Road. This ran all the way from China to the Mediterranean Sea.

Connecting Roads The Silk Road was a series of routes covering more than 4,000 miles (6,400 kilometers), a little less than the distance from present-day Chicago to Hawaii. Follow the routes on the map above titled The Silk Road.

The Silk Road followed a challenging route through mountainous country and desert land. The road passed through Persia and Mesopotamia. Finally, it turned north to the city of Antioch (AN tee ahk), in present-day Turkey. From there, traders shipped goods across the Mediterranean to Rome, Greece, Egypt, and other lands that bordered the Mediterranean.

A terra-cotta statue of a traveler on a camel, about A.D. 700

Making Silk
A scroll from the 1100s shows Chinese women beating silk fibers in a trough. Silk was used to make musical instruments, fishing line, and even paper. **Infer** *Why was the Silk Road named after this material?*

Identify Supporting Details

What details in the last paragraph on this page tell about tradition and learning during the Han dynasty?

A Route for Goods Few travelers ever journeyed the entire length of the Silk Road. Generally, goods were passed from trader to trader as they crossed Asia. With each trade along the route, the price of the goods went up. By the time the goods arrived at the end of their journey, they were very expensive.

The Silk Road got its name from **silk,** a valuable cloth originally made only in China. Han farmers had developed new methods for raising silkworms, the caterpillars that made the silk. Han workers found new ways to weave and dye the silk. These methods were closely guarded secrets. The penalty for revealing them was death.

The arrival of silk in Europe created great excitement. Wealthy Romans prized Chinese silk and were willing to pay high prices for it. And wealthy people in China would pay well for glass, horses, ivory, woolens, and linen cloth from Rome.

A Route for Ideas More than goods traveled the road. New ideas did, too. For example, missionaries from India traveled to China along a section of the road and brought the religion of Buddhism with them. By the time the Han dynasty ended, Buddhism was becoming a major religion in China.

✓ Reading Check **What are silkworms?**

Tradition and Learning

Traditional Chinese ideas flourished during the Han dynasty. People returned to the teachings of Confucius. A renewed interest in learning led one Han scholar to record the early history of China. His efforts helped the people of China understand their past.

Respect for Learning Han rulers found that during troubled times in the past, many people had lost respect for their traditions. As a way of bringing back this respect, rulers encouraged people to return to the teachings of Confucius. Rulers of the Han and later dynasties also required members of the civil service to be educated in Confucian teachings.

The arts and scholarship flourished under the Han dynasty. Expressive poetry reflected Chinese culture. Chinese scholars put together the first dictionary of the Chinese language. But the greatest advances happened in the field of history.

A History of China   Until the time of the Han dynasty, the Chinese people had little knowledge of their own history. They knew only myths that had been passed down from generation to generation. Often, these stories were in conflict with one another. No one was sure exactly when the various Chinese rulers had lived or what each had accomplished.

The scholar Sima Qian (sih MAH chen) decided to solve the problem. **Sima Qian** spent his life writing a history of China from mythical times to the reign of Wudi. Sima described his work:

> **❝I wish to examine all that encircles heaven and man. I want to probe the changes of the past and present.❞**
>
> —Sima Qian

Sima Qian's work, called *Historical Records,* is a major source of information about ancient China.

✓ **Reading Check**   **What problem did Sima Qian solve?**

Han Technology

Because the Han government was stable, the Chinese could turn their attention to improving their society. During the Han dynasty, China became the most advanced civilization in the world.

Advances in Technology   The Chinese made significant advances in farming tools and other technologies. Some of these advances are shown in the chart at the right, titled Achievements in Ancient China. During the Han dynasty, the Chinese invented many practical devices that did not reach Europe until centuries later. Among these was paper—something the world still depends on every day.

Achievements in Ancient China

The Arts
- Silk weaving
- Bronze working
- Architecture (temples and palaces)
- Poetry and history
- ▶ Jade carving

Medicine
- ◀ Acupuncture—the treatment of disease using needles
- Herbal remedies—the use of plants in the practice of medicine
- Circulatory system—the discovery that blood travels through the body

Technology
- Paper made from wood pulp
- Iron plow for breaking up soil
- Rudder—a device used to steer ships
- Seismoscope—a device that registers the occurrence of earthquakes
- Compass
- ▼ Wheelbarrow

Arts, Medicine, and Technology
The Chinese made great advances during the Han dynasty. **Analyze** *Which two inventions were especially useful to farmers? Explain your answer.*

The Invention of Paper The Chinese first used wooden scrolls and bones to keep records. Later, they wrote messages and even whole books on silk. Then, around A.D. 105, the Chinese recorded one of their greatest achievements: the invention of paper. Archaeological evidence shows that paper may have already been in use before that time. Early paper was made from materials such as tree bark, hemp, and old rags. The materials were soaked in water, beaten into pulp, and dried flat on a screen mold.

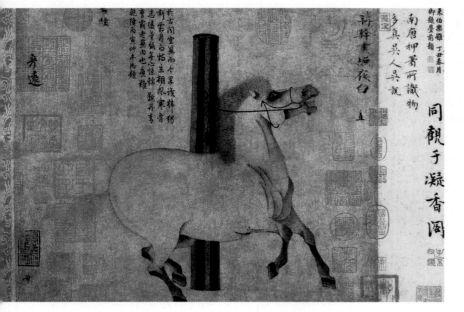

A Chinese emperor's favorite horse, named Night-Shining White, is shown in this painting from the A.D. 700s.

The availability of paper greatly influenced learning and the arts in China. After several centuries, the use of paper spread across Asia and into Europe. Eventually, paper replaced papyrus from Egypt as the material for scrolls and books.

The Han dynasty came to an end in the A.D. 200s. But its accomplishments were not forgotten. Today, people in China still call themselves "the children of Han."

✓ Reading Check **What did the Chinese write on before they invented paper?**

Section 4 Assessment

Key Terms
Review the key terms at the beginning of this section. Use each term in a sentence that explains its meaning.

Target Reading Skill
State the details that support the main idea on page 158.

Comprehension and Critical Thinking
1. (a) Locate Describe the route of the Silk Road.
(b) Infer Why were the secrets of silk-making so closely guarded?

2. (a) List In what ways did the Han dynasty show a respect for Chinese traditions?
(b) Draw Conclusions Describe the importance of Sima Qian's role in preserving Chinese traditions.
3. (a) Recall Name three important inventions or achievements during the Han dynasty.
(b) Predict How did the achievements of the Han dynasty affect later generations of Chinese people, as well as other peoples?

Writing Activity
Suppose that you are a poet living in ancient Chang'an, at one end of the Silk Road. Write a poem about what you have seen or heard about the Silk Road from living in Chang'an.

Go Online
PHSchool.com

For: An activity on ancient Chinese technology
Visit: PHSchool.com
Web Code: lbd-2504

5 Review and Assessment

◆ Chapter Summary

Terra-cotta warriors

Section 1: The Geography of China's River Valleys

- Flooding rivers, monsoon rains, and mountain and ocean barriers greatly affected China's early peoples.
- China's first known civilization, the Shang dynasty, arose in the Huang Valley.
- The family, headed by the eldest man, was at the heart of early Chinese society.

Section 2: Confucius and His Teachings

- Confucius was a poor noble from the North China Plain who became a professional teacher.
- Confucius believed that a peaceful, orderly society was possible only when rulers treated others justly.
- Confucianism reformed Chinese government by requiring that civil service workers be hired based on merit.

Confucius

Section 3: Warring Kingdoms Unite

- Several warring states became one China under Shi Huangdi of the Qin dynasty.
- China's first emperor built the Great Wall to protect the empire. He also organized local governments by dividing China into districts.
- Under the Qin dynasty, some attempts to unify China's economy and culture benefited the people, while others caused unrest.
- China's second ruling dynasty, the Han, remained in power for about 400 years. China then broke into smaller kingdoms.

Section 4: Achievements of Ancient China

- The Silk Road opened China to trade with lands to the west.
- The Han dynasty embraced the ideas of Confucius.
- The Chinese made many advances in learning and technology under the Han dynasty.

◆ Key Terms

Match each definition in Column I with the correct key term in Column II.

Column I

1. a kind of money
2. a fine yellow soil
3. a protective wall built along a river to hold back the waters
4. several generations of closely related people
5. a system of beliefs and values
6. a valuable cloth first made in China
7. a group of people who carry out the government's work
8. a local leader of armed groups

Column II

A extended family

B dike

C civil service

D loess

E currency

F philosophy

G warlord

H silk

◆ Comprehension and Critical Thinking

9. (a) **Recall** Describe the geographic setting of China's first known civilization.
(b) **Infer** Why did the early Chinese have so little contact with other ancient civilizations?
(c) **Compare and Contrast** Think about the other ancient civilizations you have read about. How were the earliest Chinese civilizations similar? How were they different?

10. (a) **Describe** According to Confucius, how should rulers and other people in authority behave?
(b) **Explain** Why did Confucius think his ideas were necessary and important?
(c) **Analyze Information** Some Chinese people thought the ideas of Confucius were dangerous. Who felt most threatened by his ideas? Explain why. How do we know that others found his ideas useful?

11. (a) **Name** Identify three actions the emperor Shi Huangdi took to unite China.
(b) **Draw Conclusions** Why is the rule of Shi Huangdi judged as harsh?
(c) **Identify Causes** How did the harsh rule of Shi Huangdi help bring about Liu Bang's rise to power?

12. (a) **Describe** What characterized the rule of the Han dynasty?

(b) **Make Generalizations** Why is the Han dynasty considered to be an important part of Chinese history?
(c) **Make Inferences** Why do people in China today call themselves "the children of Han"?

13. (a) **Identify** What was the route of the Silk Road?
(b) **Explain** How was the Silk Road used?
(c) **Apply Information** What was the importance of the Silk Road to other civilizations?

◆ Writing Activity: Language Arts

Reread the story about Confucius and the grieving woman on page 146. Many legends about Confucius were written by scholars long after his death. Use what you know about Confucius and China to write a similar brief story. Use his ideas about family or government to write the moral, or lesson, of the story.

◆ Skills Practice

Making Valid Generalizations Review the steps you followed to learn this skill. Then reread Traditional Families on page 142. Using the skills you learned, make a generalization about traditional families in ancient China. Use the steps you have learned to make sure your generalization is valid.

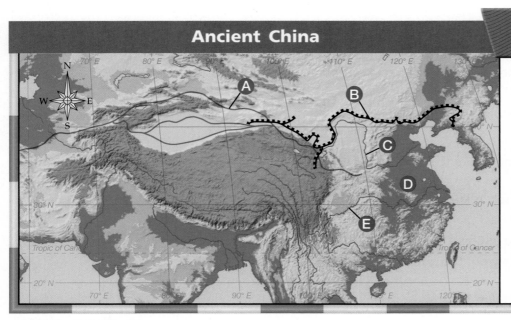

Ancient China

MAP MASTER™
Skills Activity

Place Location For each place listed below, write the letter from the map that shows its location.

1. Huang River
2. Chang River
3. North China Plain
4. Great Wall of China
5. Silk Road

Go Online
PHSchool.com Use Web Code **lbp-2544** for an **interactive map.**

Standardized Test Prep

Test-Taking Tips

Some questions on standardized tests ask you to analyze a graphic organizer. Study the concept web below. Then follow the tips to answer the sample question.

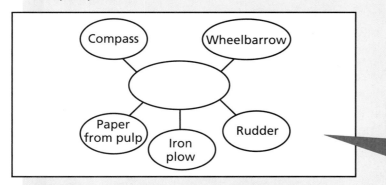

Choose the letter that best answers the question.

Which title should go in the center of the web?

A Gunpowder

B Inventions of Ancient Japan

C Inventions of Ancient China

D Technology

Think It Through The question asks for a title that describes all of the information in the smaller ovals. You can rule out A, because it does not describe all of the outer ovals. D could be a title, but it is not the *best* answer. To evaluate answers B and C, use your knowledge of history. Do you know where any of the items were first invented? If you recognize the origin of even one item shown in the web, then you know that the correct answer is C.

TIP When you study a chart or concept web, pay attention to the kind of information that goes in each part of it.

TIP Use what you already know about history, geography, government, and culture to help you answer the question.

Practice Questions

Use the tips above and other tips in this book to help you answer the following questions.

1. The Chinese called the Huang River China's Sorrow because

   A it was hard to navigate.

   B it flooded and destroyed property.

   C foreigners used it to invade China.

   D it carried no loess to use in farming.

2. What was the main goal of Confucianism?

   A to create original ideas

   B to produce written texts of philosophy

   C to bring order to society

   D to reward important people in society

3. Paper, the wheelbarrow, and iron farming tools were all invented during which dynasty?

   A the Qin   C the Shang

   B the Zheng   D the Han

Study the chart below and then answer the question that follows.

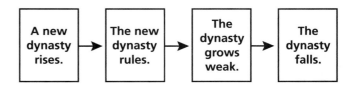

4. "Rulers lose control of the provinces" belongs under which of the headings above?

   A A new dynasty rises.

   B The new dynasty rules.

   C The dynasty grows weak.

   D The dynasty falls.

Use Web Code lba-2504 for **Chapter 5 self-test.**

Chapter

6
Ancient Greece

Chapter Preview

This chapter will introduce you to the history of ancient Greece.

Target Reading Skill

Word Analysis In this chapter you will focus on using word parts and recognizing word origins to determine the meaning of unfamiliar words in the text.

▶ The ruins of the Temple of Poseidon in Greece

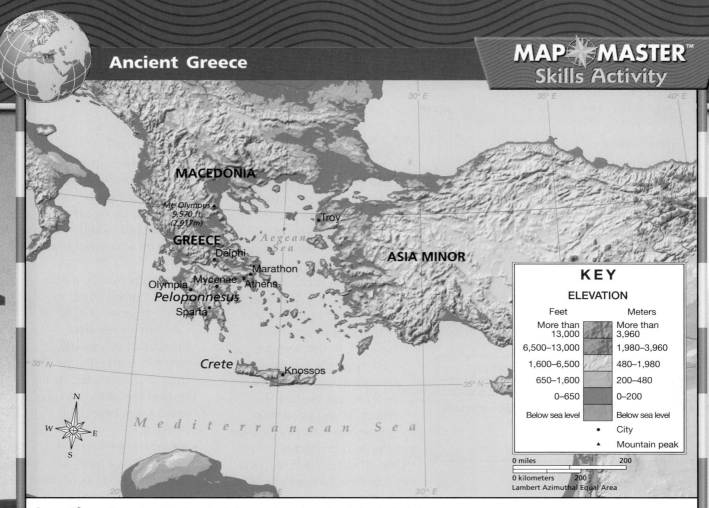

MACEDONIA

Mt. Olympus ▲
9,570 ft
(2,917m)

Troy

GREECE

Delphi

Aegean
Sea

ASIA MINOR

Marathon
Olympia Mycenae Athens
Peloponnesus
Sparta

Crete Knossos

35° N   35° N

N
W   E
S

M e d i t e r r a n e a n   S e a

KEY

ELEVATION

Feet		Meters
More than 13,000		More than 3,960
6,500–13,000		1,980–3,960
1,600–6,500		480–1,980
650–1,600		200–480
0–650		0–200
Below sea level		Below sea level
	•	City
	▲	Mountain peak

0 miles   200
0 kilometers   200
Lambert Azimuthal Equal Area

Location Examine the land of the ancient Greeks: it included the mainland and many islands in the Aegean and Mediterranean seas. The ancient Greeks also built colonies on the coast of Asia Minor, a region within present-day Turkey. **Identify** Name the major cities in ancient Greece. **Draw Conclusions** Study the map to make some guesses about how the people of ancient Greece earned their living. What role do you think the sea had in their lives? Why do you think some Greeks left ancient Greece to build cities elsewhere?

Go Online
PHSchool.com Use Web Code
lbp-2611 for step-by-step
map skills practice.

Early Greek Civilization

Prepare to Read

Objectives

In this section you will
1. Find out about the geography of Greece.
2. Learn about the rise of civilization in ancient Greece.
3. Study the beginnings of government in ancient Greece.

Taking Notes

As you read, find the details about early Greek civilization. Copy the chart below, and use it to record your findings.

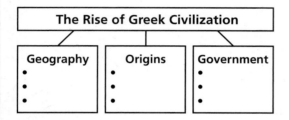

The Rise of Greek Civilization

Geography	Origins	Government
•	•	•
•	•	•
•	•	•

Target Reading Skill

Use Word Parts When you come across an unfamiliar word, break the word into parts to help you recognize and pronounce it. You may find roots, prefixes, or suffixes. A root is the base of a word. A suffix attaches to the end of a root and changes the word's part of speech. In this section, you will read the word *fortification*. The suffix *-ion* makes the word a noun. If you know the meaning of *fortify*, you can figure out what a fortification is. Break the word into a root and a suffix to learn its meaning.

Key Terms

- **peninsula** (puh NIN suh luh) *n.* an area of land almost completely surrounded by water and connected to the mainland by a narrow strip of land
- **acropolis** (uh KRAH puh lis) *n.* the fortified, or strengthened, hill of an ancient Greek city
- **aristocrat** (uh RIS tuh krat) *n.* a member of a rich and powerful family
- **tyrant** (TY runt) *n.* a ruler who takes power by force
- **democracy** (dih MAHK ruh see) *n.* a form of government in which citizens govern themselves

Following their defeat of the Titans, Zeus and his brothers and sisters battled the giants. The gods Apollo and Artemis, above left, confront a group of helmeted giants.

First there was nothing. Then came Mother Earth. The gods of Night and Day appeared next, and then starry Sky. Earth and Sky created the Twelve Titans (TYT unz). These great gods rebelled against their father Sky and took away his power. The youngest of the Titans, Cronos, ruled in his father's place. In time, Cronos had six children. The youngest, mighty Zeus (zoos), toppled Cronos from his throne.

With such stories, the people of ancient Greece described the struggles of their gods. Like their gods, the people of Greece had to struggle for power and independence. Their struggles began with the land itself.

The Geography of Greece

The land of Greece looks as if the sea had smashed it to pieces. Some pieces have drifted away to form small, rocky islands. Others seem to barely cling to the mainland. Greece is a peninsula made up of smaller peninsulas and islands. A **peninsula** is an area of land almost completely surrounded by water and connected to the mainland by a narrow strip of land. Look at the map on page 167 titled Ancient Greece. As you can see, no part of Greece is very far from the sea.

The Mountains of Greece Mountains are the major landform of Greece. Greece's islands are mostly mountain peaks. Mountains crisscross the mainland, leaving only small patches of farmland. Only about one fifth of Greece is good for growing crops. It is no wonder the Greeks became traders and sailors. At times, they left Greece to found colonies far away.

Geography and Ancient Communities The ancient Greeks were in a way all islanders. Some lived on real islands, completely surrounded by water, or on small peninsulas. Others lived on what could be thought of as land islands. Instead of water, mountains separated the people in these small communities from one another.

Because it was difficult for Greeks from different communities to meet, each community developed its own customs and beliefs. Each was more than ready to go to war to protect itself. In fact, for most of their history, the Greeks were so busy fighting among themselves that it was easy to forget that they shared a common heritage, spoke the same language, and worshiped the same gods.

✓ Reading Check **Explain why someone might say the ancient Greeks were all islanders.**

Greece's Coastline
This view of the port of Parga shows the rocky islands and mountains that are common in Greece. **Infer** *Why did many ancient Greeks become traders and sailors?*

The Rise of Greek Civilization

Early Greek civilization arose both on and off the Greek mainland. Two ancient peoples, the Minoans (mih NOH unz) and the Mycenaeans (my suh NEE unz), made important contributions to Greek civilization.

Minoan Civilization From about 3000 to about 1100 B.C., Bronze Age people called the Minoans lived on the island of Crete. Surrounded by the waters of the Aegean (ee JEE un) and Mediterranean seas, Crete was an ideal place for the Minoans to develop a broad sea-trade network. Mainland Greece and other Greek islands, Egypt, and Sicily all traded with the Minoans, who at one time dominated the Aegean.

The Minoans developed an advanced culture. Samples of Minoan writing have been found on thousands of clay tablets. Palace ruins in the ancient city of Knossos (NAHS us) on Crete hint at rooms once covered with fanciful wall paintings. Statues found within suggest that the Minoans worshiped mainly goddesses. In the middle of the 1400s B.C., Knossos was destroyed, and Minoan civilization declined. People from mainland Greece, the Mycenaeans, were the likely invaders.

The Mycenaeans After the Mycenaeans came to power, mainland and island cultures blended. However, the focus of these cultures moved to the mainland, where Mycenae was located.

Ancient Cultures
The fresco from the 1500s B.C., shown below, illustrates Minoan naval combat. A Mycenaean princess appears in the inset photo. **Conclude** *How do we know that both the Minoans and the Mycenaeans developed advanced cultures?*

At the height of their power, around 1400 B.C., the Mycenaeans controlled the Aegean Sea and parts of the Mediterranean. Like the Minoans, the Mycenaeans also used writing. Studies of the Mycenaeans' script show that they spoke an early form of Greek.

The Minoans had gained much of their power through trade. Although the Mycenaeans traded widely, they relied upon conquest to spread their power. Greek myth tells the story of the Trojan War, a long struggle between Greece and the city of Troy on the west coast of Asia Minor, in present-day Turkey. There was an actual struggle over trade in the region, though the details of the legend were invented.

The Trojan War According to the myth, Greece conquered Troy by using a trick—the Trojan Horse. Greek warriors hid inside a huge wooden horse. The horse was rolled to the city gates. Thinking it was a gift, the Trojans brought the horse into their city. During the night, the Greek soldiers climbed out of the horse and let the rest of their army into Troy. The Greeks burned and looted Troy and then returned home.

Two epics, or long storytelling poems, about the Trojan War survive today. They are the *Iliad* and the *Odyssey*. These epics may have been composed by many people, but they are credited to one poet called Homer. The poems were important to the Greeks. They taught the Greeks what their gods were like and how the noblest, or best, of their heroes behaved. Today, people think these poems came from stories memorized by several poets and passed down by word of mouth through many generations. Homer may have been the last and greatest in this line of poets.

The Dark Ages of Greece Not long after the Trojan War ended, civilization in Greece collapsed. No one knows exactly why. Life went on, but poverty was everywhere. People no longer traded beyond Greece for food and other goods. They had to depend on what they could raise or make themselves. Some were forced to move to islands or to the western part of Asia Minor. They were so concerned with survival that they even forgot the practice of writing.

These years, from the early 1100s B.C. to about 750 B.C., have been called Greece's Dark Ages. Without writing, people had to depend on word of mouth to keep their traditions and history alive. Old traditions were remembered only in the myths that were told and retold.

Links to

Science

Troy Discovered Over the years, people came to believe that Troy and the Trojan War were fictional. An amateur archaeologist, Heinrich Schliemann, disagreed. In the late 1800s, he used clues in the *Iliad* to pinpoint the location of Troy in Turkey. When he and later archaeologists dug there, they found nine layers of ruins from ancient cities, as shown below. One was possibly the Troy of the *Iliad* and the *Odyssey*.

Greece's Dark Ages were not completely bleak, however. During that time, families gradually resettled in places where they could grow crops and raise animals. Some of these family farms may have developed into villages. When families chose where to build their farms, they favored places near rocky, protected hills. There they built fortifications and other structures to protect themselves from attack. The name for the fortified hill of an ancient Greek city is **acropolis,** meaning "upper city."

Target Skill
Roots and Suffixes
If *fortify* means "strengthen," what is a fortification?

✓ **Reading Check** What happened during Greece's Dark Ages?

Governing Ancient Greece

Historians believe that sometime around 750 B.C., villages throughout Greece began joining to form cities. Each city formed near an acropolis. As these cities developed, they became city-states. Hundreds of Greek city-states formed, each one more or less independent.

The Rule of the Aristocrats The earliest rulers of city-states were probably chieftains or kings who were military leaders. By the end of Greece's Dark Ages, most city-states were ruled by **aristocrats,** members of rich and powerful families. Aristocrats controlled most of the good land. They owned horses, chariots, and the best weapons, which made them stronger than others.

A New Type of Ruler As the Greeks sailed to foreign ports, trading olive oil, marble, and other products, the city-states became richer. A middle class of merchants and artisans developed. They, too, wanted a say in the government of their cities. These people could not afford to equip themselves with horses and chariots for war. However, they could afford armor, swords, and spears. With these weapons, large groups of soldiers could fight effectively on foot. Gradually, military strength in the cities shifted from the aristocrats to the merchants and artisans.

As a result of these changes, aristocratic governments were often overthrown and replaced by rulers called tyrants. A **tyrant** was a ruler who took power by force. Tyrants were usually supported by the middle and working classes. Today, we think of tyrants as being cruel and violent. That was true of some Greek tyrants, but others ruled wisely and well.

The Aristocrats
Some wealthy ancient Greeks owned chariots such as the one shown on this vessel from about 700 B.C.
Analyze *How did the aristocrats use their wealth to gain power?*

Democracy: Rule by the People Eventually, the people of many city-states overthrew tyrants who were too harsh. Some of the cities adopted a form of government that would have a lasting effect around the world for years to come. It was called **democracy,** a form of government in which citizens govern themselves. The city-state in which democracy was most fully developed was Athens.

In the 500s B.C., a leader named Solon reformed Athen's laws. One law canceled all debts, or money owed to other people, and freed citizens who had been enslaved for having debts. Another law allowed any male citizen of Athens aged 18 or older to debate important laws. These laws and others made Athens the leading democracy of the ancient world.

Citizens of Athens might be rich or poor. However, not everyone living in ancient Athens benefited from democracy. Only about one in five Athenians was a citizen.

In Athens, only men could be citizens. A citizen had to have two parents who came from families with citizenship. Some of the people living in Athens were enslaved. These people could not take part in democracy, nor could women or men with noncitizen parents. But the men who were citizens of Athens were free and self-governing.

✓ Reading Check **Who could be granted citizenship in ancient Athens?**

Tools of Democracy
Athenians used a machine to help select juries. A colored ball (top) dropped into a kleroterion, or allotment machine (bottom), would fall at random next to the slots containing names of potential jurors. In the middle is a voting tablet used in ancient Athens. **Infer** *How do you think voting helped strengthen Athenian democracy?*

Section 1 Assessment

Key Terms
Review the key terms at the beginning of this section. Use each term in a sentence that explains its meaning.

Target Reading Skill
Find the word *location* on page 171 in the Links to Science column. If *locate* means "find," what does *location* mean?

Comprehension and Critical Thinking
1. (a) Recall Describe the geographic setting and major landforms of ancient Greece.

(b) Predict What effect do you think the geography of Greece had on the kind of communities that developed there?

2. (a) Recall Describe two important early Greek civilizations.

(b) Make Generalizations Why were poems and myths important to the ancient Greeks?

3. (a) Identify What were the three kinds of governments that developed in the Greek city-states after Greece's Dark Ages?

(b) Cause and Effect How did the rise of the middle class help the government of ancient Greece become more democratic?

Writing Activity
Write a description of the conditions in Greece during the period between the 1100s B.C. and the 700s B.C. Why are these years referred to as Greece's Dark Ages?

For: An activity on the Trojan War
Visit: PHSchool.com
Web Code: lbd-2601

Section 2

Religion, Philosophy, and the Arts

Prepare to Read

Objectives

In this section you will

1. Discover what characterized the Golden Age of Athens.
2. Learn about the religious beliefs of the ancient Greeks.
3. Find out about science, philosophy, and the arts in ancient Greece.

Taking Notes

As you read, look for important details about the religion, philosophy, and art of the ancient Greeks. Copy the outline below, and use it to record your findings.

> I. The Golden Age of Athens
>   A. Period from 479 to 431 B.C.
>   1.
>   2.
>   B. Sources of wealth
> II. Ancient Greek religious beliefs

Target Reading Skill

Use Word Parts When you see an unfamiliar word, break the word into parts to help you recognize and pronounce it. You may find roots, prefixes, or suffixes. A prefix goes before the root and changes the meaning of the word. In this section, you will come across the word *immortal*. Break it into a prefix and a root to learn its meaning.

Key Terms

- **tribute** (TRIB yoot) *n.* a regular payment made to a powerful state or nation by a weaker one
- **oracle** (AWR uh kul) *n.* in ancient Greece, a sacred site where a god or goddess was consulted; any priest or priestess who spoke for the gods
- **philosopher** (fih LAHS uh fur) *n.* someone who uses reason to understand the world; in Greece, the earliest philosophers used reason to explain natural events
- **tragedy** (TRAJ uh dee) *n.* a type of serious drama that usually ends in disaster for the main character

Pericles lived from about 495 to 429 B.C.

As leader of Athens, Pericles (PEHR uh kleez) gave a speech at a funeral of fallen soldiers. In his speech, he said of Athens,

> **"Our constitution favors the many instead of the few. That is why it is called a democracy. If we look at the laws, we see they give equal justice to all. . . . Poverty does not bar the way, if a man is able to serve the state. . . . In short, I say that as a city we are the school for all Greece."**
>
> —The History of the Peloponnesian War
> *Thucydides*

Pericles delivered his speech during the first year of a war with Sparta, another Greek city-state. Eventually, it was Sparta that ended Athens' golden age of accomplishment.

The Golden Age of Athens

The Golden Age of Athens lasted from 479 to 431 B.C. During this period, philosophy and the arts flourished in Athens, and democracy reached its highest point. The democratic government of Athens would serve as a model for future civilizations.

The Wealth of Athens During the Golden Age, Athens grew rich from trade and from silver mined by slaves in regions around the city. Athens also collected **tribute,** or a regular payment made to a powerful state or nation by a weaker one. Both Athens' allies and the states it had conquered paid tribute, fearing Athens' great strength. The tribute paid to Athens added to its wealth.

Pericles and Democracy For about 30 years during Athens' Golden Age, Pericles (c. 495–429 B.C.) was the most powerful man in Athenian politics. Well-educated and intelligent, he always tried to act in the best interests of his city. When he made speeches to the Athenians, he could move and persuade them.

Pericles was a member of an aristocratic family, but he supported democracy. Around 460 B.C., he became the leader of a democratic group. He introduced reforms that strengthened democracy. One of Pericles' reforms required the city to pay a salary to its officials. This meant that poor citizens could afford to hold public office.

✓ Reading Check **How did Pericles strengthen democracy?**

An ancient Athenian silver coin bearing an owl, a symbol of the city

Scenes of Ancient Greece
The arts flourished during Athens' Golden Age. This Greek vase was created about 470 B.C. **Conclude** *How did Athens become wealthy during the Golden Age?*

Religious Beliefs in Ancient Greece

Greeks worshiped a family of gods and goddesses called the Twelve Olympians. Each ruled different areas of human life and the natural world. The chart below titled A Family of Gods describes some of the Twelve Olympians and the areas over which they ruled.

The Greeks took great care in honoring their gods. They expressed their gratitude to them and asked them for blessings. They also tried to avoid angering the gods.

Gods and Goddesses Wherever the Greeks lived, they built temples to the gods. Since the gods had human forms, they also had many human characteristics. The gods were different from humans, however, in that they were perfect in their human forms, they had great power, and they were immortal.

Mythology tells us that the Greeks worshiped twelve great gods led by Zeus, the king of the gods. Zeus ruled both the gods and men from atop Mt. Olympus, Greece's highest mountain. In addition to the twelve great gods, the Greeks worshiped many lesser ones. They also honored mythical heroes like Achilles (uh KIL eez), who fought bravely during the Trojan War. The story of Achilles is told in the *Iliad*.

Prefixes and Roots
Target Skill If *im-* means "not," what does *immortal* mean?

Chart Skills

The Greeks considered the five gods in the table at the right to be the most powerful of the Twelve Olympians. Poseidon, Athena, Apollo, and Artemis, the goddess of the hunt, are shown in the above relief. **Identify** Who was considered to be the leader of all gods and goddesses? **Analyze** Why do you think this chart is titled "A Family of Gods"?

A Family of Gods

God or Goddess	Description
Zeus (zoos)	King of the gods and goddesses. Ruler of the sky and storms. Protector of the law.
Hera (HIHR uh)	Wife and queen to Zeus. Goddess of marriage and women.
Apollo (uh PAHL oh)	Son of Zeus. Handsome young god of poetry and music. The most widely worshiped of the Greek gods.
Athena (uh THEE nuh)	Zeus' wise daughter. Goddess of crafts. War goddess who defended her cities.
Poseidon (poh SY dun)	Zeus' brother. God of the sea, of water, and of earthquakes. Lord of horses.

Although the Greeks worshiped all their gods, each city-state honored just one of the twelve gods, in part by building a temple to that god. To honor Zeus, the city-states came together every four years for an Olympian festival and games. The modern Olympic Games are based on this tradition.

The Oracles In ancient cultures, people often looked to their gods for signs, or advice. They wanted the gods to show them how to live or how to behave. The Greeks visited **oracles,** sacred sites where a god or goddess was consulted. At these shrines, Greeks would ask the gods for advice or for predictions about the future. Sometimes the advice came through dreams. Often the answers came in the form of a riddle, delivered by a priest or a priestess believed to be able to hear the voices of the gods. Oracles of various gods were located throughout Greece. Heads of state often sought advice on governing from the oracle of the god Apollo at Delphi, an ancient town in central Greece. Because such advice was taken very seriously, the oracles had a great effect on Greek history.

✓ Reading Check **How did the Greeks honor their gods?**

Delphi
At the top is the Tholos Temple at the Sanctuary of Athena Pronaia, once the gateway to Delphi. In the vase painting above, Aegeus, a legendary Athenian king, consults a priestess at Apollo's oracle in Delphi. **Conclude** *Why did the ancient Greeks visit oracles?*

Greek Science and Philosophy

Most Greeks believed that their gods were the source of all natural events. But about 150 years before the Golden Age of Athens, some people thought about other ways besides myths to understand the world.

The Search for Knowledge You learned earlier about philosophy, which is a system of beliefs or values. **Philosophers believed that people could use the powers of the mind and reason to understand natural events.** One of the first philosophers, Thales (THAY leez), believed that water was the basic material of the world. He thought that everything was made from it. Democritus (dih MAHK ruh tus), who lived in the 400s B.C., thought that everything was made of tiny particles he called atoms. More than 2,000 years later, scientists still use his ideas about atoms.

Beginning in the 600s B.C., writers and traveling teachers called Sophists (SAHF ists) gained popularity in Greece. Sophists were skilled speakers who cleverly debated topics in public. Although they were popular in Athens, some philosophers thought Sophists were more interested in winning debates than in seeking the truth.

Socrates, Plato, and Aristotle During the Golden Age and later, several important philosophers taught in Athens. The ideas of three men, Socrates (SAHK ruh teez), Plato (PLAY toh), and Aristotle (AR is taht ul), had a lasting effect on modern learning and thinking.

Using the marketplace as his classroom, Socrates eagerly discussed wisdom and goodness with the people of Athens. He asked questions that challenged people's beliefs. His questions often frightened and angered many Athenians.

In 399 B.C., Socrates was brought to trial. The authorities accused him of dishonoring the gods and misleading young people. He was sentenced to death by forced suicide, a common sentence in Athens at the time. Socrates drank a cup of hemlock, a poison, and died.

Much of what is known about Socrates comes from the writings of Plato, one of his students. Socrates' death caused Plato to mistrust democracy. In *The Republic,* Plato wrote that society should be made up of three groups: workers, soldiers, and philosopher-rulers. Plato founded a school in Athens called the Academy, where he taught a student named Aristotle. Aristotle believed that reason should guide the pursuit of knowledge. He later founded his own school, the Lyceum.

✔ **Reading Check** **Which three important philosophers taught in Athens?**

The Acropolis
Once the religious center of Athens, the Acropolis now serves as a monument to Greek architecture.
① The Propylaia, the entrance to the Acropolis, was completed in 432 B.C.
② The Odeion (theater) of Herodes Atticus was built in A.D. 161.
③ The Erechtheion, named after a legendary king of Athens, was completed in 406 B.C. The inset photo shows the temple's south porch.
④ Completed in 438 B.C., the Parthenon was a temple to Athena, the patron goddess of Athens.
Predict *Why do you think the Athenians built the Acropolis?*

Visual and Dramatic Arts

The Greeks used visual arts, such as architecture and sculpture, to glorify and honor their gods. The Greeks are also known as the first playwrights, because they wrote the first plays.

The Parthenon The Acropolis, the religious center of Athens, had been destroyed in 480 B.C., during one of the city's many wars. Pericles decided to rebuild the Acropolis and create new buildings to glorify the city.

The builders of the new Acropolis brought Greek architecture to its highest point. Their most magnificent work was the Parthenon, a temple to the goddess Athena. The temple was made of fine marble. Rows of columns surrounded it on all four sides. Within the columns was a room that held a 40-foot (12-meter) statue of Athena, made of ivory and gold.

The great statue of Athena disappeared long ago. However, many of the sculpted scenes that decorate the inside and outside of the temple still exist. These scenes have three important characteristics. First, they are full of action. Second, the figures are carefully arranged to show balance and order. Third, the sculptures are lifelike and accurate. However, they are ideal, or perfect, views of humans and animals. The goal of Greek art was to present images of perfection in a balanced and orderly way.

Dramas Athenians were the first people to write dramas, or stories written to be performed by actors. Among the city's greatest achievements were the plays written and produced in the 400s B.C., during the Golden Age. These plays soon became popular all over the Greek world.

Some of the most famous Greek dramas were tragedies. A **tragedy** is a type of serious drama that usually ends in disaster for the main character. Between scenes in the play, a chorus chanted or sang poems. In most plays, the writer used the chorus to give background information, to comment on the events, or to praise the gods. Euripides (yoo RIP uh deez), Aeschylus (ES kih lus), and Sophocles were important authors of tragedies.

Performances of tragedies were part of contests held during religious festivals. The city chose wealthy citizens to fund these dramatic contests.

Greek actors performed in outdoor theaters, such as the one shown above at Epidauros. By using different masks, such as the one shown at the top, actors could play a variety of roles.

Comedies Comic writers also competed at the dramatic festivals. During the 400s B.C. in Athens, these writers wrote comedies that made fun of well-known citizens and politicians and also made jokes about the customs of the day. Because of the freedom in Athens, people accepted the humor and jokes. Aristophanes (a rih STAHF uh neez) is probably the best-known Greek comic playwright.

✓ Reading Check **What was the role of the chorus in Greek drama?**

Section 2 Assessment

Key Terms
Review the key terms at the beginning of this section. Use each term in a sentence that explains its meaning.

Target Reading Skill
Find *perfection* on page 179. Apply your knowledge of the prefix *im-*. What are imperfections?

Comprehension and Critical Thinking
1. (a) Define What was the Golden Age of Athens?

(b) Draw Conclusions Why do you think Pericles called Athens "the school for all Greece"?

2. (a) Explain How did the Greeks attempt to understand the world?

(b) Analyze One of the teachings of Socrates was "know thyself." What did Socrates mean when he said this?

3. (a) Identify What were the goals of Greek art?

(b) Infer What does Greek art, both visual and literary, tell us about the Greeks and their culture?

Writing Activity
Write a brief essay describing the achievements of Athenians during the Golden Age.

Writing Tip Your opinion should be the main idea of your paragraph. When writing to persuade, support your main idea with specific evidence arranged in a logical order.

3 Daily Life in Athens

Prepare to Read

Objectives

In this section you will

1. Learn about public life in Athens.
2. Find out how the people of Athens spent their time at home.
3. Study the practice of slavery and its effects in ancient Greece.

Taking Notes

As you read, look for details about daily life in ancient Greece. Copy the table below, and use it to record your findings.

Daily Life in Ancient Greece		
The Marketplace	**Life at Home**	**Slavery**
• • •	• • •	• • •

Target Reading Skill

Recognize Word Origins The origin of a word is where the word comes from. The word *splendor,* on page 182, comes from the Latin word *splendere,* which means "to shine." In *splendor*, the suffix *-or* means "quality." Use your knowledge of the origin of the word *splendor* and the context to determine what this word means.

Key Terms

- **Athens** (ATH unz) *n.* a city-state in ancient Greece; the capital of modern-day Greece
- **agora** (AG uh ruh) *n.* a public market and meeting place in an ancient Greek city; the agora of Athens when spelled with a capital *A*
- **vendor** (VEN dur) *n.* a seller of goods
- **slavery** (SLAY vur ee) *n.* condition of being owned by, and forced to work for, someone else

The light from the courtyard was still gray when the young boy awoke for school. He ate his breakfast, pulled on his cloak, and stepped outside. Soon, the women of the household would be starting the day's weaving and other chores.

On the way to school, the boy met other students. All were carrying wooden tablets covered with wax. They would write their lessons on the tablets.

After school, the boy went to the training ground. All the boys exercised and practiced wrestling and throwing a flat plate called a discus. They might watch older athletes training to compete in the Olympic Games, held in honor of Zeus.

This story shows how a boy might spend his day in ancient **Athens,** a city-state in ancient Greece. A look at daily life in ancient Athens will help you understand how many of the ancient Greeks lived.

A statue of a discus thrower

Life in Public

Ruins of the agora of ancient Corinth, Greece ▶

On their way to school, the boys passed through the Agora (AG uh ruh) of Athens. All Greek cities had **agoras,** or public markets and meeting places. Athens' Agora was probably the busiest and most interesting of them all. It was not far from the great Acropolis, which rose in splendor above it. Just as the Acropolis was the center of Athens' religious life, the Agora was the center of its public life.

Recognize Word Origins

Combine your knowledge of the Latin word *splendere* and the suffix *-or* with the context at the right to figure out the meaning of *splendor*.

The Business of Men In the morning, many Athenian men found their way to the Agora. The mild climate of Athens made it possible to carry on business in the open. In the Agora, the men talked of politics and philosophy. Sometimes they just gossiped.

As they talked, they heard the cries of **vendors,** or sellers of goods. Buyers and vendors commonly haggled, or bargained, for the best prices. The streets were lined with shops. Farmers and artisans also sold their wares from stands set up under shady trees. Just about any food an Athenian would want could be found in the Agora. Other goods were also for sale—sheep's wool, pottery, hardware, cloth, and books.

Public Buildings Temples and government buildings lined the Agora. One building was the headquarters of Athens' army. Another was a prison. A board displayed public notices such as new laws and upcoming court cases.

✓ Reading Check What business did Athenians conduct in the Agora?

Community Life
A vase from the 400s B.C. shows two Greeks discussing philosophy.
Analyze Why do you think the Agora was the center of public life in Athens?

At Home in Athens

The grand public buildings of Athens contrasted with the simplicity of people's houses, even during the Golden Age.

Private Life Throughout Greece, private homes were plain. Most were made of mud bricks, with rooms set around an open courtyard hidden from the street. The courtyard was the center of the household. Other rooms might include a kitchen, storerooms, a dining room, and bedrooms. Some homes had bathrooms. But water had to be carried to them from a public fountain.

The ancient Greeks ate simple foods. Breakfast might be just bread. For midday meals, Athenians might eat cheese or olives with the bread. Dinner might consist of fish and vegetables followed by cheese, fruit, and even cakes sweetened with honey. Most Athenians ate little meat, because there was little space or extra money to raise cattle. Even wealthy families ate meat only during religious festivals.

Women of Athens If you had walked through the Agora, you might have been surprised to see that most of the people there were men. If you had asked where the women were, an Athenian man might have replied, "At home."

Greek Games
The people of ancient Greece played a game called knucklebones, as shown in the terra-cotta figures at the top. Knucklebone playing pieces are shown above.
Predict *Use what you know about the lives of the ancient Greeks to predict where girls might gather to play a game of knucklebones.*

Painting Their Lives The Athenians were known for their beautiful pottery. They decorated vases, jars, and cups with black or reddish-tan figures. Many scenes were mythological, but others displayed scenes from Athenian daily life. For example, the pottery might show men talking together, or working at their jobs, such as the butcher, below.

Home was where most Athenian women spent their days. They had almost none of the freedoms that their husbands, sons, and fathers probably took for granted. They could not take any part in politics. Nor could they vote. They could not own property. One of the very few official roles allowed them was to be a priestess in religious ceremonies.

Running the home and family was the job of women. In some wealthy families, men and women had completely separate quarters. Women organized the spinning and weaving, looked after supplies of food and wine, and cared for young children. They also kept track of the family finances. If a family owned slaves, they were the woman's responsibility as well. She directed them, trained them, and cared for them when they were sick.

✓ Reading Check **What kinds of foods did Athenians eat?**

Slavery in Ancient Greece

Slaves worked hard throughout the city-states of Greece. No one knows for sure, but historians estimate that as many as 100,000 slaves may have lived in Athens. That is almost one third of the population at that time. **Slavery,** the condition of being owned by someone else, was common in Athens. Today, we consider slavery a crime. But free people rarely questioned the practice in ancient times, even in democratic Athens.

The Slaves of Athens
In this detail from a vase, a servant attends to a seated woman. **Draw Conclusions** *Based on what you have read, draw a conclusion about the ancient Greeks' attitudes toward slavery.*

Who Were the Slaves? Many free people were enslaved when they were captured by armies during war or by pirates while traveling on ships. Some slaves were the children of slaves. A large number of slaves in Greece were foreigners, because some Greeks were uncomfortable owning other Greeks.

The Lives of Slaves Enslaved people did many kinds of work. Some provided labor on farms. Others dug silver and other metals in the mines. Still others assisted artisans by making pottery, constructing buildings, or forging weapons and armor. Most Greek households could not function well without slaves. Household slaves cooked and served food, tended children, and wove cloth.

Household slaves may have had the easiest life. Often they were treated like members of the family. The slaves who worked in the mines suffered the most. The work was not only physically tiring, but was also extremely dangerous. Slaves who worked in the mines often did not live long.

Some slaves were able to buy their freedom, but many were not. The hard work of slaves meant that the free citizens of Athens could afford to pursue art, education, and public service.

A painting from a cup shows a male slave balancing two vessels.

✓ **Reading Check** Why were many slaves in Greece foreigners?

Section 3 Assessment

Key Terms
Review the key terms at the beginning of this section. Use each term in a sentence that explains its meaning.

Target Reading Skill
What do you think the adjective *splendid* means?

Comprehension and Critical Thinking
1. (a) Describe What activities took place in the agoras of ancient Greece?
(b) Draw Conclusions What do the agoras tell us about the culture of the ancient Greeks?

2. (a) Recall Describe the home life of the Greeks.
(b) Compare What were the responsibilities of men compared with those of women in ancient Greece? Based on that information, what conclusions can you make about ancient Greek society?
3. (a) Recall Describe the various roles of slaves in ancient Greece.
(b) Draw Inferences Free people rarely questioned slavery in ancient Greece. Why do you think that was so?

Writing Activity
Write a description of your school-day routine. How does your day compare with that of the Greek boy you read about at the beginning of this section?

Writing Tip Reread the description that begins this section. Think about how your days are similar to the boy's day and how your days are different. When you describe your own day, include both the similarities and the differences.

The Agora of Athens

In the center of town stands the town hall, a grocery store, a church, a library, and a firehouse. These buildings enclose a public square. The square looks like countless town squares throughout America and Europe, yet its roots lie in ancient Greece. The busy heart of a Greek city was called the *agora,* or "marketplace." Some agoras were laid out as squares or rectangles. The Athenian agora shown here followed a more rambling style.

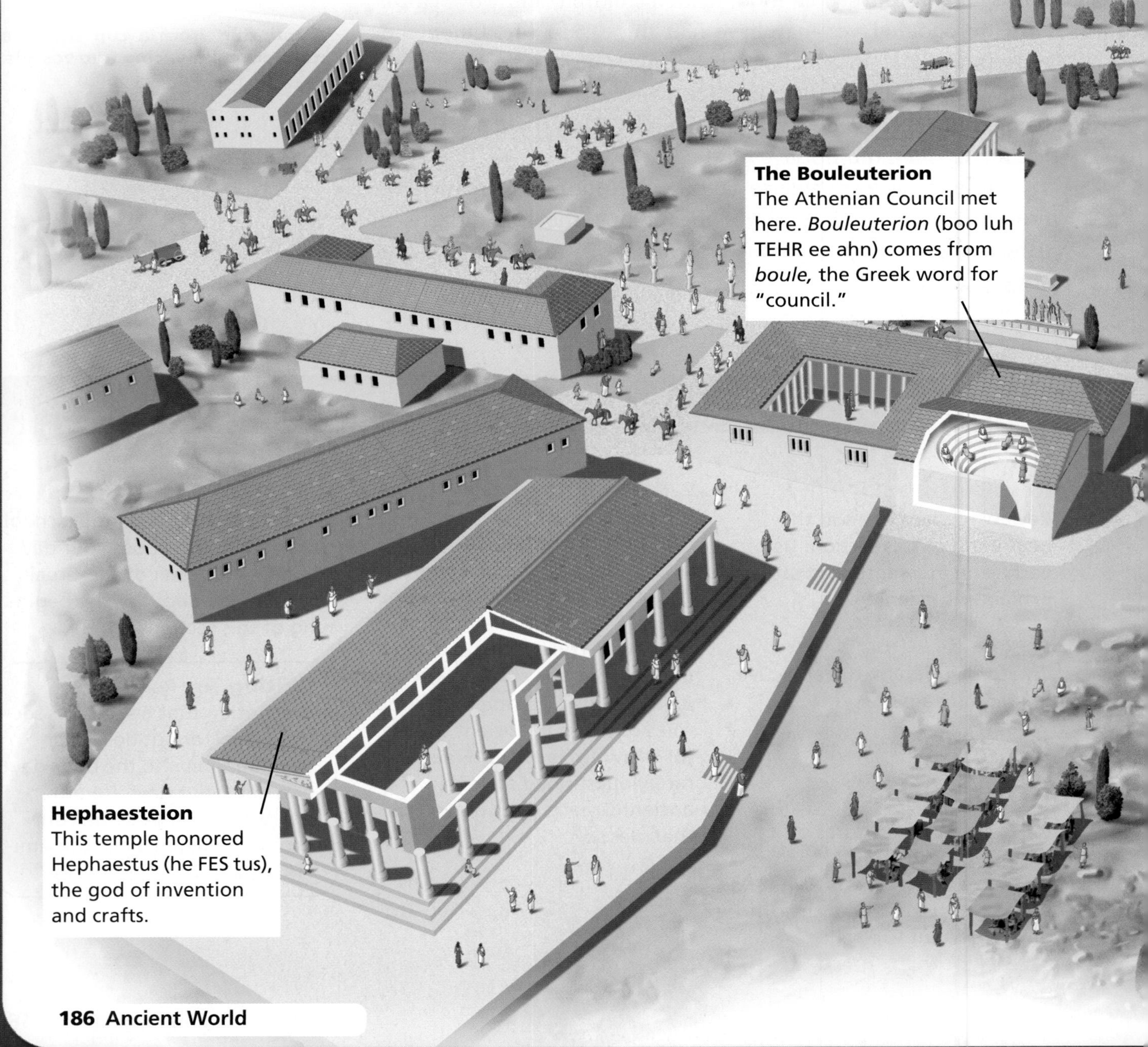

The Bouleuterion
The Athenian Council met here. *Bouleuterion* (boo luh TEHR ee ahn) comes from *boule,* the Greek word for "council."

Hephaesteion
This temple honored Hephaestus (he FES tus), the god of invention and crafts.

Hephaesteion Ruins
This temple was built in the 400s B.C. Among all the Agora ruins, it is the best preserved.

The Odeion of Agrippa
This concert hall could seat 1,000 people.

Stoa of Attalos
Merchants housed their *stoae* (STOH ee), or "shops," here.

The Tholos
Council members ate and slept in this round building.

The Athenian Marketplace The agora symbolized the Greeks' love of public participation—political, religious, economic, judicial, and scholarly. Public buildings surrounded open spaces for the exchange of news, ideas, and goods. In the shadow of the Acropolis, Athens built a magnificent agora. There, the orator Pericles spoke, and the philosopher Socrates taught and was sentenced to death. Generals rallied the city to war, and priests paid respect to the gods. There, democracy was born as Athenian citizens voted for their leaders and sat on juries. Although once adorned with fountains, gardens, and sculpture, little is left of the Agora today.

Assessment

Describe What kinds of activities took place in the Agora?

Compare In what ways is the Agora similar to the citadel section of Mohenjo-Daro (shown on pages 114–115)?

Prepare to Read

Objectives

In this section you will

1. Find out what it was like to live in the ancient city of Sparta.
2. Learn about the Persian invasion of Greece.
3. Examine other conflicts faced by the Athenian Empire.

Taking Notes

As you read, look for important details about Sparta and the fall of Athens. Copy the flowchart below, and use it to record your findings.

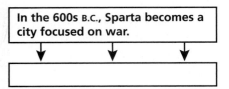

In the 600s B.C., Sparta becomes a city focused on war.

↓ ↓ ↓

Target Reading Skill

Recognize Word Origins On page 189 of this section, you will read the word *rebellion*. It contains the Latin root *-belli-*, which means "war." Consider how the word *rebellion* is used in its context. What do you think *rebellion* means?

Key Terms

- **Sparta** (SPAHR tuh) *n.* a city-state in the southern part of ancient Greece
- **helot** (HEL ut) *n.* a member of a certain class of servants in ancient Sparta
- **Peloponnesian War** (pel uh puh NEE shun wawr) *n.* (431–404 B.C.) a war fought between Athens and Sparta in ancient Greece, involving almost every other Greek city-state
- **plague** (playg) *n.* a widespread disease
- **blockade** (blah KAYD) *n.* an action taken to isolate an enemy and cut off its supplies

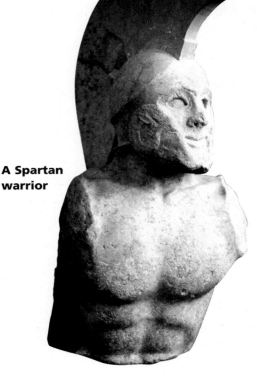

A Spartan warrior

The boy stood still and straight beside his companions as their trainer approached. "You," the trainer barked. "Are you sick? You cannot escape sword practice—and why are you holding your belly? Are you hiding something?"

The trainer gave the boy's cloak a sharp tug. It fell to the ground, freeing a fox that streaked off into the underbrush. The boy sank down to the ground, shaking. His cloak was a crimson red. His side was shredded with deep cuts and bites. The hungry boy had stolen the fox for his dinner. Hidden beneath his cloak, the fox had clawed and bitten him.

Later, the boy died from his wounds. The people of his city, Sparta, celebrated his life. He had endured terrible pain without giving any sign of his distress. To the Spartans, such behavior was the sign of true character.

This Spartan story of the boy and the fox may or may not be true. Yet it tells us much about the people of **Sparta**, a city-state in southern Greece.

Living in Sparta

If life in Athens was free and open, then life for the citizens of Sparta was the opposite. Life in Sparta was harsh. The Spartans themselves were tough, silent, and grim. Sparta's army easily equaled Athens' in the 400s B.C. However, Sparta never came close to equaling Athens' other achievements.

A City Devoted to War In its early days, Sparta seemed to be similar to other Greek cities. Then, in the 600s B.C., wars inside and outside the city led to changes in government and the way people lived. The changes turned Sparta into a powerful war machine. The city-state had made one basic rule: Always put the city's needs above your own.

Early in its history, the Spartans conquered the land around their city. They turned the conquered people into **helots** (HEL uts), or servants of Sparta. Helots did all the farm work on the land owned by Spartan citizens, freeing the Spartans to wage war. However, the helots far outnumbered the Spartans. Living in fear of a helot rebellion, the Spartans turned their city into a military society. They treated the helots very harshly.

Recognize Word Origins

Use what you know about the Latin root *-belli-* , as well as the context, to find the meaning of *rebellion* in the last paragraph.

Sparta's Ruins

The agora of Sparta once stood on the site shown below. **Analyze** *How did Sparta become a powerful war machine?*

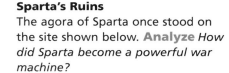

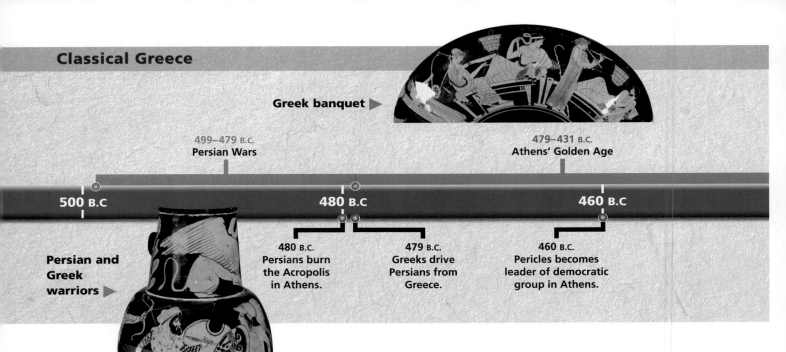

Classical Greece

Greek banquet ▶

499–479 B.C.
Persian Wars

479–431 B.C.
Athens' Golden Age

500 B.C

480 B.C

460 B.C

Persian and Greek warriors ▶

480 B.C.
Persians burn the Acropolis in Athens.

479 B.C.
Greeks drive Persians from Greece.

460 B.C.
Pericles becomes leader of democratic group in Athens.

■ Timeline Skills

The timeline above covers events that occurred during Classical Greece, an era that lasted from about 500 B.C. to 323 B.C. **Identify** What event occurred near the end of the Persian Wars?
Analyze After which war did Athens surrender to Sparta?

Growing Up in Sparta The life of every Spartan was in the hands of the government from an early age. Community leaders examined newborn infants. Those thought to be too sickly would be left to die. Military training began early for boys. At seven, a Spartan boy left his home to live in barracks with other boys. His training continued for the next 13 years.

By the age of 12, a boy had spent long hours practicing with swords and spears. He had only one cloak and a thin mat to sleep on. He could hardly live on the food he was given, so he was urged to steal. The Spartans believed that stealing would help him learn how to live off the land during a war. However, if the boy was caught, he was severely punished. After all, if a soldier was caught stealing, he would probably be killed. Boys were expected to bear pain, hardship, and punishment in silence.

Like the boys, girls also trained and competed in wrestling and spear throwing. No one expected the girls to become soldiers. But Spartans did believe that girls who grew up strong and healthy would have strong, healthy children. Spartan women had somewhat more freedoms than women in other Greek city-states. They were allowed to own land and even take part in business.

Spartan life lacked the beauty and pleasures found in Athens and some other Greek cities. But Spartan warriors were known for their skill and bravery. The Spartan fighting force played a key role in the Greek wars against the Persians, a people who lived across the Aegean Sea to the east of Greece.

✓ Reading Check **What was life like for the women of Sparta?**

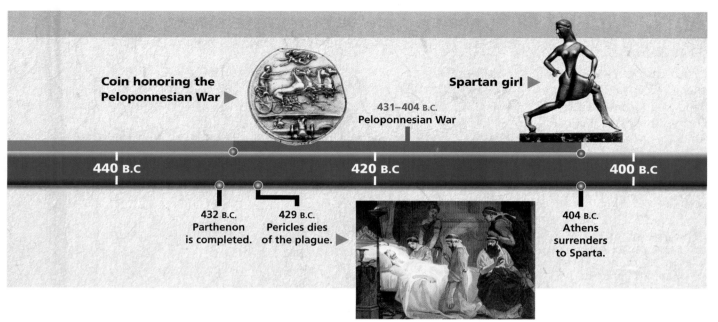

Coin honoring the Peloponnesian War ▶

Spartan girl ▶

431–404 B.C.
Peloponnesian War

440 B.C   420 B.C   400 B.C

432 B.C.
Parthenon is completed.

429 B.C.
Pericles dies of the plague. ▶

404 B.C.
Athens surrenders to Sparta.

The Persians Invade

Much of the history of the Greeks tells of wars they fought among themselves. But near the beginning of the 400s B.C., a new threat loomed: the growing might of Persia.

The Expanding Persian Empire By about the mid-500s B.C., Cyrus the Great had founded the Persian Empire. Cyrus and later rulers then extended the original empire. By 520 B.C., the Persians had gained control of the Greek colonies on the west coast of Asia Minor. See the map titled Greece and the Persian Empire on page 192.

Battle at Marathon In the fall of 490 B.C., a huge force of thousands of Persians landed in Greece itself. They gathered at Marathon, about 25 miles (40 kilometers) north of Athens. The Athenians hastily put together a small army. The Persians outnumbered them by at least two to one. For several days the armies stared tensely at each other across the plain of Marathon.

Then, without warning, the Athenians rushed the Persians, who were overwhelmed by the furious attack. By one account, the Athenians had killed 6,400 Persians and lost only 192 of their own soldiers. The Persian losses may be exaggerated. The truth is that in a short time, this tiny state had defeated the giant that had come to destroy it.

More battles with Persia followed. As a common enemy, Persia distracted the Greek city-states from fighting one another. Briefly united, the Greeks drove the Persians away.

✓ Reading Check **What happened during the battle at Marathon?**

Citizen Heroes

Spartan Soldiers

In one of the wars against the Persians, some 6,000 Greeks had to defend a mountain pass, called Thermoplylae (thur MAHP uh lee), leading into southern Greece. They faced almost 200,000 Persians. Most of the Greeks retreated, but 300 Spartan soldiers stayed to fight. The Spartans all died in the battle. They didn't hold back the Persians. But they earned undying praise for their brave sacrifice.

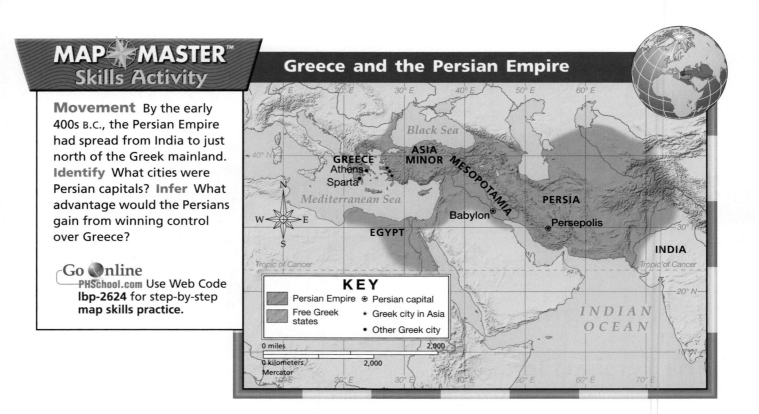

Movement By the early 400s B.C., the Persian Empire had spread from India to just north of the Greek mainland. **Identify** What cities were Persian capitals? **Infer** What advantage would the Persians gain from winning control over Greece?

Go Online
PHSchool.com Use Web Code **lbp-2624** for step-by-step map skills practice.

KEY

- Persian Empire
- Free Greek states
- ⊛ Persian capital
- ★ Greek city in Asia
- • Other Greek city

0 miles 2,000
0 kilometers 2,000
Mercator

Conflict and the Athenian Empire

After the Persians were finally defeated, the influence of Athens spread over much of eastern Greece. Athens allied itself, or became partners, with other city-states. Athens worked to strengthen democratic groups within the city-states. In time, these cities became more like subjects than allies.

Sparta and Athens at War Athens may have been a democracy at home, but it began to treat its allied city-states unfairly. At first, the allies had paid tribute to Athens for protection in case the Persians again became a threat. But later, Athens used this money for building the Parthenon and other projects. In response, the people of these city-states began to resent Athens' power. They looked to Sparta, which had not joined the alliance, to protect them. In 431 B.C., allies of Sparta and Athens fought. Thus began the **Peloponnesian War** (pel uh puh NEE shun wawr), a conflict between Athens and Sparta that lasted 27 years. It is called the Peloponnesian War because Sparta was located in Pelopponese, the southern Greek peninsula.

Greek warrior figurine ▶

The Fall of Athens Most of what we know about the Peloponnesian War comes from Greek historian Thucydides (thoo SID ih deez). Thucydides saw the war first hand. He later wrote an eyewitness account of the war. Early in the Peloponnesian War, Athens was struck by a **plague,** or widespread disease. By the time the plague ended five years later, about one third of Athens' people had died from it. Among the dead was Pericles. His death was a great blow to Athens.

Athens never recovered from its losses during the plague. In 405 B.C., the Spartans staged a **blockade,** an action taken to isolate an enemy and cut off its supplies. The Spartans surrounded and closed the harbor where Athens received food shipments. Starving and beaten, the Athenians surrendered in 404 B.C. The victorious Spartans knocked down Athens' walls. Athens never again dominated the Greek world.

✔ **Reading Check** **How did the Spartans finally defeat the Athenians?**

Athens Defeated
Shields and spears, such as those carried by the warriors above, could not spare the Athenians from the plague. **Analyze** *What factors contributed to the fall of Athens?*

Section 4 Assessment

Key Terms
Review the key terms at the beginning of this section. Use each term in a sentence that explains its meaning.

Target Reading Skill
If the suffix -*ous* means "full of," what do you think the word *rebellious* means?

Comprehension and Critical Thinking
1. (a) Recall Describe what life was like for people living in Sparta.
(b) Compare and Contrast You have read previously about life in ancient Athens. Compare life in Sparta with life in Athens.
2. (a) Describe How did the Greeks overcome the Persian invasion of 490 B.C.?
(b) Explain What do you think was at stake for the people of Athens at the Battle of Marathon?
(c) Predict How might the history of Greece have changed if Persia had won at Marathon?
3. (a) Summarize How did the Athenian Empire develop after its victory over Persia?
(b) Identify Causes In what ways did Athens contribute to its own downfall?

Writing Activity
Reread the story that begins this section. Write a report about the event from a Spartan trainer's point of view. In the report, retell the story as though you were explaining it to other Spartan officers.

Go Online
PHSchool.com

For: An activity on politics in Sparta
Visit: PHSchool.com
Web Code: lbd-2604

The teacher looked at Lisa and asked, "How did the people of Athens feel about drama?"

Lisa had read the assignment, but there wasn't anything in the book telling how Athenians felt about drama. She did remember a few facts, though. "They had a lot of theaters and put on a lot of plays. They had play-writing contests. So I guess if they had so many plays, drama must have been pretty important to them."

Greek actor's mask

Like Lisa, when you draw a conclusion, you figure out something based on the information you have read or seen. Drawing conclusions is a skill that will help you benefit from your schoolwork and anything you read.

Learn the skill

Use these steps to learn how to draw a conclusion:

 1 Gather factual information about the topic. Find out as many factual details as you can by reading about your topic and then talking with people who know about the subject.

2 Combine the facts with other information you already know. Add the information you find in your research to what you already know.

3 Write a conclusion that follows logically. A conclusion is usually an educated guess.

Practice the Skill

Turn to page 171, and reread the first four paragraphs of text in the main column. Use this information to draw conclusions about the Trojan War.

1 The text tells you about the people who may have inspired the legend of the war. It tells where the war was fought, and it describes the heroes, how they fought, and how the story was handed down to us. Choose one of these topics. Write down facts about that topic.

2 Combine whatever facts you already know with the facts you have just read. You might know something about stories of other wars or about how people react to war stories.

3 Try to form an educated guess about your topic—something that is not specifically stated in the text. Your conclusion might answer a question starting with *why*. For instance, Why has the history of the Trojan War fascinated so many people through the centuries? Check your conclusion to make sure it is supported by the facts.

Apply the Skill

Turn to page 173, and reread the four paragraphs titled Democracy: Rule by the People. Use facts from that text plus facts you already know to draw conclusions about American democracy.

The Trojan horse inside the ancient city of Troy

The Spread of Greek Culture

Prepare to Read

Objectives

In this section you will
1. Learn how Alexander the Great built his empire.
2. Find out about the age of Hellenism, when Greek culture spread to many other parts of the world.

Taking Notes

As you read, look for important details about the spread of Greek culture. Copy the table below, and use it to record your findings.

The Spread of Greek Culture	
Alexander's Empire	The Hellenistic Age
•	•
•	•
•	•

Target Reading Skill

Use Word Parts When you come across an unfamiliar word, break the word into parts to help you recognize and pronounce it. On page 197 of this section, you will come across the word *extensive*. Break it into a prefix, root, and suffix to learn its meaning. The prefix *ex-* means "out." The Latin root *-ten-* means "stretch." The suffix *-ive* means "relating to" and makes the word an adjective.

Key Terms

- **barbarian** (bar BEHR ee un) *n.* a wild and uncivilized person
- **assassinate** (uh SAS uh nayt) *v.* to murder for political reasons
- **Alexander the Great** (al ig ZAN dur thuh grayt) *n.* king of Macedonia from 336 to 323 B.C.; conquerer of Persia and Egypt and invader of India
- **Hellenistic** (hel uh NIS tik) *adj.* describing Greek history or culture after the death of Alexander the Great, including the three main kingdoms formed by the breakup of Alexander's empire

A sculpture of King Philip of Macedonia

King Philip of Macedonia (mas uh DOH nee uh) had not wasted the money he spent on Greek tutors for his son, Alexander. The boy wanted to learn as much as he could, especially about the ideas and deeds of the Greeks.

Macedonia lay just north of Greece. Alexander thought of himself as Greek and spoke the Greek language. But people who lived to the south in such cities as Athens and Sparta did not accept the Macedonians as Greeks. They thought the Macedonians were **barbarians,** or wild, uncivilized people.

Alexander's tutor was the Greek philosopher Aristotle. Alexander loved his tutor, but his role model was Achilles, the mythical warrior hero of the *Iliad*. One day, Alexander vowed, he would visit the site of Troy to honor his hero.

Alexander's Empire

Before King Philip seized power in 359 B.C., Macedonia was poor and divided. Philip united Macedonia and built an army even stronger than Sparta's. With such an army and with his talent for waging war, Philip captured one Greek city-state after another.

Death of a King Philip then planned to attack Persia. But in 336 B.C., before he could carry out his plan, he was **assassinated, or murdered for political reasons,** by a rival. At the age of 20, Alexander became king. History would know him as **Alexander the Great,** king of Macedonia from 336 to 323 B.C.

Alexander's Conquests One of Alexander's first actions was to invade the Persian Empire. Within 11 years, the Macedonian king had conquered an extensive area, including Persia, Egypt, and lands beyond the Indus River to the east.

Alexander's energy and military genius helped him succeed. He drove himself and his army hard, advancing across vast lands at remarkable speed. His soldiers wanted to return home, but they obeyed him. Wherever Alexander went, he established cities. Many of them he named after himself. Even today, there are numerous cities named Alexandria or Alexandropolis throughout western Asia. Alexander never stayed very long in the cities he conquered. He quickly pushed on, never losing a battle.

Fighting the Persian Empire
The mosaic above shows the Battle of Issus, in which Alexander the Great, at the top, defeated an army of Persians in 333 B.C. **Infer** *Why do you think Alexander became known as Alexander the Great?*

Use Word Parts
What does *extensive* mean? Does your definition make sense in the paragraph at the left?

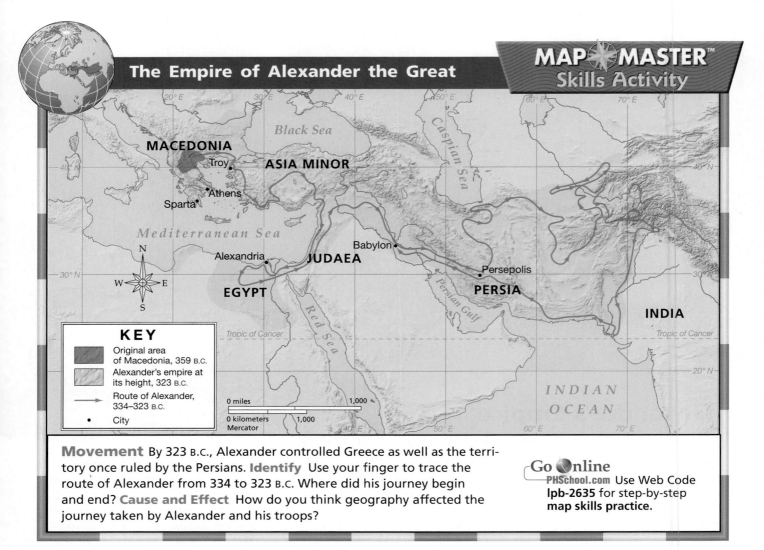

The Empire of Alexander the Great

MAP★MASTER™
Skills Activity

MACEDONIA
Troy
ASIA MINOR
Black Sea
Caspian Sea
Athens
Sparta
Mediterranean Sea
Alexandria
Babylon
JUDAEA
Persepolis
EGYPT
PERSIA
Red Sea
Persian Gulf
INDIA
INDIAN OCEAN
Tropic of Cancer

KEY
- Original area of Macedonia, 359 B.C.
- Alexander's empire at its height, 323 B.C.
- Route of Alexander, 334–323 B.C.
- • City

0 miles 1,000
0 kilometers 1,000
Mercator

Movement By 323 B.C., Alexander controlled Greece as well as the territory once ruled by the Persians. **Identify** Use your finger to trace the route of Alexander from 334 to 323 B.C. Where did his journey begin and end? **Cause and Effect** How do you think geography affected the journey taken by Alexander and his troops?

Go Online
PHSchool.com Use Web Code **lpb-2635** for step-by-step map skills practice.

A silver coin stamped with a portrait of Alexander the Great

After many years of travel and fighting, Alexander's army was exhausted. Not far beyond the Indus River, his troops became so weary that they refused to continue east. Alexander was angry, but he turned back. Alexander got as far as Babylon, where he caught a fever. In 323 B.C., only 13 years after he came to the throne, Alexander died. Like the legendary warrior Achilles, he had died young. But he had gone far beyond the deeds of his hero. His conquests spread Greek culture throughout a vast area.

✓ **Reading Check** What events caused Alexander to become king?

The Hellenistic Age

With Alexander's death, his empire began to decline. Within 50 years, the empire had broken into three main kingdoms. Each kingdom was ruled by a family that had descended from one of Alexander's commanders.

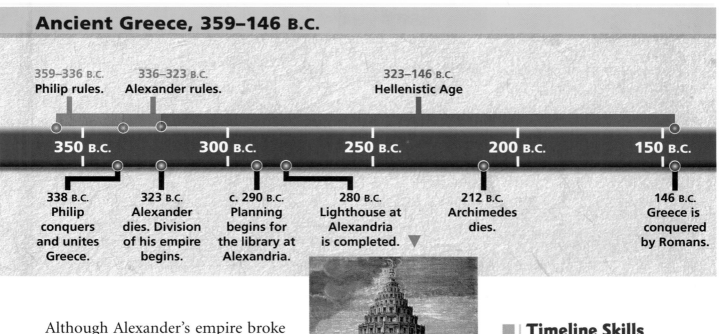

Ancient Greece, 359–146 B.C.

359–336 B.C.
Philip rules.

336–323 B.C.
Alexander rules.

323–146 B.C.
Hellenistic Age

350 B.C.   **300 B.C.**   **250 B.C.**   **200 B.C.**   **150 B.C.**

338 B.C.
Philip conquers and unites Greece.

323 B.C.
Alexander dies. Division of his empire begins.

c. 290 B.C.
Planning begins for the library at Alexandria.

280 B.C.
Lighthouse at Alexandria is completed. ▼

212 B.C.
Archimedes dies.

146 B.C.
Greece is conquered by Romans.

Although Alexander's empire broke apart, Greek culture remained alive and well in the three Hellenistic kingdoms. **Hellenistic** describes Greek history and culture after the death of Alexander the Great. *Hellenistic* comes from the word *Hellas*—the name the Greeks gave their land.

■ Timeline Skills

The Hellenistic Age began with the death of Alexander. **Identify** How long did the Hellenistic Age last? **Predict** Why do you think historians mark the end of the Hellenistic Age as 146 B.C.?

The Hellenistic Kingdoms When Alexander took control of lands, he tried not to destroy the cultures of the defeated people. He hoped that in his new cities, the local cultures would mix with Greek culture. Instead, however, Greek culture became the strongest culture in the three Hellenistic kingdoms.

The cities of the Hellenistic world were modeled after Greek cities. Greek kings ruled, and Greeks held the most important jobs. There were Greek temples and agoras. Citizens gathered at large theaters for performances of old Greek tragedies. The Greek language was spoken in the cities, although people in the countryside spoke the local languages.

Greek Culture in Egypt The greatest of all Hellenistic cities was Alexandria in Egypt. Alexander had founded this city in 332 B.C. at the edge of the Nile Delta. Alexandria became the capital of Egypt. Over the years, it grew famous as a center for business and trade. Its double harbor was dominated by a huge lighthouse that rose about 350 feet (106 meters) in the air. The tower was topped by a flame that guided ships safely into port.

Levers Probably the greatest scholar of the Hellenistic Age was Archimedes (ahr kuh MEE deez) Archimedes studied in Alexandria. He discovered that people can use pulleys and levers to lift very heavy objects. One story claims that he hoisted up a loaded ship with these devices. As shown below, he once boasted, "Give me the place to stand, and a lever long enough, and I will move the Earth."

Although all the important Hellenistic cities were centers of learning, Alexandria was the learning capital of the Greek world. Alexandria's library was the largest in the world. Scholars and writers from many lands came to use its massive collection.

Math and Science Mathematics and science also flourished at Alexandria. Around 300 B.C., a mathematician named Euclid (YOO klid) helped extend the branch of mathematics called geometry. His work helped explain the qualities of such figures as squares, angles, triangles, cubes, and cones. Mathematicians today still use Euclid's system.

Greek scientists made important contributions to astronomy. In about 250 B.C., the Greek scientist Aristarchus (ar is TAHR kus) of Samos concluded that Earth revolved around the Sun. At the time, however, most scientists believed Earth to be the center of the universe. Much later, the idea of a sun-centered universe began to gain acceptance.

In Hellenistic times, many scholars knew that Earth was round. A scholar named Eratosthenes (ehr uh TAHS thuh neez) calculated the distance around Earth. Eratosthenes used mathematics that were advanced for his time. His result was very close to the correct distance as it is known today.

✓ **Reading Check** **Why did many scholars go to Alexandria?**

Section 5 Assessment

Key Terms
Review the key terms at the beginning of this section. Use each term in a sentence that explains its meaning.

Target Reading Skill
Apply your knowledge of the prefix *ex-* and the root *-ten-*. What does *extension* mean?

Comprehension and Critical Thinking
1. (a) Recall Who was Alexander's tutor when he was young?
(b) Identify Effects How did Alexander's upbringing affect his attitudes about Greek culture?

(c) Analyze Alexander the Great wanted the cultures of the cities that he conquered to survive and mix with Greek culture. What happened instead?
2. (a) Describe What features of Greek culture could be seen in the Hellenistic kingdoms?
(b) Make Generalizations What was the importance of Alexandria, Egypt?
(c) Evaluate Describe the importance of scientific contributions made by Euclid, Eratosthenes, and Aristarchus.

Writing Activity
What do you think of Alexander's life and conquests? Write a short paragraph that supports your opinion.

Writing Tip Your opinion should be the main idea of your paragraph. When writing to persuade, support your main idea with specific evidence arranged in a logical order.

Chapter 6

Review and Assessment

◆ Chapter Summary

Section 1: Early Greek Civilization

- The geography of Greece encouraged the growth of independent communities that shared a common culture.
- The dominance of the Minoans and then the Mycenaeans was followed by a decline of Greek civilization.
- Greece's traditionally independent cities provided the foundations for government based upon rule by the people.

Section 2: Religion, Philosophy and the Arts

- During the 400s B.C., Athens enjoyed a golden age of achievement in philosophy and the arts.
- Like most ancient cultures, the Greeks were polytheistic, believing in many gods.
- Greek philosophers introduced new ways to think about the world.
- Visual arts, such as architecture and sculpture, and literary arts, such as drama, flourished during the Golden Age of Athens.

Oracle at Delphi

Section 3: Daily Life in Athens

- Business and social activities took place in the marketplaces.
- Athenians and other Greeks tended to eat simply and live in plain houses.
- It was common for Athenians to own slaves.

Playing knucklebones

Section 4: Sparta and Athens

- Life in ancient Sparta was strictly ruled by the state in order to create a powerful army.
- Although outnumbered, Athenians fought back a force of invading Persians that threatened to take over all of Greece.
- Athens grew into an empire but eventually fell to the forces of Sparta.

Section 5: The Spread of Greek Culture

- King Philip of Macedonia conquered all of Greece before he was killed in 336 B.C.
- Philip's son, known as Alexander the Great, conquered Persia, Egypt, and lands extending beyond the Indus River to the east.
- After Alexander's death, Greek culture spread to the areas he had conquered.

◆ Key Terms

Write a definition for each of the key terms listed below.

1. acropolis
2. aristocrat
3. tyrant
4. democracy
5. tribute
6. philosopher
7. tragedy
8. agora
9. plague
10. blockade
11. barbarian
12. assassinate

◆ Comprehension and Critical Thinking

13. (a) Identify Who were the Minoans and the Mycenaeans?
(b) Generalize Describe the period in Greek history that followed the dominance of the Minoans and the Mycenaeans.
(c) Infer How did the story of the Trojan War help the people of ancient Greece understand their history?

14. (a) Recall How did city-states arise in Greece?
(b) Explain Why were aristocrats replaced by tyrants as rulers of the city-states?
(c) Identify Effects How did rule by tyrants affect the city-states?

15. (a) List Name two ideas that governed ancient Greek religion.
(b) Describe What was the importance of the oracles to the Greeks?
(c) Apply Information According to Greek philosophers, how could people understand natural events?

16. (a) Generalize What was everyday life like in the Golden Age of Athens?
(b) Compare Describe the roles of free men, free women, and slaves in Athenian life.
(c) Predict A great many slaves lived and worked in ancient Athens. What would daily life have been like in Athens if slavery had not been practiced there?

17. (a) Describe How did the Spartans become skilled warriors?
(b) Sequence What events led to the Peloponnesian War?
(c) Draw Conclusions How did Athens lose its dominance over the rest of Greece?

18. (a) Recall Describe the empire of Alexander the Great before and after he died.
(b) Explain Why did Greek culture remain strong throughout the region after the empire broke apart?
(c) Predict What impact would Hellenism have on the rest of the world?

◆ Writing Activity: Government

Use at least five key terms from the chapter to write a brief poem, essay, or dialogue having to do with government in ancient Greece.

◆ Skills Practice

Drawing Conclusions Review the Skills for Life activity. Reread the passage on pages 177–178 titled Greek Science and Philosophy. Then draw conclusions about how the ideas of Greek philosophers affected later civilizations.

MAP MASTER™ Skills Activity

Ancient Greece

Place Location For each place listed below, write the letter from the map that shows its location.
1. Athens
2. Sparta
3. Macedonia
4. Crete
5. Troy
6. Marathon
7. Mycenae

Go Online
PHSchool.com Use Web Code **lbp-2645** for an **interactive map**.

Standardized Test Prep

Test-Taking Tips

Some questions on standardized tests ask you to analyze an outline. Study the outline below. Then follow the tips to answer the sample question.

> I. Solon's reforms
>   A. Outlawed slavery based on debt
>   B. Opened high offices to more citizens
>   C.
>   D. Gave the assembly more power
> II. Limited rights

TIP Use key words in the outline to help you.

Think It Through This outline is organized by major topics and subtopics. The question asks you to find subtopic C under Topic I. Answers A and C are too general. That leaves B and D. Answer D does not fit under Topic I, which is about Solon's reforms. *Reforms* means "changes" or "improvements." The correct answer is B.

TIP Think about how the text is organized in the outline. Use that information to help you answer the question.

Pick the letter that best answers the question.

Which of the following belongs in I-C?

A Later reforms under other leaders

B Let male citizens debate important laws

C Life in Athens

D Did not let women share in public life

Practice Questions

Use the tips above and other tips in this book to help you answer the following questions.

1. Why did ancient Greek communities think of themselves as separate countries?

   A They spoke different languages.

   B Each community's people came from different countries.

   C They practiced different religions.

   D Geographical features separated them from one another.

2. Most of the labor in ancient Greek households was performed by

   A slaves.   **B** philosophers.

   C girls.   **D** boys.

3. For which of the following were Spartans best known?

   A art and architecture

   B their skills in war

   C philosophy

   D having an open society

Study the outline below, and then answer the following question.

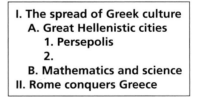

> I. The spread of Greek culture
>   A. Great Hellenistic cities
>   1. Persepolis
>   2.
>   B. Mathematics and science
> II. Rome conquers Greece

4. Which answer belongs in the space next to the number 2 in the outline above?

   A Son of King Philip

   B Died in 323 B.C.

   C Alexandria

   D Athens

Use Web Code **lba-2605** for **Chapter 6 self-test.**

The Sirens

A Greek Myth From *The Adventures of Ulysses*
Retold by Bernard Evslin

Prepare to Read

Background Information

Have you ever been persuaded to go somewhere, do something, or buy something because someone made it sound fun or exciting? Messages like these can sometimes lead people in the wrong direction.

The Sirens (SY runz) in this myth are creatures who use their songs to lead sailors to destruction. The hero, Ulysses (yoo LIS eez), is warned about the Sirens as he tries to sail home to Greece after the Trojan War.

Ulysses is the name the Roman people gave to the Greek hero Odysseus (oh DIS ee us). The tale of Ulysses and the Sirens comes from a series of tales told in Homer's *Odyssey*. The clever Ulysses had expected an easy journey home. Instead, he was delayed by adventures that tested his body and spirit.

Like Homer and other storytellers, Bernard Evslin has retold the ancient story of the Sirens in his own words. The events are the same as those in the Odyssey myth. But the author has added many details to make the story his own.

Objectives

In this selection you will
1. Learn about the Greek ideas of leadership and heroism.
2. Think about the roles temptation and danger play in this story and in people's lives.

Sculpture of a Siren

n the first light of morning Ulysses awoke and called his crew about him.

"Men," he said. "Listen well, for your lives today hang upon what I am about to tell you. That large island to the west is <u>Thrinacia</u>, where we must make a landfall, for our provisions run low. But to get to the island we must pass through a narrow strait. And at the head of this <u>strait</u> is a rocky <u>islet</u> where dwell two sisters called Sirens, whose voices you must not hear. Now I shall guard you against their singing, which would lure you to shipwreck, but first you must bind me to the mast. Tie me tightly, as though I were a dangerous captive. And no matter how I struggle, no matter what signals I make to you, do not release me, lest I follow their voices to destruction, taking you with me."

Thereupon Ulysses took a large lump of the beeswax that was used by the sail mender to slick his heavy thread and kneaded it in his powerful hands until it became soft. Then he went to each man of the crew and plugged his ears with soft wax; he <u>caulked</u> their ears so tightly that they could hear nothing but the thin pulsing of their own blood.

Thrinacia (thrih NAY shee uh) *n.* mythological island that might have been Sicily
strait (strayt) *n.* narrow water passage between two pieces of land
islet (EYE lit) *n.* small island

caulk (kawk) *v.* to stop up and make tight

Then he stood himself against the mast, and the men bound him about with rawhide, winding it tightly around his body, lashing him to the thick mast.

They had lowered the sail because ships cannot sail through a narrow strait unless there is a following wind, and now each man of the crew took his place at the great oars. The polished blades whipped the sea into a froth of white water and the ship nosed toward the strait.

Ulysses had left his own ears unplugged because he had to remain in command of the ship and had need of his hearing. Every sound means something upon the sea. But when they drew near the rocky islet and he heard the first faint <u>strains</u> of the Sirens' singing, then he wished he, too, had stopped his own ears with wax. All his strength suddenly <u>surged</u> toward the sound of those magical voices. The very hair of his head seemed to be tugging at his scalp, trying to fly away. His eyeballs started out of his head.

For in those voices were the sounds that men love:
Happy sounds like birds <u>railing</u>, sleet hailing, milk pailing....
Sad sounds like rain leaking, trees creaking, wind seeking....
Autumn sounds like leaves tapping, fire snapping, river <u>lapping</u>....
Quiet sounds like snow flaking, spider waking, heart breaking....

strain (strayn) *n.* tune

surge (surj) *v.* to rise or swell suddenly

rail (rayl) *v.* to cry, complain

lap (lap) *v.* to splash in little waves

√ Reading Check

What does Ulysses do to keep his men from hearing the voices of the Sirens?

A Greek jar showing Ulysses and his men as they encounter the Sirens

purl (purl) *v.* to make a soft murmuring sound like a flowing stream
spume (spyoom) *n.* foam

hawser (HAW zur) *n.* a large rope

About the Selection

Homer's tale of Ulysses and the Sirens is only a few dozen verses long. This version of the tale, "The Sirens," as well as many other tales from Homer's *Odyssey,* can be found in *The Adventures of Ulysses,* by Bernard Evslin. The book was published in 1969.

It seemed to him then that the sun was burning him to a cinder as he stood. And the voices of the Sirens <u>purled</u> in a cool crystal pool upon their rock past the blue-hot flatness of the sea and its lacings of white-hot <u>spume</u>. It seemed to him he could actually see their voices deepening into a silvery, cool pool and must plunge into that pool or die a flaming death.

He was filled with such a fury of desire that he swelled his mighty muscles, burst the rawhide bonds like thread, and dashed for the rail.

But he had warned two of his strongest men—Perimedes (pehr ih MEE deez) and Eurylochus (yoo RIHL uh kus)—to guard him close. They seized him before he could plunge into the water. He swept them aside as if they had been children. But they had held him long enough to give the crew time to swarm about him. He was overpowered—crushed by their numbers—and dragged back to the mast. This time he was bound with the mighty <u>hawser</u> that held the anchor.

The men returned to their rowing seats, unable to hear the voices because of the wax corking their ears. The ship swung about and headed for the strait again.

Louder now, and clearer, the tormenting voices came to Ulysses. Again he was aflame with a fury of desire. But try as he might he could not break the thick anchor line. He strained against it until he bled, but the line held.

The men bent to their oars and rowed more swiftly, for they saw the mast bending like a tall tree in a heavy wind, and they feared that Ulysses, in his fury, might snap it off short and dive, mast and all, into the water to get at the Sirens.

Now they were passing the rock, and Ulysses could see the singers. There were two of them. They sat on a heap of white bones—the bones of shipwrecked sailors—and sang more beautifully than senses could bear. But their appearance did not match their voices, for they were shaped like birds, huge birds, larger than eagles.

A Siren

They had feathers instead of hair, and their hands and feet were claws. But their faces were the faces of young girls.

When Ulysses saw them he was able to forget the sweetness of their voices because their look was so fearsome. He closed his eyes against the terrible sight of these bird-women perched on their heap of bones. But when he closed his eyes he could not see their ugliness, then their voices maddened him once again, and he felt himself straining against the bloody ropes. He forced himself to open his eyes and look upon the monsters, so that the terror of their bodies would blot the beauty of their voices.

But the men, who could only see, not hear the Sirens, were so <u>appalled</u> by their <u>aspect</u> that they swept their oars faster and faster, and the black ship scuttled past the rock. The Sirens' voices sounded fainter and fainter and finally died away.

When Perimedes and Eurylochus saw their captain's face lose its madness, they unbound him, and he signaled to the men to unstop their ears. For now he heard the whistling gurgle of a whirlpool, and he knew that they were approaching the narrowest part of the strait, and must pass between <u>Scylla</u> and <u>Charybdis</u>.

appall (uh PAWL) *v.* to horrify
aspect (AS pekt) *n.* the way something looks
Scylla (SIL uh) *n.* a monster who ate sailors passing through the Straits of Messina, between Italy and Sicily
Charybdis (kuh RIB dis) *n.* a monster in the form of a deadly whirlpool near Scylla

✓ **Reading Check**

What are the Sirens doing on their rocky islet?

Review and Assessment

Thinking About the Selection

1. (a) **Identify** What are the Sirens?
(b) **Apply Information** Why do you think temptation is sometimes described as a "siren song"?
2. (a) **Recall** What fears does Ulysses have about the voyage?
(b) **Infer** Give two reasons Ulysses leaves his own ears unplugged during the voyage.
(c) **Draw Conclusions** Do you think Ulysses is a good leader? Explain why or why not.

Writing Activity

Retell the Story in a Different Form "The Sirens" is in the form of a short story. Use another form of writing to retell it. You might choose to make it into a poem. You could retell it as a movie script with dialog and scene descriptions. Or, you might write an instruction manual for sailors to follow when they have to travel near the Sirens.

About the Author

Homer Although "The Sirens" is retold here by Bernard Evslin, the tale was made famous by Homer. Homer was a Greek poet who lived around 750 B.C. Scholars believe that he drew on legends passed down by word of mouth to compose the epic poems the *Iliad* and the *Odyssey*.

Chapter Preview

In this chapter you will learn about civilization and government in ancient Rome.

 Target Reading Skill

Sequencing In this chapter you will learn about sequence, the order in which a series of events occurs.

▶ The ruins of Ephesus (EF ih sus), a Roman city in Asia Minor

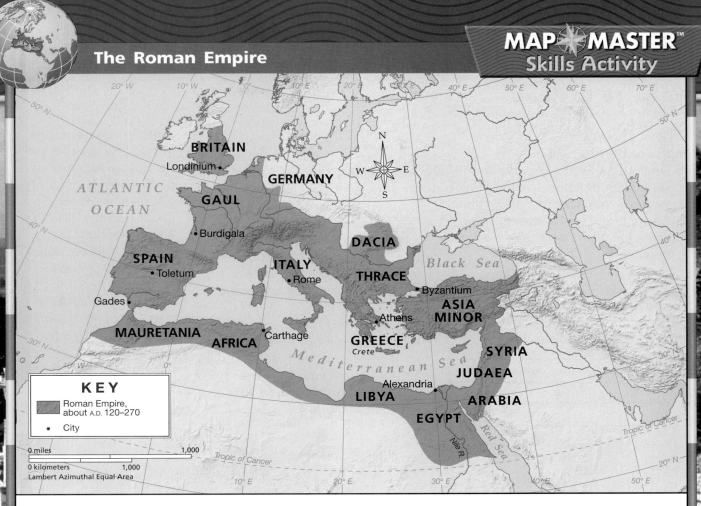

The Roman Empire

BRITAIN
Londinium •

ATLANTIC
OCEAN

GERMANY

N
W ✦ E
S

GAUL

• Burdigala

DACIA

Black Sea

SPAIN
• Toletum

ITALY
• Rome

THRACE

• Byzantium

Gades •

GREECE
Crete

ASIA
MINOR

• Athens

MAURETANIA

AFRICA

• Carthage

Mediterranean Sea

SYRIA

JUDAEA

Alexandria •

ARABIA

LIBYA

EGYPT

Tropic of Cancer

Nile R.

Red Sea

KEY

Roman Empire,
about A.D. 120–270

• City

0 miles   1,000
0 kilometers   1,000
Lambert Azimuthal Equal Area

Tropic of Cancer

Location The Roman Empire set boundaries, built cities, and influenced place names that are used in the present day. Africa, as shown here, was originally the name for a Roman province. The name later came to refer to an entire continent. **Identify** Find Londinium on the map. What is this city's name today? Refer to the Atlas on page 254 if needed. **Predict** What difficulties do you think the Romans may have had in governing such a large empire?

Go Online
PHSchool.com Use Web Code
lbp-2711 for step-by-step
map skills practice.

The Roman Republic

Prepare to Read

Objectives

In this section you will

1. Find out about the geography and early settlement of Rome.
2. Examine characteristics of the Roman Republic and why it was founded.
3. Learn about the decline of the Roman Republic.

Taking Notes

As you read, look for details about the history of the Roman Republic. Copy the chart below, and record your findings in it.

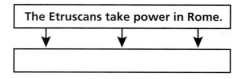

The Etruscans take power in Rome.

Target Reading Skill

Identify Sequence A sequence is the order in which a series of events occurs. Use the chart at the left to track the events discussed in this section. Use arrows to show how one event leads to the next.

Key Terms

- **republic** (rih PUB lik) *n.* a government in which citizens who have the right to vote select their leaders

- **consul** (KAHN sul) *n.* one of two officials who led the Roman Republic
- **patrician** (puh TRISH un) *n.* a member of an upper-class family in the Roman Republic
- **plebeian** (plih BEE un) *n.* an ordinary citizen in the Roman Republic
- **veto** (VEE toh) *n.* the rejection of any planned action or rule by a person in power
- **dictator** (DIK tay tur) *n.* a ruler who has total control of the government

In ancient times, young Romans were told a legend about the founding of their state. The main characters in the story were twin brothers, Romulus and Remus. They were the children of a princess and Mars, the Roman god of war. A jealous king feared that the twins would someday seize power from him. He ordered them to be drowned. However, a mother wolf rescued the infants. Then a shepherd found the twins and raised them as his own. The twins grew up, killed the king, and went off to build their own city. At a place where seven hills rise above the Tiber River, they founded the city of Rome.

The Tiber River in Rome

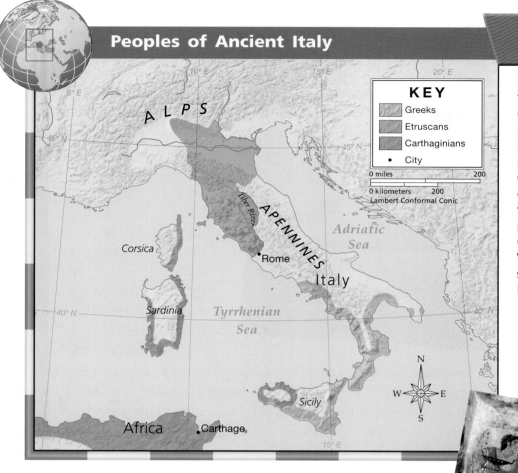

Peoples of Ancient Italy
KEY
Greeks
Etruscans
Carthaginians
City
0 miles 200
0 kilometers 200
Lambert Conformal Conic
ALPS
APENNINES
Tiber River
Adriatic Sea
Tyrrhenian Sea
Corsica
Sardinia
Sicily
Rome
Italy
Africa
Carthage
N
S
E
W
10° E
15° E
20° E
5° E
45° N
40° N

MAP MASTER™ Skills Activity

Movement It is not known for certain where the Etruscans originated, but they came to power in Rome about 600 B.C.
Identify What groups of people are identified on the map?
Conclude Note the location of Carthage. Why do you think the Carthaginians settled in parts of Sardinia and Sicily? Greece is southeast of Italy. Why do you think the Greeks settled in the southern part of Italy?

Go Online
PHSchool.com Use Web Code **lbp-2721** for step-by-step **map skills practice.**

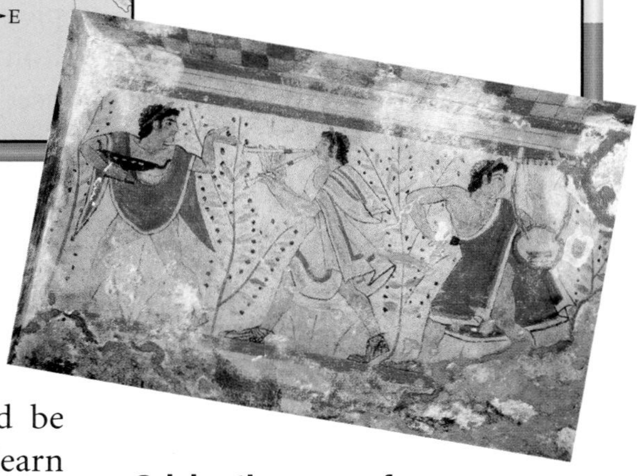

Celebration scene from an Etruscan tomb painting

Rome's Geography

We can learn much from the story of Rome's founding—even if it is mostly legend. We learn that the Romans valued loyalty and justice. People who broke the law would be severely punished, just as the king was punished. We also learn that the Romans believed that having the favor of the gods was very important.

Geographical Advantages The first people who settled on Rome's seven hills were not thinking about building a great empire. They chose that site because it seemed to be a good place to live. The hills made the area easy to defend. The soil was fertile, and the area had a good source of water. From the mountains of central Italy, the Tiber River flowed through Rome before emptying into the Tyrrhenian (tih REE nee un) Sea. But as time passed, the people of Rome discovered that the location of their city gave them other advantages. Rome was at the center of the long, narrow peninsula we now call Italy. Italy was at the center of the Mediterranean Sea. And the Mediterranean Sea was at the center of the known Western world.

The Etruscans We know very little about the people who actually founded Rome. However, we do know that their first settlements date from about the 900s B.C. Rome grew slowly, as the Romans fought their neighbors for more land.

About 600 B.C., a group of people, the Etruscans (ih TRUS kunz), took power in Rome. Many examples of Etruscan writing have been found. They show that Etruscans spoke a language unlike most others in ancient Italy, including Latin, the language of the Romans. For a time, Etruscan kings ruled Rome. However, in 509 B.C., the Romans revolted and drove the Etruscans from power.

Although the Romans defeated the Etruscans, they adopted Etruscan ideas. For example, many of the Roman gods were originally Etruscan. The Romans even borrowed the Greek alphabet that the Etruscans used. The Roman garment called the toga also came from the Etruscans.

An Etruscan tomb sculpture from about 510 B.C.

✓ **Reading Check** What is known about the Etruscans?

Romans Form a Republic

After driving the last Etruscan king from the throne, the Romans vowed never again to put so much trust in kings. They wanted a government that did not rely on the will of one ruler.

How the Republic Worked The Romans created a new form of government, a republic. In a **republic,** citizens who have the right to vote select their leaders. The leaders rule in the name of the people. The Roman Republic was led by two chief officials, called **consuls.** However, the most powerful part of the government was a group called the senate. The senate advised the consuls on foreign affairs, laws, and finances, among other things. Consuls almost always took the senate's advice.

At first, the senate was made up of only 300 men called patricians. A **patrician** was a member of a wealthy, upper-class family in the Roman Republic. The consuls were also patricians. Ordinary citizens were known as **plebeians.** In the early republic, plebeians could not hold office or be senators. In 367 B.C., a new law said that at least one consul had to be a plebeian. From that point on, plebeians could also be senators.

Links to
Government

Benefits of Office Roman consuls were allowed the use of a *sella curulis,* the Latin name for a special chair of office, in addition to twelve lictors, or attendants. The chair was usually made of ivory and had curved legs. Roman officials sat on such chairs when passing judgment. Lictors guarded the consuls and escorted them in public.

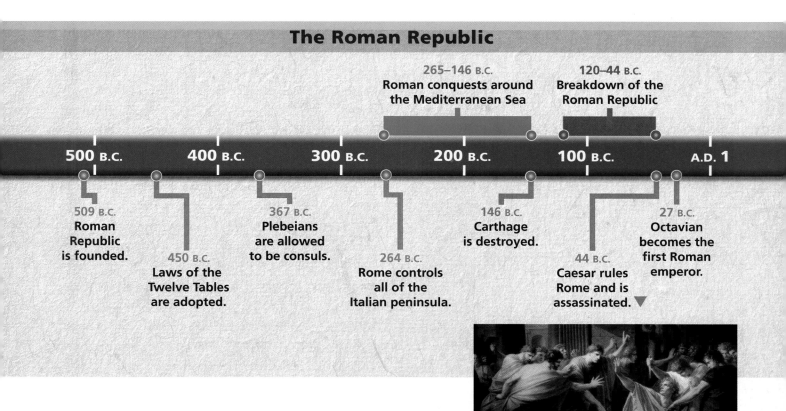

The Roman Republic

265–146 B.C.
Roman conquests around the Mediterranean Sea

120–44 B.C.
Breakdown of the Roman Republic

500 B.C.   **400** B.C.   **300** B.C.   **200** B.C.   **100** B.C.   **A.D. 1**

509 B.C.
Roman Republic is founded.

450 B.C.
Laws of the Twelve Tables are adopted.

367 B.C.
Plebeians are allowed to be consuls.

264 B.C.
Rome controls all of the Italian peninsula.

146 B.C.
Carthage is destroyed.

44 B.C.
Caesar rules Rome and is assassinated. ▼

27 B.C.
Octavian becomes the first Roman emperor.

The power of the consuls was limited. Consuls ruled for one year only. Also, power was divided equally between the consuls. Both had to agree before the government could take any action. If only one consul said "Veto" ("I forbid it"), the matter was dropped. A **veto** is the rejection of any planned action by a person in power. Today, we use *veto* to mean the rejection of a bill by the President of the United States or a state governor.

The Romans knew that their government might fail if the two consuls disagreed in an emergency. For that reason, Roman law allowed that a dictator could be appointed for six months to handle an emergency. A **dictator** is a ruler who has total control of the government.

Patricians Versus Plebeians Within about 250 years, Rome had conquered almost all of Italy. As Rome grew wealthy from conquest, troubles arose between the patricians and the plebeians.

Many patricians benefited from Rome's conquests. They took riches from the people they defeated. These riches helped them buy land from small farmers to create huge farms for themselves. Slaves brought back from conquest worked on these farms. As a result, plebeian farmers found themselves without work. The cities, especially Rome, were filled with jobless plebeians. Mistrustful of the patrician senate, plebeians formed groups to protect their own interests.

■ **Timeline Skills**

The Roman Republic lasted for almost 500 years. **Identify** By what year did Rome control the Italian peninsula? **Analyze** About how long did the republic's main period of conquests around the Mediterranean Sea last? What event occured near the end of that period?

Identify Sequence
Read the paragraphs at the left. What important events caused the plebeians to mistrust the patricians?

Eventually, angry plebeians refused to fight in the Roman army. It was then that the patricians gave in to one of the main demands of the plebeians—a written code of laws called the Laws of the Twelve Tables. The Twelve Tables applied equally to all citizens. Despite this victory, the plebeians never had as much power as the patricians.

Master of the Mediterranean While patricians and plebeians fought for power in Rome, Roman armies conquered new territories under a policy of imperialism, the practice of gaining control over foreign lands and peoples. Roman armies invaded territories controlled by Carthage, a North African city in the present-day country of Tunisia. After a series of bloody wars, the armies destroyed Carthage and its empire. They gradually seized control of Spain. Other Roman armies conquered Greece. Then, the Romans turned their attention to conquering the people of Gaul, who lived in present-day France and nearby lands.

√ Reading Check **What complaints did the plebeians have against the patricians?**

Roman Conquest
The Mediterranean city of Carthage falls to the Romans in the above painting, *The Capture of Carthage,* by Giovanni Battista Tiepolo. After the attack, Carthage burned for 17 days. **Summarize** *How was the Roman army able to control the Mediterranean?*

The Decline of the Republic

By 120 B.C., Rome was in trouble. Over the next 75 years, a number of generals gathered private armies and fought for power. Consuls no longer respected each other's veto power. Rome fell into civil disorder, with private armies roaming the streets and murdering their enemies. As Rome seemed about to break up, Julius Caesar arose as a strong leader.

The Rise of Julius Caesar Caesar was eager for power. From 58 to 51 B.C., he had led his army in conquering Gaul. His strong leadership won him the loyalty of his troops. They would follow him anywhere—even back to Rome to seize power.

In 49 B.C., Caesar returned to Italy. War broke out between Caesar and the senate. Caesar won the war and became dictator of the Roman world in 48 B.C. Recall that under Roman law, a dictator could rule for only six months. Caesar's rule, however, was to last longer. Although some elements of the republic remained, Caesar ruled with great power. In 45 B.C., he became the only consul. In 44 B.C., he became dictator for life. Caesar made many important government reforms. But many senators hated the idea that Rome seemed to be once again ruled by a king.

The Death of a Dictator On March 15, 44 B.C., Caesar attended a meeting of the senate. At the meeting, a group of senators gathered around Caesar. Suddenly, they drew knives and stabbed him. He fell to the ground, dead. Caesar had been a strong leader, but many Romans felt that he had gone too far, and too fast, in gathering power.

From Republic to Empire Civil war followed soon after Caesar's death. When war ended 13 years later, Caesar's adopted son, Octavian, held power. In 27 B.C., the senate awarded Octavian the title Augustus, which means "highly respected." He was the first emperor of Rome.

The Roman Republic had lasted nearly 500 years. The government worked well for much of that time. As a republic, Rome had grown from a city-state to a holder of vast territories. Rome had the largest elected government the world had seen to that point. But it finally faltered and died. With Augustus, the Roman Empire was born. A civilization that had raised a republic would live under absolute rule for about the next 500 years.

✓ Reading Check **What events followed the death of Julius Caesar?**

A statue of Julius Caesar

Section 1 Assessment

Key Terms
Review the key terms at the beginning of this section. Use each term in a sentence that explains its meaning.

Target Reading Skill
Place these events in the correct order: Romans form a republic; the Etruscans take power; the Romans defeat the Etruscans.

Comprehension and Critical Thinking
1. (a) Recall Describe the geography and early settlement of Rome.

(b) Explain Why did the Romans overthrow the Etruscans?
2. (a) List What were some of the important features of the Roman Republic?
(b) Analyze Why did the Romans want the republic to have two consuls rather than one?
3. (a) Identify Describe the features of the rule of Julius Caesar.
(b) Draw Conclusions Why did the Roman senate resent Caesar's growing power?

Writing Activity
Julius Caesar was a strong leader, but his leadership angered the Roman senate. Write a list of pros and cons about Caesar's leadership.

> **Writing Tip** Your writing is most effective when you know how you feel about a given topic. Having a strong opinion will help you form your list of pros and cons. What do you admire about Julius Caesar? What aspects of his leadership do you dislike?

The Roman Soldier

The Roman soldier was a citizen and a professional, committed to serving on the battlefield for at least 25 years. Away from his homeland for years at a time and forbidden to marry during his service, he formed strong bonds of loyalty to his commander and his comrades. If he survived to complete his dangerous service, he could expect to be well rewarded with land or money.

Pocket Sundial
This travel-sized Roman sundial was used to keep time.

Making Camp Foot soldiers, called legionaries (LEE juh nehr eez), sometimes marched 20 miles a day, weighed down by about 70 pounds (32 kilograms) of armor and gear. At the end of their march, the legion, or army, would make a temporary camp. Scouts traveled ahead of the legion to choose a level piece of land near a water source, such as a river or a stream. When the legionaries arrived, some stood guard while others set to work building ramparts—banks of earth to protect them from attack. First they cut strips of turf from the ground. Then they dug trenches about 10 feet (3 meters) deep. The earth piled up from the trenches formed the ramparts, which were then covered with turf. Finally, stakes driven into the ramparts created a fence. Inside the camp, tents were pitched in orderly rows. The entire job probably took about two hours.

Ruins of a Roman military camp built near the Dead Sea in Israel

Armor
Various styles of armor were introduced throughout the army's history.

Tools
The men used pickaxes and turf cutters to build the camp's defenses.

Centurions
These officers led the legionaries into battle and directed them in their duties.

Iron Tools
Roman soldiers used many different kinds of tools. The axe (left) and a hook (right) used to lift cauldrons from a fire date from the A.D. 100s.

Assessment

Describe What types of challenges did legionaries face during their service in the Roman army?

Generalize Why do you think Roman soldiers developed a strong sense of loyalty to the army during their service?

Prepare to Read

Objectives

In this section you will
1. Learn about the rule of the Roman Empire and the empire's conquered peoples.
2. Examine the influence of Greece on Rome.
3. Find out about Roman advances in architecture, technology, and science.
4. Learn about the laws of Rome.

Taking Notes

As you read, find main ideas and details about the Roman Empire. Copy the outline below, and use it to record your findings. Expand the outline as needed.

> I. Governing the empire
>   A. Boundaries and territory
>   1.
>   2.
>   B. Augustus
> II. Greek influence on Rome

Target Reading Skill

Recognize Signal Words
Signal words point out relationships among ideas or events. This section discusses ideas about the Roman Empire. To help keep the order of events clear, look for words like *when, first, before, during this time, after,* and *in [date]* that signal the order in which events took place.

Key Terms

- **Pax Romana** (paks roh MAH nah) *n.* the period of stability and prosperity in the Roman Empire, lasting from 27 B.C. to A.D. 180; "Roman peace"
- **province** (PRAH vins) *n.* a unit of an empire or a country; area of the Roman Empire ruled by a governor, who was supported by an army
- **Colosseum** (kahl uh SEE um) *n.* a large amphitheater built in Rome around A.D. 70; site of contests and combats between people and animals
- **aqueduct** (AK wuh dukt) *n.* a structure that carries water over long distances

The Arch of Constantine, erected in Rome about A.D. 315

In his epic the *Aeneid,* the poet Virgil says that other cultures may produce beautiful art or learned philosophers and astronomers. But Romans are most fit to govern, he says, and will do so wisely and with fairness.

> **❝For you, O Roman, it is due to rule the peoples of your Empire.**
> **These are your arts: to impose peace and morality. To spare the subject [powerless] and subdue [control] the proud.❞**
>
> —*Virgil*

In his poem, Virgil expresses his hopes for Rome and its rule under Augustus, the first emperor of Rome. Many Romans probably agreed with Virgil's opinions and shared his hopes for the empire.

Ruling an Empire

When Augustus came to power after Caesar's death, Roman control had already spread far beyond Italy. Imperialism continued under Augustus and the emperors who followed, as Rome gained even more territory. Find the territory controlled by the Romans on the map titled The Roman Empire on page 209.

The Power of Augustus With the rule of Augustus, a period of stability and prosperity known as the **Pax Romana,** or "Roman peace" began. The Pax Romana lasted for about 200 years. During this time, people and goods traveled easily within the empire, and trade with Asia and Africa thrived.

Augustus was an intelligent ruler. When he was struggling for power, he often ignored the senate and its laws. But after he won control, he changed his manner. He showed great respect for the senate and was careful to avoid acting like a king. He did not want to have the same fate as Julius Caesar.

Governing Conquered Peoples The Roman rulers treated conquered peoples wisely. They took some slaves after a conquest, but most of the conquered people remained free. To govern, they divided their empire into provinces. Each **province,** or area of the empire, had a Roman governor supported by an army. Often, the Romans built a city in a new province to serve as its capital.

Generally, the Romans did not force their way of life on conquered peoples. They allowed them to follow their own religions. Local rulers were allowed to run the daily affairs of government. As long as there was peace, Roman governors did not interfere in conquered peoples' lives. Rather, they kept watch over them.

Rome wanted peaceful provinces in which the conquered people would supply the empire with the raw materials it needed, buy Roman goods, and pay taxes. Many of the conquered people adopted Roman ways. Many learned to speak Latin, the language of the Romans, and to worship Roman gods.

Economic Measures
Augustus issued new coins to promote trade and ordered a census, or population count, to improve tax collection. Below, goods captured from wars increased the empire's wealth. **Generalize** *What was the condition of the Roman economy during the rule of Augustus?*

In the stone sculpture above, Marcus Aurelius pardons the barbarians whose attacks weakened the Roman Empire.

Target Skill

Recognize Signal Words What words and phrases in the first paragraph on this page signal sequence?

The Five "Good Emperors" In A.D. 14, Augustus died. Although the Pax Romana continued after his death, good, bad, and terrible emperors ruled for the next 82 years. Two of the worst emperors during this time were Caligula (kuh LIG yuh luh) and Nero. Caligula was a cruel, unfair ruler. Nero murdered his half-brother, his mother, and his wife, among others.

In A.D. 96, Rome entered what is called the age of the "five good emperors." The five emperors—Nerva, Trajan, Hadrian (HAY dree un), Antoninus Pius (PY us), and Marcus Aurelius (aw REE lee us)—gained the support of the senate and ruled fairly.

Perhaps the greatest of these five emperors was Hadrian, who ruled from A.D. 117 to 138. He issued a code of laws, making laws uniform throughout the empire. Hadrian reorganized the army so that soldiers were allowed to defend their home provinces. This gave them a greater sense of responsibility. Hadrian also encouraged learning.

The last of the "good emperors," Marcus Aurelius, chose his son Commodus to follow him. Commodus ruled with great brutality, or cruelty. His reign ended the age of peace and prosperity known as the Pax Romana.

✓ **Reading Check** Why was Hadrian considered to be one of the five "good emperors"?

The Greek Influence on Rome

The Romans had long admired Greek achievements. Many Romans visited Greece to study Greek art, architecture, and ideas about government.

Adoption of Greek Religion
The sculpture, right, is of Dionysus, the Greek god of fruitfulness and vegetation. The Romans worshiped Dionysus and called him Bacchus.
Compare *What did Greek and Roman religion have in common?*

Religion Greek religion influenced the Roman religion. Like the Greeks, Romans practiced polytheism and offered prayers and sacrifices to their gods. Many Roman gods and goddesses had Greek counterparts. For example, the Roman god of the sky, Jupiter, shared characteristics with the Greek god Zeus. The Roman goddess of arts and trades, Minerva, can be compared with the Greeks' Athena. The Romans also adopted heroes from Greek mythology, such as Heracles—Hercules to the Romans. As their empire spread, Romans appealed to and adopted other foreign gods as well.

The Roman Aqueduct

The Romans built aqueducts to bring fresh water to the city. Sources of water had to be at elevations higher than the city, as pumping was not a practical way of moving water. Engineers tunneled through mountains and bridged valleys to create a gradual, even slope. Follow the numbers to see how the water flowed from the mountains to the city.

Roman Arches
Water traveled through hollow passages in the stonework, which was supported by arches.

2 Water pressure carries water across the valley and up the other side, to a pool at a lower elevation.

3 To maintain a gentle slope, arches carry the water high above the ground.

1 Water from mountain springs flows into a collecting pool. Mud and gravel settle out.

4 The water runs underground in tunnels and trenches.

5 Aqueducts bound for different parts of the city cross at this tower.

6 The water runs into a settling pool. From there, smaller channels carry it to public baths and fountains.

Keeping the Water Fresh
Around four out of every five miles of aqueduct ran underground. Underground tunnels kept the water fresh, by keeping out dirt and animals. The Roman government did not allow anyone to damage an aqueduct, pollute the water, or use it for private consumption.

Fountain

ANALYZING IMAGES
Why were the arches built high above the land?

Building on Ideas Greeks and Romans both valued learning, but in different ways. The Greeks were interested in ideas. They sought to learn truths about the world through reason. The Romans were more interested in using the ideas of the Greeks to build things. The Romans developed outstanding architecture and engineering skills. With these skills, they built their empire.

Architecture and Technology

Early Roman art and architecture copied the Etruscans. Later, the Romans studied and copied Greek sculpture and architecture. They then developed their own style.

The Roman Style Roman statues and buildings were heavier and stronger in style than those of the Greeks. Using arches, Romans were able to build larger structures. Most large buildings were built of bricks covered with thin slabs of marble. An important development was a new building material—concrete. Concrete is a mix of stone, sand, cement, and water, which dries as hard as a rock. Concrete helped the Romans construct buildings that were far taller than any built before.

The Colosseum Possibly the greatest Roman building was the **Colosseum**, the site of contests and combats between people and animals. This giant arena held 50,000 spectators. It was so well built that the floor of the arena could be flooded for mock naval battles using real people in actual boats. Stairways and ramps ran through the building. There were even elevators to carry wild animals from dens below the floor to the arena.

Roads and Aqueducts Do you know the saying "All roads lead to Rome"? In Roman times, all the major roads of the empire did lead to Rome. The Roman road system covered a distance equal to twice the distance around Earth at the Equator. The map on page 7 of the World Overview shows this network of roads.

Romans were famous for their **aqueducts**, structures that carried water over long distances. The aqueducts were huge lines of arches, often many miles long. A channel along the top carried water from the countryside to the cities. Roman aqueducts tunneled through mountains and spanned valleys. Some are still in use today. To learn more, see Eyewitness Technology on page 221.

√ Reading Check **What are some characteristics of Roman buildings?**

The Laws of Rome

Like Roman roads, Roman laws spread throughout the empire. The Roman senator Cicero (SIS uh roh) said that laws "cannot be bent by influence, or broken by power, or spoiled by money."

A later ruler named Justinian (jus TIN ee un) used Roman laws to create a famous code of justice. Here are a few laws from that code.

> **"No one suffers a penalty for what he thinks. No one may be forcibly removed from his own house. The burden of proof is upon the person who accuses. In inflicting penalties, the age and inexperience of the guilty party must be taken into account."**
>
> —*Justinian's Code*

Roman laws continued to be passed down to other cultures, including our own. Other Roman ideas of justice are also basic to our system of laws. For example, persons accused of crimes had the right to face their accusers. If there were any doubt about a person's guilt, he or she would be judged innocent.

✔ **Reading Check** **Recall two laws from Justinian's Code.**

Roman Justice
In the tomb carving below, the Roman senate participates in a ceremony dedicated to the consul taking office. **Conclude** *What do you think Justinian meant when he wrote, "No one suffers a penalty for what he thinks"?*

Section 2 Assessment

Key Terms
Review the key terms at the beginning of this section. Use each term in a sentence that explains its meaning.

Target Reading Skill
Review the text on page 219 that follows the heading The Power of Augustus. Find the signal words related to the sequence of events discussed in the text.

Comprehension and Critical Thinking
1. (a) Describe At its height, what area did the Roman Empire cover?

(b) Explain How did Rome handle the difficulties of governing its large empire?

2. (a) List What did the Romans learn from the Greeks?

(b) Find the Main Idea How did the technological achievements of the Romans help them strengthen their empire?

3. (a) Name What was Justinian's Code?

(b) Draw Conclusions What did Cicero mean when he said that the law "cannot be bent by influence, or broken by power, or spoiled by money"?

(c) Compare How do Cicero's ideas compare with the ideas contained in Justinian's Code?

Writing Activity
Write a job description for the governor of a Roman province. Include ideas about how the governor should treat the people of the province.

For: An activity on the Roman Empire
Visit: PHSchool.com
Web Code: lbd-2702

Prepare to Read

Objectives

In this section you will
1. Learn about the social classes that existed in ancient Rome.
2. Find out what characterized family life in ancient Rome.
3. Examine the practice of slavery in Rome.

Taking Notes

As you read, notice details about the daily life of the ancient Romans. Copy the concept web below, and use it to record your findings.

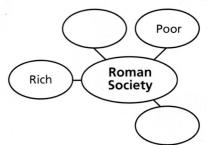

Target Reading Skill

Recognize Sequence Signal Words As you have learned, signal words point out relationships among ideas or events. This section discusses daily life and customs in ancient Rome. Customs and ways of life changed during Roman history. To help keep ideas and the order of events clear, look for words and phrases that either signal sequence or suggest a time period.

Key Terms

- **villa** (VIL uh) *n.* a large country estate; an important source of food for ancient Rome
- **circus** (SUR kus) *n.* an arena in ancient Rome; also the show held there
- **gladiator** (GLAD ee ay tur) *n.* a person in ancient Rome who fought in an arena for the entertainment of the public; usually a slave

An ancient wall painting from Pompeii, Italy

At the height of its glory, Rome had perhaps the most beautiful monuments and public buildings in the world. Wealth and goods flowed into Rome from all parts of the empire. Tourists and merchants flocked to the city. Its marketplaces and shops had more goods than any other city.

Rome could also be noisy and crowded. One Roman complained of narrow streets "jammed with carts and their complaining drivers." Another writer, the poet Martial (MAHR shul), complained,

> **❝ Before it gets light, we have the bakers. Then it's the hammering of the artisans all day. There's no peace or quiet in this city! ❞**
>
> —*Martial*

Roman Social Classes

Roman society was made up of a few rich people and many poor free people and slaves. A majority of poor Romans were either slaves or jobless. Most of Rome's jobless survived only with the support of the government.

A Life of Luxury The rich often had elegant homes in the city. They also owned large country estates, called **villas.** Some wealthy families had huge villas in the provinces, where much of the food for the empire was grown.

Wealthy Romans were famous for their excesses. A Roman historian describes the eating habits of Aulus Vitellius (OH lus vuh TEL ee us), emperor for only six months in A.D. 69.

> **"** He used to have three, or four, heavy meals a day. . . . He had himself invited to a different house for each meal. The cost to the host was never less than 400,000 coins a time. **"**
>
> —*Suetonius*

Of course, few Romans could afford to eat like an emperor. Still, the wealthy were known for their feasts. Often they served game, perhaps partridge or wild boar. For very special occasions, they might serve exotic dishes such as flamingo or ostrich. A special treat was dormouse—a type of rodent—cooked in honey. Roman feasts often included entertainment by musicians, dancers, and poets.

An ancient Roman glass flask shaped like a bunch of grapes

The Roman Villa
In this drawing, the roof is cut away to show the inside of a Roman villa.
Analyze Images *In what ways is the Roman villa below different from homes that you are familiar with?*
❶ Study
❷ Bedroom
❸ Dining room
❹ Kitchen

Another Way of Life for the Poor In Rome, most people lived in poorly built, rundown housing. Many lived in tall apartment houses with no running water, toilets, or kitchens. Rubbish and human waste were often dumped out the window. Because most houses were made of wood, fires were frequent and often fatal. The worst, in A.D. 64, destroyed most of the city.

Bread and Circuses Poor citizens needed wheat for bread to survive. When wheat harvests were bad, or when grain shipments from overseas were late, the poor often rioted. To prevent this, the emperors provided free grain to the poor. They also provided spectacular shows. The shows were held in the Colosseum or in arenas called **circuses.** Thus, the shows came to be called circuses, too.

The circuses could be violent. Romans, rich and poor, packed the arenas to watch the events. These events included animals fighting other animals, animals fighting humans, and humans fighting humans. Clowns might also have entertained, or there might even have been a public execution of a criminal. The highlights of the day were the fights between **gladiators,** people who fought for the entertainment of others in ancient Rome. Most gladiators were slaves who had been captured in battle. However, a few were free men—and some women—who fought professionally.

Gladiator Battles Before the battles, the gladiators paraded onto the floor of the arena. On at least one occasion—a battle of condemned criminals—the gladiators approached the emperor's box and shouted, "Hail Emperor! Those who are about to die salute you." However, it is unknown if all battles began this way.

Battles ended when one gladiator was dead or dying, or disarmed and on the ground. A wounded gladiator's life might be spared if he had fought well. It is commonly thought that the crowd waved handkerchiefs to appeal to the emperor to spare the loser. Although it is widely believed that thumbs pointed down signaled death, some historians believe instead that thumbs pointed up meant death by the sword.

Not all Romans approved of these brutal sports. The writer and philosopher Seneca noted, "It's sheer murder. In the morning, men are thrown to the lions or bears. At noon, they are thrown to the spectators."

✓ Reading Check **What events took place in Roman circuses?**

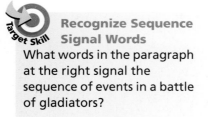

A Roman gladiator's helmet

Target Skill **Recognize Sequence Signal Words**
What words in the paragraph at the right signal the sequence of events in a battle of gladiators?

The Roman Family

Despite these brutal sports, many Romans had strong traditional values. Most of all, they valued family life. Roman writings are filled with stories of happy families and dedication and love.

Government Support The Roman government provided family support, usually to the upper classes, in various ways. Under Julius Caesar, for example, fathers of three or more children received land from the government. Freeborn mothers of three children, and freed slaves who had four children, were given certain privileges. At the same time, unmarried men over 20 and couples who had no children suffered political and financial penalties. These measures were designed to encourage the upper classes to increase the size of their families and to continue their family names.

The Roman Household Under Roman law, the father had absolute power over the entire household. He owned his wife, children, slaves, and furniture. In the early days, he could sell a son or daughter into slavery. Later, this power was limited.

The amount of freedom a woman in ancient Rome enjoyed depended on her husband's wealth and status. Wealthy women had a great deal of independence. Women had a strong influence on their families. The mothers or wives of some Roman emperors gained great political power.

✓ **Reading Check** What rights did men and women have in ancient Rome?

Links to
Language Arts

The Latin Language The Latin language is the source of today's French, Italian, Spanish, Portuguese, and Romanian languages. About half of all English words have a Latin origin. Some came directly from Latin, such as *legal, computer,* and *library*. Others came into the English language from French, after French invaders conquered England in 1066.

Ancient Roman Cookery
The Roman diet included the foods, herbs, and spices shown below. Fish and meats were seasoned with *garum*, a fermented fish sauce. Cooks used a pestle and mortar to grind foods into pastes and powders, an often slow and difficult task.
Compare *How is the Roman diet similar to ours today?*

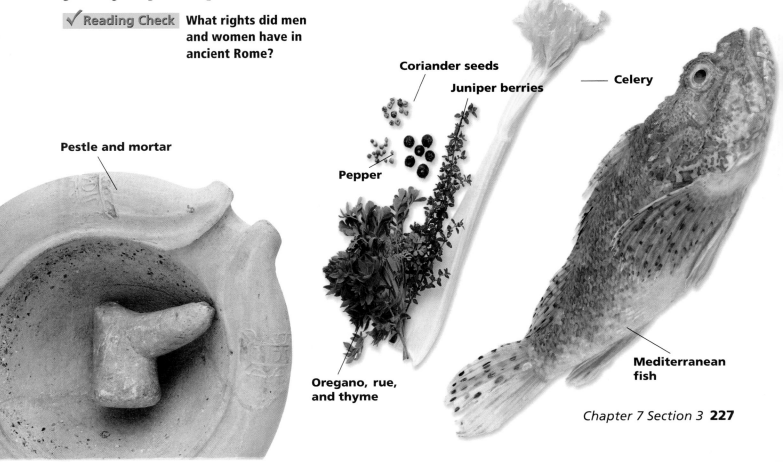

Pestle and mortar

Coriander seeds

Juniper berries

Celery

Pepper

Oregano, rue, and thyme

Mediterranean fish

Slavery in Rome

Slavery was common in ancient Rome. Almost every wealthy family owned slaves. About a third of Italy's people were slaves by 50 B.C. Few owners paid slaves for their work, but they often looked after household slaves.

Slaves had almost no rights. Yet relationships between household slaves and their owners were sometimes trusting and friendly. These slaves helped raise children and provided companionship. Sometimes they rose to important positions in the households of wealthy owners.

Household slaves received the best treatment. Other slaves often led short, brutal lives. Slaves who worked on farms sometimes worked chained together during the day and slept in chains at night. Slaves in copper, tin, and iron mines worked under terrible conditions. Gladiator slaves risked death every time they fought in an arena. Roman warships were powered by slaves trained as rowers.

Some slaves were able to save tips or wages and buy their freedom. These might be slaves with very special skills, such as gladiators and chariot racers. Such former slaves sometimes became famous and wealthy.

✓ Reading Check Who owned slaves in ancient Rome?

Artifacts of Slavery ▶
At the top right is a bronze plaque naming a freed slave, Hedone, her former master, Marcus Crassus, and Feronia, a goddess popular with freed slaves. Beneath it is a figure of a weeping kitchen slave holding a mortar. **Analyze** *What was the importance of slaves in Roman society?*

Section 3 Assessment

Key Terms
Review the key terms at the beginning of this section. Use each term in a sentence that explains its meaning.

Target Reading Skill
Reread The Roman Household on page 227. Find the words that signal a sequence of events in Roman lawmaking.

Comprehension and Critical Thinking
1. (a) Recall Describe the living conditions of the rich and of the poor of ancient Rome.

(b) Infer Why was it in the interests of the Roman government to feed and entertain its people?

2. (a) Describe What was family life like for the ancient Romans?

(b) Evaluate Information Romans valued peaceful family life, but they also enjoyed watching violent combat in Roman arenas. What does this tell us about the Romans?

3. (a) Name What kinds of work did slaves do in ancient Rome?

(b) Predict How do you think abolishing slavery would have affected Roman society?

Writing Activity
In this section, you read the reaction of the writer Seneca to a circus. Write an editorial that describes how you might react to a Roman circus.

Writing Tip Before you begin, read an editorial on any subject from your local or school newspaper. Critique the editorial for style and content. Next, write your editorial on Roman circuses, paying special attention to the style and content of what you write.

Christianity and the Roman Empire

Prepare to Read

Objectives

In this section you will
1. Find out about the rise of Christianity in the Roman Empire.
2. Learn about the spread of Christianity and its effect on the Roman Empire.

Taking Notes

As you read, write details that relate the rise and spread of Christianity and the effects of Christianity on the Roman Empire. Copy the flowchart below, and use it to record your findings.

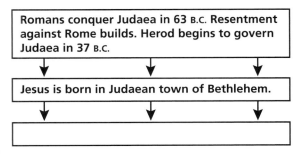

Romans conquer Judaea in 63 B.C. Resentment against Rome builds. Herod begins to govern Judaea in 37 B.C.

Jesus is born in Judaean town of Bethlehem.

Target Reading Skill

Identifying Sequence A sequence is the order in which a series of events occurs. You can track a sequence of events by listing the events in the order in which they happened. As you read this section, list the events that led from the rise of Christianity in Judaea to its spread throughout the Roman Empire. Use the chart at the left to record the sequence of events.

Key Terms

- **Jesus** (JEE zus) *n.* (c. 4 B.C.–A.D. 29) founder of Christianity; believed by his followers to be the Messiah
- **messiah** (muh SY uh) *n.* a savior in Judaism and Christianity
- **disciple** (dih SY pul) *n.* a follower of a person or a belief
- **epistle** (ee PIS ul) *n.* a letter; in the Christian Bible, any of the letters written by disciples to Christian groups
- **martyr** (MAHR tur) *n.* a person who dies for a particular cause

According to the Bible, a Jewish religious teacher named Jesus spoke these words to his followers,

> **" Blessed are the poor in spirit, for theirs is the kingdom of heaven. . . .**
> **Blessed are the lowly, for they shall inherit the Earth. . . .**
> **Blessed are those who are persecuted in the cause of right, for theirs is the kingdom of heaven. "**
>
> —*the Sermon on the Mount*

This sermon and its meaning are an important part of the religion called Christianity. Jesus was the founder of Christianity. In the beginning, the followers of Christianity were often the poor and slaves. Over time, Christianity spread throughout the entire Roman Empire.

A book illustration of Jesus healing a paralyzed man

Links to Language Arts

Sign of the Fish A secret sign that Christians used to identify one another was a simple image of a fish. How did a fish come to be an early Christian symbol? Each letter of the Greek word for fish, *ichthys,* was the first letter of a word in a Greek phrase. The phrase meant "Jesus Christ, Son of God, Savior." Symbols such as the fish and cross-shaped anchor, left, marked Christian tombs.

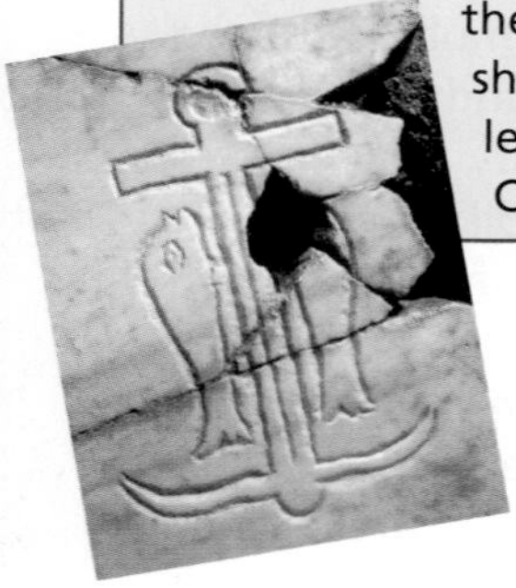

The Beginnings of Christianity

Christianity was one of many religions in the vast Roman Empire. The empire contained many lands with different languages, customs, and religions. The Romans were tolerant toward the people in these lands. They allowed them to follow their own religions. But the people Rome conquered also had to show loyalty to Roman gods and to the emperor.

Unrest in Judaea The Romans conquered the Jewish homeland of Judaea in 63 B.C. At first, they respected the Jews' right to worship their God. But many Jews resented foreign rule. Some believed that a **messiah,** or savior, would come to bring justice and freedom to the land. As opposition to Roman rule grew, the Romans struck back with harsh punishments. In 37 B.C., the Roman senate appointed a new ruler of Judaea named Herod (HEHR ud). It was during Herod's reign that Jesus was born in the Judaean town of Bethlehem.

Stories about what Jesus taught and how he lived are found in the New Testament, a part of the Christian Bible. After Jesus died, his **disciples,** or followers, told stories about his life and teaching. Between 40 and 70 years after his death, four of these stories—believed to have been written by men named Matthew, Mark, Luke, and John—came to be accepted by Christians as true descriptions of Jesus' life and work. These writings are known as the four Gospels.

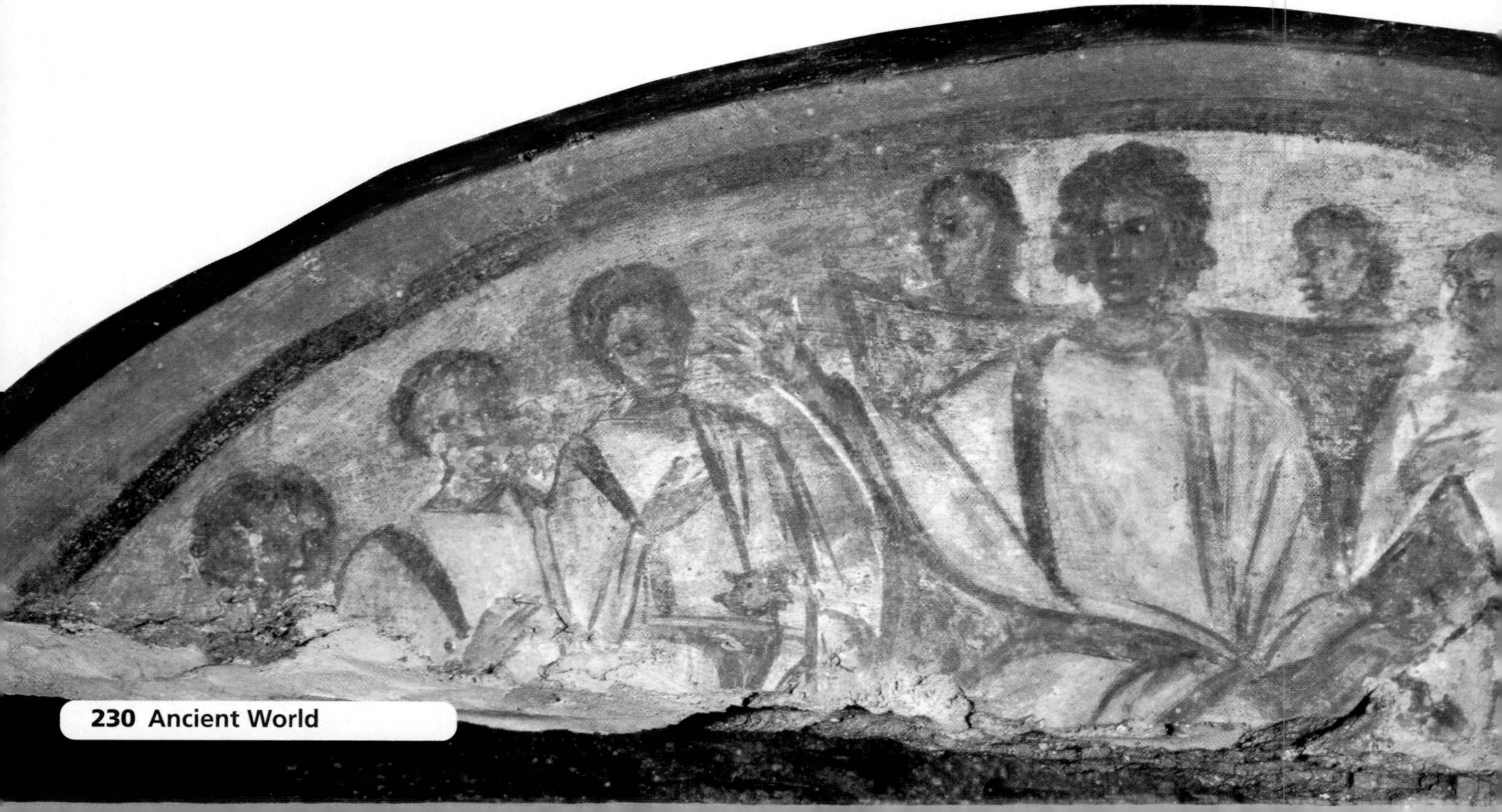

Christian Beliefs According to the New Testament, Jesus grew up in Nazareth and learned to be a carpenter. He began teaching when he was about 30 years old. Christian tradition holds that for three years, Jesus traveled from place to place, preaching to Jews who lived in the countryside. Much of what he taught was part of the Jewish tradition he learned as he was growing up. Like all Jewish teachers, Jesus preached that there is only one true God.

Read again the words from the sermon that begin this section. The ideas expressed in this sermon are important Christian beliefs. According to the Gospels, Jesus taught that God is loving and forgiving. He told his followers, "love the Lord your God with all your heart . . . and love your neighbor as yourself." He promised that people who believe in him and follow his teachings will have everlasting life. His followers believed that Jesus was their messiah.

Fears of Christianity Jesus' teachings alarmed many people. Some complained to the Romans that Jesus was teaching that God was greater than the emperor. Fearing that he might lead an armed revolt against the government, the Roman governor condemned Jesus to death. He was crucified, or put to death by being nailed to a large wooden cross. According to the Gospels, Jesus rose from the dead and spoke to his disciples, telling them to spread his teachings.

 Identify Sequence What events led to the execution of Jesus?

✓ Reading Check   **Why did some Jewish people resent Roman rule?**

Jesus and His Disciples
This scene is painted on the wall of a Roman catacomb, an underground passageway. Many early Christians— and people of other faiths— buried their dead in the Roman catacombs.
Analyze Images *Use what you know about the life of Jesus to identify him and his disciples in the painting. Explain your reasoning.*

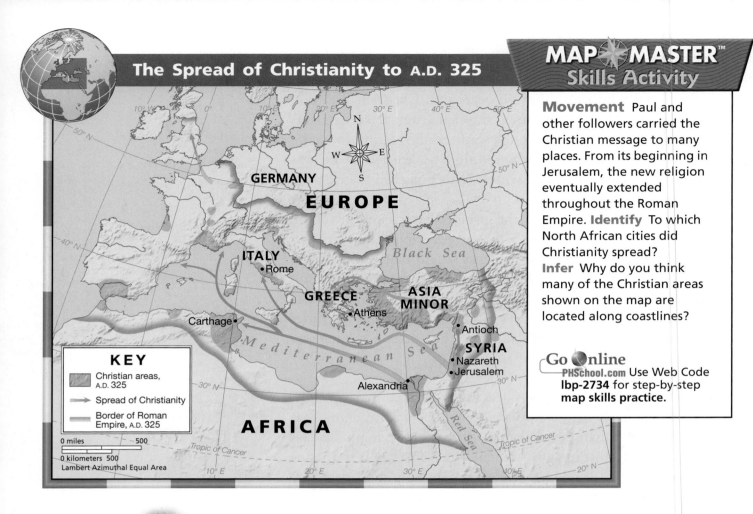

Movement Paul and other followers carried the Christian message to many places. From its beginning in Jerusalem, the new religion eventually extended throughout the Roman Empire. **Identify** To which North African cities did Christianity spread? **Infer** Why do you think many of the Christian areas shown on the map are located along coastlines?

KEY
- Christian areas, A.D. 325
- → Spread of Christianity
- Border of Roman Empire, A.D. 325

0 miles 500
0 kilometers 500
Lambert Azimuthal Equal Area

Go Online
PHSchool.com Use Web Code **lbp-2734** for step-by-step **map skills practice.**

Christianity Spreads

The Greek equivalent of the word *messiah* was *christos*. Many educated people of that day spoke Greek. As these people accepted Jesus' teachings, they began calling him Christ. After his death, his followers, called Christians, spread the new religion from Jerusalem to Antioch in Syria, and finally to Rome itself.

The Letters of Paul One of the most devoted followers of Jesus' teachings was a Jew whose original name was Saul. Saul was well educated and spoke Greek, the common language of the eastern Roman Empire. According to the New Testament, Saul at first rejected the Christian message. One day, however, he believed he had a vision in which Jesus spoke to him. After this experience, Saul changed his name to Paul and carried Christianity to the cities around the Mediterranean, spreading Jesus' teachings as he traveled.

Paul's writings also helped turn the Christian faith into an organized religion. Paul wrote many **epistles** (ee PIS ulz), or letters, to Christian groups in distant cities. Some of these epistles became a part of the Christian Bible.

Above is a painting of Paul from the 1500s by Marco Pino. At the right is another image of Paul, painted in the 200s in Rome.

Rome Burns Because Christians refused to worship Roman gods or the emperor, many Roman officials began to view them as enemies of the empire. Under the emperor Nero, the first official campaign against the Christians began in A.D. 64. One night, a fire started in some shops in Rome. The fire spread and burned for nine days, leaving much of the city in ruins.

According to some accounts, Nero blamed the Christians. He ordered the arrest of Christians, who were sent to their deaths. According to tradition, Paul was imprisoned and then killed.

The Appeal of Christianity At times over the next 250 years, the Romans tormented Christians. During these years, the Roman Empire began to lose its power. To explain the decline, the Romans sometimes blamed the Christians.

Still, Christianity spread throughout the empire. Its message of hope for a better life after death appealed to many. The help that Christian communities gave to widows, orphans, and the poor also attracted followers.

Emperor Diocletian (dy uh KLEE shun), who ruled from A.D. 284 to 305, outlawed Christian services and put many believers to death. Nonetheless, many Romans admired the Christians. They saw them as martyrs and heroes. A **martyr** is someone who dies for a particular cause. By the A.D. 200s, over 50,000 Romans had accepted the Christian faith.

✓ **Reading Check** How did the Romans regard early Christians?

Christian Martyr
According to tradition, Saint Agnes, shown below, died for her beliefs during the persecution of Christians by Diocletian. **Evaluating Information** Why did some Romans think the early Christians were heroes?

Section 4 Assessment

Key Terms
Review the key terms at the beginning of this section. Use each term in a sentence that explains its meaning.

Target Reading Skill
Place these events in the correct order: Diocletian rules, Jesus dies, and Nero campaigns against the Christians.

Comprehension and Critical Thinking
1. (a) Describe What ideas did Jesus teach?

(b) Infer Why did Jesus' ideas attract so many followers?
(c) Draw Conclusions Why do you think the Roman governor had Jesus put to death?
2. (a) Recall To whom did Paul write his epistles?
(b) Explain How did Paul's writings affect Christianity?
(c) Identify Cause and Effect Although the Roman government tormented Christians, the new religion spread throughout the empire. Explain why.

Writing Activity
You are a Roman citizen who has just learned about Christianity. Write a paragraph describing what you now know about the religion.

Writing Tip Write your description from the Roman's point of view. Remember, the Romans believed in many gods. In your writing, be sure to consider how these beliefs would influence the point of view of your speaker.

Skills for Life
Comparing and Contrasting

Suppose your teacher gave you this extra-credit project: Write a paper comparing and contrasting the ancient empire of Rome with China during the Qin dynasty.

To compare means to find similarities. (Sometimes people use *to compare* to mean to find similarities *and* differences. Be sure to ask your teachers what they mean when they ask you to compare.) You also know that *to contrast* means to find differences. For this project, you need to find out how Rome and China were alike and how they were different.

Learn the Skill

Whenever you are asked to compare and contrast, follow these steps:

1 **Identify a topic and purpose.** What do you want to compare, and for what purpose? For example, you may want to:
   • make a choice
   • understand a topic
   • discover patterns
   • show that items are more alike or more different

2 **Identify categories of comparison, and fill in details for each category.** You will need to take notes. You may want to organize your notes in a chart. Make a column for each item you want to compare, and make a row for each category of comparison. Then fill in specific information under each of your categories.

3 **Identify similarities and differences.** If you make a chart, you can mark an *S* for similar or a *D* for different items.

4 **Draw conclusions.** Write a sentence telling whether the items you're comparing have more similarities or more differences.

Practice the Skill

Use the chart below to practice comparing and contrasting.

1 Examine the headings in the chart below to identify the chart's topic and its purpose.

2 What are the main categories of comparison in the chart? How do the details shown support each category?

3 Fill in *S* or *D* in the last column of the chart to identify the similarities and the differences between the two empires.

4 As you write your conclusion, keep in mind the topic and the purpose of the chart.

The remains of an ancient Roman road in Sicily

The Roman Empire and the Qin Dynasty

Characteristic	Roman Empire	Qin Dynasty	Similar or Different
Length of empire	About 520 years (44 B.C.–A.D. 476)	About 15 years (221–206 B.C.)	
Major characteristics	• Built a network of roads • Created local governments • Established code of laws • Created a money system (currency) • Supported literature and the arts	• Built a network of roads • Created local governments • Established code of laws • Created a money system (currency) • Restricted the freedoms of scholars	
Religion or philosophy	Roman religion; later Christianity	Philosophy of legalism	

An ancient Chinese road

Apply the Skill

Use the steps on this page to compare and contrast features of Roman life with life in the United States today. Take notes or put your comparisons in a chart. Write a sentence that draws a conclusion about your findings.

Prepare to Read

Objectives

In this section you will

1. Learn about what caused the decline of the Roman Empire.
2. Find out how the Roman government came to accept Christianity.
3. Examine the events that marked the defeat of Rome.

Taking Notes

As you read, take notes on the causes that led to the division of the Roman Empire, and the events afterward that led to the fall of the empire. Copy the cause-and-effect chart below, and use it to record your findings.

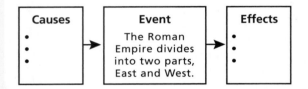

Causes	Event	Effects
• • •	The Roman Empire divides into two parts, East and West.	• • •

 Target Reading Skill

Identify This section discusses events related to the decline and fall of the Roman Empire. Use the Causes box in the chart at the left to note the sequence of events that led to the division of the Roman Empire. Use the Effects box to note the events that followed the division.

Key Terms

- **Constantine** (KAHN stun teen) (c. A.D. 286–337) *n.* emperor of Rome from A.D. 312 to 337; encouraged the spread of Christianity
- **mercenary** (MUR suh neh ree) *n.* a soldier who serves for pay in a foreign army
- **inflation** (in FLAY shun) *n.* an economic situation in which there is more money with less value

The head from a statue of Emperor Constantine that originally stood 30 feet (9 meters) high

The Roman emperor and his troops paused on the banks of the Tiber River. The enemy waited across the river. A battle was about to begin. **Constantine** (KAHN stun teen), emperor of Rome from A.D. 312 to A.D. 337, looked up and saw a cross in the sky. Written in Latin above the cross was the message, "By this [sign] you shall conquer."

Constantine's army went on to win an overwhelming victory. Because Jesus had died on a cross, Constantine believed he owed his victory to the God of the Christians. He vowed to become a Christian himself.

This story was told by a historian who lived during the reign of Constantine. Historians today debate whether he actually had this religious experience—or whether it is just legend. However, Constantine is known for strongly encouraging the spread of Christianity throughout the Roman Empire.

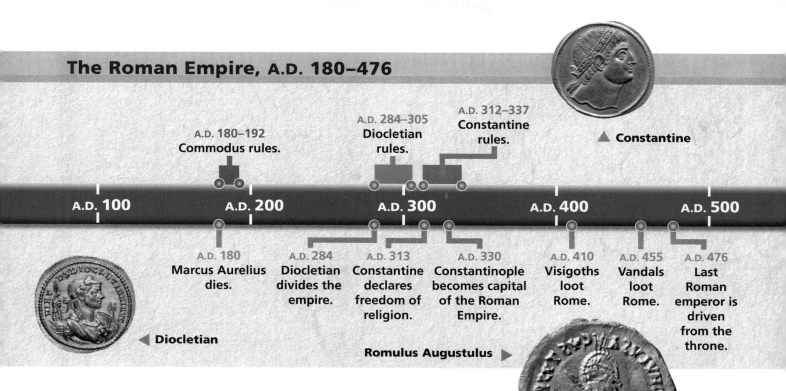

The Roman Empire, A.D. 180–476

Constantine

A.D. 180–192
Commodus rules.

A.D. 284–305
Diocletian rules.

A.D. 312–337
Constantine rules.

A.D. **100**   A.D. **200**   A.D. **300**   A.D. **400**   A.D. **500**

A.D. 180
Marcus Aurelius dies.

A.D. 284
Diocletian divides the empire.

A.D. 313
Constantine declares freedom of religion.

A.D. 330
Constantinople becomes capital of the Roman Empire.

A.D. 410
Visigoths loot Rome.

A.D. 455
Vandals loot Rome.

A.D. 476
Last Roman emperor is driven from the throne.

◀ Diocletian

Romulus Augustulus ▶

The Decline of the Empire

The Christian Church provided comfort and authority at a time when the mighty Roman Empire was on the edge of disaster. By the time Constantine took power, he could do little to stop the empire's fall.

The decline had begun many years before, when Marcus Aurelius died. The emperor, known for his wisdom, had left his son Commodus in power in A.D. 180. Commodus was not a wise choice. He was a savage ruler who loved the bloodshed of the gladiators. To strengthen his position as ruler, he bribed the army to support him.

The decline of the Roman Empire began under Commodus. Historians do not agree on any one main cause for this decline. Generally, they believe that the following problems together led to Rome's end.

Weak, Corrupt Rulers After Commodus, Roman emperors were almost always successful generals and not politicians. They often stole money from the treasury. They used the money to make themselves rich and to bribe the soldiers. Under these emperors, the government and the economy lost stability. The senate lost power. Would-be rulers gained the throne by violence. Between A.D. 180 and A.D. 284, Rome had 29 emperors. Most were assassinated.

■ **Timeline Skills**

The timeline entries above show the decline and collapse of the Roman Empire. **Identify** Who ruled the Roman Empire from A.D. 180 to 192? **Analyze** What event brought about the beginning of the rule of Commodus?

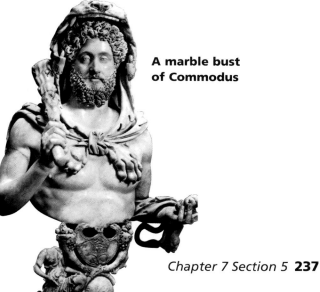

A marble bust of Commodus

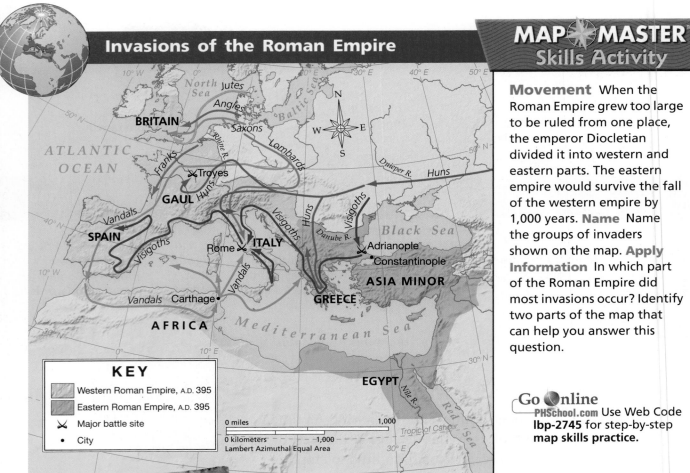

Invasions of the Roman Empire

ATLANTIC OCEAN

North Sea

Baltic Sea

Jutes
Angles
BRITAIN
Saxons
Lombards
Rhine R.
Franks
✗ Troyes
GAUL Huns
Huns
Vandals
SPAIN
Visigoths
Visigoths
Rome ✗ ITALY
Vandals
Vandals Carthage •
AFRICA
Dnieper R. Huns
Huns
Visigoths
Danube R.
Black Sea
Adrianople
• Constantinople
ASIA MINOR
GREECE
Mediterranean Sea
EGYPT
Nile R.
Red Sea
Tropic of Cancer

KEY
Western Roman Empire, A.D. 395
Eastern Roman Empire, A.D. 395
✗ Major battle site
• City

0 miles 1,000
0 kilometers 1,000
Lambert Azimuthal Equal Area

Movement When the Roman Empire grew too large to be ruled from one place, the emperor Diocletian divided it into western and eastern parts. The eastern empire would survive the fall of the western empire by 1,000 years. **Name** Name the groups of invaders shown on the map. **Apply Information** In which part of the Roman Empire did most invasions occur? Identify two parts of the map that can help you answer this question.

Go Online
PHSchool.com Use Web Code **lbp-2745** for step-by-step map skills practice.

A marble carving of a Roman soldier fighting an enemy

A Mercenary Army   Once the Roman army had been made up of citizen soldiers willing to defend their land. Now the army was filled with **mercenaries,** foreign soldiers who served for pay. Mercenaries are motivated by money, not by loyalty to any cause. They often change sides if it is to their personal advantage. Rome's strength had depended on a strong army loyal to the empire. Such an army was now just a memory.

The Size of the Empire   The Roman Empire had grown too big to be ruled from one place. Tribes that the Romans had conquered earlier now invaded the empire. Many conquered territories regained their independence. The Roman army now had to spend its time defending the empire instead of extending its authority into new areas. The loss of former territories and an inability to gain new territories caused the empire to shrink.

Serious Economic Problems   After Rome stopped conquering new lands, no new sources of wealth were available. The empire struggled to pay its army, one that often refused to fight. To raise money, taxes were increased. In the meantime, the people of the empire suffered severe unemployment.

Food was in short supply, so the price of food went up. To pay for food, the government decided to produce more coins. The value of the coins depended on the amount of silver in them. But since the government did not have much silver, it put less in each coin. This resulted in **inflation,** an economic situation in which there is more money, but the money has less value. If inflation is not controlled, money will buy less and less. Roman coins soon became worthless.

Identify Sequence What is the order of events that led to the decline in value of Roman coins?

Efforts to Stop the Decline Some emperors tried hard to stop the steady decline of the Roman Empire. Diocletian worked to strengthen Rome. He enlarged the army and built new forts at the borders. He also improved the system of collecting taxes. This brought in more money to pay the army. Diocletian divided the empire into two parts to make it easier to control. He ruled over the wealthier east, and he appointed a co-emperor who ruled over the west.

✓ Reading Check **What problems did having a mercenary army cause the empire?**

The Romans Accept Christianity

Diocletian and his co-emperor stepped down in A.D. 305. A struggle for power followed. For seven years, generals fought each other to lead Rome until one—Constantine—won the power to rule. As you read earlier, Constantine claimed that the Christian God had helped his army win the battle for the control of Rome. A year later, Constantine proclaimed freedom of worship for people in the empire. Under Constantine, Rome would no longer persecute the Christians. Christianity soon became the official religion of the Roman Empire—the one accepted by the government.

During Constantine's 25 years as emperor, he worked to strengthen the Christian church. In 330, Constantine moved his capital to the city of Byzantium (bih ZAN tee um) in present-day Turkey. He renamed the city Constantinople. The power of the empire was now firmly in the east.

✓ Reading Check **What city became the new capital of the Roman Empire?**

Christianity in the Empire
Below is the church of St. John the Theologian in Ephesus, an ancient city whose ruins are located in present-day Turkey. Ephesus was an early base of Christianity within the Roman Empire. **Infer** *How did Christianity become accepted by the government of Rome?*

Vandals Today, we call someone who destroys property and valuable objects a vandal. The Vandals were one of the Germanic tribes that invaded the Roman Empire. They looted Rome in A.D. 455, stealing artwork and other highly prized items. Their name came to be linked with this kind of damaging behavior.

A helmet of the Anglo-Saxons, descendants of Germanic invaders

The Defeat of Rome

Constantine had struggled to keep the empire together. But the forces pulling it apart were too great. After his death, northern invaders swept across Rome's borders. Today, we call these people Germanic tribes. The Romans called them barbarians. In the past, the Roman army had been able to defeat these tribes. Now, however, they could not stop them. In the A.D. 400s, the Germanic tribes overwhelmed the empire. One tribe, the Visigoths, captured and looted Rome in 410. The Vandals, another Germanic tribe, took Rome in 455. The Roman emperor was almost powerless.

The last Roman emperor was 14-year-old Romulus Augustulus. His name recalled more than 1,000 years of Roman glory. But the boy emperor did not win glory for himself. In 476, a German general seized control of Rome and sent the boy to live with his relatives in southern Italy. After Romulus Augustulus, no emperor ruled over Rome and the western part of the empire.

However, even after Rome fell, the eastern part of the empire remained strong. Its capital, Constantinople, remained the center of another empire, the Byzantine Empire, for another thousand years.

✓ Reading Check **Who was Romulus Augustulus, and what was his fate?**

Section 5 Assessment

Key Terms
Review the key terms at the beginning of this section. Use each term in a sentence that explains its meaning.

Target Reading Skill
Place these events in the correct order: Christianity becomes the official religion of the empire, Commodus rules, the Visigoths capture Rome.

Comprehension and Critical Thinking
1. (a) Identify Causes List the factors that contributed to the decline of the Roman Empire.

(b) Identify Effects Examine your list of factors from part (a). What effect did each of these factors have on the health and stability of the empire?
2. (a) Describe What did the emperor Constantine do to show he accepted Christianity?
(b) Draw Conclusions Why did Constantine try to strengthen the Christian church?
3. (a) Recall What events led to the fall of Rome?
(b) Analyze Information Why was the Roman army unable to resist the invading armies of the northern tribes?

Writing Activity
Today, we think of the fall of the Western Roman Empire in A.D. 476 as a great turning point in history. However, some historians think most people in those days hardly noticed any change. Why do you think that might have been true?

Go Online
PHSchool.com

For: An activity on the decline of the Roman Empire
Visit: PHSchool.com
Web Code: lbd-2705

Review and Assessment

◆ Chapter Summary

Section 1: The Roman Republic
- Rome's geographic setting helped the city grow into an important civilization.
- Rome's early ruling people, the Etruscans, were eventually overthrown.
- Romans formed a republic in reaction to Etruscan rule.
- Julius Caesar took over the weakened republic and became Rome's dictator.

Section 2: The Roman Empire
- Ruling the expanding Roman Empire became a challenge for Augustus and other emperors who followed him.
- The Greeks influenced Roman learning and Roman religion.
- The Romans were masters at creating large public buildings and road networks.
- Roman law spread throughout the empire and continues to influence civilizations today.

The Colosseum

Section 3: Roman Daily Life
- A few people in ancient Rome were wealthy, but many people were poor, and were either slaves or jobless.
- Roman law gave fathers absolute authority over their households.
- Slavery was common in ancient Rome.

Section 4: Christianity and the Roman Empire
- According to the Christian Bible, Jesus' followers believed that he was their savior, sent to help bring them justice and freedom.
- After Jesus' death, Christianity spread throughout the Roman Empire.

Section 5: The Fall of Rome
- Political and economic problems brought about the decline of the Roman Empire.
- Christianity became the official state religion under the emperor Constantine.
- Germanic tribes invaded Rome in the A.D. 400s, and Rome's last emperor stepped down in 476.

◆ Key Terms

Fill in the blanks with the correct key terms.

1. A _____ was an ordinary citizen in the ancient Roman Republic.
   - **A** patrician
   - **B** plebeian
   - **C** dictator
   - **D** martyr

2. A(n) _____ was an arena in ancient Rome.
   - **A** villa
   - **B** aqueduct
   - **C** circus
   - **D** province

3. A _____ was one of two officials who led the Roman Republic.
   - **A** consul
   - **B** plebeian
   - **C** dictator
   - **D** martyr

4. A(n) _____ is someone who follows a person or a belief.
   - **A** epistle
   - **B** gladiator
   - **C** disciple
   - **D** patrician

5. A _____ is a soldier who serves for pay in a foreign army.
   - **A** gladiator
   - **B** disciple
   - **C** dictator
   - **D** mercenary

6. A(n) _____ is the rejection of any planned action or rule by a person in power.
   - **A** Pax Romana
   - **B** republic
   - **C** veto
   - **D** inflation

◆ Comprehension and Critical Thinking

7. (a) Describe How was Rome governed in the time of the republic?
(b) Identify Cause and Effect What led to the decline of the Roman Republic and how did the decline affect the governing of Rome?

8. (a) Recall What events led to the rise of both Julius and Augustus Caesar?
(b) Compare and Contrast Compare the way the Roman senate felt about Julius Caesar with the way they felt about Augustus. Why did they kill Caesar, but later support Augustus?

9. (a) Explain How did the Roman Empire govern its conquered territories?
(b) Draw Inferences Why was Rome interested in keeping peace in its conquered territories?

10. (a) Identify What contributions did Romans make to law, technology, and architecture?
(b) Generalize What was the importance of these contributions?

11. (a) List Give examples of the ways the rich, the poor, and slaves lived in ancient Rome.

(b) Summarize How did the Roman circuses bring the rich, the poor, and slaves together?

12. (a) Recall What were some of Jesus' teachings?
(b) Draw Conclusions Why did poor Romans and slaves find Christianity appealing?

13. (a) Describe What were the strengths and weaknesses of the Roman Empire?
(b) Identify Effects What good and bad effects resulted from the great size of the Roman Empire?

◆ Writing Activity: Government

Write a speech, addressed to the Roman senate, that is either for or against Augustus as emperor.

◆ Skills Practice

Comparing and Contrasting Review the steps you followed to learn this skill. Create a chart to help identify the similarities and differences between the decline of the Roman Republic and the fall of the Roman Empire. Use your findings to draw conclusions about those events.

MAP MASTER™ Skills Activity

Place Location For each place listed below, write the letter from the map that shows its location.

1. Rome
2. Mediterranean Sea
3. Gaul
4. Judaea
5. Britain
6. Greece
7. Constantinople
8. Carthage

Go Online
PHSchool.com Use Web Code **lbp-2755** for step-by-step **map skills practice.**

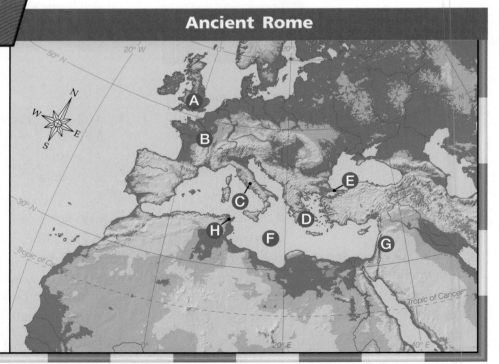

Ancient Rome

Standardized Test Prep

Test-Taking Tips

Some questions on standardized tests ask you to analyze a timeline. Study the timeline below. Then follow the tips to answer the question.

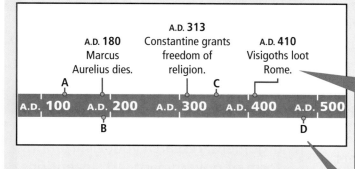

Think It Through As you look over the timeline, ask yourself, *When did the last emperor rule Rome?* It must have happened near the end of the Roman Empire; so you can rule out A and B. Even if you don't know the exact date, you can make a thoughtful guess. The last emperor's rule took place *after* the Visigoths looted Rome. The correct answer is D.

TIP When you read a timeline, line up each event with the nearest date. Make sure you can read a date for each point on the timeline.

TIP Carelessness costs points on multiple-choice tests. Think about each date and event on the timeline carefully.

Choose the letter that best answers the question.

Where would "The last Roman emperor is driven from power" go on the timeline?

A point A
B point B
C point C
D point D

Practice Questions

Use the tips above and other tips in this book to help you answer the following questions.

1. In the Roman Republic, what happened if the republic faced an emergency?
   A A dictator was appointed.
   B A third consul was appointed.
   C The senate made the final decision.
   D All citizens voted.

2. The Romans were heavily influenced by the
   A Greeks.
   B Chinese.
   C Persians.
   D plebeians.

3. The letters that Paul wrote, called epistles, became part of
   A the Torah.
   B Hadrian's laws.
   C the Roman alphabet.
   D the Christian Bible.

Study the timeline below, and then answer the question that follows.

63 B.C. Romans conquer Judaea.		A.D. 330 Empire's capital moves to Byzantium.
100 B.C. A.D.1 A.D.100 A.D. 200 A.D. 300 A.D. 400		
27 B.C. Beginning of Roman Empire		A.D. 476 Fall of Rome

4. Which emperor is associated with the event that took place in A.D. 330?
   A Augustus
   B Constantine
   C Commodus
   D Marcus Aurelius

Go Online PHSchool.com
Use Web Code lba-2705 for **Chapter 7 self-test.**

Projects

Create your own projects to learn more about the ancient world. At the beginning of this book, you were introduced to these Guiding Questions for studying the chapters and special features. But you can also find answers to these questions by doing projects on your own or with a group. Use the questions to find topics you want to explore further. Then try the projects described on this page or create your own.

1. **Geography** How did physical geography affect the growth of ancient civilizations?

2. **History** What historical accomplishments is each civilization known for?

3. **Culture** What were the beliefs and values of ancient peoples?

4. **Government** How did ancient peoples develop governments?

5. **Economics** How did ancient peoples develop economic systems?

Project

STAGE A DEBATE

Researching Ancient Civilizations
Which of the civilizations in this book made the greatest contributions to the modern world? Stage a debate with representatives from each civilization. To support your argument, research your civilization's form of government, art, inventions, language, science, and literature. Visual aids such as pictures and posters could make your arguments more convincing.

Colossal statue of a seated Buddha at Kyaikpun Pagoda, Burma (Myanmar)

Project

CREATE A TRAVEL GUIDE

Travel the Ancient World
As you study each civilization in this book, write a chapter for a travel guide to the world of ancient times. Create a map for each place, and write about its geography and history. Include a picture of a special place or an interesting feature of each civilization that is a "must see" for travelers. When you have finished all of the chapters, combine them to make a travel guidebook.

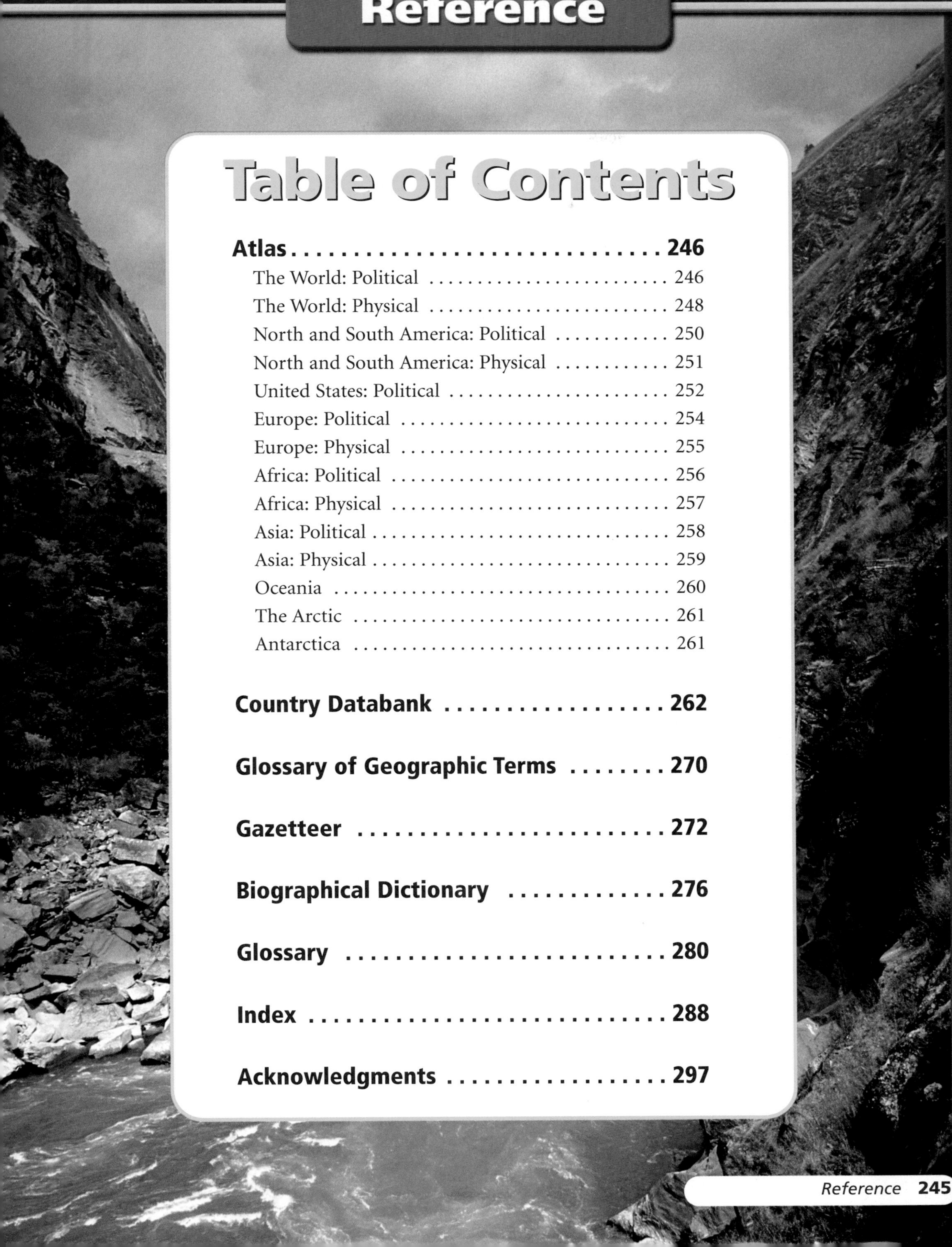

Reference

Table of Contents

The World: Political

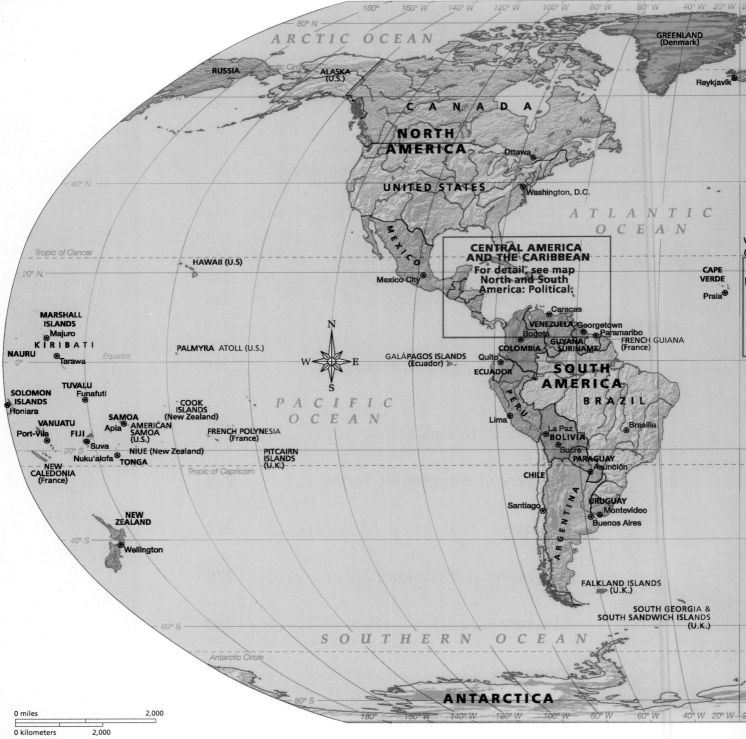

GREENLAND
(Denmark)

Reykjavík

RUSSIA

ALASKA
(U.S.)

ARCTIC OCEAN

Arctic Circle

CANADA

NORTH
AMERICA

UNITED STATES

Ottawa

Washington, D.C.

ATLANTIC
OCEAN

MEXICO

Tropic of Cancer

HAWAII (U.S)

20° N

Mexico City

CENTRAL AMERICA
AND THE CARIBBEAN
For detail, see map
North and South
America: Political.

CAPE
VERDE

Praia

MARSHALL
ISLANDS
Majuro

KIRIBATI

NAURU

PALMYRA ATOLL (U.S.)

Equator

Tarawa

N

GALÁPAGOS ISLANDS
(Ecuador)

Caracas

VENEZUELA Georgetown
Bogotá   Paramaribo
COLOMBIA GUYANA FRENCH GUIANA
         SURINAME   (France)

Quito
ECUADOR

SOUTH
AMERICA

BRAZIL

TUVALU
Funafuti

SOLOMON
ISLANDS
Honiara

W   E

Lima

PERU

VANUATU

SAMOA
Apia AMERICAN
SAMOA
(U.S.)

COOK
ISLANDS
(New Zealand)

FRENCH POLYNESIA
(France)

S

Brasília

La Paz
BOLIVIA
Sucre

PACIFIC
OCEAN

Port-Vila

FIJI

Suva

NIUE (New Zealand)

PITCAIRN
ISLANDS
(U.K.)

PARAGUAY
Asunción

20° S

Nuku'alofa TONGA

Tropic of Capricorn

NEW
CALEDONIA
(France)

CHILE

URUGUAY
Montevideo

Santiago

ARGENTINA

Buenos Aires

NEW
ZEALAND

40° S

Wellington

FALKLAND ISLANDS
(U.K.)

SOUTH GEORGIA &
SOUTH SANDWICH ISLANDS
(U.K.)

60° S

SOUTHERN OCEAN

Antarctic Circle

80° S

ANTARCTICA

0 miles   2,000

0 kilometers   2,000

Robinson

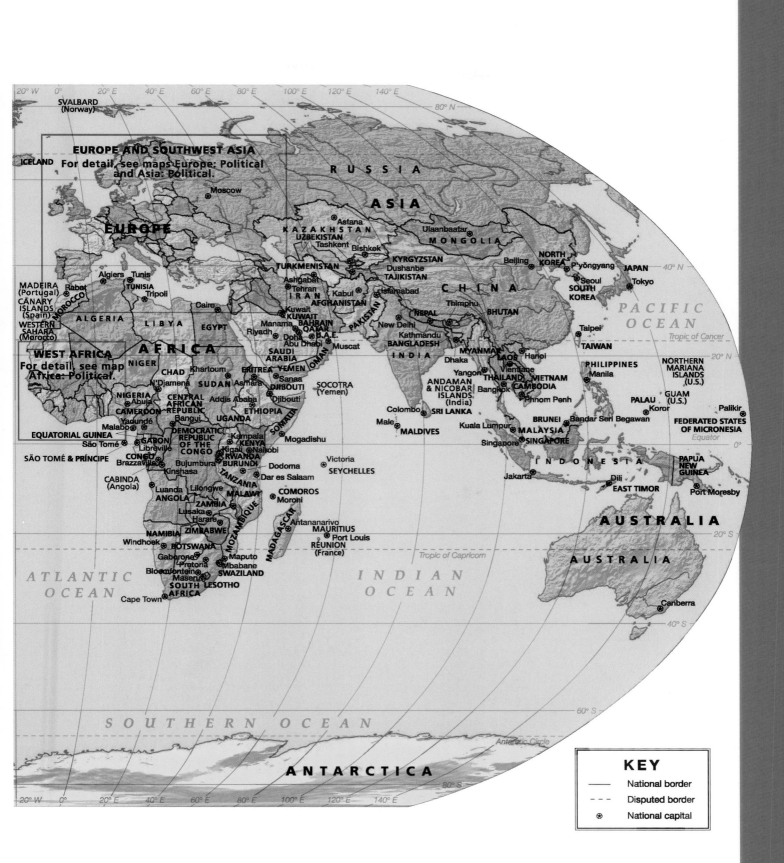

The World: Physical

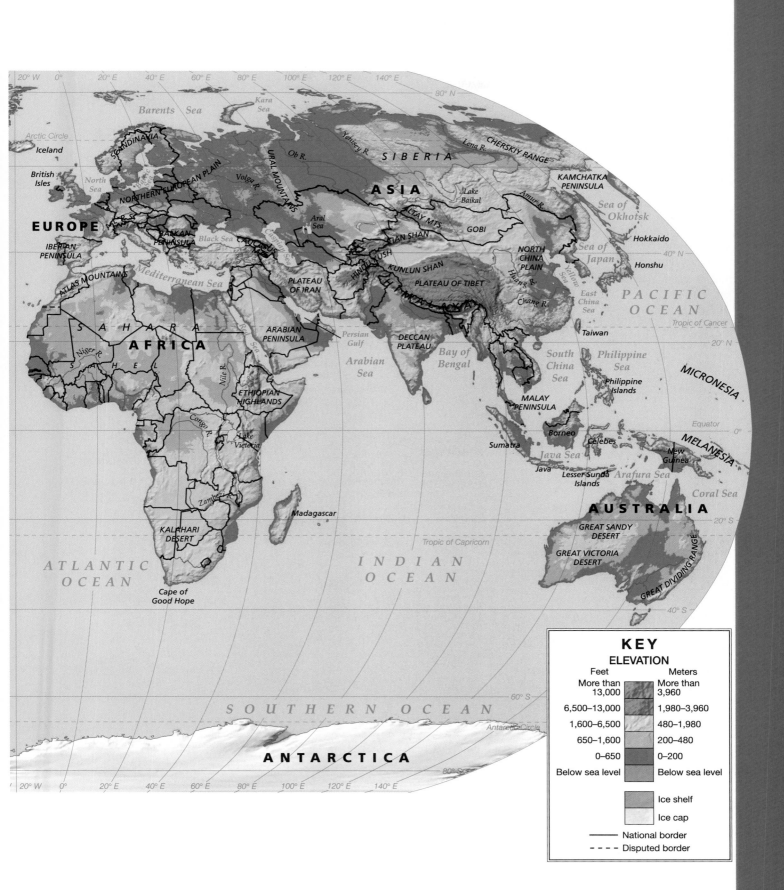

20° W 0° 20° E 40° E 60° E 80° E 100° E 120° E 140° E

80° N

Barents Sea

Arctic Circle

Kara Sea

Iceland

SCANDINAVIA

British Isles

North Sea

NORTHERN EUROPEAN PLAIN

Volga R.

Ob R.

Yenisey R.

SIBERIA

Lena R.

CHERSKIY RANGE

KAMCHATKA PENINSULA

URAL MOUNTAINS

ASIA

Lake Baikal

ALTAY MTS

Sea of Okhotsk

Hokkaido

40° N

EUROPE

BALKAN PENINSULA

Black Sea

CAUCASUS

Caspian Sea

Aral Sea

TIAN SHAN

GOBI

Amur R.

NORTH CHINA PLAIN

Sea of Japan

Honshu

IBERIAN PENINSULA

ATLAS MOUNTAINS

Mediterranean Sea

PLATEAU OF IRAN

HINDU KUSH

KUNLUN SHAN

PLATEAU OF TIBET

HIMALAYA

Huang R.

Chang R.

Yellow Sea

East China Sea

PACIFIC OCEAN

Tropic of Cancer

SAHARA

AFRICA

Niger R.

SAHEL

ARABIAN PENINSULA

Red Sea

Persian Gulf

DECCAN PLATEAU

Arabian Sea

Bay of Bengal

Taiwan

20° N

South China Sea

Philippine Sea

MICRONESIA

Nile R.

ETHIOPIAN HIGHLANDS

Philippine Islands

Congo R.

Lake Victoria

MALAY PENINSULA

Equator 0°

MELANESIA

Sumatra

Borneo

Celebes

Java Sea

New Guinea

Zambezi R.

Java

Lesser Sunda Islands

Arafura Sea

Coral Sea

Madagascar

AUSTRALIA

20° S

KALAHARI DESERT

GREAT SANDY DESERT

ATLANTIC OCEAN

Tropic of Capricorn

INDIAN OCEAN

GREAT VICTORIA DESERT

GREAT DIVIDING RANGE

Cape of Good Hope

40° S

60° S

SOUTHERN OCEAN

Antarctic Circle

ANTARCTICA

80° S

20° W 0° 20° E 40° E 60° E 80° E 100° E 120° E 140° E

KEY

ELEVATION

Feet		Meters
More than 13,000		More than 3,960
6,500–13,000		1,980–3,960
1,600–6,500		480–1,980
650–1,600		200–480
0–650		0–200
Below sea level		Below sea level

Ice shelf

Ice cap

—— National border

- - - Disputed border

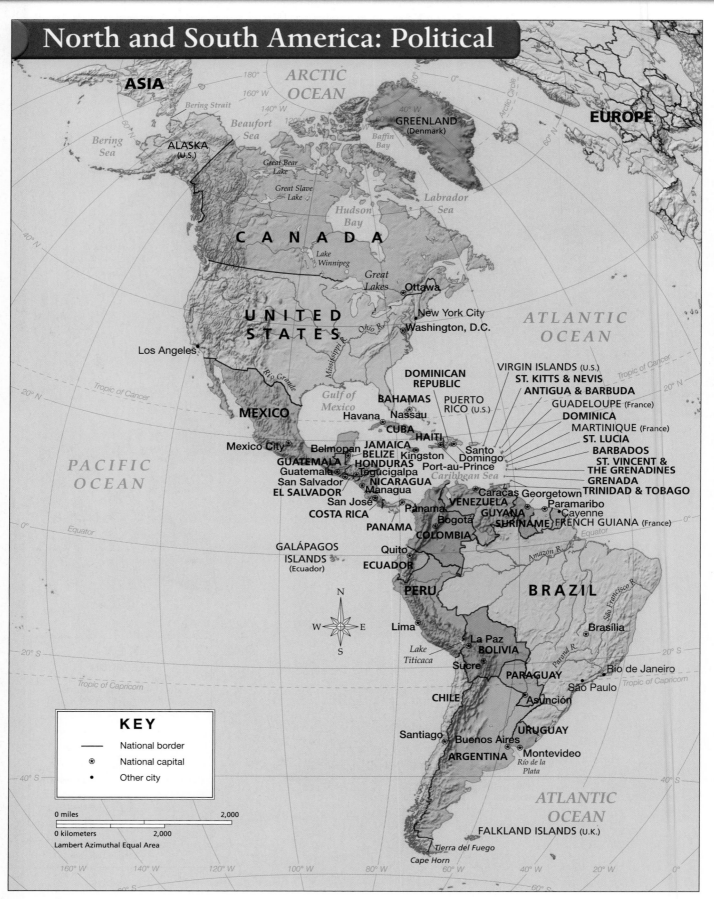

North and South America: Political

ASIA

ARCTIC OCEAN

180°
160° W
140° W
Bering Strait
60° N

Bering Sea

ALASKA (U.S.)

Beaufort Sea

Baffin Bay

GREENLAND (Denmark)
40° W
0°
Arctic Circle
60° N

EUROPE

Great Bear Lake

Great Slave Lake

Labrador Sea

Hudson Bay

C A N A D A

40° N

40° N

Lake Winnipeg

Great Lakes

Ottawa

New York City
Washington, D.C.

ATLANTIC OCEAN

U N I T E D   S T A T E S

Ohio R.

Mississippi

Los Angeles

Río Grande

20° N

Tropic of Cancer

DOMINICAN REPUBLIC

VIRGIN ISLANDS (U.S.)
ST. KITTS & NEVIS
ANTIGUA & BARBUDA

Tropic of Cancer

20° N

Gulf of Mexico

BAHAMAS

PUERTO RICO (U.S.)

GUADELOUPE (France)

MEXICO

Havana   Nassau

DOMINICA

CUBA

MARTINIQUE (France)
ST. LUCIA

Mexico City

Belmopan

JAMAICA

HAITI

Santo
Domingo

BARBADOS

PACIFIC OCEAN

Guatemala

BELIZE

Kingston

Port-au-Prince

ST. VINCENT &
THE GRENADINES

GUATEMALA
San Salvador

HONDURAS
Tegucigalpa

Caribbean Sea

GRENADA

EL SALVADOR

NICARAGUA
Managua

TRINIDAD & TOBAGO

San José

Panama

Caracas   Georgetown
VENEZUELA

Paramaribo
Cayenne

COSTA RICA

PANAMA

Bogotá

GUYANA
SURINAME

FRENCH GUIANA (France)

0°

Equator

COLOMBIA

Equator

0°

GALÁPAGOS
ISLANDS
(Ecuador)

Quito

ECUADOR

Amazon R.

B R A Z I L

São Francisco R.

PERU

Lima

Brasília

N

20° S

W   E

S

Lake
Titicaca

La Paz
BOLIVIA

Paraná R.

Tropic of Capricorn

Sucre

Rio de Janeiro

Tropic of Capricorn

PARAGUAY

São Paulo

CHILE

Asunción

KEY

National border

National capital

Other city

URUGUAY

Santiago

Buenos Aires

Montevideo

ARGENTINA

Río de la
Plata

0 miles   2,000

0 kilometers   2,000

Lambert Azimuthal Equal Area

40° S

ATLANTIC
OCEAN

40° S

FALKLAND ISLANDS (U.K.)

Tierra del Fuego
Cape Horn

160° W   140° W   120° W   100° W   80° W   60° W   40° W   20° W   0°

60° S

North and South America: Physical

ASIA

ARCTIC OCEAN

EUROPE

Bering Strait

Beaufort Sea

Greenland

Bering Sea

Mt. McKinley 20,320 ft (6,194 m)

Baffin Bay

Aleutian Islands

Alaska Range

Gulf of Alaska

Mackenzie R.

Great Bear Lake

Great Slave Lake

Davis Strait

Baffin Island

Labrador Sea

ROCKY MOUNTAINS

GREAT PLAINS

CANADIAN SHIELD

Newfoundland

Lake Winnipeg

Missouri R.

Great Lakes

Hudson Bay

Colorado R.

Mississippi R.

Ohio R.

Appalachian Mts.

ATLANTIC OCEAN

Tropic of Cancer

Baja California

Rio Grande

Sierra Madre Occidental

Sierra Madre Oriental

Yucatán Peninsula

Gulf of Mexico

Cuba

Hispaniola

Lesser Antilles

Gulf of California

Greater Antilles

Caribbean Sea

PACIFIC OCEAN

Isthmus of Panama

Orinoco R.

Guiana Highlands

Galápagos Islands

Equator

AMAZON BASIN

Amazon R.

São Francisco R.

ANDES

Brazilian Highlands

Lake Titicaca

KEY

ELEVATION

Feet	Meters
More than 13,000	More than 3,960
6,500–13,000	1,980–3,960
1,600–6,500	480–1,980
650–1,600	200–480
0–650	0–200

Ice cap

National border

Tropic of Capricorn

ANDES

Gran Chaco

Paraguay R.

Paraná R.

Aconcagua 22,834 ft (6,960 m)

Pampas

Río de la Plata

0 miles 2,000

0 kilometers 2,000

Lambert Azimuthal Equal Area

Patagonia

ATLANTIC OCEAN

Falkland Islands

Tierra del Fuego

Cape Horn

N W E S

United States: Political

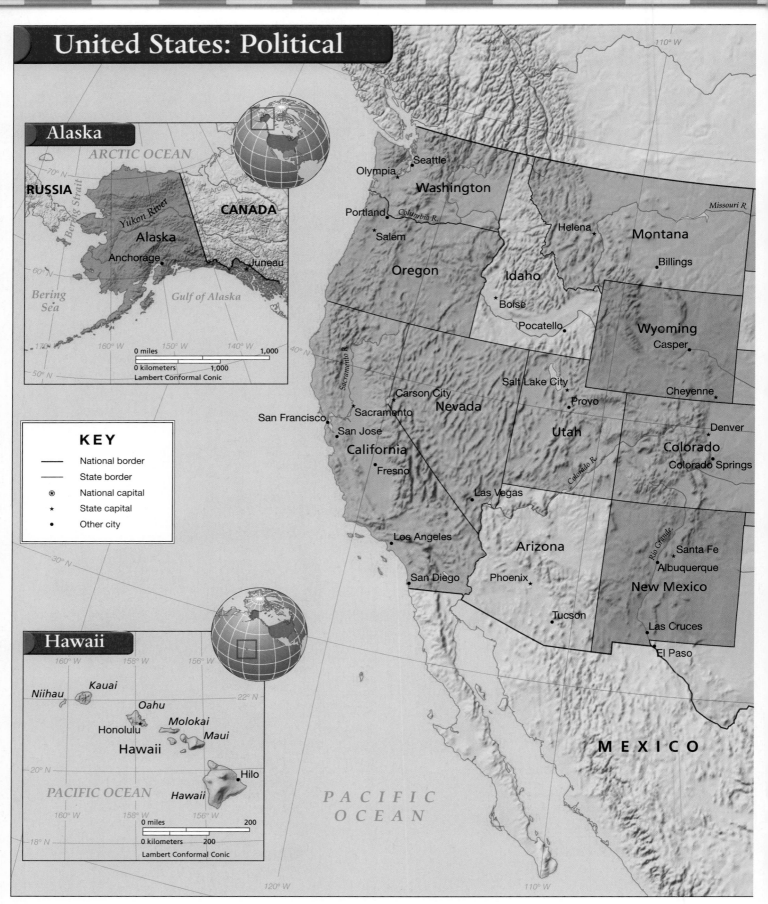

ARCTIC OCEAN

RUSSIA

CANADA

Yukon River

Arctic Circle

70° N

Alaska

Anchorage

Juneau

60° N

Bering
Sea

Gulf of Alaska

Bering Strait

0 miles   1,000
150° W
0 kilometers   1,000
140° W
160° W
Lambert Conformal Conic
50° N

KEY

——	National border
——	State border
⊛	National capital
★	State capital
•	Other city

Seattle
Olympia
Washington
Portland   Columbia R.
Salem   Helena   Montana
Oregon   Idaho   Billings
Boise
Pocatello   Wyoming
Carson City   Casper
Sacramento   Salt Lake City   Cheyenne
San Francisco   Nevada   Provo
San Jose   Denver
California   Utah   Colorado
Fresno   Colorado Springs
Colorado R.
Las Vegas
Arizona   Santa Fe
Los Angeles   Rio Grande   Albuquerque
San Diego   Phoenix   New Mexico
Tucson   Las Cruces
El Paso

Sacramento R.
Missouri R.

110° W
100°
40° N
30° N

M E X I C O

Hawaii

160° W   158° W   156° W

Niihau   Kauai
Oahu   22° N
Molokai
Honolulu Maui
Hawaii

PACIFIC OCEAN   Hilo
Hawaii

160° W   158° W   156° W
20° N
18° N

0 miles   200
0 kilometers   200
Lambert Conformal Conic

P A C I F I C
O C E A N

120° W   110° W

CANADA

North Dakota
Bismarck
Fargo

Minnesota

South Dakota
Pierre
Minneapolis
St. Paul

Sioux Falls

Lake Superior

Wisconsin

Michigan

Lake Huron

Lake Ontario

Maine
Augusta

Vermont
Montpelier
Portland

New Hampshire
Concord

Albany
Boston

New York
Providence
Hartford

Massachusetts
Rhode Island
Connecticut

Buffalo

Iowa
Des Moines

Nebraska
Omaha
Lincoln

Milwaukee
Madison

Grand Rapids
Lansing

Detroit

Lake Erie

Cleveland
Pittsburgh

Harrisburg

Pennsylvania

New York City

New Jersey
Trenton
Philadelphia
Delaware
Dover

Chicago

Cedar Rapids

Fort Wayne

Ohio
Columbus

Baltimore
Washington, D.C.
Annapolis
Maryland

Illinois

Indiana
Indianapolis

Springfield

Cincinnati
Ohio R.

West
Virginia

District of Columbia
Richmond

Kansas City
Topeka
Jefferson City

St. Louis

Louisville

Frankfort

Charleston

Virginia
Norfolk

Kansas

Arkansas R.

Wichita

Missouri

Kentucky

Raleigh

Oklahoma
Tulsa

Oklahoma City

Arkansas

Nashville
Knoxville

Tennessee

North Carolina
Charlotte

South Carolina
Columbia

ATLANTIC
OCEAN

Red R.

Fort Smith
Little Rock

Memphis

Tennessee R.

Atlanta

Charleston

Dallas
Fort Worth

Mississippi

Birmingham

Georgia
Columbus

Savannah

Texas

Jackson

Alabama
Montgomery

Austin

Shreveport
Louisiana

Baton Rouge
Gulfport
New Orleans

Mobile

Tallahassee

Jacksonville

San Antonio
Houston

Florida
Orlando

Tampa

Gulf of Mexico

N
W E
S

Miami

0 miles   250
0 kilometers   250
Lambert Azimuthal Equal Area

Lake Michigan
Mississippi R.
Missouri R.
Mississippi R.

100° W   90° W   80° W   70° W
50° N
40° N
30° N

Europe: Political

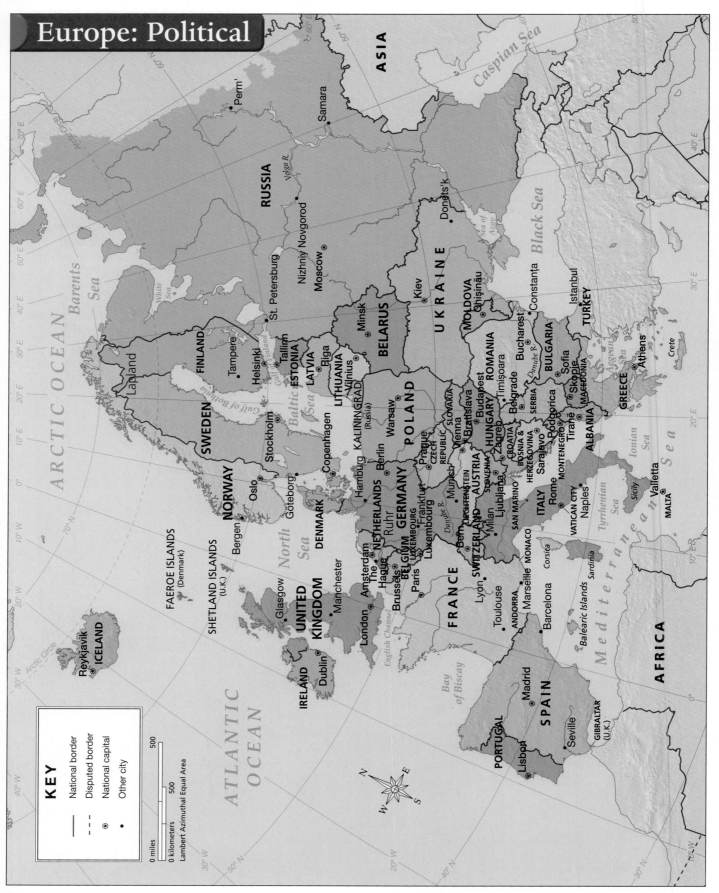

KEY

National border
Disputed border
⊛ National capital
• Other city

0 miles 500
0 kilometers 500
Lambert Azimuthal Equal Area

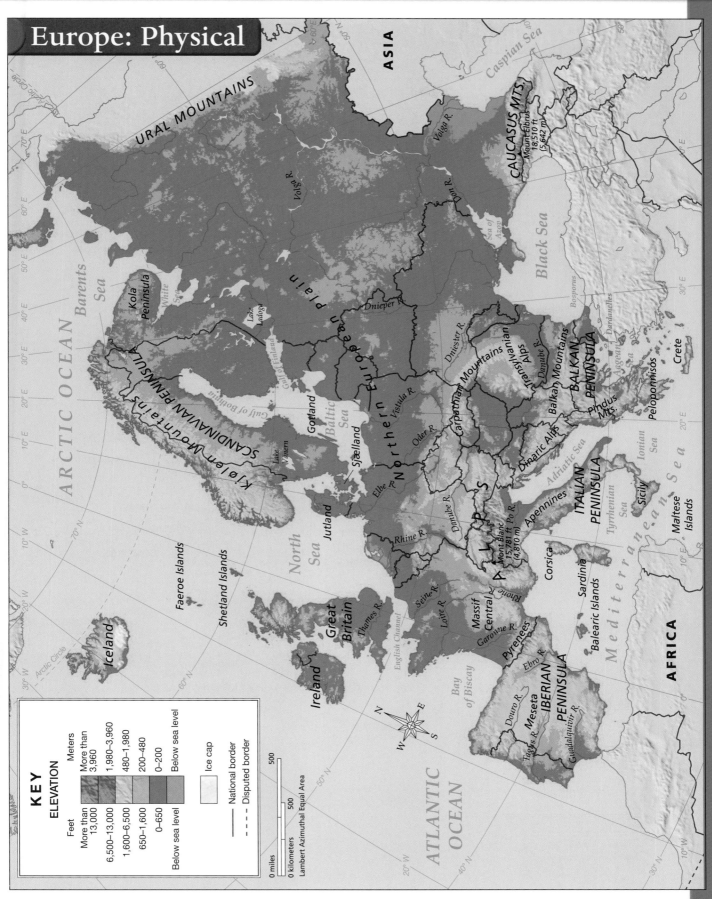

Europe: Physical

URAL MOUNTAINS

Caspian Sea

CAUCASUS MTS.

Mount Elbrus
18,510 ft
(5,642 m)

Barents Sea

Kola Peninsula

White Sea

Volga R.

Volga R.

Don R.

Sea of Azov

Black Sea

ARCTIC OCEAN

Lake Ladoga

Gulf of Finland

Dnieper

Bosporus

Dardanelles

SCANDINAVIAN PENINSULA

Kjølen Mountains

Gulf of Bothnia

Baltic Sea

Gotland

Lake Vänern

Sjælland

Dniester R.

Carpathian Mountains

Transylvanian Alps

Danube R.

Balkan Mountains

BALKAN PENINSULA

Aegean Sea

Crete

European Plain

Northern

Vistula R.

Oder R.

Elbe R.

Dinaric Alps

Adriatic Sea

Pindus Mts.

Peloponnisos

North Sea

Jutland

Danube R.

Apennines

ITALIAN PENINSULA

Ionian Sea

Sicily

Maltese Islands

Faeroe Islands

Shetland Islands

Great Britain

Thames R.

Rhine R.

Seine R.

A L P S

Mont Blanc
15,781 ft
(4,810 m)

Po R.

Rhône R.

Corsica

Tyrrhenian Sea

Sardinia

Balearic Islands

Mediterranean Sea

English Channel

Ireland

Loire R.

Massif Central

Garonne R.

Pyrenees

Ebro R.

IBERIAN PENINSULA

Arctic Circle

Iceland

Bay of Biscay

Meseta

Douro R.

Tagus R.

Guadalquivir R.

ATLANTIC OCEAN

AFRICA

N
E
W
S

KEY

ELEVATION

Feet	Meters
More than 13,000	More than 3,960
6,500–13,000	1,980–3,960
1,600–6,500	480–1,980
650–1,600	200–480
0–650	0–200
Below sea level	Below sea level

Ice cap

—— National border

-- -- Disputed border

0 miles   500
0 kilometers   500
Lambert Azimuthal Equal Area

Africa: Political

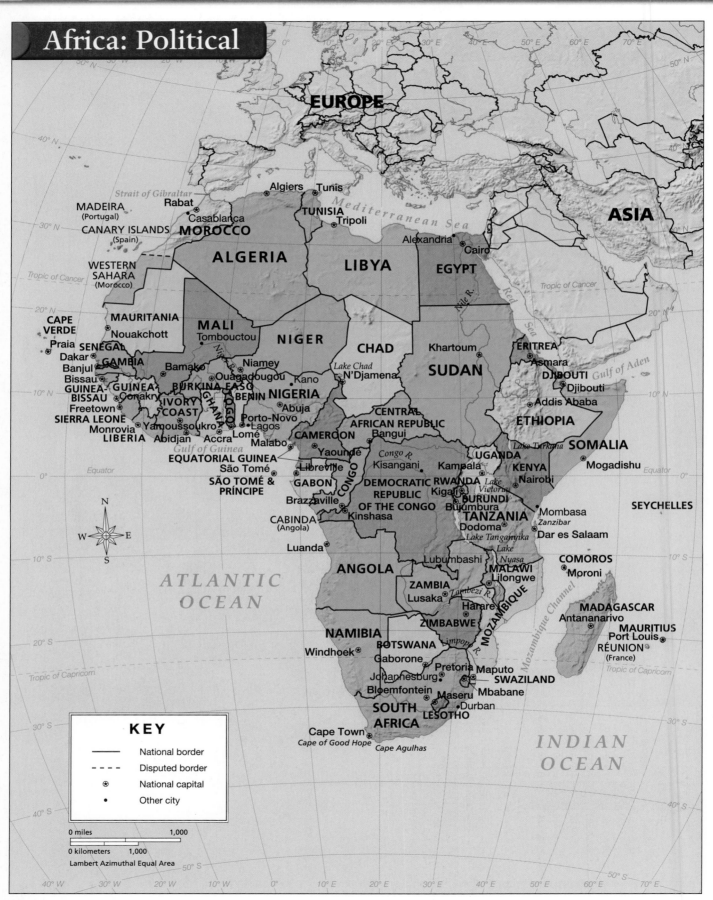

EUROPE

ASIA

Strait of Gibraltar
MADEIRA (Portugal)
Rabat
Algiers • Tunis
CANARY ISLANDS (Spain)
Casablanca
Mediterranean Sea
TUNISIA
Tripoli
MOROCCO
Alexandria • Cairo

WESTERN SAHARA (Morocco)
Tropic of Cancer

ALGERIA
LIBYA
EGYPT
Nile R.
Red Sea
Tropic of Cancer

CAPE VERDE
MAURITANIA
Nouakchott
MALI
Tombouctou
NIGER
CHAD
Khartoum
ERITREA
Asmara
Praia
SENEGAL
Dakar
GAMBIA
Niger R.
Niamey
Lake Chad
N'Djamena
SUDAN
DJIBOUTI
Djibouti
Gulf of Aden
Banjul
Bamako
Bissau
Ouagadougou
Kano
GUINEA-BISSAU
GUINEA
Conakry
BURKINA FASO
BENIN
NIGERIA
Abuja
CENTRAL AFRICAN REPUBLIC
Bangui
Addis Ababa
Freetown
IVORY COAST
GHANA
TOGO
Porto-Novo
Lagos
ETHIOPIA
SIERRA LEONE
Yamoussoukro
Lomé
Malabo
CAMEROON
Monrovia
Abidjan
Accra
Yaoundé
Lake Turkana
SOMALIA
LIBERIA
Gulf of Guinea
EQUATORIAL GUINEA
São Tomé
Libreville
Congo R.
Kisangani
UGANDA
Kampala
KENYA
Mogadishu
Equator
SÃO TOMÉ & PRÍNCIPE
GABON
CONGO
DEMOCRATIC REPUBLIC OF THE CONGO
RWANDA
Kigali
Lake Victoria
Nairobi
Brazzaville
BURUNDI
Bujumbura
SEYCHELLES
CABINDA (Angola)
Kinshasa
TANZANIA
Dodoma
Mombasa
Zanzibar
Dar es Salaam
Luanda
Lake Tanganyika
Lake Nyasa
COMOROS
Moroni
ANGOLA
Lubumbashi
MALAWI
Lilongwe

ATLANTIC OCEAN

ZAMBIA
Lusaka
Zambezi R.
MOZAMBIQUE
MADAGASCAR
Antananarivo
MAURITIUS
Port Louis
Harare
ZIMBABWE
Mozambique Channel
RÉUNION (France)
NAMIBIA
BOTSWANA
Limpopo R.
Windhoek
Gaborone
Pretoria
Maputo
SWAZILAND
Johannesburg
Mbabane
Bloemfontein
Maseru
Durban
SOUTH AFRICA
LESOTHO
Cape Town
Cape of Good Hope
Cape Agulhas

INDIAN OCEAN

N W E S

KEY

——	National border
- - -	Disputed border
⊛	National capital
•	Other city

0 miles 1,000
0 kilometers 1,000
Lambert Azimuthal Equal Area

Africa: Physical

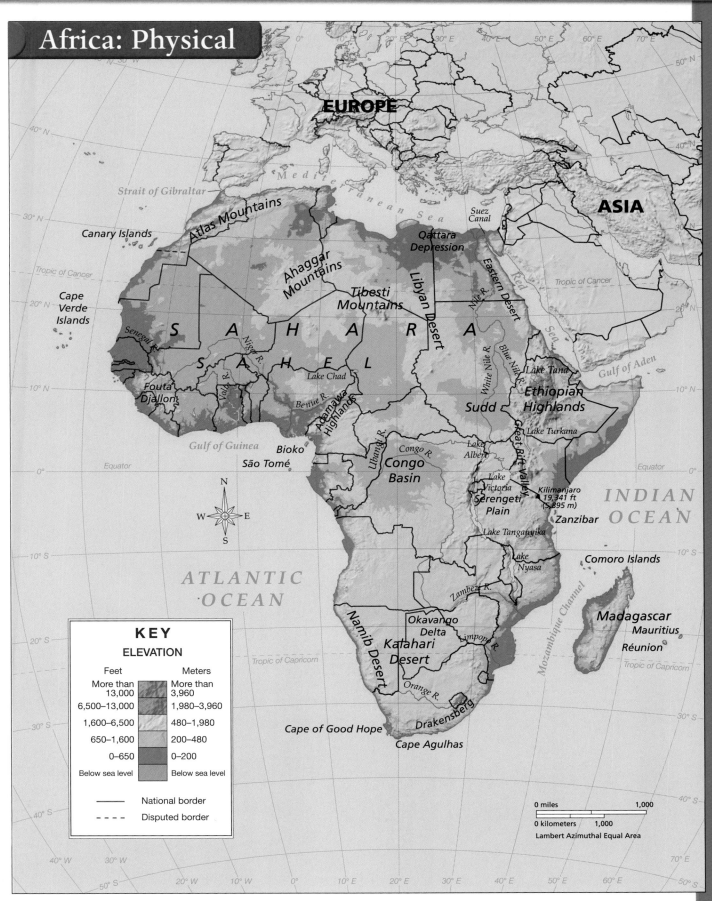

EUROPE

ASIA

Strait of Gibraltar

Canary Islands

Atlas Mountains

Mediterranean Sea

Suez Canal

Qattara Depression

Tropic of Cancer

Cape Verde Islands

Ahaggar Mountains

Tibesti Mountains

Libyan Desert

Eastern Desert

Tropic of Cancer

S A H A R A

Senegal R.

Niger R.

S A H E L

Lake Chad

Benue R.

Volta R.

White Nile R.

Blue Nile R.

Nile R.

Red Sea

Lake Tana

Ethiopian Highlands

Gulf of Aden

Fouta Djallon

Gulf of Guinea

Bioko

São Tomé

Adamawa Highlands

Ubangi R.

Congo R.

Congo Basin

Lake Albert

Lake Victoria

Sudd

Great Rift Valley

Lake Turkana

Equator

Serengeti Plain

Kilimanjaro 19,341 ft (5,895 m)

Zanzibar

Equator

INDIAN OCEAN

N
W   E
S

Lake Tanganyika

ATLANTIC OCEAN

Lake Nyasa

Comoro Islands

Namib Desert

Okavango Delta

Kalahari Desert

Zambezi R.

Limpopo R.

Madagascar

Mauritius

Réunion

Mozambique Channel

Tropic of Capricorn

Tropic of Capricorn

Orange R.

Drakensberg

Cape of Good Hope

Cape Agulhas

KEY
ELEVATION

Feet	Meters
More than 13,000	More than 3,960
6,500–13,000	1,980–3,960
1,600–6,500	480–1,980
650–1,600	200–480
0–650	0–200
Below sea level	Below sea level

————— National border

– – – – Disputed border

0 miles   1,000

0 kilometers   1,000

Lambert Azimuthal Equal Area

Asia: Political

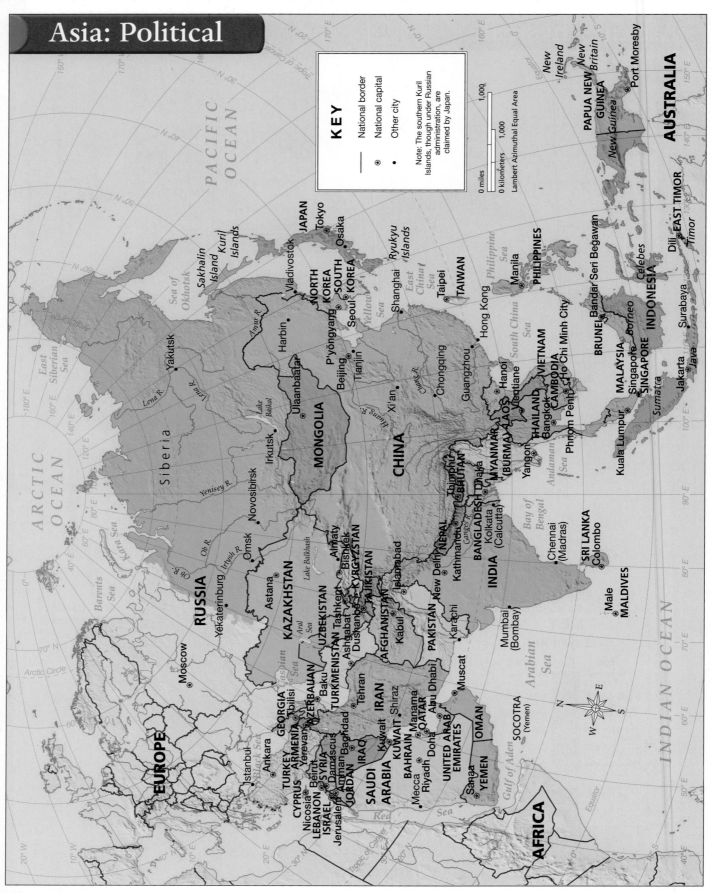

KEY
— National border
⊛ National capital
• Other city

Note: The southern Kuril Islands, though under Russian administration, are claimed by Japan.

0 miles 1,000
0 kilometers 1,000
Lambert Azimuthal Equal Area

PACIFIC OCEAN

ARCTIC OCEAN

East Siberian Sea

Kara Sea

Barents Sea

Sea of Okhotsk

Sakhalin Island

Kuril Islands

JAPAN
Tokyo
Osaka
Vladivostok
NORTH KOREA
P'yŏngyang
SOUTH KOREA
Seoul
Harbin
Amur R.
Yakutsk
Lena R.

RUSSIA
Siberia
Irkutsk
Lake Baikal
Novosibirsk
Omsk
Yenisey R.
Ob R.
Yekaterinburg
Moscow
Astana
Irtysh R.

MONGOLIA
Ulaanbaatar

CHINA
Beijing
Tianjin
Xi'an
Chongqing
Guangzhou
Shanghai
Hong Kong
Huang R.
Chang R.

Ryukyu Islands
East China Sea
TAIWAN
Taipei
Yellow Sea

Philippine Sea
PHILIPPINES
Manila

South China Sea
VIETNAM
Hanoi
Ho Chi Minh City
LAOS
Vientiane
CAMBODIA
Phnom Penh
THAILAND
Bangkok
MYANMAR (BURMA)
Yangon
Andaman Sea

BRUNEI
Bandar Seri Begawan
MALAYSIA
Kuala Lumpur
SINGAPORE
Singapore
Borneo
Celebes
INDONESIA
Sumatra
Jakarta
Surabaya
Java

PAPUA NEW GUINEA
Port Moresby
New Guinea
New Ireland
New Britain
AUSTRALIA
EAST TIMOR
Dili
Timor

KAZAKHSTAN
Aral Sea
Lake Balkhash
UZBEKISTAN
Tashkent
Almaty
Bishkek
KYRGYZSTAN
TAJIKISTAN
Dushanbe
TURKMENISTAN
Ashgabat
Caspian Sea

AFGHANISTAN
Kabul
PAKISTAN
Islamabad
Karachi

NEPAL
Kathmandu
BHUTAN
Thimphu
BANGLADESH
Dhaka
Ganges R.

INDIA
New Delhi
Mumbai (Bombay)
Kolkata (Calcutta)
Chennai (Madras)
Bay of Bengal

SRI LANKA
Colombo
MALDIVES
Male

GEORGIA
Tbilisi
ARMENIA
Yerevan
AZERBAIJAN
Baku
Black Sea

TURKEY
Ankara
Istanbul
CYPRUS
Nicosia
LEBANON
Beirut
SYRIA
Damascus
ISRAEL
Jerusalem
Amman
JORDAN
Baghdad
IRAQ

IRAN
Tehran
Shiraz

KUWAIT
Kuwait
BAHRAIN
Manama
QATAR
Doha
UNITED ARAB EMIRATES
Abu Dhabi
OMAN
Muscat

SAUDI ARABIA
Riyadh
Mecca
YEMEN
Sana
SOCOTRA (Yemen)
Gulf of Aden
Red Sea

Arabian Sea

INDIAN OCEAN

EUROPE

AFRICA

Tropic of Cancer
Arctic Circle
Equator

Asia: Physical

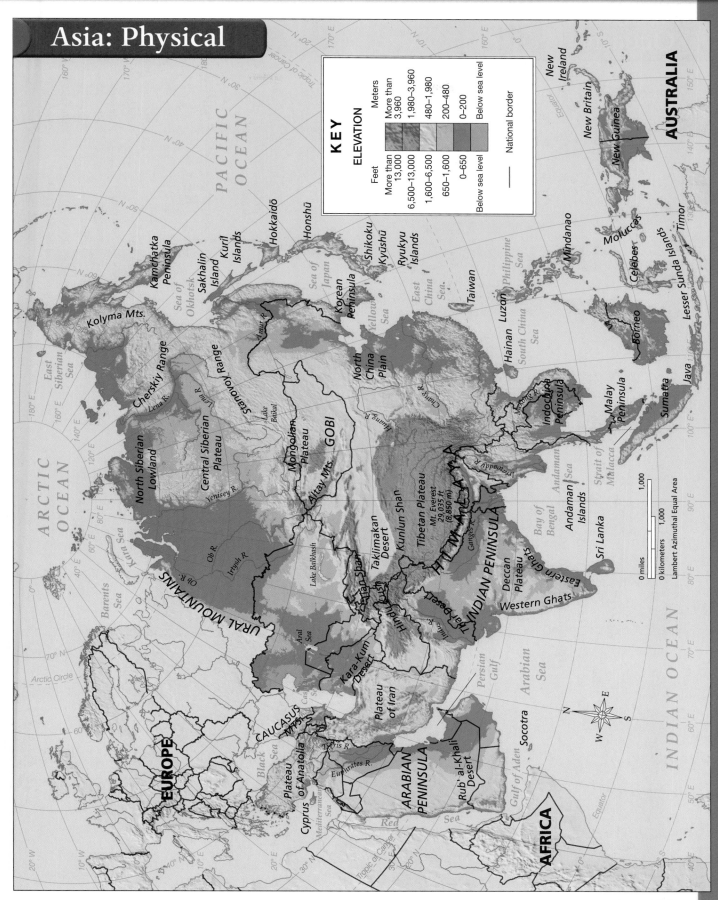

KEY

ELEVATION

Feet	Meters
More than 13,000	More than 3,960
6,500–13,000	1,980–3,960
1,600–6,500	480–1,980
650–1,600	200–480
0–650	0–200
Below sea level	Below sea level

— National border

PACIFIC OCEAN

ARCTIC OCEAN

East Siberian Sea

Sea of Okhotsk

Kamchatka Peninsula

Kolyma Mts.

Cherskiy Range

Stanovoy Range

Kuril Islands

Sakhalin Island

Hokkaidō

Honshū

Sea of Japan

Korean Peninsula

Shikoku

Kyūshū

Ryukyu Islands

North Siberian Lowland

Central Siberian Plateau

Lake Baikal

Mongolian Plateau

GOBI

Altay Mts.

Lena R.

Yenisey R.

Amur R.

Yellow Sea

North China Plain

Huang R.

Chang R.

East China Sea

Taiwan

Philippine Sea

Mindanao

New Ireland

New Britain

New Guinea

AUSTRALIA

Ural Mountains

Ob R.

Irtysh R.

Aral Sea

Lake Balkhash

Tian Shan

Taklimakan Desert

Kunlun Shan

Tibetan Plateau

Mt. Everest 29,035 ft (8,850 m)

HIMALAYA

Ganges R.

Mekong R.

Irrawaddy R.

Indochina Peninsula

Hainan

South China Sea

Luzon

Malay Peninsula

Strait of Malacca

Borneo

Celebes

Moluccas

Lesser Sunda Islands

Timor

Java

Sumatra

Andaman Sea

Andaman Islands

Bay of Bengal

Deccan Plateau

Eastern Ghats

Western Ghats

INDIAN PENINSULA

Thar Desert

Indus R.

Hindu Kush

Kara-Kum Desert

Plateau of Iran

Sri Lanka

Caspian Sea

CAUCASUS MTS.

Plateau of Anatolia

Cyprus

Black Sea

Mediterranean Sea

Tigris R.

Euphrates R.

ARABIAN PENINSULA

Rub' al-Khali Desert

Persian Gulf

Arabian Sea

Socotra

Gulf of Aden

Red Sea

INDIAN OCEAN

EUROPE

AFRICA

Barents Sea

Kara Sea

Arctic Circle

0 miles 1,000

0 kilometers 1,000

Lambert Azimuthal Equal Area

Oceania

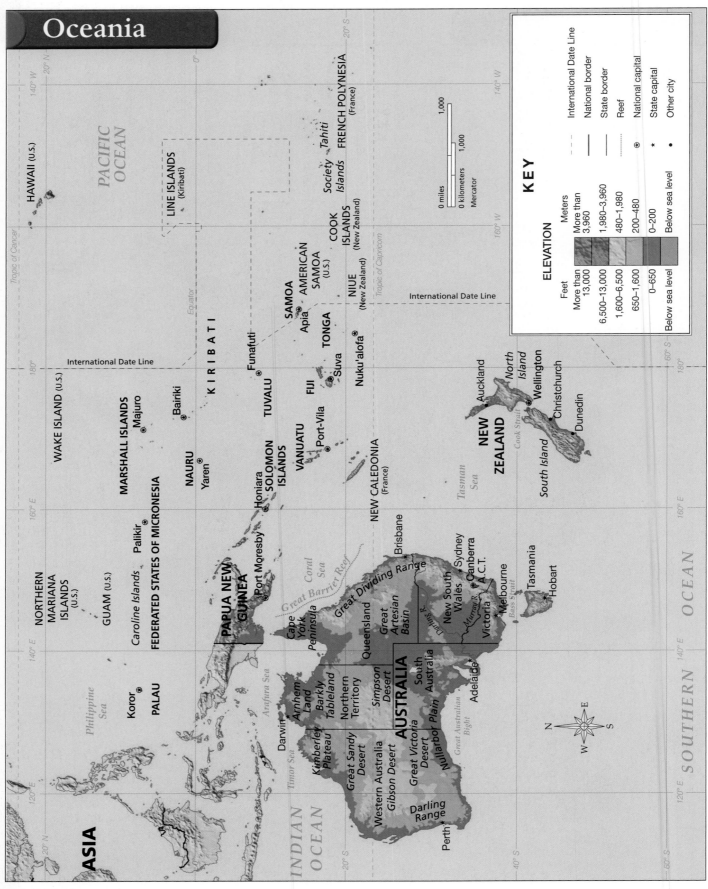

PACIFIC OCEAN

HAWAII (U.S.)

Tropic of Cancer

LINE ISLANDS
(Kiribati)

FRENCH POLYNESIA
(France)

Tahiti
Society
Islands

COOK
ISLANDS
(New Zealand)

Tropic of Capricorn

AMERICAN
SAMOA
(U.S.)

SAMOA
Apia

NIUE
(New Zealand)

TONGA
Nuku'alofa

International Date Line

KEY

ELEVATION

Feet	Meters
More than 13,000	More than 3,960
6,500–13,000	1,980–3,960
1,600–6,500	480–1,980
650–1,600	200–480
0–650	0–200
Below sea level	Below sea level

International Date Line
National border
State border
Reef
National capital
State capital
Other city

0 miles 1,000
0 kilometers 1,000
Mercator

*Philippine
Sea*

Koror
PALAU

NORTHERN
MARIANA
ISLANDS
(U.S.)

GUAM (U.S.)

Caroline Islands   Palikir
FEDERATED STATES OF MICRONESIA

WAKE ISLAND (U.S.)

MARSHALL ISLANDS
Majuro

Bairiki

NAURU
Yaren

K I R I B A T I

Funafuti

TUVALU

International Date Line

SOLOMON
ISLANDS
Honiara

FIJI
Suva

VANUATU
Port-Vila

NEW CALEDONIA
(France)

**PAPUA NEW
GUINEA**
Port Moresby

*Coral
Sea*

Great Barrier Reef

Brisbane

Great Dividing Range

Queensland

Great
Artesian
Basin

New South
Wales

Murray R.
Darling R.

Sydney
Canberra
A.C.T.

Melbourne
Victoria

Bass Strait

Tasmania
Hobart

*Tasman
Sea*

New
North
Island
Auckland
Wellington

Cook Strait

**NEW
ZEALAND**

South Island

Christchurch
Dunedin

ASIA

Arafura Sea

Timor Sea

Darwin

Arnhem
Land

Kimberley
Plateau

Barkly
Tableland

Northern
Territory

Simpson
Desert

South
Australia

Great Sandy
Desert

Western Australia
Gibson Desert

Great Victoria
Desert

Nullarbor Plain

Adelaide

AUSTRALIA

Great Australian Bight

Cape
York
Peninsula

Darling
Range

Perth

**INDIAN
OCEAN**

SOUTHERN   OCEAN

N
W E
S

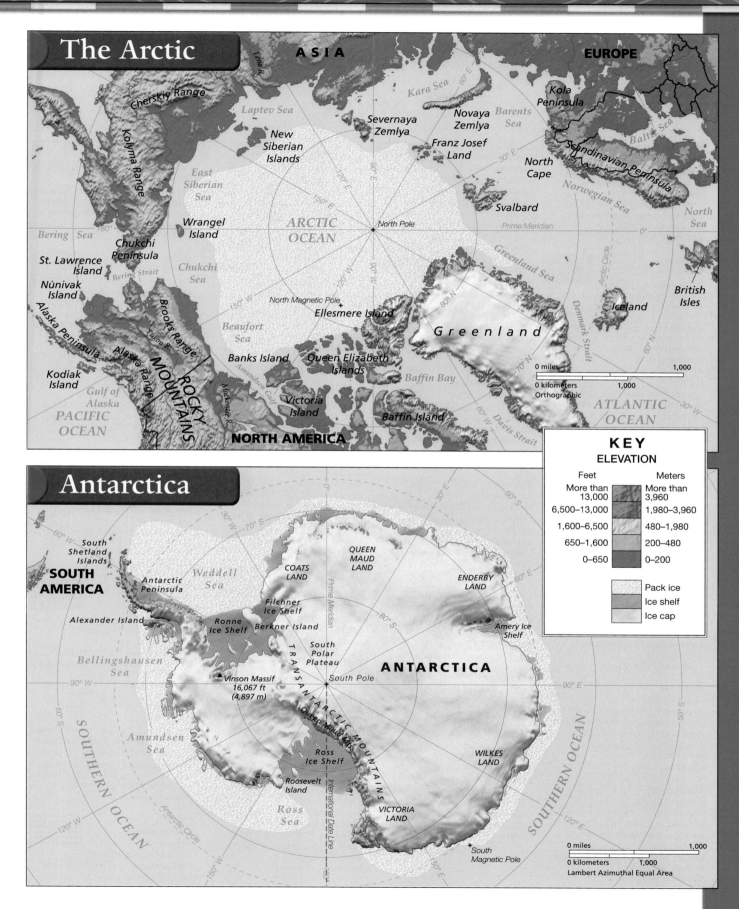

The Arctic

ASIA   EUROPE

Lena R.

Cherskiy Range

Kolyma Range

Laptev Sea

Kara Sea

Severnaya Zemlya

New Siberian Islands

Novaya Zemlya

Franz Josef Land

Barents Sea

Kola Peninsula

Baltic Sea

East Siberian Sea

Scandinavian Peninsula

North Cape

Wrangel Island

ARCTIC OCEAN

North Pole

Svalbard

Norwegian Sea

Prime Meridian

North Sea

Bering Sea

Chukchi Peninsula

St. Lawrence Island

Chukchi Sea

Greenland Sea

Arctic Circle

Iceland

British Isles

Nunivak Island

North Magnetic Pole

Ellesmere Island

Greenland

Denmark Strait

Alaska Peninsula

Brooks Range

Yukon R.

Beaufort Sea

Banks Island

Queen Elizabeth Islands

Baffin Bay

Kodiak Island

Alaska Range

ROCKY MOUNTAINS

Mackenzie R.

Amundsen Gulf

Victoria Island

Baffin Island

Davis Strait

0 miles 1,000
0 kilometers 1,000
Orthographic

Gulf of Alaska

PACIFIC OCEAN

NORTH AMERICA

ATLANTIC OCEAN

Antarctica

SOUTH AMERICA

South Shetland Islands

Antarctic Peninsula

Weddell Sea

COATS LAND

QUEEN MAUD LAND

ENDERBY LAND

Alexander Island

Filchner Ice Shelf

Ronne Ice Shelf

Berkner Island

Prime Meridian

Amery Ice Shelf

Bellingshausen Sea

South Polar Plateau

ANTARCTICA

TRANSANTARCTIC MOUNTAINS

Vinson Massif 16,067 ft (4,897 m)

South Pole

Queen Maud Mts.

SOUTHERN OCEAN

Amundsen Sea

Ross Ice Shelf

WILKES LAND

Roosevelt Island

VICTORIA LAND

Ross Sea

South Magnetic Pole

Antarctic Circle

0 miles 1,000
0 kilometers 1,000
Lambert Azimuthal Equal Area

SOUTHERN OCEAN

KEY
ELEVATION

Feet		Meters
More than 13,000		More than 3,960
6,500–13,000		1,980–3,960
1,600–6,500		480–1,980
650–1,600		200–480
0–650		0–200

Pack ice

Ice shelf

Ice cap

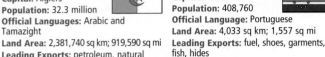

Africa

Algeria
Capital: Algiers
Population: 32.3 million
Official Languages: Arabic and Tamazight
Land Area: 2,381,740 sq km; 919,590 sq mi
Leading Exports: petroleum, natural gas, petroleum products
Continent: Africa

Angola
Capital: Luanda
Population: 10.6 million
Official Language: Portuguese
Land Area: 1,246,700 sq km; 481,551 sq mi
Leading Exports: crude oil, diamonds, refined petroleum products, gas, coffee, sisal, fish and fish products, timber, cotton
Continent: Africa

Benin
Capital: Porto-Novo
Population: 6.9 million
Official Language: French
Land Area: 110,620 sq km; 42,710 sq mi
Leading Exports: cotton, crude oil, palm products, cocoa
Continent: Africa

Botswana
Capital: Gaborone
Population: 1.6 million
Official Language: English
Land Area: 585,370 sq km; 226,011 sq mi
Leading Exports: diamonds, copper, nickel, soda ash, meat, textiles
Continent: Africa

Burkina Faso
Capital: Ouagadougou
Population: 12.6 million
Official Language: French
Land Area: 273,800 sq km; 105,714 sq mi
Leading Exports: cotton, animal products, gold
Continent: Africa

Burundi
Capital: Bujumbura
Population: 6.4 million
Official Languages: Kirundi and French
Land Area: 25,650 sq km; 9,903 sq mi
Leading Exports: coffee, tea, sugar, cotton, hides
Continent: Africa

Cameroon
Capital: Yaoundé
Population: 16.1 million
Official Languages: English and French
Land Area: 469,440 sq km; 181,251 sqmi
Leading Exports: crude oil and petroleum products, lumber, cocoa, aluminum, coffee, cotton
Continent: Africa

Cape Verde
Capital: Praia
Population: 408,760
Official Language: Portuguese
Land Area: 4,033 sq km; 1,557 sq mi
Leading Exports: fuel, shoes, garments, fish, hides
Location: Atlantic Ocean

Central African Republic
Capital: Bangui
Population: 3.6 million
Official Language: French
Land Area: 622,984 sq km; 240,534 sq mi
Leading Exports: diamonds, timber, cotton, coffee, tobacco
Continent: Africa

Chad
Capital: N'Djamena
Population: 9 million
Official Languages: Arabic and French
Land Area: 1,259,200 sq km; 486,177 sq mi
Leading Exports: cotton, cattle, gum arabic
Continent: Africa

Comoros
Capital: Moroni
Population: 614,382
Official Languages: Arabic, Comoran, and French
Land Area: 2,170 sq km; 838 sq mi
Leading Exports: vanilla, ylang-ylang, cloves, perfume oil, copra
Location: Indian Ocean

Congo, Democratic Republic of the
Capital: Kinshasa
Population: 55.2 million
Official Language: French
Land Area: 2,267,600 sq km; 875,520 sq mi
Leading Exports: diamonds, copper, coffee, cobalt, crude oil
Continent: Africa

Congo, Republic of the
Capital: Brazzaville
Population: 3.3 million
Official Language: French
Land Area: 341,500 sq km; 131,853 sq mi
Leading Exports: petroleum, lumber, sugar, cocoa, coffee, diamonds
Continent: Africa

Djibouti
Capital: Djibouti
Population: 472,810
Official Languages: Arabic and French
Land Area: 22,980 sq km; 8,873 sq mi
Leading Exports: reexports, hides and skins, coffee (in transit)
Continent: Africa

Egypt
Capital: Cairo
Population: 70.7 million
Official Language: Arabic
Land Area: 995,450 sq km; 384,343 sq mi
Leading Exports: crude oil and petroleum products, cotton, textiles, metal products, chemicals
Continent: Africa

Equatorial Guinea
Capital: Malabo
Population: 498,144
Official Languages: Spanish and French
Land Area: 28,050 sq km; 10,830 sq mi
Leading Exports: petroleum, timber, cocoa
Continent: Africa

Eritrea
Capital: Asmara
Population: 4.5 million
Official Language: Tigrinya
Land Area: 121,320 sq km; 46,842 sq mi
Leading Exports: livestock, sorghum, textiles, food, small manufactured goods
Continent: Africa

Ethiopia
Capital: Addis Ababa
Population: 67.7 million
Official Language: Amharic
Land Area: 1,119,683 sq km; 432,310 sq mi
Leading Exports: coffee, qat, gold, leather products, oilseeds
Continent: Africa

Gabon
Capital: Libreville
Population: 1.2 million
Official Language: French
Land Area: 257,667 sq km; 99,489 sq mi
Leading Exports: crude oil, timber, manganese, uranium
Continent: Africa

Gambia
Capital: Banjul
Population: 1.5 million
Official Language: English
Land Area: 10,000 sq km; 3,861 sq mi
Leading Exports: peanuts and peanut products, fish, cotton lint, palm kernels
Continent: Africa

Ghana
Capital: Accra
Population: 20.2 million
Official Language: English
Land Area: 230,940 sq km; 89,166 sq mi
Leading Exports: gold, cocoa, timber, tuna, bauxite, aluminum, manganese ore, diamonds
Continent: Africa

Guinea
Capital: Conakry
Population: 7.8 million
Official Language: French
Land Area: 245,857 sq km; 94,925 sq mi
Leading Exports: bauxite, alumina, gold, diamonds, coffee, fish, agricultural products
Continent: Africa

Guinea-Bissau
Capital: Bissau
Population: 1.4 million
Official Language: Portuguese
Land Area: 28,000 sq km; 10,811 sq mi
Leading Exports: cashew nuts, shrimp, peanuts, palm kernels, lumber
Continent: Africa

Ivory Coast
Capital: Yamoussoukro
Population: 16.8 million
Official Language: French
Land Area: 318,000 sq km; 122,780 sq mi
Leading Exports: cocoa, coffee, timber, petroleum, cotton, bananas, pineapples, palm oil, cotton, fish
Continent: Africa

Kenya
Capital: Nairobi
Population: 31.3 million
Official Languages: Swahili and English
Land Area: 569,250 sq km; 219,787 sq mi
Leading Exports: tea, horticultural products, coffee, petroleum products, fish, cement
Continent: Africa

Lesotho
Capital: Maseru
Population: 2.2 million
Official Languages: Sesotho and English
Land Area: 30,355 sq km; 11,720 sq mi
Leading Exports: manufactured goods (clothing, footwear, road vehicles), wool and mohair, food and live animals
Continent: Africa

Liberia
Capital: Monrovia
Population: 3.3 million
Official Language: English
Land Area: 96,320 sq km; 37,189 sq mi
Leading Exports: rubber, timber, iron, diamonds, cocoa, coffee
Continent: Africa

Libya

Capital: Tripoli
Population: 5.4 million
Official Language: Arabic
Land Area: 1,759,540 sq km;
679,358 sq mi
Leading Exports: crude oil, refined petroleum products
Location: Indian

Madagascar

Capital: Antananarivo
Population: 16.5 million
Official Languages: French and Malagasy
Land Area: 581,540 sq km;
224,533 sq mi
Leading Exports: coffee, vanilla, shellfish, sugar, cotton cloth, chromite, petroleum products
Location: Indian Ocean

Malawi

Capital: Lilongwe
Population: 10.7 million
Official Languages: English and Chichewa
Land Area: 94,080 sq km; 36,324 sq mi
Leading Exports: tobacco, tea, sugar, cotton, coffee, peanuts, wood products, apparel
Continent: Africa

Mali

Capital: Bamako
Population: 11.3 million
Official Language: French
Land Area: 1,220,000 sq km;
471,042 sq mi
Leading Exports: cotton, gold, livestock
Continent: Africa

Mauritania

Capital: Nouakchott
Population: 2.8 million
Official Language: Arabic
Land Area: 1,030,400 sq km;
397,837 sq mi
Leading Exports: iron ore, fish and fish products, gold
Continent: Africa

Mauritius

Capital: Port Louis
Population: 1.2 million
Official Language: English
Land Area: 2,030 sq km;
784 sq mi
Leading Exports: clothing and textiles, sugar, cut flowers, molasses
Location: Indian Ocean

Morocco

Capital: Rabat
Population: 31.2 million
Official Language: Arabic
Land Area: 446,300 sq km;
172,316 sq mi
Leading Exports: phosphates and fertilizers, food and beverages, minerals
Continent: Africa

Mozambique

Capital: Maputo
Population: 19.6 million
Official Language: Portuguese
Land Area: 784,090 sq km;
302,737 sq mi
Leading Exports: prawns, cashews, cotton, sugar, citrus, timber, bulk electricity
Continent: Africa

Namibia

Capital: Windhoek
Population: 1.8 million
Official Language: English
Land Area: 825,418 sq km;
318,694 sq mi
Leading Exports: diamonds, copper, gold, zinc, lead, uranium, cattle, processed fish, karakul skins
Continent: Africa

Niger

Capital: Niamey
Population: 11.3 million
Official Language: French
Land Area: 1,226,700 sq km;
489,073 sq mi
Leading Exports: uranium ore, livestock products, cowpeas, onions
Continent: Africa

Nigeria

Capital: Abuja
Population: 129.9 million
Official Language: English
Land Area: 910,768 sq km;
351,648 sq mi
Leading Exports: petroleum and petroleum products, cocoa, rubber
Continent: Africa

Rwanda

Capital: Kigali
Population: 7.4 million
Official Languages: Kinyarwanda, French, and English
Land Area: 24,948 sq km; 9,632 sq mi
Leading Exports: coffee, tea, hides, tin ore
Continent: Africa

São Tomé and Príncipe

Capital: São Tomé
Population: 170,372
Official Language: Portuguese
Land Area: 1,001 sq km; 386 sq mi
Leading Exports: cocoa, copra, coffee, palm oil
Location: Atlantic Ocean

Senegal

Capital: Dakar
Population: 10.6 million
Official Language: French
Land Area: 192,000 sq km;
74,131 sq mi
Leading Exports: fish, groundnuts (peanuts), petroleum products, phosphates, cotton
Continent: Africa

Seychelles

Capital: Victoria
Population: 80,098
Official Languages: English and French
Land Area: 455 sq km; 176 sq mi
Leading Exports: canned tuna, cinnamon bark, copra, petroleum products (reexports)
Location: Indian Ocean

Sierra Leone

Capital: Freetown
Population: 5.6 million
Official Language: English
Land Area: 71,620 sq km; 27,652 sq mi
Leading Exports: diamonds, rutile, cocoa, coffee, fish
Continent: Africa

Somalia

Capital: Mogadishu
Population: 7.8 million
Official Languages: Somali and Arabic
Land Area: 627,337 sq km;
242,215 sq mi
Leading Exports: livestock, bananas, hides, fish, charcoal, scrap metal
Continent: Africa

South Africa

Capital: Cape Town, Pretoria, and Bloemfontein
Population: 43.6 million
Official Languages: Eleven official languages: Afrikaans, English, Ndebele, Pedi, Sotho, Swazi, Tsonga, Tswana, Venda, Xhosa, and Zulu
Land Area: 1,219,912 sq km;
471,008 sq mi
Leading Exports: gold, diamonds, platinum, other metals and minerals, machinery and equipment
Continent: Africa

Sudan

Capital: Khartoum
Population: 37.1 million
Official Language: Arabic
Land Area: 2,376,000 sq km;
917,374 sq mi
Leading Exports: oil and petroleum products, cotton, sesame, livestock, groundnuts, gum arabic, sugar
Continent: Africa

Swaziland

Capital: Mbabane
Population: 1.1 million
Official Languages: English and siSwati
Land Area: 17,20 sq km; 6,642 sq mi
Leading Exports: soft drink concentrates, sugar, wood pulp, cotton yarn, refrigerators, citrus and canned fruit
Continent: Africa

Tanzania

Capital: Dar es Salaam and Dodoma
Population: 37.2 million
Official Languages: Swahili and English
Land Area: 886,037 sq km;
342,099 sq mi
Leading Exports: gold, coffee, cashew nuts, manufactured goods, cotton
Continent: Africa

Togo

Capital: Lomé
Population: 5.2 million
Official Language: French
Land Area: 54,385 sq km; 20,998 sq mi
Leading Exports: cotton, phosphates, coffee, cocoa
Continent: Africa

Tunisia

Capital: Tunis
Population: 9.8 million
Official Language: Arabic
Land Area: 155,360 sq km;
59,984 sq mi
Leading Exports: textiles, mechanical goods, phosphates and chemicals, agricultural products, hydrocarbons
Continent: Africa

Uganda

Capital: Kampala
Population: 24.7 million
Official Language: English
Land Area: 199,710 sq km;
77,108 sq mi
Leading Exports: coffee, fish and fish products, tea, gold, cotton, flowers, horticultural products
Continent: Africa

Zambia

Capital: Lusaka
Population: 10.1 million
Official Language: English
Land Area: 740,724 sq km;
285,994 sq mi
Leading Exports: copper, cobalt, electricity, tobacco, flowers, cotton
Continent: Africa

Zimbabwe

Capital: Harare
Population: 11.3 million
Official Language: English
Land Area: 386,670 sq km;
149,293 sq mi
Leading Exports: tobacco, gold, iron alloys, textiles and clothing
Continent: Africa

Asia and the Pacific

Afghanistan

Capital: Kabul
Population: 27.8 million
Official Languages: Pashtu and Dari
Land Area: 647,500 sq km;
250,000 sq mi
Leading Exports: agricultural products, hand-woven carpets, wool, cotton, hides and pelts, precious and semiprecious gems
Continent: Asia

Armenia

Capital: Yerevan
Population: 3.3 million
Official Language: Armenian
Land Area: 29,400 sq km; 10,965 sq mi
Leading Exports: diamonds, scrap metal, machinery and equipment, brandy, copper ore
Continent: Asia

Australia

Capital: Canberra
Population: 19.6 million
Official Language: English
Land Area: 7,617,930 sq km;
2,941,283 sq mi
Leading Exports: coal, gold, meat, wool, alumina, iron ore, wheat, machinery and transport equipment
Continent: Australia

Azerbaijan

Capital: Baku
Population: 7.8 million
Official Language: Azerbaijani
Land Area: 86,100 sq km; 33,243 sq mi
Leading Exports: oil and gas, machinery, cotton, foodstuffs
Continent: Asia

Bahrain

Capital: Manama
Population: 656,397
Official Language: Arabic
Land Area: 665 sq km; 257 sq mi
Leading Exports: petroleum and petroleum products, aluminum, textiles
Continent: Asia

Bangladesh

Capital: Dhaka
Population: 133.4 million
Official Language: Bengali
Land Area: 133,910 sq km; 51,705 sq mi
Leading Exports: garments, jute and jute goods, leather, frozen fish and seafood
Continent: Asia

Bhutan

Capital: Thimphu
Population: 2.1 million
Official Language: Dzongkha
Land Area: 47,000 sq km; 18,147 sq mi
Leading Exports: electricity, cardamom, gypsum, timber, handicrafts, cement, fruit, precious stones, spices
Continent: Asia

Brunei

Capital: Bandar Seri Begawan
Population: 350,898
Official Language: Malay
Land Area: 5,270 sq km; 2,035 sq mi
Leading Exports: crude oil, natural gas, refined products
Continent: Asia

Cambodia

Capital: Phnom Penh
Population: 12.8 million
Official Language: Khmer
Land Area: 176,520 sq km; 68,154 sq mi
Leading Exports: timber, garments, rubber, rice, fish
Continent: Asia

China

Capital: Beijing
Population: 1.29 billion
Official Languages: Mandarin and Chinese
Land Area: 9,326,410 sq km; 3,600,927 sq mi
Leading Exports: machinery and equipment, textiles and clothing, footwear, toys and sports goods, mineral fuels
Continent: Asia

Cyprus

Capital: Nicosia
Population: 767,314
Official Languages: Greek and Turkish
Land Area: 9,240 sq km; 3,568 sq mi
Leading Exports: citrus, potatoes, grapes, wine, cement, clothing and shoes
Location: Mediterranean Sea

East Timor

Capital: Dili
Population: 952,618
Official Languages: Tetum and Portuguese
Land Area: 15,007 sq km; 5,794 sq mi
Leading Exports: coffee, sandalwood, marble
Continent: Asia

Fiji

Capital: Suva
Population: 856,346
Official Language: English
Land Area: 18,270 sq km; 7,054 sq mi
Leading Exports: sugar, garments, gold, timber, fish, molasses, coconut oil
Location: Pacific Ocean

Georgia

Capital: Tbilisi
Population: 5 million
Official Languages: Georgian and Abkhazian
Land Area: 69,700 sq km; 26,911 sq mi
Leading Exports: scrap metal, machinery, chemicals, fuel reexports, citrus fruits, tea, wine, other agricultural products
Continent: Asia

India

Capital: New Delhi
Population: 1.05 billion
Official Languages: Hindi and English
Land Area: 2,973,190 sq km; 1,147,949 sq mi
Leading Exports: textile goods, gems and jewelry, engineering goods, chemicals, leather manufactured goods
Continent: Asia

Indonesia
Capital: Jakarta
Population: 231.3 million
Official Language: Bahasa Indonesia
Land Area: 1,826,440 sq km; 705,188 sq mi
Leading Exports: oil and gas, electrical appliances, plywood, textiles, rubber
Continent: Asia

Iran
Capital: Tehran
Population: 66.6 million
Official Language: Farsi
Land Area: 1,636,000 sq km; 631,660 sq mi
Leading Exports: petroleum, carpets, fruits and nuts, iron and steel, chemicals
Continent: Asia

Iraq

Capital: Baghdad
Population: 24.7 million
Official Language: Arabic
Land Area: 432,162 sq km; 166,858 sq mi
Leading Exports: crude oil
Continent: Asia

Israel
Capital: Jerusalem
Population: 6.0 million
Official Language: Hebrew, Arabic
Land Area: 20,330 sq km; 7,849 sq mi
Leading Exports: machinery and equipment, software, cut diamonds, agricultural products, chemicals, textiles and apparel
Continent: Asia

Japan
Capital: Tokyo
Population: 127 million
Official Language: Japanese
Land Area: 374,744 sq km; 144,689 sq mi
Leading Exports: motor vehicles, semiconductors, office machinery, chemicals
Continent: Asia

Jordan

Capital: Amman
Population: 5.3 million
Official Language: Arabic
Land Area: 91,971 sq km; 35,510 sq mi
Leading Exports: phosphates, fertilizers, potash, agricultural products, manufactured goods, pharmaceuticals
Continent: Asia

Kazakhstan

Capital: Astana
Population: 16.7 million
Official Language: Kazakh
Land Area: 2,669,800 sq km; 1,030,810 sq mi
Leading Exports: oil and oil products, ferrous metals, machinery, chemicals, grain, wool, meat, coal
Continent: Asia

Kiribati

Capital: Bairiki (Tarawa Atoll)
Population: 96,335
Official Language: English
Land Area: 811 sq km; 313 sq mi
Leading Exports: copra, coconuts, seaweed, fish
Location: Pacific Ocean

Korea, North

Capital: Pyongyang
Population: 22.3 million
Official Language: Korean
Land Area: 120,410 sq km; 46,490 sq mi
Leading Exports: minerals, metallurgical products, manufactured goods (including armaments), agricultural and fishery products
Continent: Asia

Korea, South

Capital: Seoul
Population: 48.3 million
Official Language: Korean
Land Area: 98,190 sq km; 37,911 sq mi
Leading Exports: electronic products, machinery and equipment, motor vehicles, steel, ships, textiles, clothing, footwear, fish
Continent: Asia

Kuwait

Capital: Kuwait City
Population: 2.1 million
Official Language: Arabic
Land Area: 17,820 sq km; 6,880 sq mi
Leading Exports: oil and refined products, fertilizers
Continent: Asia

Kyrgyzstan
Capital: Bishkek
Population: 4.8 million
Official Languages: Kyrgyz and Russian
Land Area: 191,300 sq km; 73,861sq mi
Leading Exports: cotton, wool, meat, tobacco, gold, mercury, uranium, hydropower, machinery, shoes
Continent: Asia

Laos

Capital: Vientiane
Population: 5.8 million
Official Language: Lao
Land Area: 230,800 sq km; 89,112 sq mi
Leading Exports: wood products, garments, electricity, coffee, tin
Continent: Asia

Lebanon

Capital: Beirut
Population: 3.7 million
Official Language: Arabic
Land Area: 10,230 sq km; 3,950 sq mi
Leading Exports: foodstuffs and tobacco, textile, chemicals, precious stones, metal and metal products, electrical equipment and products, jewelry, paper and paper products
Continent: Asia

Malaysia
Capital: Kuala Lumpur and Putrajaya
Population: 22.7 million
Official Language: Bahasa Malaysia
Land Area: 328,550 sq km; 126,853 sq mi
Leading Exports: electronic equipment, petroleum and liquefied natural gas, wood and wood products, palm oil, rubber, textiles, chemicals
Continent: Asia

Maldives
Capital: Malé
Population: 320,165
Official Language: Dhivehi (Maldivian)
Leading Exports: fish, clothing
Location: Indian Ocean

Marshall Islands
Capital: Majuro
Population: 73,360
Official Languages: Marshallese and English
Land Area: 181.3 sq km; 70 sq mi
Leading Exports: copra cake, coconut oil, handicrafts
Location: Pacific Ocean

Micronesia, Federated States of

Capital: Palikir (Pohnpei Island)
Population: 135,869
Official Language: English
Land Area: 702 sq km; 271 sq mi
Leading Exports: fish, garments, bananas, black pepper
Location: Pacific Ocean

Mongolia
Capital: Ulaanbaatar
Population: 2.6 million
Official Language: Khalkha Mongolian
Land Area: 1,555,400 sq km; 600,540 sq mi
Leading Exports: copper, livestock, animal products, cashmere, wool, hides, fluorspar, other nonferrous metals
Continent: Asia

Myanmar (Burma)
Capital: Rangoon (Yangon)
Population: 42.2 million
Official Language: Burmese (Myanmar)
Land Area: 657,740 sq km; 253,953 sq mi
Leading Exports: apparel, foodstuffs, wood products, precious stones
Continent: Asia

Nauru
Capital: Yaren District
Population: 12,329
Official Language: Nauruan
Land Area: 21 sq km; 8 sq mi
Leading Exports: phosphates
Location: Pacific Ocean

Nepal

Capital: Kathmandu
Population: 25.9 million
Official Language: Nepali
Land Area: 136,800 sq km; 52,818 sq mi
Leading Exports: carpets, clothing, leather goods, jute goods, grain
Continent: Asia

New Zealand

Capital: Wellington
Population: 3.8 million
Official Languages: English and Maori
Land Area: 268,680 sq km; 103,737 sq mi
Leading Exports: dairy products, meat, wood and wood products, fish, machinery
Location: Pacific Ocean

Oman
Capital: Muscat
Population: 2.7 million
Official Language: Arabic
Land Area: 212,460 sq km; 82,030 sq mi
Leading Exports: petroleum, reexports, fish, metals, textiles
Continent: Asia

Pakistan

Capital: Islamabad
Population: 147.7 million
Official Languages: Urdu and English
Land Area: 778,720 sq km; 300,664 sq mi
Leading Exports: textiles (garments, cotton cloth, and yarn), rice, other agricultural products
Continent: Asia

Palau
Capital: Koror
Population: 19,409
Official Languages: English and Palauan
Land Area: 458 sq km; 177 sq mi
Leading Exports: shellfish, tuna, copra, garments
Location: Pacific Ocean

Papua New Guinea

Capital: Port Moresby
Population: 5.2 million
Official Language: English
Land Area: 452,860 sq km; 174,849 sq mi
Leading Exports: oil, gold, copper ore, logs, palm oil, coffee, cocoa, crayfish, prawns
Location: Pacific Ocean

Philippines

Capital: Manila
Population: 84.5 million
Official Languages: Filipino and English
Land Area: 298,170 sq km; 115,123 sq mi
Leading Exports: electronic equipment, machinery and transport equipment, garments, coconut products
Continent: Asia

Qatar

Capital: Doha
Population: 793,341
Official Language: Arabic
Land Area: 11,437 sq km; 4,416 sq mi
Leading Exports: petroleum products, fertilizers, steel
Continent: Asia

Samoa

Capital: Apia
Population: 178,631
Official Languages: Samoan and English
Land Area: 2,934 sq km; 1,133 sq mi
Leading Exports: fish, coconut oil cream, copra, taro, garments, beer
Location: Pacific Ocean

Saudi Arabia

Capital: Riyadh and Jiddah
Population: 23.5 million
Official Language: Arabic
Land Area: 1,960,582 sq km; 756,981 sq mi
Leading Exports: petroleum and petroleum products
Continent: Asia

Singapore

Capital: Singapore
Population: 4.5 million
Official Languages: Malay, English, Mandarin, Chinese, and Tamil
Land Area: 683 sq km; 264 sq mi
Leading Exports: machinery and equipment (including electronics), consumer goods, chemicals, mineral fuels
Continent: Asia

Solomon Islands

Capital: Honiara
Population: 494,786
Official Language: English
Land Area: 27,540 sq km; 10,633 sq mi
Leading Exports: timber, fish, copra, palm oil, cocoa
Location: Pacific Ocean

Sri Lanka

Capital: Colombo
Population: 19.6 million
Official Language: Sinhala, Tamil, and English
Land Area: 64,740 sq km; 24,996 sq mi
Leading Exports: textiles and apparel, tea, diamonds, coconut products, petroleum products
Continent: Asia

Syria

Capital: Damascus
Population: 17.2 million
Official Language: Arabic
Land Area: 184,050 sq km; 71,062 sq mi
Leading Exports: crude oil, textiles, fruits and vegetables, raw cotton
Continent: Asia

Taiwan
Capital: Taipei
Population: 22.5 million
Official Language: Mandarin Chinese
Land Area: 32,260 sq km; 12,456 sq mi
Leading Exports: machinery and electrical equipment, metals, textiles, plastics, chemicals
Continent: Asia

Tajikistan

Capital: Dushanbe
Population: 6.7 million
Official Language: Tajik
Land Area: 142,700 sq km; 55,096 sq mi
Leading Exports: aluminum, electricity, cotton, fruits, vegetables, oil, textiles
Continent: Asia

Thailand
Capital: Bangkok
Population: 62.5 million
Official Language: Thai
Land Area: 511,770 sq km; 197,564 sq mi
Leading Exports: computers, transistors, seafood, clothing, rice
Continent: Asia

Tonga
Capital: Nuku'alofa
Population: 106,137
Official Languages: Tongan and English
Land Area: 718 sq km; 277 sq mi
Leading Exports: squash, fish, vanilla beans, root crops
Location: Pacific Ocean

Turkey
Capital: Ankara
Population: 67.3 million
Official Language: Turkish
Land Area: 770,760 sq km; 297,590 sq mi
Leading Exports: apparel, foodstuffs, textiles, metal manufactured goods, transport equipment
Continent: Asia

Turkmenistan
Capital: Ashgabat
Population: 4.7 million
Official Language: Turkmen
Land Area: 488,100 sq km; 188,455 sq mi
Leading Exports: gas, oil, cotton fiber, textiles
Continent: Asia

Asia and the Pacific (continued)

Tuvalu

Capital: Fongafale
Population: 10,800
Official Language: English
Land Area: 26 sq km; 10 sq mi
Leading Exports: copra, fish
Location: Pacific Ocean

United Arab Emirates

Capital: Abu Dhabi
Population: 2.4 million
Official Language: Arabic
Land Area: 82,880 sq km; 32,000 sq mi
Leading Exports: crude oil, natural gas, reexports, dried fish, dates
Continent: Asia

Uzbekistan

Capital: Tashkent
Population: 25.5 million
Official Language: Uzbek
Land Area: 425,400 sq km; 164,247 sq mi
Leading Exports: cotton, gold, energy products, mineral fertilizers, ferrous metals, textiles, food products, automobiles
Continent: Asia

Vanuatu

Capital: Port-Vila
Population: 196,178
Official Languages: English, French, and Bislama
Land Area: 12,200 sq km; 4,710 sq mi
Leading Exports: copra, kava, beef, cocoa, timber, coffee
Location: Pacific Ocean

Vietnam

Capital: Hanoi
Population: 81.1 million
Official Language: Vietnamese
Land Area: 325,320 sq km; 125,621 sq mi
Leading Exports: crude oil, marine products, rice, coffee, rubber, tea, garments, shoes
Continent: Asia

Yemen
Capital: Sanaa
Population: 18.7 million
Official Language: Arabic
Land Area: 527,970 sq km; 203,849 sq mi
Leading Exports: crude oil, coffee, dried and salted fish
Continent: Asia

Europe and Russia

Albania

Capital: Tiranë
Population: 3.5 million
Official Language: Albanian
Land Area: 27,398 sq km; 10,578 sq mi
Leading Exports: textiles and footwear, asphalt, metals and metallic ores, crude oil, vegetables, fruits, tobacco
Continent: Europe

Andorra

Capital: Andorra la Vella
Population: 68,403
Official Language: Catalan
Land Area: 468 sq km; 181 sq mi
Leading Exports: tobacco products, furniture
Continent: Europe

Austria
Capital: Vienna
Population: 8.2 million
Official Language: German
Land Area: 82,738 sq km; 31,945 sq mi
Leading Exports: machinery and equipment, motor vehicles and parts, paper and paperboard, metal goods, chemicals, iron and steel, textiles, foodstuffs
Continent: Europe

Belarus

Capital: Minsk
Population: 10.3 million
Official Languages: Belarussian and Russian
Land Area: 207,600 sq km; 80,154 sq mi
Leading Exports: machinery and equipment, mineral products, chemicals, textiles, food stuffs, metals
Continent: Europe

Belgium

Capital: Brussels
Population: 10.3 million
Official Languages: Dutch and French
Land Area: 30,230 sq km; 11,172 sq mi
Leading Exports: machinery and equipment, chemicals, metals and metal products
Continent: Europe

Bosnia and Herzegovina

Capital: Sarajevo
Population: 4.0 million
Official Language: Serbo-Croat
Land Area: 51,129 sq km; 19,741 sq mi
Leading Exports: miscellaneous manufactured goods, crude materials
Continent: Europe

Bulgaria

Capital: Sofía
Population: 7.6 million
Official Language: Bulgarian
Land Area: 110,550 sq km; 42,683 sq mi
Leading Exports: clothing, footwear, iron and steel, machinery and equipment, fuels
Continent: Europe

Croatia
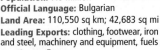
Capital: Zagreb
Population: 4.4 million
Official Language: Croatian
Land Area: 56,414 km; 21,781 sq mi
Leading Exports: transport equipment, textiles, chemicals, foodstuffs, fuels
Continent: Europe

Czech Republic

Capital: Prague
Population: 10.3 million
Official Language: Czech
Land Area: 78,276 sq km; 29,836 sq mi
Leading Exports: machinery and transport equipment, intermediate manufactured goods, chemicals, raw materials and fuel
Continent: Europe

Denmark

Capital: Copenhagen
Population: 5.4 million
Official Language: Danish
Land Area: 42,394 sq km; 16,368 sq mi
Leading Exports: machinery and instruments, meat and meat products, dairy products, fish, chemicals, furniture, ships, windmills
Continent: Europe

Estonia

Capital: Tallinn
Population: 1.4 million
Official Language: Estonian
Land Area: 43,211 sq km; 16,684 sq mi
Leading Exports: machinery and equipment, wood products, textiles, food products, metals, chemical products
Continent: Europe

Finland

Capital: Helsinki
Population: 5.2 million
Official Languages: Finnish and Swedish
Land Area: 305,470 sq km; 117,942 sq mi
Leading Exports: machinery and equipment, chemicals, metals, timber, paper, pulp
Continent: Europe

France

Capital: Paris
Population: 59.8 million
Official Language: French
Land Area: 545,630 sq km; 310,668 sq mi
Leading Exports: machinery and transportation equipment, aircraft, plastics, chemicals, pharmaceutical products, iron and steel, beverages
Continent: Europe

Germany

Capital: Berlin
Population: 83 million
Official Language: German
Land Area: 349,223 sq km; 134,835 sq mi
Leading Exports: machinery, vehicles, chemicals, metals and manufactured goods, foodstuffs, textiles
Continent: Europe

Greece

Capital: Athens
Population: 10.6 million
Official Language: Greek
Land Area: 130,800 sq km; 50,502 sq mi
Leading Exports: food and beverages, manufactured goods, petroleum products, chemicals, textiles
Continent: Europe

Holy See (Vatican City)
Capital: Vatican City
Population: 900
Official Languages: Latin and Italian
Land Area: 0.44 sq km; 0.17 sq mi
Leading Exports: no information available
Continent: Europe

Hungary

Capital: Budapest
Population: 10.1 million
Official Language: Hungarian
Land Area: 92,340 sq km; 35,652 sq mi
Leading Exports: machinery and equipment, other manufactured goods, food products, raw materials, fuels and electricity
Continent: Europe

Iceland
Capital: Reykjavík
Population: 279,384
Official Language: Icelandic
Land Area: 100,250 sq km; 38,707 sq mi
Leading Exports: fish and fish products, animal products, aluminum, diatomite, ferrosilicon
Location: Atlantic Ocean

Ireland

Capital: Dublin
Population: 3.9 million
Official Languages: Irish Gaelic and English
Land Area: 68,890 sq km; 26,598 sq mi
Leading Exports: machinery and equipment, computers, chemicals, pharmaceuticals, live animals, animal products
Continent: Europe

Italy

Capital: Rome
Population: 57.7 million
Official Language: Italian
Land Area: 294,020 sq km; 113,521 sq mi
Leading Exports: fruits, vegetables, grapes, potatoes, sugar beets, soybeans, grain, olives, beef, diary products, fish
Continent: Europe

Latvia
Capital: Riga
Population: 2.4 million
Official Language: Latvian
Land Area: 63,589 sq km; 24,552 sq mi
Leading Exports: wood and wood products, machinery and equipment, metals, textiles, foodstuffs
Continent: Europe

Liechtenstein

Capital: Vaduz
Population: 32,842
Official Language: German
Land Area: 160 sq km; 62 sq mi
Leading Exports: small specialty machinery, dental products, stamps, hardware, pottery
Continent: Europe

Lithuania

Capital: Vilnius
Population: 3.6 million
Official Language: Lithuanian
Land Area: 65,200 sq km; 25,174 sq mi
Leading Exports: mineral products, textiles and clothing, machinery and equipment, chemicals, wood and wood products, foodstuffs
Continent: Europe

Luxembourg

Capital: Luxembourg
Population: 448,569
Official Languages: Luxembourgish, French, and German
Land Area: 2,586 sq km; 998 sq mi
Leading Exports: machinery and equipment, steel products, chemicals, rubber products, glass
Continent: Europe

Macedonia, The Former Yugoslav Republic of

Capital: Skopje
Population: 2.1 million
Official Languages: Macedonian and Albanian
Land Area: 24,856 sq km; 9,597 sq mi
Leading Exports: food, beverages, tobacco, miscellaneous manufactured goods, iron and steel
Continent: Europe

Malta

Capital: Valletta
Population: 397,499
Official Languages: Maltese and English
Land Area: 316 sq km; 122 sq mi
Leading Exports: machinery and transport equipment, manufactured goods
Location: Mediterranean Sea

Moldova
Capital: Chişinău
Population: 4.4 million
Official Language: Moldovan
Land Area: 33,371 sq km; 12,885 sq mi
Leading Exports: foodstuffs, textiles and footwear, machinery
Continent: Europe

Monaco
Capital: Monaco
Population: 31,987
Official Language: French
Land Area: 1.95 sq km; 0.75 sq mi
Leading Exports: no information available
Continent: Europe

Montenegro

Capital: Podgorica
Population: 620,145
Official Language: Serbian
Land Area: 13,812 sq km; 5,333 sq mi
Leading Exports: food products
Continent: Europe

Netherlands

Capital: Amsterdam and The Hague
Population: 16.1 million
Official Language: Dutch
Land Area: 33,883 sq km; 13,082 sq mi
Leading Exports: machinery and equipment, chemicals, fuels, foodstuffs
Continent: Europe

Norway

Capital: Oslo
Population: 4.5 million
Official Language: Norwegian
Land Area: 307,860 sq km; 118,865 sq mi
Leading Exports: petroleum and petroleum products, machinery and equipment, metals, chemicals, ships, fish
Continent: Europe

Poland
Capital: Warsaw
Population: 38.6 million
Official Language: Polish
Land Area: 304,465 sq km; 117,554 sq mi
Leading Exports: machinery and transport equipment, intermediate manufactured goods, miscellaneous manufactured goods, food and live animals
Continent: Europe

Portugal

Capital: Lisbon
Population: 10.1 million
Official Language: Portuguese
Land Area: 91,951 sq km; 35,502 sq mi
Leading Exports: clothing and footwear, machinery, chemicals, cork and paper products, hides
Continent: Europe

Romania
Capital: Bucharest
Population: 22.3 million
Official Language: Romanian
Land Area: 230,340 sq km; 88,934 sq mi
Leading Exports: textiles and footwear, metals and metal products, machinery and equipment, minerals and fuels
Continent: Europe

Russia

Capital: Moscow
Population: 145 million
Official Language: Russian
Land Area: 16,995,800 sq km; 6,592,100 sq mi
Leading Exports: petroleum and petroleum products, natural gas, wood and wood products, metals, chemicals, and a wide variety of civilian and military manufactured goods
Continents: Europe and Asia

San Marino
Capital: San Marino
Population: 27,730
Official Language: Italian
Land Area: 61 sq km; 24 sq mi
Leading Exports: building stone, lime, wood, chestnuts, wheat, wine, baked goods, hides, ceramics
Continent: Europe

Serbia

Capital: Belgrade
Population: 9.4 million
Official Language: Serbian
Land Area: 88,361 sq km; 34,116 sq mi
Leading Exports: food and live animals, manufactured goods, raw materials
Continent: Europe

Slovakia

Capital: Bratislava
Population: 5.4 million
Official Language: Slovak
Land Area: 48,800 sq km; 18,842 sq mi
Leading Exports: machinery and transport equipment, intermediate manufactured goods, miscellaneous manufactured goods, chemicals
Continent: Europe

Slovenia

Capital: Ljubljana
Population: 1.9 million
Official Language: Slovene
Land Area: 20,151 sq km; 7,780 sq mi
Leading Exports: manufactured goods, machinery and transport equipment, chemicals, food
Continent: Europe

Spain
Capital: Madrid
Population: 40.1 million
Official Languages: Spanish, Galician, Basque, and Catalan
Land Area: 499,542 sq km; 192,873 sq mi
Leading Exports: machinery, motor vehicles, foodstuffs, other consumer goods
Continent: Europe

Europe and Russia (continued)

Sweden

Capital: Stockholm
Population: 8.9 million
Official Language: Swedish
Land Area: 410,934 sq km; 158,662 sq mi
Leading Exports: machinery, motor vehicles, paper products, pulp and wood, iron and steel products, chemicals
Continent: Europe

Switzerland

Capital: Bern
Population: 7.3 million
Official Languages: German, French, and Italian
Land Area: 39,770 sq km; 15,355 sq mi
Leading Exports: machinery, chemicals, metals, watches, agricultural products
Continent: Europe

Ukraine

Capital: Kiev
Population: 48.4 million
Official Language: Ukrainian
Land Area: 603,700 sq km; 233,090 sq mi
Leading Exports: ferrous and nonferrous metals, fuel and petroleum products, machinery and transport equipment, food products
Continent: Europe

United Kingdom

Capital: London
Population: 59.8 million
Official Languages: English and Welsh
Land Area: 241,590 sq km; 93,278 sq mi
Leading Exports: manufactured goods, fuels, chemicals, food, beverages, tobacco
Continent: Europe

Latin America

Antigua and Barbuda
Capital: Saint John's
Population: 67,448
Official Language: English
Land Area: 442 sq km; 171 sq mi
Leading Exports: petroleum products, manufactured goods, machinery and transport equipment, food and live animals
Location: Caribbean Sea

Argentina

Capital: Buenos Aires
Population: 37.8 million
Official Language: Spanish
Land Area: 2,736,690 sq km; 1,056,636 sq mi
Leading Exports: edible oils, fuels and energy, cereals, feed, motor vehicles
Continent: South America

Bahamas
Capital: Nassau
Population: 300,529
Official Language: English
Land Area: 10,070 sq km; 3,888 sq mi
Leading Exports: fish and crawfish, rum, salt, chemicals, fruit and vegetables
Location: Caribbean Sea

Barbados
Capital: Bridgetown
Population: 276,607
Official Language: English
Land Area: 431 sq km; 166 sq mi
Leading Exports: sugar and molasses, rum, other foods and beverages, chemicals, electrical components, clothing
Location: Caribbean Sea

Belize

Capital: Belmopan
Population: 262,999
Official Language: English
Land Area: 22,806 sq km; 8,805 sq mi
Leading Exports: sugar, bananas, citrus, clothing, fish products, molasses, wood
Continent: North America

Bolivia
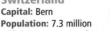
Capital: La Paz and Sucre
Population: 8.5 million
Official Language: Spanish, Quechua, and Aymara
Land Area: 1,084,390 sq km; 418,683 sq mi
Leading Exports: soybeans, natural gas, zinc, gold, wood
Continent: South America

Brazil

Capital: Brasília
Population: 176 million
Official Language: Portuguese
Land Area: 8,456,510 sq km; 3,265,059 sq mi
Leading Exports: manufactured goods, iron ore, soybeans, footwear, coffee, autos
Continent: South America

Chile
Capital: Santiago
Population: 15.5 million
Official Language: Spanish
Land Area: 748,800 sq km; 289,112 sq mi
Leading Exports: copper, fish, fruits, paper and pulp, chemicals
Continent: South America

Colombia
Capital: Bogotá
Population: 41 million
Official Language: Spanish
Land Area: 1,038,700 sq km; 401,042 sq mi
Leading Exports: petroleum, coffee, coal, apparel, bananas, cut flowers
Continent: South America

Costa Rica

Capital: San José
Population: 3.8 million
Official Language: Spanish
Land Area: 51,660 sq km; 19,560 sq mi
Leading Exports: coffee, bananas, sugar, pineapples, textiles, electronic components, medical equipment
Continent: North America

Cuba

Capital: Havana
Population: 11.2 million
Official Language: Spanish
Land Area: 110,860 sq km; 42,803 sq mi
Leading Exports: sugar, nickel, tobacco, fish, medical products, citrus, coffee
Location: Caribbean Sea

Dominica
Capital: Roseau
Population: 73,000
Official Language: English
Land Area: 754 sq km; 291 sq mi
Leading Exports: bananas, soap, bay oil, vegetables, grapefruit, oranges
Location: Caribbean Sea

Dominican Republic

Capital: Santo Domingo
Population: 8.7 million
Official Language: Spanish
Land Area: 48,380 sq km; 18,679 sq mi
Leading Exports: ferronickel, sugar, gold, silver, coffee, cocoa, tobacco, meats, consumer goods
Location: Caribbean Sea

Ecuador
Capital: Quito
Population: 13.5 million
Official Language: Spanish
Land Area: 276,840 sq km; 106,888 sq mi
Leading Exports: petroleum, bananas, shrimp, coffee, cocoa, cut flowers, fish
Continent: South America

El Salvador

Capital: San Salvador
Population: 6.4 million
Official Language: Spanish
Land Area: 20,720 sq km; 8,000 sq mi
Leading Exports: offshore assembly exports, coffee, sugar, shrimp, textiles, chemicals, electricity
Continent: North America

Grenada
Capital: Saint George's
Population: 89,211
Official Language: English
Land Area: 344 sq km; 133 sq mi
Leading Exports: bananas, cocoa, nutmeg, fruit and vegetables, clothing, mace
Location: Caribbean Sea

Guatemala
Capital: Guatemala City
Population: 13.3 million
Official Language: Spanish
Land Area: 108,430 sq km; 41,865 sq mi
Leading Exports: coffee, sugar, bananas, fruits and vegetables, cardamom, meat, apparel, petroleum, electricity
Continent: North America

Guyana
Capital: Georgetown
Population: 698,209
Official Language: English
Land Area: 196,850 sq km; 76,004 sq mi
Leading Exports: sugar, gold, bauxite/alumina, rice, shrimp, molasses, rum, timber
Continent: South America

Haiti

Capital: Port-au-Prince
Population: 7.1 million
Official Language: French and French Creole
Land Area: 27,560 sq km; 10,641 sq mi
Leading Exports: manufactured goods, coffee, oils, cocoa
Location: Caribbean Sea

Honduras

Capital: Tegucigalpa
Population: 6.6 million
Official Language: Spanish
Land Area: 111,890 sq km; 43,201 sq mi
Leading Exports: coffee, bananas, shrimp, lobster, meat, zinc, lumber
Continent: North America

Jamaica

Capital: Kingston
Population: 2.7 million
Official Language: English
Land Area: 10,831 sq km; 4,182 sq mi
Leading Exports: alumina, bauxite, sugar, bananas, rum
Location: Caribbean Sea

Mexico

Capital: Mexico City
Population: 103.4 million
Official Language: Spanish
Land Area: 1,923,040 sq km; 742,486 sq mi
Leading Exports: manufactured goods, oil and oil products, silver, fruits, vegetables, coffee, cotton
Continent: North America

Nicaragua
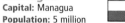

Capital: Managua
Population: 5 million
Official Language: Spanish
Land Area: 120,254 sq km; 46,430 sq mi
Leading Exports: coffee, shrimp and lobster, cotton, tobacco, beef, sugar, bananas, gold
Continent: North America

Panama

Capital: Panama City
Population: 2.9 million
Official Language: Spanish
Land Area: 75,990 sq km; 29,340 sq mi
Leading Exports: bananas, shrimp, sugar, coffee, clothing
Continent: North America

Paraguay

Capital: Asunción
Population: 5.9 million
Official Language: Spanish
Land Area: 397,300 sq km; 153,398 sq mi
Leading Exports: electricity, soybeans, feed, cotton, meat, edible oils
Continent: South America

Peru

Capital: Lima
Population: 28 million
Official Languages: Spanish and Quechua
Land Area: 1,280,000 sq km; 494,208 sq mi
Leading Exports: fish and fish products, gold, copper, zinc, crude petroleum and byproducts, lead, coffee, sugar, cotton
Continent: South America

Saint Kitts and Nevis

Capital: Basseterre
Population: 38,736
Official Language: English
Land Area: 261 sq km; 101 sq mi
Leading Exports: machinery, food, electronics, beverages, tobacco
Location: Caribbean Sea

Saint Lucia

Capital: Castries
Population: 160,145
Official Language: English
Land Area: 606 sq km; 234 sq mi
Leading Exports: bananas, clothing, cocoa, vegetables, fruits, coconut oil
Location: Caribbean Sea

Saint Vincent and the Grenadines

Capital: Kingstown
Population: 116,394
Official Language: English
Land Area: 389 sq km; 150 sq mi
Leading Exports: bananas, eddoes and dasheen, arrowroot starch, tennis racquets
Location: Caribbean Sea

Suriname

Capital: Paramaribo
Population: 436,494
Official Language: Dutch
Land Area: 161,470 sq km; 62,344 sq mi
Leading Exports: alumina, crude oil, lumber, shrimp and fish, rice, bananas
Continent: South America

Trinidad and Tobago

Capital: Port-of-Spain
Population: 1.2 million
Official Language: English
Land Area: 5,128 sq km; 1,980 sq mi
Leading Exports: petroleum and petroleum products, chemicals, steel products, fertilizer, sugar, cocoa, coffee, citrus, flowers
Location: Caribbean Sea

Uruguay

Capital: Montevideo
Population: 3.4 million
Official Language: Spanish
Land Area: 173,620 sq km; 67,100 sq mi
Leading Exports: meat, rice, leather products, wool, vehicles, dairy products
Continent: South America

Venezuela

Capital: Caracas
Population: 24.3 million
Official Language: Spanish
Land Area: 882,050 sq km; 340,560 sq mi
Leading Exports: petroleum, bauxite and aluminum, steel, chemicals, agricultural products, basic manufactured goods
Continent: South America

United States and Canada

Canada

Capital: Ottawa
Population: 31.9 million
Official Languages: English and French
Land Area: 9,220,970 sq km; 3,560,217 sq mi
Leading Exports: motor vehicles and parts, industrial machinery, aircraft, telecommunications equipment, chemicals, plastics, fertilizers, wood pulp, timber, crude petroleum, natural gas, electricity, aluminum
Continent: North America

United States
Capital: Washington, D.C.
Population: 281.4 million
Official Language: English
Land Area: 9,158,960 sq km; 3,536,274 sq mi
Leading Exports: capital goods, automobiles, industrial supplies and raw materials, consumer goods, agricultural products
Continent: North America

SOURCE: CIA World Factbook Online, 2002

Glossary of Geographic Terms

basin
an area that is lower than surrounding land areas; some basins are filled with water

bay
a body of water that is partly surrounded by land and that is connected to a larger body of water

butte
a small, high, flat-topped landform with cliff-like sides

▲ **butte**

canyon
a deep, narrow valley with steep sides; often with a stream flowing through it

cataract
a large waterfall or steep rapids

◄ **cataract**

delta
a plain at the mouth of a river, often triangular in shape, formed where sediment is deposited by flowing water

flood plain
a broad plain on either side of a river, formed where sediment settles during floods

glacier
a huge, slow-moving mass of snow and ice

hill
an area that rises above surrounding land and has a rounded top; lower and usually less steep than a mountain

island
an area of land completely surrounded by water

isthmus
a narrow strip of land that connects two larger areas of land

mesa
a high, flat-topped landform with cliff-like sides; larger than a butte

mountain
a landform that rises steeply at least 2,000 feet (610 meters) above surrounding land; usually wide at the bottom and rising to a narrow peak or ridge

▶ **glacier**

◀ **delta**

mountain pass
a gap between mountains

peninsula
an area of land almost completely surrounded by water but connected to the mainland

plain
a large area of flat or gently rolling land

plateau
a large, flat area that rises above the surrounding land; at least one side has a steep slope

river mouth
the point where a river enters a lake or sea

strait
a narrow stretch of water that connects two larger bodies of water

tributary
a river or stream that flows into a larger river

valley
a low stretch of land between mountains or hills; land that is drained by a river

volcano
an opening in Earth's surface through which molten rock, ashes, and gases escape from the interior

▶ **volcano**

Gazetteer

A

Acropolis (37°58' N, 23°43' E) a hill in Athens, Greece, on which many temples and other archaeological sites are located, p. 179

Africa (10° N, 22° E) the world's second-largest continent, surrounded by the Mediterranean Sea, the Atlantic Ocean, and the Red Sea, p. 11

Alexandria (31°12' N, 29° 54' E) an ancient Hellenistic city in Egypt, p. 199

Andes (20° S, 67° W) a mountain system extending along the western coast of South America, p. 18

Anyang (36°6' N, 114°21' E) capital of the Shang dynasty in ancient China, p. 26

Arabian Peninsula (25° N, 45° E) a peninsula of Southwest Asia, on which are located the present-day nations of Saudi Arabia, Yemen, Oman, the United Arab Emirates, Qatar, Bahrain, and Kuwait, p. 102

Arctic Circle (66°30' N) a line of latitude around Earth near the North Pole, p. 18

Asia (50° N, 100° E) the world's largest continent, surrounded by the Arctic Ocean, the Pacific Ocean, the Indian Ocean, and Europe, p. 26

Asia Minor (39° N, 32° E) a peninsula in western Asia, between the Black Sea and the Mediterranean Sea; in present-day Turkey, p. 44

Assyria a historical kingdom of northern Mesopotamia around present-day Iraq and Turkey, p. 42

Athens (37°58' N, 23°43' E) a city-state in ancient Greece; the capital city of present-day Greece, p. 173

B

Babylonia (32° N, 44° E) an ancient region around southeastern Mesopotamia and between the Tigris and Euphrates rivers; present-day Iraq, p. 43

Bangladesh (24° N, 90° E) a country in South Asia, p. 109

C

Cairo (30°3' N, 31°15' E) the capital and largest city of Egypt, located on the Nile River, p. 77

Canaan a region occupied by the ancient Israelites, later known as Judaea, located between the Syrian Desert and the Mediterranean Sea; today encompassing Israel and the West Bank, p. 56

Carthage (36°52' N, 10°20' E) an ancient city on the northern coast of Africa that controlled much of the North African coast and other Mediterranean territories; now a suburb of the city of Tunis, p. 214

Chang River (32° N, 121° E) the longest river in China and Asia and the third-longest river in the world (also called the Yangtze River), p. 139

Chang'an (34°15' N, 108°52' E) a city in northern China; in ancient times the eastern end of the Silk Road; also called Xi'an, p. 159

Chile (30° S, 71° W) a country in South America, p. 18

China (35° N, 105° E) a country in East Asia, p. 138

Colosseum (41°54' N, 12°29' E) a large amphitheatre built in Rome around A.D. 70; site of contests and combats between people and animals, p. 222

Constantinople (41°1' N, 28°58' E) formerly the ancient city of Byzantium, renamed in A.D. 330 after the Roman emperor, Constantine, who made it the new capital of the Eastern Roman, or Byzantine, Empire; now Istanbul, Turkey, p. 239

Crete (35°15' N, 25° E) an island of Greece, southeast of the mainland, home to the ancient Minoan civilization, p. 170

D

Damascus (33°30' N, 36°18' E) the capital and largest city of Syria, p. 7

E

East Africa an eastern region of the continent of Africa that is made up of the countries of Burundi, Kenya, Rwanda, Tanzania, Uganda, and Somalia, p. 16

Egypt (27° N, 30° E) a country in North Africa, pp. 26, 70

Euphrates River (31° N, 47° E) a river that flows south from Turkey through Syria and Iraq, pp. 26, 36

Europe (50° N, 28° E) the world's second-smallest continent, a peninsula of the Eurasian landmass bounded by the Arctic Ocean, the Atlantic Ocean, the Mediterranean Sea, and Asia, p. 26

F

Fertile Crescent a region in Southwest Asia; site of the world's first civilizations, p. 36

G

Ganges River (23°22' N, 90°32' E) a river in northern India and Bangladesh that flows from the Himalaya Mountains to the Bay of Bengal, p. 110

Gaul a region inhabited by the ancient Gauls, including present-day France and parts of Belgium, Germany, and Italy, p. 214

Giza (30°1' N, 31°13' E) an ancient city of Upper Egypt; site of the Sphinx and the Great Pyramid, p. 86

Gobi Desert (43° N, 105° E) a desert in Mongolia and northern China, p. 137

Great Wall of China (41° N, 117° E) a wall that extends about 1,400 miles across northern China; built in the third century B.C., p. 137

Greece (39° N, 22° E) a country in Mediterranean Europe; site of a great ancient civilization, p. 168

Gupta Empire an empire that ruled northern India in the 300s and 400s A.D., p. 132

H

Harappa (30°38' N, 72°52' E) an ancient city of the Indus civilization; a village in present-day Pakistan, p. 110

Himalayas (28° N, 84° E) a mountain system of south central Asia that extends along the border between India and Tibet and through Pakistan, Nepal, and Bhutan, p. 108

Hindu Kush (36° N, 72° E) a mountain range in central Asia, p. 110

Huang River (38° N, 118° E) the second-longest river in China, beginning in Tibet and emptying into the Yellow Sea, pp. 26, 139

I

India (20° N, 77° E) a large country in South Asia, p. 108

Indian Ocean (10° S, 70° E) the world's third-largest ocean, lying between Africa, Asia, and Australia, p. 109

Indus River (24° N, 68° E) a river that flows from Tibet through India and Pakistan into the Indian Ocean. Its valley was the home of India's earliest civilization, pp. 26, 110.

Iran (32° N, 53° E) a country in Southwest Asia, p. 46

Iraq (33° N, 44° E) a country in Southwest Asia, p. 66

Israel (32° N, 35° E) an ancient kingdom of the Hebrews; a present-day country in Southwest Asia, p. 60

Italy (43° N, 13° E) a country in southern Europe, p. 211

J

Japan (36° N, 138° E) an island country in the Pacific Ocean off the east coast of Asia, p. 125

Jerusalem (31°46' N, 35°14' E) the capital city of present-day Israel; a holy city for Jews, Christians, and Muslims, p. 57

Judaea (31°35' N, 35° E) a Roman province centered on the ancient region of Judah, located in present-day Israel and the Israeli-occupied territories, p. 230

Judah the name of the southern half of the Kingdom of the Israelites (the northern half retaining the name Israel), with Jerusalem its capital; later called Judaea, p. 57

K

Kemet the term used by ancient Egyptians to describe their land, meaning "the black land," a reference to the dark soil left by the Nile River, p. 73

Kerma an ancient Nubian city; a market town in present-day Sudan, p. 99

Knossos (35°20' N, 25°10' E) an ancient city on the island of Crete, pp. 26, 170

Korea the present-day nations of the Democratic People's Republic of Korea (North Korea) (40° N, 127° E) and the Republic of Korea (South Korea) (37° N, 128° E), which occupy the Korean peninsula in East Asia, p. 125

L

Lake Nasser (22°40' N, 32° E) a lake located in southeast Egypt and northern Sudan, formed by the construction of the Aswan Dam on the Nile River, p. 74

Lower Egypt (31° N, 31° E) an area in ancient and present-day Egypt, in the northern Nile River region, p. 72

Lower Nubia an ancient region in northern Africa extending from the Nile Valley in Egypt to present-day Sudan, specifically, between the first and second Nile cataracts, p. 99

M

Macedonia (41° N, 23° E) an ancient kingdom on the Balkan Peninsula in southeastern Europe, the site of the present-day nation of Macedonia, northern Greece, and southwest Bulgaria, p. 196

Marathon a village in ancient Greece, northeast of Athens, where the ancient Greeks defeated the Persians in 490 B.C., p. 191

Maurya Empire the Indian empire founded by Chandragupta; empire that began with his kingdom in northeastern India and spread to most of northern and central India, p. 128

Mediterranean Sea (35° N, 20° E) the large sea that separates Europe and Africa, p. 36

Memphis (29°51' N, 31°15' E) an ancient city in Lower Egypt; capital of many ancient Egyptian dynasties, pp. 26, 77

Meroë a city of ancient Nubia in present-day Sudan, p. 99

Mesopotamia (34° N, 44° E) an ancient region between the Tigris and Euphrates rivers in Southwest Asia, p. 35

Mohenjo-Daro (27°18' N, 68°15' E) an ancient city on the banks of the Indus River in southern Pakistan, pp. 26, 110

Mycenae an ancient city on the mainland of Greece, home to one of Greece's earliest civilizations, p. 170

N

Napata one of the three most powerful Nubian kingdoms, located between the third and fourth cataracts of the Nile River in Upper Nubia, p. 99

New Babylonian Empire a revival of the old Babylonian empire stretching from the Persian Gulf to the Mediterranean Sea, p. 45

Nile River (30°10' N, 31°6' E) the longest river in the world, flowing through northeastern Africa into the Mediterranean Sea, pp. 13, 70

North China Plain a large plain in East Asia, built up by soil deposits of the Huang River, p. 139

Nubia (21° N, 33° E) a desert region and ancient kingdom in the Nile River Valley, on the site of present-day southern Egypt and northern Sudan, p. 71

P

Pakistan (30° N, 70° E) a country in South Asia between India and Afghanistan; officially, the Islamic Republic of Pakistan, p. 109

Parthenon (37°58' N, 23°43' E) the chief temple of the Greek goddess Athena on the hill of the Acropolis in Athens, Greece, p. 179

Peloponnese (38° N, 22° E) a large peninsula in southern Greece, p. 192

Persian Empire an empire centered in modern Iran that covered the Fertile Crescent, Egypt, Asia Minor, and parts of Central Asia and India, p. 46

Persian Gulf (27° N, 51° E) an arm of the Arabian Sea, located between the Arabian Peninsula and southwest Iran, p. 36

Phoenicia (34° N, 36° E) an ancient region in present-day Lebanon, p. 53

R

Rome (41°58' N, 12°40' E) the capital city of Italy; the capital of the ancient Roman Empire, p. 210

S

Sahara (26° N, 13° E) the largest tropical desert in the world, covering almost all of North Africa, p. 73

Silk Road an ancient trade route between China and Europe, p. 158

Sinai Peninsula (29°30' N, 34° E) a peninsula on the northern end of the Red Sea that links southwest Asia with northeast Africa, p. 55

Sparta (37°5' N, 22°27' E) an ancient city-state in Greece, pp. 174, 188

Sumer the site of the earliest known civilization, located in Mesopotamia, in present-day southern Iraq; later became Babylonia, p. 34

Syria (35° N, 38° E) a country in Southwest Asia, p. 81

T

Tiber River (42° N, 12° E) a major river in Italy that rises in the mountains of central Italy and empties into the Tyrrhenian Sea; flows through Rome, p. 211

Tibet (32° N, 88° E) a historical region of central Asia north of the Himalayas; currently under Chinese control, p. 125

Tigris River (31° N, 47° E) a river in Iraq and Turkey, pp. 26, 36

Troy (39°57' N, 26°15' E) an ancient city in north-western Anatolia, the Asian part of Turkey; the site of the mythical Trojan War, p. 171

Tyre (33°16' N, 35°11' E) a rich trade port and the major city of Phoenicia, located on the eastern Mediterranean Sea in present-day southern Lebanon, p. 52

U

Upper Egypt (26° N, 32° E) an area in ancient and present-day Egypt in the Nile Valley, south of the river's delta and the 30th northern parallel, p. 72

Upper Nubia an ancient region in northeastern Africa that extended from the Nile Valley in Egypt to present-day Sudan, specifically, between the second and sixth cataracts, p. 71

Ur (30°57' N, 46°9' E) a city of ancient Sumer in southern Mesopotamia, located in present-day southeast Iraq, pp. 26, 36

V

Vietnam (16° N, 108° E) a country located in Southeast Asia, p. 125

Biographical Dictionary

A

Abraham (AY bruh ham) the first leader of the Israelites, who, according to the Torah, led his family to Canaan, where he became the founder of a new nation, p. 55

Akhenaton (ah keh NAH tun) king of ancient Egypt from about 1379–1362 B.C.; tried to impose monotheism; lost much of Egypt's territory; changed his name from Amenhotep IV, p. 84

Alexander the Great (al ig ZAN dur thuh grayt) (356–323 B.C.) the king of Macedonia from 336 to 323 B.C.; conquerer of Persia and Egypt and invader of India, p. 197

Archimedes (ahr kuh MEE deez) (born 290 B.C.) a Greek inventor and mathematician; calculated the surface area and volume of a sphere, p. 200

Aristarchus (ar is TAHR kus) (c. 310–230 B.C.) a Greek astronomer who was the first to hold the theory that Earth moves around the sun, p. 200

Aristotle (AR is taht ul) (384–322 B.C.) a Greek philosopher who was a student of Plato and became a famous teacher; wrote about and taught logic, politics, science, and poetry; author of works that became the basis for medieval church scholarship, p. 178

Asoka (uh SOH kuh) (died c. 232 B.C.) Chandragupta's grandson and last major emperor of India's Maurya Empire; credited with having built the greatest empire in India's history; helped spread Buddhism, p. 130

Augustus (aw GUS tus) (63 B.C.–A.D. 14) the first Roman emperor; ruled after Julius Caesar's death in 44 B.C. until his own death; named Octavian, he was awarded the title of Augustus in 27 B.C., pp. 215, 219

Aurelius, Marcus (aw REE lee us, MAHR kus) (A.D. 121–180) a Roman emperor, generally tolerant, and promoter of humanitarian causes, p. 220

C

Caesar, Julius (SEE zur, JOOL yus) (c. 100–44 B.C.) a Roman political and military leader; assassinated by Roman senators, p. 214

Caligula (kuh LIG yuh luh) (A.D. 12–41) a Roman emperor (A.D. 37–41) believed to be insane for much of his rule, p. 220

Champollion, Jean François (shahm poh LYOHN, zhahn frahn SWAH) (A.D. 1790–1832) a French scholar; first to decode Egyptian hieroglyphics, p. 94

Chandragupta (chun druh GUP tuh) (died c. 297 B.C.) founded India's Maurya Empire in 321 B.C.; unified most of India under one ruler, p. 128

Cicero (SIS uh roh) (106–43 B.C.) Roman orator, author, philosopher, and politician, p. 223

Cleopatra VII (klee oh PA truh) Macedonian queen who ruled Egypt from 51 to 30 B.C., p. 81

Commodus (KAHM uh dus) (A.D. 161–192) Roman emperor who succeeded his father, Marcus Aurelius; a poor ruler whose reign marked the beginning of the decline of the Roman Empire, p. 220

Confucius (kun FYOO shus) (551–479 B.C.) a Chinese philosopher and teacher, pp. 143, 146

Constantine (KAHN stun teen) (c. A.D. 278–337) the emperor of Rome from A.D. 312 to 337; encouraged the spread of Christianity, p. 236

Constantine

D

David (DAY vid) (died c. 972 B.C.) the king of the Israelites from about 1012 to 972 B.C.; unified the Jews into a settled nation and established a capital at the city of Jerusalem, p. 57

Deborah (DEB uh ruh) (c. 1100s B.C.) a judge and prophet in the Jewish Bible, p. 62

Democritus (dih MAHK ruh tus) (c. 460–c. 370 B.C.) a Greek philosopher who proposed that the universe is made up of atoms, p. 177

Diocletian (dy uh KLEE shun) (A.D. 245–316) emperor of Rome from A.D. 284 to 305; reorganized the Roman government, p. 233

E

Eratosthenes (ehr uh TAHS thuh neez) (c. 275–c. 195 B.C.) a Greek scholar who headed the library at Alexandria; a noted astronomer who wrote about many subjects, p. 200

Etruscans (ih TRUS kunz) an ancient people who lived in Etruria in Italy from at least 650 B.C. to about 500 B.C.; lived before the Romans and influenced their culture, p. 212

Euclid (YOO klid) (c. 300 B.C.) a Greco-Roman mathematician; known for the *Elements*, a book on geometry, p. 200

G

Gautama, Siddhartha (GOW tuh muh, sih DAHR tuh) (born after 500 B.C. and died before 350 B.C.) the founder of Buddhism; a prince who left his family and gave up his wealth to try to find the cause of human suffering; also known as the Buddha, p. 121

H

Hadrian (HAY dree un) (A.D. 76–138) the emperor of Rome from A.D. 117 to 138; one of Rome's greatest emperors; worked to unify the empire, p. 220

Hammurabi (hah muh RAH bee) (died 1750 B.C.) the king of Babylon from about 1792 to 1750 B.C.; creator of the Babylonian Empire; established one of the oldest codes of law, pp. 43, 47

Hatshepsut (haht SHEP soot) (died c. 1458 B.C.) the stepmother of Thutmose III; ruled Egypt as regent and then as pharaoh; achieved economic success, especially in trade, p. 76

Herodotus (huh RAHD uh tus) (c. 484–420 B.C.) a Greek author who traveled throughout the known world; wrote about the wars between Greece and Persia in the *History*, the first major historical work of ancient times, p. 70

Homer (HOH mur) (c. 800 B.C.) a Greek poet; credited with composing the epics the *Iliad* and the *Odyssey*, p. 171

I

Iceman (EYES man) one of the best-preserved bodies from prehistory that has ever been found; discovered in the Ötztal Alps on the border between Austria and Italy in 1991; believed to be from Europe's Copper Age (4000–2200 B.C.); also called Ötzi, p. 10

J

Jesus (JEE zus) (c. 6–4 B.C.–c. A.D. 30) the founder of Christianity; believed by Christians to be the Messiah; executed by the Roman government; believed to have spoken to his followers after his death, and to have later risen bodily to heaven, p. 229

Justinian (jus TIN ee un) (A.D. 483–565) a Byzantine emperor, responsible for codifying Roman law; influenced all later laws, p. 223

L

Laozi (LOW dzuh) (c. 500s B.C.) a Chinese philosopher and the founder of Taoism, p. 149

Liu Bang (LYOH bahng) the founder of the Han dynasty of China in 202 B.C.; born a peasant; stabilized the government and promoted education, p. 154

M

Martial (MAHR shul) (c. A.D. 40–104) a Roman poet who wrote poems about the early Roman Empire, p. 224

Menes (MEE neez) the legendary founder of the first Egyptian dynasty; according to tradition, unified Upper and Lower Egypt, around 3100 B.C. or earlier, and founded the capital of Memphis; possibly King Narmer of the carving known as the Narmer Palette, p. 77

Moses (MOH zuz) (c. 1200s B.C.) the Israelite leader who, according to the Torah, led the Israelites from Egypt to Canaan; said to have received the Ten Commandments from God, p. 56

N

Narmer (NAHR mur) the Egyptian king honored in the carving known as the Narmer Palette, celebrating the unification of Upper and Lower Egypt; possibly the King Menes of Egyptian legend, p. 77

Nebuchadnezzar II (neb yuh kud NEZ ur) (c. 630–561 B.C.) the king of the New Babylonian Empire from about 605 to 561 B.C., p. 45

Nero (NEE roh) (c. A.D. 37–68) the Roman emperor from A.D. 54 to 68; known for his cruel treatment of the Christians, p. 220

O

Octavian (ahk TAY vee un) (63 B.C.–A.D. 14) Rome's first emperor; strong leader whose rule led to peace and wealth; also known as Augustus, p. 215

P

Paul (pawl) (died c. A.D. 64) a disciple of Jesus, spent his later life spreading Jesus' teachings; helped turn Christianity into an organized religion, p. 232

Pericles (PEHR uh kleez) (c. 495–429 B.C.) an Athenian leader; played a major role in the development of democracy and the Athenian empire, p. 174

Philip (FIL ip) (382–336 B.C.) a king of Macedonia; seized power in 359 B.C.; conquered the Greek city-states; father of Alexander the Great, p. 196

Plato (PLAY toh) (c. 427–347 B.C.) a Greek philosopher and student of Socrates; founded the Academy of Athens and wrote *The Republic*, p. 178

Ptolemy V (TAHL uh mee) (died 180 B.C.) king of ancient Egypt from 205 to 180 B.C.; his ascension to the throne is recorded on the Rosetta Stone, p. 94

R

Ramses II (RAM seez) (died 1224 B.C.) a king of ancient Egypt from 1292 to 1225 B.C.; known for great splendor and the building of monuments during his reign, p. 74

Romulus Augustulus (RAHM yuh lus oh GUS chuh lus) (died c. A.D. 476) the last Roman emperor; ruled from A.D. 475 to 476, p. 240

S

Sargon II (SAHR gahn) (died 705 B.C.) a king of Assyria from 722 to 705 B.C.; conquered Babylonia and founded the last great Assyrian dynasty, p. 42

Saul (sawl) the first king of the Israelites, p. 57

Seneca (SEN ih kuh) (c. 4 B.C.–A.D. 65) a writer, philosopher, and statesman of ancient Rome, p. 226

Shi Huangdi (shur hwahng DEE) (c. 259–210 B.C.) the founder of the Qin dynasty and China's first emperor, ruled from about 221 to 210 B.C., p. 151

Sima Qian (sih MAH chen) (c. 145 – 85 B.C.) a Chinese scholar, astronomer, and historian; wrote the most important history of ancient China, *Historical Records*, p. 161

Socrates (SAHK ruh teez) (c. 470–399 B.C.) an Athenian philosopher of the late 400s B.C.; taught by using a method of questioning; helped form many values of Western culture; put to death for challenging Athenian values, p. 178

Solomon (SAHL uh mun) (died c. 932 B.C.) the king of the Israelites from about 972 to 932 B.C., after his father King David; built cities, a temple, and established foreign trade and alliances, p. 57

Solon (SOH lun) (c. 630–560 B.C.) an Athenian statesman; made Athens more democratic, p. 173

T

Taharka (tuh HAHR kuh) a prince of Nubia; became king of Nubia and Egypt in 690 B.C., p. 98

Thales (THAY leez) (c. 636–546 B.C.) a Greek philosopher, the first recorded Western philosopher; first to look for ways to explain the physical world other than mythological explanations, p. 177

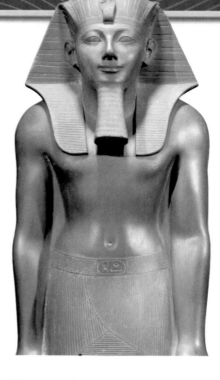

Thutmose III

Thutmose III (thoot MOH suh) the stepson of Hatshepsut; considered the greatest pharaoh of the New Kingdom of Egypt; expanded the empire to include Syria and Nubia; reigned from about 1479 to 1425 B.C., p. 80

Tutankhamen (toot ahng KAH mun) a king of ancient Egypt from about 1333 to 1323 B.C.; well known because the excavation of his tomb in 1922 provided new knowledge about Egyptian art and history, p. 79

V

Virgil (VUR jul) (70–19 B.C.) a Roman poet and the author of the *Aeneid*, an epic that glorifies Roman ideals in the age of Augustus, p. 218

W

Wudi (woo dee) (c. 156–86 B.C.) the Chinese emperor from 140 to 86 B.C.; expanded the Chinese empire under the Han dynasty; made Confucianism the state religion, p. 154

Glossary

This glossary lists key terms and other useful terms from the book.

A

absolute power (AB suh loot POW ur) *n.* complete control over someone or something, p. 77

acropolis (uh KRAH puh lis) *n.* the fortified, or strengthened, hill of an ancient Greek city; the acropolis of Athens when spelled with a capital *A*, p. 172

A.D. the abbreviation for the Latin term, *Anno Domini*, or "in the year of the Lord"; used with dates, p. 14

afterlife (AF tur lyf) *n.* a life after death, p. 82

agora (AG uh ruh) *n.* a public market and meeting place in an ancient Greek city; the agora of Athens when spelled with a capital *A*, p. 182

ahimsa (uh HIM sah) *n.* the Hindu idea of nonviolence, p. 119

Alexander the Great (al ig ZAN dur thuh grayt) *n.* the king of Macedonia from 336 to 323 B.C.; conqueror of Persia and Egypt and invader of India, p. 197

alphabet (AL fuh bet) *n.* a set of symbols that represent the sounds of a language, p. 54

ancestor (AN ses tur) *n.* a person from whom one is descended, especially of a generation earlier than a grandparent, p. 16

aqueduct (AK wuh dukt) *n.* a structure that carries water over long distances, p. 222

archaeologist (ahr kee AHL uh jist) *n.* a scientist who examines objects such as bones and tools to learn about past peoples and cultures, p. 11

architecture (AHR kuh tek chur) *n.* the art and work of designing and constructing buildings or other large structures; the style and design of a building, p. 27

aristocrat (uh RIS tuh krat) *n.* a member of a rich and powerful family, p. 172

artisan (AHR tuh zun) *n.* a worker who is especially skilled in crafting items by hand, pp. 25, 100

assassinate (uh SAS uh nayt) *v.* to murder for political reasons, p. 197

astronomer (uh STRAHN uh mur) *n.* a scientist who studies the stars and other objects in the sky, p. 94

Athens (ATH unz) *n.* a city-state in ancient Greece; the capital of present-day Greece, p. 181

avatar (av uh TAHR) *n.* a representation of a Hindu god or goddess in human or animal form, p. 117

B

Babylon (BAB uh lahn) *n.* the capital of Babylonia; a city of great wealth and luxury, p. 43

barbarian (bahr BEHR ee un) *n.* a wild and uncivilized person, p. 196

barge (bahrj) *n.* a large, flat-bottomed boat, p. 87

battering ram (BAT ur ing ram) *n.* a weapon having a wooden beam mounted on wheels; used to knock down walls or buildings, p. 45

bazaar (buh ZAHR) *n.* a market selling different kinds of goods, p. 43

B.C. the abbreviation for "before Christ"; used with dates, p. 14

blockade (blah KAYD) *n.* an action taken to isolate an enemy and cut off its supplies, p. 193

boomerang (BOOM ur ang) *n.* a flat, curved object, traditionally made of wood, that can be thrown so that it returns to the thrower, p. 70

brahman (BRAH mun) *n.* a single spiritual power that, according to Hinduism, lives in everything, p. 117

bronze (brahnz) *n.* a yellowish-brown alloy of copper, tin, and traces of other metals, p. 27

Buddhism (BOOD iz um) *n.* a religion based on the teachings of Buddha; characterized by the belief that enlightenment comes from within rather than from worshipping gods, p. 121

C

canal (kuh NAL) *n.* a waterway dug into the earth or modified by people to transport water or people, or to provide drainage, p. 24

caravan (KA ruh van) *n.* a group of travelers journeying together, p. 43

caste (kast) *n.* a social class of people, p. 113

catacombs (KAT uh kohmz) *n.* an underground cemetery of many tunnels and passageways, p. 231

cataract (KAT uh rakt) *n.* a large waterfall or steep rapids, p. 71

Chandragupta (chun druh GUP tuh) *n.* (died C. 297 B.C.) the founder of India's Maurya Empire in 321 B.C.; unified most of India under one ruler, p. 128

chieftain (CHEEF tun) *n.* a leader or head of a group, such as a clan or a tribe, p. 172

Christianity (kris chee AN uh tee) *n.* the Christian religion, based on the life and teachings of Jesus and on the Christian holy book, the Bible, p. 229

circa (SUR kuh) *prep.* the Latin word meaning "about"; often abbreviated as *c.*, p. 14

circus (SUR kus) *n.* an arena in ancient Rome; also the show held there, p. 226

citadel (SIT uh del) *n.* a fortress in a city, p. 110

city-state (SIH tee stayt) *n.* a city that is also a separate, independent state, p. 37

civilization (sih vuh luh ZAY shun) *n.* a society with cities, a central government run by official leaders, and workers who specialize in certain jobs, leading to social classes; characterized by writing, art, and architecture, p. 27

civil service (SIV ul SUR vis) *n.* the group of people whose job is to carry out the work of the government, p. 150

code (kohd) *n.* an organized list of laws or rules, p. 48

Colosseum (kahl uh SEE um) *n.* a large amphitheater built in Rome around A.D. 70; site of contests and combats between people and animals, p. 222

Confucius (kun FYOO shus) *n.* (551–479 B.C.) a Chinese philosopher and teacher; originator of Confucianism, greatly influenced Chinese life, pp. 143, 146

conqueror (KAHN kur ur) *n.* a person who uses force to gain control of other people, land, or possessions, p. 43

Constantine (KAHN stun teen) *n.* (c. A.D. 278–337) the emperor of Rome from A.D. 312 to 337; encouraged the spread of Christianity, p. 236

consul (KAHN sul) *n.* one of two officials who led the ancient Roman Republic, p. 212

convert (kun VURT) *v.* to change one's beliefs; in particular, to change from one religion to another, p. 130

covenant (KUV uh nunt) *n.* a promise made by God; a binding agreement, p. 61

culture (KUL chur) *n.* the language, religious beliefs, values, customs, and other ways of life shared by a group of people, p. 11

cuneiform (kyoo NEE uh fawrm) *n.* a form of writing that uses groups of wedges and lines; used to write several languages of the Fertile Crescent, p. 50

currency (KUR un see) *n.* the kind of money used by a group or a nation, p. 153

D

dam (dam) *n.* a barrier across a waterway to control the level of water, p. 24

Dead Sea Scrolls (ded see skrohlz) *n.* ancient parchment manuscripts containing the earliest version of the first few books of the Bible, p. 61

delta (DEL tuh) *n.* a triangular-shaped plain at the mouth of a river, formed when sediment is deposited by flowing water, p. 72

democracy (dih MAHK ruh see) *n.* a form of government in which citizens govern themselves, p. 173

descendant (dee SEN dunt) *n.* child, grandchild, great-grandchild (and so on) of an ancestor, p. 60

dharma (DAHR muh) *n.* the religious and moral duties of Hindus, p. 119

diaspora (dy AS pur uh) *n.* the scattering of people who have a common background or beliefs, p. 64

dictator (DIK tay tur) *n.* a ruler who has total control of the government, p. 213

dike (dyk) *n.* a protective wall that controls or holds back water by a river, p. 140

disciple (dih SY pul) *n.* a follower of a person or belief, p. 230

district (DIS trikt) *n.* an area set by law for a particular purpose; an area having particular characteristics, p. 152

domesticate (duh MES tih kayt) *v.* to adapt wild plants for human use; to tame wild animals and breed them for human use, p. 20

drama (DRAH muh) *n.* a type of literary work, such as a play, that tells a story and is written to be performed by actors, p. 180

dynasty (DY nus tee) *n.* a series of rulers from the same family or ethnic group, p. 77

E

emperor (EM pur ur) *n.* a ruler of widespread lands, p. 151

empire (EM pyr) *n.* many territories and people controlled by one government, p. 43

epistle (ee PIS ul) *n.* a letter; in the Christian Bible, letters written by disciples to Christian groups, p. 232

exile (EK syl) *v.* to force someone to live in another place or country, p. 57

extended family (ek STEN did FAM uh lee) *n.* closely related people of several generations, p. 142

F

famine (FAM in) *n.* a time when there is so little food that many people starve, p. 56

Fertile Crescent (FUR tul KRES unt) *n.* a region in Southwest Asia; site of the world's first civilizations, p. 36

finances (FY nan siz) *n.* the amounts of money or money-related resources a person has; the management of money, p. 184

floodwaters (FLUD wah turz) *n.* water from a flood; generally used to describe floods caused in the spring by excess water from rain and melting snow, p. 24

G

geography (jee AHG ruh fee) *n.* the study of Earth's surface and the processes that shape it, p. 13

Giza (GEE zuh) *n.* an ancient Egyptian city; site of the Great Pyramid, p. 86

gladiator (GLAD ee ay tur) *n.* in ancient Rome, a person who fought in an arena for the entertainment of the public; usually a slave, p. 226

god (gahd) *n.* a being considered to be the creator or ruler of the universe or parts of the universe; the object of worship in some cultures and societies, p. 37

goddess (GAHD is) *n.* a female being considered to be the creator or ruler of the universe or parts of the universe; the object of worship in some cultures and societies, p. 37

Gospels (GAHS pulz) *n.* in the Christian Bible, the books of Matthew, Mark, Luke, and John, which are the first four books of the New Testament, p. 230

Gupta Empire (GOOP tuh EM pyr) *n.* an empire in northern India, p. 132

H

Hammurabi (hah muh RAH bee) *n.* (died 1750 B.C.) the King of Babylon from about 1792 to 1750 B.C.; creator of the Babylonian Empire; established one of the oldest codes of law, p. 43

Hammurabi's Code (hah muh RAH beez kohd) *n.* a set of laws created by Babylonian king Hammurabi, telling his people how to live and settle conflicts, p. 47

Hellenistic (hel uh NIS tik) *adj.* having to do with history or Greek-influenced culture in the Middle East and countries bordering the Mediterranean Sea after the death of Alexander the Great, p. 199

helot (HEL ut) *n.* a member of a certain class of servants in ancient Sparta, p. 189

herbalism (HUR bul iz um) *n.* the practice of creating medicines from plants, p. 95

hieroglyphs (HY ur oh glifs) *n.* pictures and other written symbols that stand for ideas, things, or sounds, p. 93

Hinduism (HIN doo iz um) *n.* a religion developed in India, introduced by the Aryans, and based on sacred books called the Vedas and Upanishads; recognizes many gods as different aspects of one supreme being, p. 116

history (HIS tuh ree) *n.* the written and other recorded events of people, p. 11

hominid (HAHM uh nid) *n.* a modern human or a member of an earlier group that may have included ancestors or relatives of modern humans, p. 16

hunter-gatherers (HUN tur GATH ur urz) *n.* people who gather wild food and hunt animals to survive, pp. 17, 22

I

Iliad (IL ee ud) *n.* a Greek epic, credited to the poet Homer, telling about quarrels among Greek leaders in the last year of the Trojan War, p. 171

immortal (ih MAWR tul) *n.* someone or something that lives forever, p. 176

imperialism (im PIHR ee ul iz um) *n.* the practice of gaining control over foreign lands and peoples, p. 214

inflation (in FLAY shun) *n.* an economic situation in which there is more money with less value, p. 239

irrigation (ihr uh GAY shun) *n.* a method of supplying land with water through a network of canals, p. 24

Islam (IS lahm) *n.* the religion practiced by Muslims; based on the teachings of the prophet Muhammad and on the holy book of Islam, the *Quran*, p. 64

J

Jesus (JEE zus) *n.* (c. 4 B.C.–A.D. 29) founder of Christianity; believed by Christians to be the Messiah; crucified by the Roman government, p. 229

Judaism (JOO day iz um) *n.* the religion of the Jewish people, which developed from ancient Israelite beliefs; based on belief in one God and the teachings of the Hebrew Bible, p. 60

L

landform (LAND fawrm) *n.* an area of Earth's surface with a definite shape; examples include mountains and hills, p. 169

linen (LIN un) *n.* a smooth, strong cloth made of the fibers of the flax plant, p. 82

Liu Bang (LYOH bahng) *n.* the founder of the Han dynasty of China in 202 B.C.; born a peasant; stabilized the government and promoted education, p. 154

loess (LOH es) *n.* a yellow-brown soil, p. 140

Lower Nubia (LOH ur NOO bee uh) *n.* an ancient region in northern Africa extending from the Nile Valley in Egypt to present-day Sudan, specifically, between the first and second Nile cataracts, p. 99

M

martyr (MAHR tur) *n.* a person who dies for a cause he or she believes in, p. 233

Maurya Empire (MOWR yuh EM pyr) *n.* Indian empire founded by Chandragupta, beginning with his kingdom in northeastern India and spreading to most of northern and central India, p. 128

meditate (MED uh tayt) *v.* to focus the mind inward in order to find spiritual awareness or relaxation, p. 122

mercenary (MUR suh neh ree) *n.* a soldier who serves for pay in a foreign army, p. 238

merchant (MUR chunt) *n.* a person who buys or sells goods for a profit; person who runs a store or business, p. 28

messiah (muh SY uh) *n.* a savior in Judaism and Christianity, p. 230

Middle Kingdom (MID ul KING dum) *n.* the period from about 1991 to 1786 B.C., during which Dynasty 12 ruled ancient Egypt, p. 77; a name for the land of ancient China, p. 139

migrate (MY grayt) *v.* to move from one place to settle in another area, p. 112

mina (MY nuh) *n.* a unit of weight or money used in ancient Greece and Asia, p. 47

missionary (MISH un ehr ee) *n.* a person who spreads his or her religious beliefs to others, p. 123

monotheism (MAHN oh thee iz um) *n.* the belief in one god, p. 55

monsoon (mahn SOON) *n.* a strong, seasonal wind that blows across East Asia, p. 109

moral (MAWR ul) *adj.* acting in a way that is considered good and just by a society's standards, p. 131

Moses (MOH zuz) *n.* (c. 1200s B.C.) Israelite leader who, according to the Torah, led the Israelites from Egypt to Canaan; said to have received the Ten Commandments from God, p. 61

mummy (MUM ee) *n.* a dead body preserved in lifelike condition, p. 84

myth (mith) *n.* a traditional story; in some cultures, a legend that explains people's beliefs, p. 38

N

New Babylonian Empire (noo bab uh LOH nee un EM pyr) *n.* a revival of the old Babylonian empire stretching from the Persian Gulf to the Mediterranean Sea, p. 45

New Kingdom (noo KING dum) *n.* the period from about 1567 to 1085 B.C., during which dynasties 18, 19, and 20 ruled ancient Egypt, p. 77

New Stone Age (noo stohn ayj) *n.* the later part of the Stone Age during which people began to grow their own foods and lived in the same place year after year, p. 19

nirvana (nur VAH nuh) *n.* the lasting peace that Buddhists seek by giving up selfish desires, p. 123

noble (NOH bul) *n.* in certain societies, a person of high rank; in early civilizations, members of the upper class who were government officials, p. 48

nomad (NOH mad) *n.* a person who has no settled home, p. 18

Nubia (NOO bee uh) *n.* a desert region and ancient kingdom in the Nile River Valley, on the site of present-day southern Egypt and northern Sudan, p. 71

O

Odyssey (AHD ih see) *n.* a Greek epic, credited to the poet Homer, describing the adventures of the hero Odysseus after the Trojan War, p. 171

Old Kingdom (ohld KING dum) *n.* the period from about 2686 to 2181 B.C., during which dynasties 3, 4, and 5 ruled ancient Egypt, p. 77

Old Stone Age (ohld stohn ayj) *n.* the early part of the Stone Age during which people learned to hunt in groups, discovered how to use fire, and became nomads, p. 17

oracle (AWR uh kul) *n.* in ancient Greece, a sacred site where a god or goddess was consulted; any priest or priestess who spoke for the gods, p. 177

oral traditions (AWR ul truh DISH unz) *n.* stories passed down through generations by word of mouth, p. 12

ore (awr) *n.* a mineral or a combination of minerals mined for the production of metals, p. 99

P

papyrus (puh PY rus) *n.* an early form of paper made from a reedlike plant found in the marshy areas of the Nile delta, p. 93

patrician (puh TRISH un) *n.* a member of a wealthy, upper-class family in the Roman Republic, p. 212

Pax Romana (paks roh MAH nah) *n.* the period of stability and prosperity in the Roman Empire, lasting from 27 B.C. to A.D. 180; "Roman peace," p. 219

peasant (PEZ unt) *n.* a member of a class that makes its living through small-scale farming and labor, p. 91

Peloponnesian War (pel uh puh NEE shun wawr) *n.* (431–404 B.C.) a war fought for 27 years between Athens and Sparta in ancient Greece that involved almost every Greek city-state, p. 192

peninsula (puh NIN suh luh) *n.* an area of land almost completely surrounded by water and connected to a mainland by a narrow strip of land, p. 169

Persian Empire (PUR zhun EM pyr) *n.* an empire centered in modern Iran that covered the Fertile Crescent, Egypt, Asia Minor, and parts of Central Asia and India, p. 46

pharaoh (FEHR oh) *n.* a king of ancient Egypt, p. 76

philosopher (fih LAHS uh fur) *n.* someone who uses reason to understand the world, pp. 146, 177

philosophy (fih LAHS uh fee) *n.* a system of beliefs and values, p. 148

plague (playg) *n.* a widespread disease, p. 193

playwright (PLAY ryt) *n.* a person who writes dramas; also called a dramatist, p. 180

plebeian (plih BEE un) *n.* an ordinary citizen in the ancient Roman Republic, p. 212

polytheism (PAHL ih thee iz um) *n.* the belief in many gods, p. 38

prehistory (pree HIS tuh ree) *n.* before history; the events in the period of time before writing was invented, p. 11

prophet (PRAHF it) *n.* a religious teacher who is regarded as speaking for God or a god, p. 63

province (PRAH vins) *n.* a unit of an empire; in the Roman Empire each one having a governor supported by an army, p. 219

pyramid (PIH ruh mid) *n.* a huge building with four sloping triange-shaped sides; built as a royal tomb in Egypt, p. 86

Q

quarry (KWAWR ee) *n.* a site where large holes are dug into the ground and stone is collected by digging, cutting, or other means, p. 87

R

rapids (RAP idz) *n.* a very fast-moving part of a river, p. 70

rebellion (rih BEL yun) *n.* an organized resistance to the government or other authority, p. 189

reeds (reedz) *n.* tall, hollow-stemmed grasses that grow in wet places, p. 93

regent (REE junt) *n.* someone who rules for a child until the child is old enough to rule, p. 80

reincarnation (ree in kahr NAY shun) *n.* the rebirth of the soul in the body of another living being, p. 119

republic (rih PUB lik) *n.* a type of government in which citizens who have the right to vote select their leaders, p. 212

Roman Empire (ROH mun EM pyr) *n.* an empire lasting from 27 B.C. to A.D. 476, whose boundaries changed over time; at its greatest extent stretching from Britain to North Africa and the Persian Gulf, p. 215

Rosetta Stone (roh ZET uh stohn) *n.* an ancient tablet covered with Egyptian and Greek hieroglyphics; provided a key to deciphering hieroglyphics, p. 94

rubble (RUB ul) *n.* irregularly shaped pieces of rock or other materials, p. 45

S

sandstorm (SAND stawrm) *n.* a strong wind that carries clouds of sand and dust as it blows, p. 158

scribe (skryb) *n.* a professional writer, p. 34

senate (SEN it) *n.* the governing council of ancient Rome and the later Roman Empire, p. 212

Shi Huangdi (shur hwahng DEE) *n.* (c. 259–210 B.C.) the founder of the Qin dynasty and China's first emperor, ruled from about 221 to 210 B.C., p. 151

silk (silk) *n.* a valuable cloth originally made only in China from threads spun by caterpillars called silkworms, p. 160

Silk Road (silk rohd) *n.* an ancient trade route between China and Europe, p. 158

silt (silt) *n.* fine soil found on river bottoms, p. 72

Sima Qian (sih MAH chen) *n.* (c. 145–85 B.C.) a Chinese scholar, astronomer, and historian; wrote the most important history of ancient China, *Historical Records*, p. 161

slavery (SLAY vur ee) *n.* the condition of being owned by, and forced to work for, someone else, p. 184

social class (SOH shul klas) *n.* a group, or class, that is made up of people with similar backgrounds, income, and ways of living, p. 28

society (suh SY uh tee) *n.* a group of people distinct from other groups, who share a common culture, p. 12

Sparta (SPAHR tuh) *n.* a city-state in the southern part of ancient Greece, p. 188

spiritual (SPIH rih choo ul) *n.* concerned with religious or sacred matters, p. 122

Stone Age (stohn ayj) *n.* a period of time during which people made lasting tools and weapons mainly from stone; the earliest known period of human culture, p. 17

subcontinent (SUB kahn tih nunt) *n.* a large landmass that juts out from a continent; for example, India, p. 109

surplus (SUR plus) *n.* more of a thing or product than is needed, p. 25

T

Taoism (DOW iz um) *n.* a religious philosophy of simple and selfless living, based on the writings of the Chinese philosopher, Laozi, p. 149

Ten Commandments (ten kuh MAND munts) *n.* according to the Bible, a code of laws given to the Israelites by God, p. 56

terra cotta (TEHR uh KAHT uh) *n.* a hard, ceramic-like clay used in pottery and building construction, p. 151

timeline (TYM lyn) *n.* a simple diagram showing how dates and events relate to one another, p. 14

tolerance (TAHL ur uns) *n.* freedom from prejudice, p. 131

topsoil (TAHP soyl) *n.* the layer of soil on the top of the ground, p. 36

Torah (TOH ruh) *n.* the most sacred text of the early Israelites; recorded their laws and history, p. 55

trade (trayd) *n.* buying and selling goods; an exchange of one thing for another, p. 27

tragedy (TRAJ uh dee) *n.* a type of serious drama that ends in disaster for the main character, p. 180

tribute (TRIB yoot) *n.* regular payment made to a powerful state or nation by a weaker one, p. 175

Trojan War (TROH jun wawr) *n.* in Greek epic poems and myths, a ten-year war between Greece and the city of Troy in Asia Minor, p. 171

tyrant (TY runt) *n.* a ruler in ancient Greece who took power by force, with the support of the middle and working classes, p. 172

U

Upanishads (oo PAN uh shadz) *n.* one of the Hindu religious texts; written in the style of questions by students and answers by teachers, p. 119

Upper Nubia (UP ur NOO bee uh) *n.* an ancient region in northeastern Africa in present-day Sudan, p. 99

V

Vedas (VAY duz) *n.* a series of religious texts, written in Sanskrit by the Aryan peoples; later a basis for Hinduism, p. 113

vendor (VEN dur) *n.* a seller of goods, p. 182

veto (VEE toh) *n.* the rejection of any planned action or rule by a person in power; the Latin word for "forbid," p. 213

villa (VIL uh) *n.* a country estate usually owned by a wealthy family; an important source of food and wealth for ancient Rome, p. 225

W

warlord (WAWR lawrd) *n.* a local leader of an armed group, p. 155

welfare (WEL fair) *n.* health, happiness, and good fortune; financial or other aid provided to people, especially by the state, p. 118

Wudi (woo dee) *n.* (c. 156–86 B.C.) the Chinese emperor from 140 to 86 B.C., p. 154

Z

ziggurat (ZIG oo rat) *n.* a temple of the ancient Sumerians and Babylonians, made of terraces connected by ramps and stairs, roughly in the shape of a pyramid, p. 38

Zoroastrianism (zoh roh AS tree un iz um) *n.* a religion that developed in ancient Persia, p. 46

A ziggurat

Index

The *m*, *g*, or *p* following some page numbers refers to maps *(m)*, charts, diagrams, tables, timelines, or graphs *(g)*, or pictures *(p)*.

A

A.D., 14, 280
Abraham, 55, 60, 61, 276
absolute power, 77–78, 129, 280
Abu Simbel, 74
acropolis, 172, 272, 280
Aegean Sea, 167*m*
Africa, 209*m*, 247*m*, 249*m*, 272, M10*m*, M11*m*
  physical map, 257*m*
  political map, 256*m*
afterlife, 82, 82*p*, 84–87, 84*p*, 85*p*, 86*p*, 87*p*, 280.
agora, 182, 186–187, 186*p*, 187*p*, 280
agriculture, 19, 19*m*
ahimsa, 119, 280
Ajanta, 132*p*
Akhenaton, 84
Akkad, 39
Alexander the Great, 81, 196–198, 197*p*, 198*m*, 198*p*, 199, 276, 280
Alexandria, Egypt, 199–200, 272
alphabet, 54, 54*g*, 280
ancestor, 16, 280
Andes Mountains, 251*m*, 272
Anyang, 26*g*, 272
aqueducts, 221, 221*p*, 222, 280
Arabian Peninsula, 102, 259*m*, 272
archaeologists, 11, 59, 171, 280
arches, 222, 222*p*
Archimedes, 200, 276
architecture, 91, 280
  Golden Rectangle, 179, 179*p*
  of the Roman Empire, 218*p*, 222, 222*p*
Aristarchus, 200, 276
aristocrats, 172, 172*p*, 280
Aristophanes, 180

Aristotle, 178, 196, 276
art
  of ancient China, 154, 154*p*, 162*p*
  of Egypt, 70*p*, 71*p*, 78*g*, 83, 83*p*, 90, 90*p*, 91
  Greek, 179, 179*p*, 181*p*, 182*p*, 184, 184*p*
  of hunter-gatherers, 23*p*
  of Kerma culture, 100, 100*p*
  Roman, 224*p*
artisans, 25, 27, 28, 28*p*, 100, 100*p*, 115, 172, 280
Aryans, 112–113
Asia, 247*m*, 249*m*, 258*m*, 259*m*, 272
Asia Minor, 33*m*, 167*m*, 171, 209*m*, 272
Asoka, 130–131, 130*m*, 276
assassination, 197, 280
Assyria, 42, 43, 43*p*, 44, 45*p*, 57, 272
astronomy, 46, 94, 200, 280
Athena, 176*g*, 179, 220
Athens, 173, 272, 280
  daily life in, 181–185, 182*p*, 183*p*, 184*p*, 185*p*
  fall of, 193
  Golden Age of, 175, 175*p*, 180
  Persian Empire and, 191, 192*m*
  Sparta and, 192–193, 192*m*, 193*p*
Augustus, 215, 219–220, 219*p*, 276
avatar, 117, 280

B

B.C., 14, 280
Babylon, 43, 46, 280
Babylonia, 39, 43*m*, 44, 45, 46, 272
Bactria, 157
Bangladesh, 109
barbarians, 196, 280
Bay of Bengal, 107*m*, 109*m*, 110, 272
bazaar, 43, 75, 280
Bible, 229, 230, 232
Black Sea, 6, 6*m*
blockade, 193, 280
Blue Nile, 71. *See also* Nile River; White Nile
Book of the Dead, 93*p*

Brahma, 117, 119, 120, 280
Brahmans, 113
bronze, 27, 75, 79, 98*p*, 154, 155*p*, 280
Bronze Age, 27, 170
Buddha, 121*p*, 122–123, 123*p*, 244*p*
Buddhism, 280
  Asoka and, 130–131
  Hinduism and, 121, 122, 124–125, 132
  in India, 121–127, 121*p*
  practice of, 122–123, 122*g*
  spread of, 124*m*, 125, 135, 160
Burma, 244*p*, 258*m*
Byzantium, 239, 240, 272

C

Caesar, Julius, 213*g*, 214–215, 227, 277
Cairo, 77, 272
Caligula, 220, 276
Canaan, 33*m*, 55*m*, 56, 61, 272
canals, 111, 281
Cao Pei, 155
caravans, 43, 75, 158, 158*p*, 159*p*, 281
Carthage, 209*m*, 211*m*, 213*g*, 214, 214*p*, 272
caste system, 113, 281
catacombs, 231*p*, 281
Çatal Hüyük, 25*p*
cataract, 71, 75, 270, 281
Central America, 20, 246*m*
Chaldeans, 44, 45, 57
Champollion, Jean François, 94, 276
Chandragupta, 128–130, 129*p*, 276, 281
Chang River, 137*m*, 139, 272
Chang'an, 2*m*, 256, 157*m*, 272
Chile, 18
China, 137*m*, 258*m*
  achievements of, 158–162, 158*p*, 159*m*, 160*p*, 161*g*, 162*p*
  art of, 154, 154*p*, 162*p*
  Buddhism in, 124*m*, 125, 131
  cities in, 26, 26*g*
  civil service, 150

cuneiform, 50–51, 50*p*, 51*g*, 281
currency, 153, 281
Cyrus the Great, 45, 191

D

dam, 24, 282
Damascus, 7
David, king of the Israelites, 57, 277
Dead Sea, 273
Dead Sea Scrolls, 61*p*, 282
death, 11
  in Egypt, 82, 82*p*, 84–87, 84*p*, 85*p*, 86*p*, 87*p*
  in Kerma culture, 100
  See also afterlife; Great Sphinx; mummification; pyramids
debates, 244
Deborah (judge), 62, 277
decimal point, 132
Deir el-Bahri, 80*p*
Delphi, 177, 177*p*
delta, 13, 72, 74, 270, 271*p*, 282
democracy, 173, 173*p*, 175, 178, 282
Democritus, 177, 277
demotic script, 94, 94*p*
descendant, 60, 282
Deuteronomy, 60
dharma, 119, 282
diaspora, 63*m*, 64, 282
dictator, 213, 214, 282
dike, 140, 282
Diocletian, 233, 238*m*, 239, 277
Dionysus, 220*p*
disciples, 230, 230*p*–231*p*, 282
district, 152, 282
domestication, 20–21, 282
drama, 194, 282
  Greek, 180, 180*p*
dynasty, 77, 141, 141*p*, 282
  Han dynasty, 154–155, 160–162
  Qin dynasty, 151–153, 154*m*
  Wei dynasty, 155

E

East Africa, 71, 273
Eastern Desert, 73
economy
  in ancient China, 153
  inflation, 239
  of the Roman Empire, 219, 219*p*, 238–239
education
  in ancient China, 160–161
  Babylonian, 46
  in Sumer, 34
Egypt, 3*m*, 69*m*, 256*m*, 273
  architecture of, 91
  art of, 70, 71*p*, 78*g*, 83, 83*p*, 90, 90*p*, 91
  cities in, 26, 26*g*
  civil war in, 81
  culture of, 90–95
  death in, 82, 82*p*, 84–87
  farming in, 92
  food of, 88, 88*p*, 89*p*
  geography of, 13, 70–75
  Greek culture in, 199–200
  Israelites in, 56
  kingdoms of, 77, 78–81, 79*m*
  medicine in, 89, 89*p*
  Nile River and, 70, 70*p*, 71p, 72
  Nubia and, 98–99, 99*p*
  pharaohs of, 76–81, 84
  pyramids of, 88–89
  religion in, 82–87, 92
  science in, 94–95
  slavery in, 91, 91*p*
  social classes in, 91–92
  timeline of, 78
  trade routes of, 97*m*
  women of, 80, 81, 92, 92*p*
  writing systems in, 93–94
empire, 43, 282
Epidauros, 180*p*
epistles, 232, 282
Eratosthenes, 200, 277
ethics, 63
Ethiopia, 71, 256*m*
Etruscans, 211*m*, 211*p*, 212, 212*p*, 222, 277

Euclid, 200, 277
Euphrates River, 5*m*, 5*p*, 26, 31, 35–36, 35*m*, 35*p*, 50, 73, 273
Euripides, 180
Europe, 247*m*, 249*m*, 273
  physical map, 255*m*
  political map, 254*m*
  Silk Road, 158–160
exile, 57, 282
Exodus, 56, 60
extended family, 142, 282

F

families, 25
  in ancient China, 142–143
  in the Roman Empire, 227
famine, 56, 73, 282
farming
  in China, 141, 161
  in Egypt, 92
  in Indus Valley, 112*p*
  in Mesopotamia, 40–41
  in New Stone Age, 19–21
  in Nubia, 74
  techniques, 20*p*, 139*p*
fertile, 20, 140, 282
Fertile Crescent, 5, 33*m*, 36, 66*m*, 273, 282
  geography of, 35–36
finances, 184, 282
floods, 24, 36, 73, 140
food, 62
  of ancient Greece, 183
  of Egypt, 88, 88*p*, 89*p*
  of the Roman Empire, 225, 227*p*
France, 214, 254*m*

G

Ganges River, 107*m*, 109*m*, 110, 117*p*, 273
Ganges Valley, 112
Gaul, 209*m*, 214, 273
Gautama, Siddhartha, 121–123, 121*p*, 277
Genesis, 60
geography, 13, 282

in Nubia, 75, 75*p*, 98, 102
Phoenician, 53–54, 53*m*
Silk Road, 158–160, 159*m*, 275, 286
tribute, 175, 287
Trojan Horse, 171, 195*p*
Trojan War, 171, 171*p*, 195, 287
Troy, 171, 171*p*, 275
Turkey, 25*p*, 167*m*, 171, 239, 239*p*, 254*m*, 258*m*
Tutankhamen, King, 79, 79*p*, 84, 84*p*, 279
Twelve Olympians, 176
Twelve Titans, 168, 168*p*
tyrant, 172, 287
Tyre, 52, 54, 275
Tyrrhenian Sea, 211, 211*m*

U

Ulysses, 204–207
Upanishads, 119, 287
Upper Egypt, 72, 74, 77, 275
Upper Nubia, 71, 99, 100*m*, 275, 287
Ur, 26*g*, 36*p*, 275
Urartu, 42

V

Vandals, 240
Vedas, 113, 116, 287
vendors, 182, 287
veto, 213, 287
Vietnam, 125, 258*m*, 275
villas, 225, 225*p*, 287
Virgil, 218, 279
Vishnu, 117, 118, 124, 124*p*
Visigoths, 240
Vitellius, Aulus, 225
volcanoes, 16, 271, 271*p*

W

warlords, 155, 287
Warring States, 141
water resources
in India, 111
of Roman Empire, 221, 221*p*
weapons
of hunter-gatherers, 22*p*
of India, 112
Roman, 217*p*
Wei dynasty, 155
West Africa, 12*p*
White Nile, 71
women
of ancient China, 142
early farming by, 19
of Egypt, 80, 81, 92, 92*p*
of Greece, 183–184, 190
Hindu, 120*p*
Judaism and, 62
Nubian, 102, 102*p*
of the Roman Empire, 227
writing skills
compare and contrast, RW4
descriptive, 95, 102, 113, 125, 143, 173, 185
dialogue, 120
editorial, 228
epitaphs, 46
essays, 180
evaluating your, RW5
explain a process, RW4
explain cause and effect, RW4
expository essays, RW4
government, 202, 242
job description, 223
journal, 21, 39, 75, 87, 150
language arts, 104, 134, 164
legal, 51
letters, 64
list of pros and cons, 215
list of questions, 155
list of rules, 132

math, 66
messages, 134
narrative essays, RW2
paragraphs, 81, 200, 233
persuasive essays, RW3
poetry, 57, 104, 162
point of view, 39, 193
reports, 193
research papers, RW4–RW5
science, 30
social studies, RW2–RW5
songs, 57
speech writing, 28, 242
stories, 13, 164
travel guide, 244
writing systems, 11–12, 34
Chinese, 141, 141*p*, 153, 162
in Egypt, 93–94, 93*g*
of Mesopotamia, 49–51
Minoan, 170
Mycenaean, 171
in Nubia, 102
Wudi, 154, 156, 159, 279, 287

X

Xiongnu warriors, 156–157

Y

Yellow River, 140, 140*p*
yoga, 120
Yuezhi, 156, 157

Z

Zagros Mountains, 5*m*, 33*m*
Zeus, 168, 176, 176*g*, 177, 220
Zhang Qian, 156–157
Zhao Zheng, 152
Zhou dynasty, 141
ziggurat, 38, 38*p*, 287
Zikirtu, 42
Zoroastrianism, 46

Acknowledgments

Cover Design
Pronk&Associates

Staff Credits
The people who made up *World Studies* ©05 team—representing design services, editorial, editorial services, educational technology, marketing, market research, photo research and art development, production services, project office, publishing processes, and rights & permissions—are listed below. Bold type denotes core team members.

Greg Abrom, Ernie Albanese, Rob Aleman, Susan Andariese, **Rachel Avenia-Prol,** Leann Davis Alspaugh, Penny Baker, Barbara Bertell, **Peter Brooks,** Rui Camarinha, John Carle, **Lisa Del Gatto,** Paul Delsignore, Kathy Dempsey, Anne Drowns, Deborah Dukeshire, Marlies Dwyer, **Frederick Fellows,** Paula C. Foye, Lara Fox, Julia Gecha, **Mary Hanisco,** Salena Hastings, Lance Hatch, Kerri Hoar, **Beth Hyslip,** Katharine Ingram, Nancy Jones, John Kingston, Deborah Levheim, Constance J. McCarty, **Kathleen Mercandetti,** Art Mkrtchyan, Ken Myett, **Mark O'Malley,** Jen Paley, Ray Parenteau, **Gabriela Pérez Fiato,** Linda Punskovsky, Kirsten Richert, **Lynn Robbins,** Nancy Rogier, Bruce Rolff, Robin Samper, Siri Schwartzman, Mildred Schulte, **Malti Sharma,** Lisa Smith-Ruvalcaba, Roberta Warshaw, Sarah Yezzi

Additional Credits
Jonathan Ambar, Tom Benfatti, Lisa D. Ferrari, Paul Foster, Florrie Gadson, Phil Gagler, Ella Hanna, Jeffrey LaFountain, Karen Mancinelli, Michael McLaughlin, Lesley Pierson, Debi Taffet, Linda Westerhoff

DK The DK Designs team who contributed to *World Studies* © 05 were as follows: Hilary Bird, Samantha Borland, Richard Czapnik, Nigel Duffield, Heather Dunleavy, Cynthia Frazer, James A. Hall, Lucy Heaver, Rose Horridge, Paul Jackson, Heather Jones, Ian Midson, Marie Ortu, Marie Osborn, Leyla Ostovar, Ralph Pitchford, Ilana Sallick, Pamela Shiels, Andrew Szudek, Amber Tokeley.

DK Maps
Maps and globes were created by **DK Cartography**. The team consisted of Tony Chambers, Damien Demaj, Julia Lunn, Ed Merritt, David Roberts, Ann Stephenson, Gail Townsley, Iorwerth Watkins

Illustrations
Kenneth Batelman: 80; KJA-artists.com: 22, 22–23, 40, 40–41, 88, 88–89, 114, 114–115, 156, 156–157, 157, 186, 186–187, 200, 216, 216–217; Jill Ort: 213, 237, 243; Jen Paley: 10, 15, 16, 24, 25, 26, 34, 42, 47, 49, 51, 52, 54, 60, 70, 76, 78, 82, 90, 93, 98, 108, 116, 120m, 121, 122, 127, 128, 138, 146, 151, 153, 158, 161, 165, 168, 174, 176, 181, 188, 190–191, 196, 199, 203, 210, 218, 224, 229, 235, 236; Lisa Smith-Ruvalcaba: 148

Photos
Cover Photos
tl, Philip Rostron/Masterfile Corporation; **tm,** Ancient Art and Architecture collection Ltd./Bridgeman Art Library; **tr,** Sandro Vannini/Corbis/Magma; **b,** D. E. Cox/Stone/Getty Images, Inc.

Title Page
D. E. Cox/Stone/Getty Images Inc.

Table of Contents
iv, Vanni Archive/Corbis; **v,** George Holton/Photo Researchers, Inc.; **vi,** Woodfin Camp & Associates; **vii,** Réunion des Musées Nationaux/Art Resource, NY; **ix,** Burstein Collection/Corbis; **xi,** Hideo Hagal/HAGA/The Image Works

Learning With Technology
xiii, Discovery School Channel

Reading and Writing Handbook
RW, Michael Newman/PhotoEdit; **RW1,** Walter Hodges/Getty Images, Inc.; **RW2,** Digital Vision/Getty Images, Inc.; **RW3,** Will Hart/PhotoEdit; **RW5,** Jose Luis Pelaez, Inc./Corbis

MapMaster Skills Handbook
M, James Hall/Dorling Kindersley; **M1,** Mertin Harvey/Gallo Images/Corbis; **M2–3 m,** NASA; **M2–3,** (globes) Planetary Visions; **M6 tr,** Mike Dunning/Dorling Kindersley; **M5 br,** Barnabas Kindersley/Dorling Kindersley; **M10 b,** Bernard and Catherine Desjeux/Corbis; **M11,** Hutchison Library; **M12 b,** Pa Photos; **M13 r,** Panos Pictures; **M14 l,** Macduff Everton/Corbis; **M14 t,** MSCF/NASA; **M15 b,** Ariadne Van Zandbergen/Lonely Planet Images; **M16 l,** Bill Stormont/Corbis; **M16 b,** Pablo Corral/Corbis; **M17 t,** Les Stone/Sygma/Corbis; **M17 b,** W. Perry Conway/Corbis

Guiding Questions
1 t, Bettman/Corbis; **1 b,** Richard Haynes

World Overview
2 tr, Dallas and John Heaton/Corbis; **3 tr,** Jonathan Blair/Corbis; **3 bl,** Gianni Dagli Orti/Corbis; **4 t,** David Samuel Robbins/Corbis; **5 b,** Nik Wheeler/Corbis; **6 tr,** Staatliche Antikensammlung und Glyptothek, Munich, Germany/ Bridgeman Art Library, London/New York; **7 tr,** A. Woolfitt/Robert Harding Picture Library

Chapter One
8–9, Philip & Karen Smith/Getty Images, Inc.; **10,** Sygma/Corbis; **11 l,** South Tyrol Archaeology Museum; **11 m,** National Geographic Image Collection; **11 r,** South Tyrol Archaeology Museum; **12 t,** George Holton/Photo Researchers, Inc.; **12 b,** M. & E. Bernheim/Woodfin Camp & Associates; **13,** James Strachan/Getty Images, Inc.; **14 t,** Wolfgang Kaehler/Corbis; **14 b,** The British Museum, London, UK/Dorling Kindersley; **15 l,** The Granger Collection, New York; **15 r,** Richard T. Nowitz/Corbis; **16,** John Reader/Science Photo Library/Photo Researchers, Inc.; **17 t,** The Museum of London/Dorling Kindersley; **17 b,** Peter Johnson/ Corbis; **18 t,** Discovery Channel School; **18 b,** Lauren Goodsmith/The Image Works; **20 t,** Peter Adams/Index Stock Imagery, Inc.; **20 b,** Robert S. Peabody Museum of Archaeology, Phillips Academy, Andover, Massachusetts. All Rights Reserved; **21,** J. C. Stevenson/Animals Animals/Earth Scenes; **22 bl,** Lauros/ Giraudon/Bridgeman Art Library; **22 bm,** Lynton Gardiner/American Museum of Natural History/Dorling Kindersley; **22 br–23 bl,** The Granger Collection, New York; **23 tl,** Peter H. Buckley/Pearson Education/Prentice Hall College; **23 tr,** D. Finnin/C. Chesek/American Museum of Natural History/Dorling Kindersley; **23 br,** Ashmolean Museum, Oxford, UK/Bridgeman Art Library; **24,** James R. Holland/Stock Boston/PictureQuest; **25,** Pictures of Record, Inc.; **26,** SuperStock, Inc.; **27 both,** University Museum of Archaeology and Anthropology, Cambridge, UK/Dorling Kindersley; **28,** Erich Lessing/Art Resource, NY; **29 t,** SuperStock, Inc.; **29 b,** J. C. Stevenson/Animals Animals/Earth Scenes

Chapter Two
32–33, Ed Kashi Photography/Independent Photography Network; **34,** The British Museum/Dorling Kindersley; **35,** Nik Wheeler/Corbis; **36–37 b,** The British Museum, London, UK/Bridgeman Art Library; **37 t,** Discovery Channel School; **38 t,** Victor J. Boswell/Oriental Institute Museum/University of Chicago; **38 b,** Hirmer Fotoarchiv; **39,** Bridgeman Art Library; **41 t,** The Art Archive/Egyptian Museum Turin/Dagli Orti; **41 m,** Erich Lessing/Art Resource, NY; **41 b,** Ashmolean Museum, Oxford, UK/Bridgeman Art Library; **42,** Musée du Louvre, Paris/SuperStock, Inc.; **43,** Erich Lessing/Art Resource, NY; **44–45,** The British Museum, London, UK; **46,** The Art Archive, Musée du Louvre, Paris/Dagli Orti; **47,** The Art Archive/Musée du Louvre, Paris/Dagli Orti; **48,** Scala/Art Resource, NY; **49,** Giraudon/Art Resource, NY; **50 t both,** The Granger Collection, New York; **50 b,** Steve Gorton/Dorling Kindersley; **52 t, 52 m,** Courtesy of P'til Tekhelet, The Association for the Promotion and Distribution of Tekhelet, Jerusalem, Israel; **52 b,** Dr. Davis S. Reese; **53,** Chris Howson/Dorling Kindersley; **54,** Michael Holford Photographs; **56,** Hideo Hagal/HAGA/The Image Works; **57,** Hulton/Getty Images, Inc.; **58 l,** Bob Daemmrich/The Image Works; **58 r,** Eyewire Collection/Getty Images, Inc.; **59,** Giraudon/Art Resource, NY; **60,** PhotoEdit; **61 t,** The Granger Collection, New York; **61 b,** The British Museum, London, UK/Dorling Kindersley; **62,** www.asap.co.il; **64,** Erich Lessing/Art Resource, NY; **65 t,** The British Museum, London, UK/Dorling Kindersley; **65 b,** Scala/Art Resource, NY

Chapter Three
68–69, Erich Lessing/Art Resource, NY; **70,** Werner Forman/Art Resource, NY; **71 t,** Bettmann/Corbis; **71 b,** Discovery Channel School; **72–73 b,** Wolfgang Kaehler Photography; **73 t,** John Elk III/Lonely Planet Images; **74,** Richard Nowitz Photography; **75,** Museum of Fine Arts, Boston: Harvard University – Museum of Fine Arts Expedition 21.318; **76,** Araldo de Luca/Corbis **77, 79,** The Art Archive/Egyptian Museum, Cairo/Dagli Orti; **80,** Miles Ertman/Masterfile Corporation; **81, 82,** Erich Lessing/Art Resource, NY; **83 l,** Réunion des Musées Nationaux/Art Resource, NY; **83 m,** The British Museum, London, UK/Dorling Kindersley; **83 r,** Scala/Art Resource, NY; **84 l,** Manchester Museum/Dorling Kindersley; **84 r,** Sandro Vannini/Corbis; **85 tr, 85 b,** Dorling Kindersley; **85 tl,** L. Mayer/Mary Evans Picture Library; **86,** Paul Solomon/Woodfin Camp & Associates; **87,** Erich Lessing/Art Resource, NY; **88,** Kenneth Garrett/National Geographic Image Collection; **89,** Peter Hayman/The British Museum, London, UK/Dorling Kindersley; **90,** National Geographic Image Collection; **91,** Erich

Lessing/Art Resource, NY; **92 l,** Gianni Dagli Orti/Corbis; **92 r,** Robert Frerck/ Odyssey Productions, Inc.; **93,** Scala/Art Resource, NY; **94 t,** The British Museum, London, UK/Bridgeman Art Library; **94 bl,** The Granger Collection, New York; **94 br,** Lauros/Giraudon/Bridgeman Art Library; **95,** The Art Archive/Musée du Louvre, Paris/Dagli Orti; **96 t,** Scala/Art Resource, NY; **96 b,** Topham/The Image Works; **98,** The Granger Collection, New York; **99,** Archivo Iconografico, S. A./Corbis; **100,** Museum of Fine Arts, Boston: Harvard University–Museum of Fine Arts Expedition 13.4081 and 13.40469; **101 t,** Topham/The Image Works; **101 b,** Tim Kendall; **102,** from K. Lepsius, *Denkmaeler aus Aegypten und Aethiopien ...* (Berlin Nicolaische Buchhandlung, 1842–45), Abt. 5, pl. 56; **103 t,** Werner Forman/Art Resource, NY; **103 b,** The Granger Collection, New York

Chapter Four

106–107, Dinodia; **108–109,** Zane Williams/Panoramic Images; **110 t,** Bridgeman Art Library; **110 b,** Jehangir Gazdar/Woodfin Camp & Associates; **111 t,** Charles & Josette Lenars/Corbis; **111 b,** Woodfin Camp & Associates; **112,** Chris Lisle/Corbis; **113,** Victoria & Albert Museum, London/Art Resource, NY; **115,** Harappan National Museum of Karachi, Karachi, Pakistan/Bridgeman Art Library; **116,** Corbis Digital Stock; **117,** Jacob Halaska/Index Stock Imagery, Inc.; **118–119,** Lindsay Hebberd/Woodfin Camp & Associates; **119 t,** The British Museum, London, UK/Bridgeman Art Library; **120,** Eve Arnold/Magnum Photos; **121,** Lee Boltin/Boltin Picture Library; **122–123,** John W. Banagan/Getty Images, Inc.; **124,** Ashmolean Museum; **125,** Hugh Sitton/Getty Images, Inc.; **126,** AP/Wide World Photos/Aijaz Rahi; **127,** Russ Lappa; **128,** Flammarion/Musée Guimet, Paris, France/Bridgeman Art Library; **129,** Burstein Collection/Corbis; **131 t,** Discovery Channel School; **131 b,** Chris Lisle/Corbis; **132,** R. Ashworth/Ancient Art & Architecture Collection, Ltd.; **133 t,** Jehangir Gazdar/Woodfin Camp & Associates; **133 bl,** The British Museum, London, UK/Bridgeman Art Library; **133 br,** Burstein Collection/Corbis

Chapter Five

136–137, David Allan Brandt/Getty Images, Inc.; **138,** Wolfgang Kaehler Photography; **139 t,** The Granger Collection, New York; **139 b,** AP/Wide World Photos/Greg Baker; **140 t,** Chris Stowers/Panos Pictures; **140 b,** Gina Corrigan/Robert Harding World Imagery; **141,** H. Rogers/Trip Photographic; **142 t,** The Granger Collection, New York; **142 b,** The Great Bronze Age of China/ Metropolitan Museum; **143,** Réunion des Musées Nationaux/Art Resource, NY; **144, 145 t,** Michael Newman/PhotoEdit; **145 b,** Julia Waterlow, Eye Ubiquitous/ Corbis; **146,** Victoria Vebell Bruck; **147, 148 tl,** The Granger Collection, New York; **148 ml,** Reed Kaestner/Corbis; **148 tr,** Carlos Spaventa/Getty Images, Inc.; **148 br,** The Art Archive/The British Museum London, UK; **148 bl,** Bettmann/Corbis; **149 t,** Bonnie Kamin/PhotoEdit; **149 b,** Archives Charmet/Bridgeman Art Library; **150,** Bridgeman Art Library; **151,** Keren Su/China Span; **152 t,** Alvis Upitis/SuperStock, Inc.; **152 b,** Discovery Channel School; **153 t,** Giraudon/Art Resource, NY; **153 b,** Réunion des Musées Nationaux/Art Resource, NY; **154,** The British Museum, London, UK/Bridgeman Art Library; **155,** Giraudon/Bridgeman Art Library; **157,** The Art Archive/Musée Cernuschi Paris/Dagli Orti; **158,** Keren Su/China Span; **159,** Réunion des Musées/Art Resource, NY; **160 t,** The Granger Collection, New York; **160 b,** Cary Wolinsky/Aurora & Quanta Productions, Inc.; **161 t,** The British Museum London, UK /Dorling Kindersley; **161 m,** Alan Hills and Geoff Brightling/Dorling Kindersley; **161 b,** Geoff Brightling/Dorling Kindersley; **162,** The Metropolitan Museum of Art, Purchase, The Dillon Fund, 1977. (1977–78) Photograph by Malcom Varon. Photograph ©1990 The Metropolitan Museum of Art; **163 t,** China Span; **163 b,** The Granger Collection, New York

Chapter Six

166–167, Picture Finders, Ltd./Leo De Wys Stock Photo Agency/eStock Photography; **168,** Erich Lessing/Art Resource, NY; **169,** Colin Paterson/SuperStock, Inc.; **170 both,** Gianni Dagli Orti/Corbis; **171,** Ulf Sjostedt/Getty Images, Inc.; **172 l,** Réunion des Musées Nationaux/Art Resource, NY; **172 r,** The British Museum London, UK/Dorling Kindersley; **173 t, 173 b,** The Art Archive/Agora Museum, Athens/Dagli Orti; **174,** The Granger Collection, New York; **175 t,** The British Museum London, UK/Dorling Kindersley; **175 b,** The Art Archive/Archaeological Museum Spina Ferrara/Dagli Orti; **176,** David Lees/Corbis; **177 t,** Steve Vidler/SuperStock, Inc.; **177 b,** Bridgeman Art Library; **178 t,** Peter Wilson; **178–179 b,** Vanni Archive/Corbis; **180 t,** The Art Archive/Archaeological Museum Piraeus/Dagli Orti; **180 b,** The Art Archive/Dagli Orti; **181,** Scala/Art Resource, NY; **182 t,** Anthony Miles/Bruce Coleman, Inc.; **182 b,** The Art Archive/Musée du Louvre, Paris/Dagli Orti; **183 t,** The Granger Collection, New York; **183 b,** Deborah Lustgarten; **184 t,** Réunion des Musées Nationaux/Art Resource, NY; **184 b,** The British Museum London, UK /Dorling Kindersley; **185,** The Art Archive/Agora Museum, Athens/Dagli Orti; **187,** Erich Lessing/Art Resource, NY; **188,** Gian Berto Vanni/Art Resource, NY; **189,** The Art Archive/Dagli Orti; **190 l,** Erich Lessing/Art Resource, NY; **190 r,** The British Museum London, UK; **191 l,** Numismatic Museum, Athens; **191 m, 191 r,** The Granger Collection, New York; **192 l,** Discovery Channel School; **192 r, 193,** The British Museum

London, UK/Dorling Kindersley; **194 t,** The Art Archive/The British Museum London, UK /Eileen Tweedy; **194 b,** David Young-Wolff/PhotoEdit; **195,** Bettmann/Corbis; **196,** Gianni Dagli Orti/Corbis; **197 t,** The Granger Collection, New York; **197 b,** David Lees/Corbis; **198,** Lee Boltin/Boltin Picture Library; **199, 201 t,** The Granger Collection, New York; **201 b,** Bridgeman Art Library; **204,** Alinari/Regione Umbria/Art Resource, NY; **205,** Ivor Kerslake/The British Museum, London, UK/Dorling Kindersley; **206,** Erich Lessing/Art Resource, NY; **207 t,** Joe Malone Agency/Jon Arnold Images/Alamy Images; **207 b,** Gustavo Tomsich/Corbis

Chapter Seven

208–209, David McLain/Aurora Photos; **210,** Enzo & Paolo Ragazzini/Corbis; **211,** Scala/Art Resource, NY; **212,** The Granger Collection, New York; **213,** The Art Archive; **214,** The Metropolitan Museum of Art, Rogers Fund, 1965 (65.183.2) Photograph ©1984 The Metropolitan Museum of Art; **215,** Bettmann/Corbis; **216 t, 216 b,** Erich Lessing/Art Resource, NY; **217,** The Art Archive/Museo Civico Riva del Garda/Dagli Orti; **218,** Richard T. Nowitz/Corbis; **219 t,** Stock Montage; **219 b,** The British Museum London, UK/Dorling Kindersley; **220 t,** Nimatallah/Art Resource, NY; **220 b,** Araldo de Luca/Corbis; **221 t,** Max Alexander/Dorling Kindersley; **221 b,** Dorling Kindersley; **222,** Dallas and John Heaton/Corbis; **223,** The Art Archive/ Museo della Civilta Romana, Rome/Dagli Orti; **224,** The Metropolitan Museum of Art; **225,** The British Museum London, UK /Dorling Kindersley; **226,** Réunion des Musées Nationaux/Art Resource, NY; **227 l,** The British Museum London, UK/Dorling Kindersley; **227 m, 227 r,** Dorling Kindersley; **228 l,** Discovery Channel School; **228 r,** The British Museum London, UK /Dorling Kindersley; **229,** Erich Lessing/Art Resource, NY; **230 t, 230–231 b,** Scala/Art Resource, NY; **232 l,** Arte & Immagini srl/Corbis; **232 r,** The Art Archive/Dagli Orti; **233,** The Art Archive/ Palazzo Barberini, Rome/Dagli Orti; **234,** Spencer Grant/PhotoEdit; **235 t,** The Art Archive/Dagli Orti; **235 b,** Panorama Images/The Image Works; **236,** Robert Frerck/ Odyssey Productions, Inc.; **237 l,** The Granger Collection, New York; **237 tr,** The British Museum London, UK /Dorling Kindersley; **237 mr,** Bridgeman Art Library; **237 br,** Alinari/Art Resource, NY; **238,** Reunion des Musées Nationaux/Art Resource, NY; **239,** Vanni Archive/Corbis; **240,** The Granger Collection, New York; **241,** Dallas and John Heaton/Corbis

Projects

244 t, Richard Haynes; **244 b,** Richard Bickel/Corbis

Reference

245, Liu Liqun/Corbis

Glossary of Geographic Terms

270 t, A & L Sinibaldi/Getty Images, Inc.; **270 b,** John Beatty/Getty Images, Inc.; **270–271 b,** Spencer Swanger/Tom Stack & Associates; **271 t,** Hans Strand/Getty Images, Inc; **271 m,** Paul Chesley/Getty Images, Inc.

Biographical Dictionary

276, The British Museum London, UK /Dorling Kindersley; **279,** Erich Lessing/ Art Resource, NY

Glossary

281, Dallas and John Heaton/Corbis; **282,** Erich Lessing/Art Resource, NY; **285,** Bridgeman Art Library; **287,** Hirmer Fotoarchiv

Text

Chapter Two

43, Excerpt from *A History of the Ancient World, Fourth Edition,* by Chester G. Starr. Copyright © 1991 by Oxford University Press. **47,** Excerpt from *Everyday Life in Babylonia and Assyria,* by H.W.F. Saggs. Copyright © 1965 by H.W.F. Saggs. **49,** Excerpt from The Code of Hammurabi, translated by L. W. King, from The Avalon Project at Yale Law School. Copyright © 1996–2003 The Avalon Project at Yale Law School. **60,** Excerpt from *The Living Torah: The Five Books of Moses and Haftarot* by Rabbi Aryeh Kaplan. Copyright © 1981by Rabbi Aryeh Kaplan.

Chapter Four

114, Excerpt from the Rig-Veda, 11.33, verses 1–3 adapted from *Hinduism* by V. P. (Hemant) Kanitkar. Text © V. P. (Hemant) Kanitkar 1989.

Chapter Six

174, *"The Sirens"* Excerpt from *The Peloponnesian War,* by Thucydides. Copyright © 1951 by Random House, Inc. **204–207,** Excerpt from *The Adventures of Ulysses* by Bernard Evslin. Copyright © 1969 by Scholastic Inc.

Chapter Seven

218, Excerpt from the *Aneid,* by Virgil from The Roman Empire in the First Century from PBS Online. Copyright © 1995–2004 Public Broadcasting Service (PBS). All rights reserved.

Note: Every effort has been made to locate the copyright owner of material used in this textbook. Omissions brought to our attention will be corrected in subsequent editions.